THE *Luxury Guide* TO
Walt Disney World

THE Luxury Guide TO
Walt Disney World

How to Get the Most Out of the
Best Disney Has to Offer

Cara Goldsbury

Bowman Books
SAN ANTONIO, TEXAS

First printing 2003

ISBN 0-9726972-2-5
LCCN 2002116273

ATTENTION CORPORATIONS, UNIVERSITIES, COLLEGES, AND PROFESSIONAL ORGANIZATIONS: Quantity discounts are available on bulk purchases of this book for educational, gift purposes, or as premiums for increasing magazine subscriptions or renewals. Special books or book excerpts can also be created to fit specific needs. For information, please contact Bowman Books, P.O. Box 15309, San Antonio, TX 78212; ph. 210-215-4288; www.luxurydisneyguide.com.

TABLE OF CONTENTS

ACKNOWLEDGMENTS

To Robert and Ben who lovingly support all my endeavors and to Lauren, my daughter and longtime Disney companion, whose enthusiasm for "the Happiest Place on Earth" has been my inspiration.

INTRODUCTION

Walt Disney World.

These three words instantly fill the mind with images of Peter Pan, Mickey Mouse, Cinderella, and Snow White. For children they send the imagination soaring to places only dreamed of in their wildest fantasies. For adults they offer a trip back to the idyllic innocence of childhood when nothing was unattainable and the world was filled with unlimited possibilities. What other place could be all this to so many people?

Walt Disney World is a destination that renews hopes and dreams, an adventure of the heart, true magic. Disney's four theme parks are so totally distinct it's almost like taking a different vacation each day of your visit. Enhancing the experience are Disney-themed hotels, capable of transporting you to a unique time and place. Where else can you travel to Polynesia, or early 20th-century New England, or a lodge in deepest Africa? With only a small percentage of its 27,000 acres fully developed, its gorgeous grounds are dotted with numerous lakes, wetlands, and stunningly landscaped resorts and parks. With so many delightful diversions you might not know where to begin. Allow this guidebook to step in and show you the way.

Is it possible for sophisticated travelers to really enjoy themselves in the land of Mickey Mouse? Absolutely! This unique travel guide—overflowing with tips and techniques for a splendid vacation—is designed for those who wish to tour Walt Disney World but also want to reside in luxurious resorts and dine at only the best restaurants. I'm prepared to direct you in planning a visit in which each day comes with the best Disney has to offer. Together we will arrange a relatively stress-free vacation by utilizing each component of this travel guide to best suit your needs. Together we will decide the most convenient time of year for your vacation, which resort best fits your party, how to obtain the finest room at the lowest possible price, where to dine, and much, much more. Helpful tips throughout can make the difference between a mediocre trip and a fantastic one. Let's get going!

Attractions:

* — Run of the mill
** — Worth a look
*** — Rather good
**** — Outstanding

Price categories for standard through concierge level rooms for 1 night, excluding tax, studio through 3-bedroom villas at home-away-from-home resorts:

$ — $200 or less
$$ — $201 to 350
$$$ — $351 to 500
$$$$ — $501 to 700
$$$$$ — $701 to 1,900

Price categories for an adult dinner entree or buffet, excluding tax and tip:

$ — $10 or less
$$ — $11 to 15
$$$ — $16 to 25
$$$$ — $26 and over

CHAPTER 1

Planning Your Trip

The most successful vacations are those that are carefully planned and researched months ahead of time. In fact, the planning is, for some, half the fun. Disney is so extensive and offers so many choices to fit the personalities of so many types of vacationers that it demands at least some forethought. You'll discover a wealth of options, some perfect for just about everyone, others ridiculously silly for some but perfect for others. If you neglect to do your homework, you won't know what your choices are, resulting in disappointment and frustration. The outcome can mean the difference between a smooth trip or an exasperating one.

Begin by reading this book cover to cover. Then send off for a free Disney vacation planning video or CD-ROM (phone **800-515-9450** or visit **www.disneyworld.com** to order), call the **Orlando/Orange County Convention and Visitors Bureau (800-551-0181** or **407-363-5871)** for maps of the area as well as a visitor's guide on the many area attractions, and for those interested in visiting **Universal Orlando** (and you should be) call **800-837-2273** or visit **www.universalorlando.com.** Search the Internet at the following sites for detailed information and tips. And remember, the help of a good travel agent may be the key to your best vacation ever.

Disney Internet Sites

Be sure to log on to some of the many Disney-related sites on the Internet where you will find thousands of tips along with pictures, menus, and much, much more.

- **www.luxurydisneyguide.com**—continual updates to this guidebook along with Disney, Universal, and SeaWorld information and photos.
- **www.disneyworld.com**—Walt Disney World's official website with a wealth of information useful in planning your trip. Especially helpful are diagrams of guestrooms, park hours, and up-to-date ticket pricing.
- **www.wdwinfo.com**—Pete Werner's unofficial site has loads of enlightening information and the best Disney discussion group around.
- **www.wdwig.com**—Fabulous for up-to-date detailed information including complete Disney restaurant menus.
- **www.wdwmagic.com**—Loads of information on upcoming Disney attractions and plenty of park photos.
- **www.mouseplanet.com**—Practical advice and reader reviews.
- **www.disneytrips.com**—Practical information, reader restaurant reviews, and a discussion site.
- **www.mousesavers.com**—A running list of current discounts available at WDW and Universal resorts.
- **www.universalorlando.com**—Official site of Universal Orlando with park hours, ticket purchasing options, theme park attractions, hotel information, and much more.
- **www.seaworld.com**—SeaWorld's official site.
- **www.discoverycove.com**—Discovery Cove's official site.

When to Go

Always a tough decision. Is it best to go in summer when the children are out of school knowing full well the parks will be sweltering and jam-packed, or in a slower season when the parks are half-empty but with shortened operating hours in which to tour them? How about over a long holiday weekend, or would it be best to simply take the children out of school? These are all questions you must weigh, all questions that will help you reach a decision best for you and your family.

Each season has its pros and its cons. The busy season brings congested parks, long lines, and higher hotel rates but also greatly extended park hours and nightly fireworks and parades at the Magic Kingdom. The slower seasons bring half-filled parks, little waiting in line, and lower hotel rates along with later opening times, earlier closing times, attractions that are closed for rehab, and often the elimination of the nighttime parade and fireworks at the Magic Kingdom. For me, hands down, I will always choose a slower season. If you can stand the guilt and your children are good students, take them out of school—do whatever to avoid the busiest times of the year. If not, the summer months or holidays are certainly better than nothing and, with a bit of planning and a lot of energy, can be more than enjoyable.

The following guidelines may not be exact since each year has different Florida resident offers, special celebrations, conventions, and so forth that affect crowd size. Use them as a general guide to avoiding the parks at their worst.

Park Attendance

Busiest—President's Day week • the last 3 weeks of Mar (staggered spring break around the country) to the week after Easter • the second week of June to the third week of Aug • Thanksgiving weekend • the week of Christmas to just after New Year's

Busy—The last 2 weeks of Feb (avoid President's Day week) to the first part of Mar before the onset of spring break • the month of Oct (a big convention month and the PGA Golf Classic) • the week after Easter until the second week of June

Least busy—The second week of Jan to the first week of Feb (avoiding the Martin Luther King holiday weekend in Jan) • the third week of Aug to the beginning of Oct • the month of Nov excluding Thanksgiving weekend • the week after Thanksgiving until the week of Christmas, a special time when the parks and resorts are festively decorated for the holidays

The Weather at WDW

Weather in Orlando can be quite unpredictable. Summer brings uncomfortably muggy and warm days with almost daily afternoon showers while winter offers many days of beautiful sunshine along with the occasional cold snap. Peak hurricane season begins in August and runs through October, so be prepared for a washout (just about every store in the parks sells inexpensive rain ponchos for that unexpected afternoon shower). The best months of the year with delightfully mild and low humidity weather, relatively small amounts of rainfall, and no danger of hurricanes are November, April, and most of the time in early May. Before leaving call **407-824-4104** for weather information or check one of the many excellent weather sites on the Internet.

MONTH	AVERAGE HIGH TEMP	AVERAGE LOW TEMP	AVERAGE RAINFALL (INCHES)
January	71	49	2.3
February	73	50	3
March	78	55	3.2
April	83	59	1.8
May	88	66	3.6
June	91	72	7.3
July	92	73	7.3
August	92	73	6.8
September	90	72	6
October	85	66	2.4
November	79	58	2.3
December	73	51	2.2

Travel Tips for the Busiest of Times

If at all possible, avoid like the plague the summer months and most importantly any major holiday at Walt Disney World. The busiest holidays are President's Day, the 2 weeks surrounding Easter, July 4th, Thanksgiving weekend, and Christmas through New Year's. Memorial Day is a toss-up, with the only exception to the rule being Labor Day, Columbus Day, and Veteran's Day when parks are crowded but not unbearable.

Remember to use priority seating and Fastpass whenever possible, and pick a resort close to the parks for easy access and midday breaks.

When parks reach full capacity, and they do during the busiest of times, only Disney resort guests are allowed in, making it even more important to stay on property if visiting in high season. For guests staying off-property, arriving at the parks well before opening time when a large percentage of Disney resort guests are still sleeping will almost assure you of getting in. Although they will never release this information in advance, Disney sometimes opens earlier than official opening time during holiday periods when they anticipate record crowds.

What to Pack

Think casual! Park attire is appropriate throughout Disney with the exception of the more stylish resort restaurants (see individual restaurant descriptions). In the warmer months of April through October bring shorts, light-colored short-sleeve or sleeveless shirts (darker colors really attract the heat), comfortable walking shoes (bring two pairs to switch off), socks, sunglasses, hat, bathing suit and cover-up, water resistant footwear, and a rain jacket. Women should bring a fanny pack or light backpack; nothing's worse than lugging a heavy purse around all day. For evenings away from the park at one of the more sophisticated dining venues, women should plan on wearing a sundress or casual pants and top with sandals; men will be comfortable in khakis and a short-sleeve casual shirt with loafers or sandals. Only at Victoria and Albert's and Dux is a jacket required for men.

The remaining months are anyone's guess. The weather is usually mild, but bring an assortment of casual clothing in the form of shorts, jeans, and comfortable pants along with short and long-sleeve shirts, a sweater, hat, sunglasses, bathing suit and cover-up (pools are heated), rain jacket, a light coat, and of course comfortable walking shoes and socks. For evenings away from the parks, women should wear smartly casual transitional clothing with a light jacket and men slacks or khakis and long-sleeve shirts. Florida is known (particularly Nov–Mar) for unexpected cold fronts that will find you in shorts one day and a winter jacket the next, although it never gets uncomfortably hot. Don't get caught off guard or you will find yourself with an unwanted Mickey Mouse wardrobe. Most importantly, always check the Internet for a weather forecast or call **Disney Weather** at **407-824-4104** before packing for your trip.

Water-resistant footwear and fast-drying clothes are desirable at the Animal Kingdom (you will get quite wet on the Kali River Rapids) and most importantly at Universal's Islands of Adventure where several rides will give you a thorough soaking. And don't forget plenty of sunscreen, film, and batteries, all of which can be purchased almost anywhere in Disney but at a premium price.

How Long Should I Plan on Staying?

With four major theme parks at Walt Disney World, two more at Universal Orlando, SeaWorld, specialty parks like Discovery Cove, and several water parks, a long weekend will barely give you a taste of the many attractions in the area. Staying 7 days or more allows enough time to truly enjoy much of what Orlando has to offer. In one week you'll have time to visit all four of Disney's theme parks, spend a day at Universal, hit one of the water parks, and still have a day left over to relax by the pool and rest your feet. Ten days would really be a treat, allowing a trip to both SeaWorld and Discovery Cove plus a bit of time to stop and smell the roses.

Of course, if you can only spare a long weekend, go for it. You will certainly have some tough decisions to make. With only 3 days for touring, go when the parks are not as crowded and plan on visiting the Magic Kingdom, Epcot, and either the Animal Kingdom or Disney MGM Studios with a trip in mind for the following year to pick up all you've missed.

Should I Rent a Car?

Does driving in an unknown place make you uneasy? Do you plan on visiting just the Disney parks or would you also like to go to SeaWorld and Universal? Will you be staying at a resort serviced by the monorail or a more isolated one? Would you like to dine at other resorts or do you see yourself eating at the parks or simply staying put at your hotel? All these factors play a large part in your decision.

The drive from the airport on the new Central Florida GreeneWay is a no-brainer and finding your way around Disney is easy. Traffic is fairly light and there's excellent signage. However, if driving a car in new situations tends to be a nerve-racking experience, use Disney's more-than-adequate transportation system.

If your plans include a stay at the Animal Kingdom Lodge, Old Key West, Wilderness Lodge, the Villas at Disney's Wilderness Lodge, or an off-site property, renting a car provides you with many more options. If you plan to visit Universal Studios, SeaWorld, or Kennedy Space Center, a car is the best choice.

No matter what your plans, a car is usually the best option for traveling to the Animal Kingdom or Disney MGM Studios (parks not serviced by the monorail), the water parks, or for evening restaurant-hopping at many of the excellent resort dining spots. However, you may find it simpler to use Disney transportation when traveling to Downtown Disney where you may want to spend the evening enjoying Pleasure Island without the worry of driving afterward or on weekends when parking can be difficult. You may want to try Disney transportation for a day or two and, if it doesn't work for you, then rent a car. Alamo offers free shuttle service to their Car Care Center location near the Magic Kingdom, and many non-Disney hotels have car rental desks in their lobbies.

Those who would like to sample some of Disney's excellent resort restaurants will find it very time-consuming, not to mention very complex, to resort-hop using Disney transportation. It requires a trip to an open park or Downtown Disney and then another bus to the resort and the same thing back again (of course you can take a cab). Staying at one of the Magic Kingdom resorts with easy monorail access to both the Magic Kingdom and Epcot or at one of the Epcot Resorts, just a walk or boat launch away from Epcot and Disney–MGM Studios, will greatly expand your restaurant choices.

A car is a must at any of the non-Disney properties where transportation options are quite inconvenient. Don't let them tell you differently. Transportation from the off-site properties is inconvenient at best, offering only the bare necessities. The only exception is the hotels on Universal property, extremely convenient to the Universal theme parks and CityWalk; if Universal is all you plan on doing, a car is really not necessary.

In short, you will probably be using a combination of Disney transportation and a car for added convenience. And if you're like me and hate waiting for public transportation, rent a car to save hours of frustration.

Tips for Disney newcomers

- Slow down and enjoy the magic. Resist the urge to see everything at breakneck speed, slowing down long enough to enjoy the many amenities at your resort (you certainly paid enough for them). You can't possibly see it all, so think of this as your first trip to Disney, not your last. There will be time to pick up all the things you missed on the next trip.

- Plan ahead. Decide before your vacation what your priorities are and make a plan of action.

- Get to the parks early! It's amazing, particularly in the busy season, how many of the popular rides you can knock off before half the "World" gets out of bed.

- Take time for a rest in the middle of the day, particularly if you have children in tow and the parks are open late. Stay at one of the Magic Kingdom or Epcot resorts, allowing a return to your room in the middle of the day for a nap or dip in the pool.

- If breakfast at Cinderella's Royal Table in the Magic Kingdom is tops on your child's list, you *must*—I repeat *must*—call exactly 60 days prior at 7 A.M. Orlando time for priority seating or risk missing this highly coveted breakfast. The only time you might get away with sleeping in and booking a bit later in the day is during the extremely slow season.

- Always come prepared for an afternoon shower during the rainy summer months even if the sky looks perfectly clear in the morning. Rent a locker to store your rain gear, circling back if skies start to look threatening. If you're caught unprepared, just about every store in the parks sells inexpensive rain ponchos.

- If a lounge chair is a priority at the water parks, you must arrive at opening time to secure one.

- Use Fastpass, Disney's nifty timesaving device offered at all four theme parks, saving hours in line (see the Fastpass section for each park).

- Utilize priority seating, especially in the busier times of year (see pages 321-322 for a more detailed explanation), to save hours of waiting and frustration.

- Allow plenty of time to reach the theme parks each morning. It's easy to miss your breakfast priority seating when enough time has not been allocated.

- Be spontaneous. If something catches your eye, even if it's not on your daily list of things to do, stop and explore or you may miss something wonderful.

- Be attuned to the limitations of your children. If they're tired, take a break; if their feet hurt, get them a stroller (forget that they outgrew one years ago); if a ride scares them, don't force the issue. It will make your day and the day of other park visitors a lot less stressful.

- If your party likes to split up, bring pagers, two-way radios, or cell phones to keep in touch.

- Wear broken-in, comfortable footwear. Better yet, bring two pairs and rotate them. Nothing is worse than blisters on your first day, then having to nurse them for the remainder of your vacation.

Arrival Information

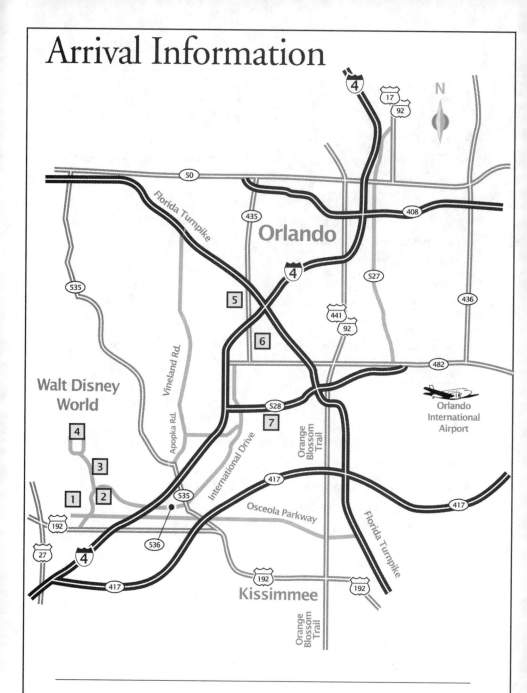

1. Animal Kingdom
2. Disney-MGM Studios
3. EPCOT
4. Magic Kingdom
5. Universal Orlando
6. Wet 'n Wild
7. Sea World of Florida

CHAPTER 2

Arrival at Disney World

GETTING TO WALT DISNEY WORLD

By Car

Walt Disney World is located off Interstate 4, 25 miles southwest of Orlando and west of the Florida Turnpike. From Interstate 95, U.S. Highway 1, or southbound on the Florida Turnpike, take I-4 west and follow the signs to the correct WDW exit for your resort or theme park destination. Visitors coming from southbound Interstate 75 need to take the Turnpike south to I-4 west and follow the signs to WDW. Those traveling northbound on the Turnpike should take the Osceola Parkway that will lead directly to WDW.

Once inside WDW, excellent signage will direct you to all destinations; however, you'll need to know what area your resort belongs to in order to find your way. The Contemporary, Grand Floridian, Polynesian, Wilderness Lodge, and the Villas at Wilderness Lodge are located in the Magic Kingdom Resort Hotels area. The Boardwalk Inn and Villas, Yacht and Beach Club, Beach Club Villas, and Walt Disney Swan and Dolphin Hotels are in the Epcot Resort Hotels area. The Animal Kingdom Lodge sits in the Animal Kingdom area and Old Key West in the Downtown Disney Resort Hotels area.

From the Airport

Excellent signage and a new toll road from the airport make for an easy 25-minute drive. Take the South Exit out of the airport to toll road State Route 417 South, also known as the Central Florida GreeneWay, and follow the signage to Walt Disney World and your resort or theme park destination. The drive is approximately 22 miles. Avoid the north route out of the airport to toll Highway 528 (unless your destination is Universal Orlando), also known as the Beeline Expressway, and then to I-4 during rush hour traffic. It's the old route before the new toll road, one often jammed with traffic and only slightly shorter.

Airport Transportation

For personalized service, book private car or limousine transfers prior to your departure from **Tiffany Towncars** at **888-838-2161** (www.tiffanytowncar.com), **Florida Towncars** at **800-525-7246** (www.floridatowncar.com), **Atlantis Limousine** at **407-592-7433** (www.atlantislimo.com), or **Advantage Limousine** at **800-438-4114** (www.advantagelimo.com). Towncars are $80–95 round-trip and limousines run approximately $200–300 round-trip (depending on the size of your party). Your driver will meet you at baggage claim. A customary 15–20% gratuity should be considered and reservations are mandatory.

Mears Transportation offers van service to all Disney hotels. Arrangements can be made in advance by calling **800-759-5219** or on arrival at the Mears desk on the second level of the airport. Return reservations should be made at least 24 hours prior by calling **407-423-5566**. The price is $28 round-trip per adult and $20 for children (those under age 4 are free). With three or more people in your party it will cost about the same for a Towncar, a wiser and certainly more comfortable alternative. Because Mears makes several stops at different resorts, add at least a half hour to your trip. You can always take a taxi, but you'll find it's not the best choice with cab fares averaging over $90 round-trip.

Car Rental

Alamo Rent A Car, the official car rental company of WDW, can be found at both the airport and at the Car Care Center near the Magic Kingdom with free shuttle service provided to and from your hotel. For convenience, stick with the companies located on airport property (**National, Alamo, Budget, Avis, and Dollar**) whose cars are parked a quick walk away from the baggage claim area. Off-property car companies include **Thrifty** and **Hertz.** All of the above have another location somewhere in the vicinity of Walt Disney World.

For something more luxurious, try the Hertz Prestige Collection, which stocks Jaguars, Volvos, and Land Rovers. Specific models may be reserved and a complimentary NeverLost navigational system is included.

DISNEY TRANSPORTATION

Disney's complimentary transportation system, designed for the exclusive use of Disney resort guests (although no ID is required to ride), is in most cases extremely efficient. A handy transportation map is available on check-in. Taxis can be found at every resort and theme park. For more information call **407-WDW-RIDE.**

Bus Transportation

Disney has an extensive and extremely reliable system of over 700 clean, air-conditioned buses traversing the extent of the property. Designed for the exclusive use of Disney's registered guests, buses depart approximately every 20 minutes, carrying guests to all four theme parks, both water parks, Downtown Disney, and all resort hotels. Some are direct while others require a change at either the Ticket and Transportation Center (more commonly know as the TTC), Disney's central hub located near the Magic Kingdom, or Downtown Disney.

One advantage of bus transportation is the convenient drop-off directly in front of the park entrance translating into no parking hassles and no waiting for a tram to the park entrance. The downside occurs after park closing when quite a line forms; consider leaving just a few minutes before the fireworks are over or hanging out to shop at one of the stores near the exit.

Getting easily from one resort to another is one of Disney's glaring problems. Those staying at one of the Magic Kingdom or Epcot resorts have many choices within walking distance or a monorail ride away, but those utilizing bus transportation find the only way to accomplish this feat is to take the quickest form of transportation to the nearest theme park and then bus to the resort of choice. Of course, this only works during theme park operating hours. Late at night it's necessary to bus to Downtown Disney and then to the resort. For example, it takes a good hour and a half to travel between say the Yacht Club Resort and Wilderness Lodge. Only by renting a car or hiring a taxi can this situation be avoided.

Monorail

Twelve monorails, each holding 300 passengers, travel over 13 miles of track at up to 40 mph on three lines: the monorail between Epcot and the Ticket and Transportation Center (TTC), the express monorail to the Magic Kingdom, and the Magic Kingdom Resorts monorail. All use the TTC as their central hub. Monorails traveling counterclockwise around the Seven Seas Lagoon offer a nonstop ride between the TTC and the Magic Kingdom. Monorails running clockwise stop at the Grand Floridian, the Polynesian, the Contemporary, and the TTC. Between Epcot and the Magic Kingdom is a lovely ride with easy access between the parks.

Tip: If the operator's car is empty of visitors, ask the cast member on duty at the monorail stop about the possibility of riding up front. Up to four people at a time are allowed.

Boat Service

Ferryboats at the TTC transport visitors to the Magic Kingdom. The Magic Kingdom is also accessible by water taxi from the Polynesian, Grand Floridian, and the Wilderness Lodge and Villas. Both Epcot and Disney–MGM Studios are accessible by water taxi from Boardwalk Inn and Villas, Yacht and Beach Club, Beach Club Villas, and the Walt Disney World Swan and Dolphin. Downtown Disney is accessible from the Old Key West Resort by water taxi.

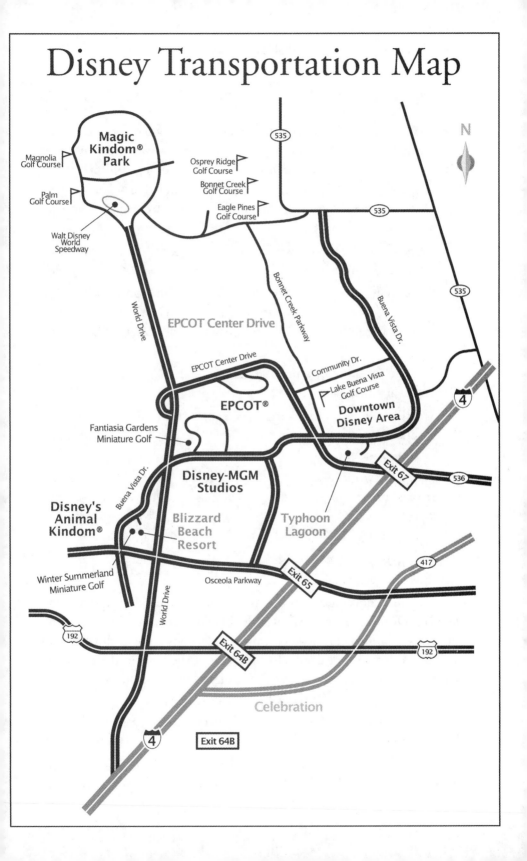

Tips for romance

- If traveling with children, plan an evening or two on your own at a romantic restaurant or a night on the town at Downtown Disney. Leave the kids at one of Disney's excellent resort childcare centers. If your child is under 4 or not potty trained, call **Kid's Nite Out** at **407-827-5444** for in-room childcare (reservations must be made in advance).

- Consider springing for two rooms. Disney guarantees connecting rooms for families with children.

- Bring along a bottle of wine to enjoy in your room or on your balcony. The bottled wine selections at the Disney resort shops are either sparse or nil. Of course, room service usually has a nice selection.

- Arrange for a couples massage at the Grand Floridian Spa in a candlelit room.

- Watch the evening fireworks spectacular from one of the resort beaches. Perfect spots can be found at the beaches of the Polynesian, Grand Floridian, and the Yacht and Beach Club.

- Take a Fireworks Cruise from one of the Magic Kingdom or Epcot resorts; bring along a bottle of champagne, two glasses, and enjoy!

BASIC DISNEY REFERENCE GUIDE

Alcoholic beverages—You'll find alcohol served at every park and hotel on Disney property, except at the Magic Kingdom. The legal drinking age in Florida is 21; however, most of Disney's lounges allow minors as long as they do not drink alcohol or sit at the bar. Bottles of liquor, wine, and beer can be purchased in at least one shop in every WDW resort and/or from room service.

ATM machines—Located at each park as well as in or near the lobby of each resort.

Car care and gasoline—Exxon has three stations in Disney World open 24 hours: on Floridian Way near the Magic Kingdom, across from

Downtown Disney's Pleasure Island, and at the entrance to the Boardwalk across from MGM Studios. For car repair, go to the **AAA Car Care Center** adjoining the Exxon station near the Magic Kingdom open Mon–Sat (**407-824-0976**). If your car becomes disabled while on Disney property, AAA offers complimentary towing to the Car Care Center; just contact **security** by calling **407-824-4777**.

Childcare—Disney childcare choices include the **Cub's Den** at Wilderness Lodge, the **Sandcastle Club** at the Yacht and Beach Club Resort, the **Mouseketeer Club** at the Grand Floridian and the Contemporary, **Simba's Cubhouse** at the Animal Kingdom Lodge, **Camp Dolphin** at the Swan and Dolphin Resort, and the **Never Land Club** at the Polynesian (my favorite), all offering childcare services for potty-trained children ages 4–12. See individual resort descriptions for detailed information. Open to Disney resort guests only. Reservations should be made at least 24 hours in advance by calling **407-WDW-DINE**.

The off-property resorts offer excellent childcare facilities. At the Grand Cypress Resort (the Hyatt Regency and the Villas of Grand Cypress) is Camp Hyatt and at Gaylord Palms you'll find La Petite Academy Kids Station.

For in-room or drop-off services, Disney recommends **Kid's Nite Out**. Call **407-827-5444** at least 24 hours in advance. All employees receive a very thorough background check.

Dietary requests— Dietary requests such as kosher, vegetarian, low-salt, or low-fat can be accommodated at most Disney full-service restaurants if requested at least 24 hours in advance. Most full-service and many counter-service restaurants offer at least one vegetarian choice, which I have tried to reflect in my entree examples in the restaurant section.

Environmental awareness—Disney's environmental commitment is more than commendable. Their efforts include the recycling of over 30% of waste, distribution of prepared, unserved food to local missions, collection of food waste for compost production, purchasing of recycled products and products with reduced packaging, using reclaimed water for irrigation, and recycling containers in every guestroom and throughout the parks.

Flowers and such—Flowers as well as fruit baskets, snack food baskets, cheese trays, and wine can be delivered anywhere on Disney property between 8 A.M.–8 P.M. Call **407-827-3505.**

Groceries—The closest full-service grocery store is 24-hour Goodings Supermarket located in the Crossroads Shopping Center near Downtown Disney. A very small selection is also available at the Gourmet Pantry at the Downtown Disney Marketplace and at each home-away-from-home resort.

Guests with disabilities—Most buses and all ferryboats and monorails as well as many park attractions are wheelchair accessible. Special parking areas are available at all four theme parks, and valet parking is free Thurs–Mon after 5:30 P.M. at Downtown Disney to guests with disabilities. Wheelchairs and electric controlled vehicles (ECVs) may be rented in limited quantities at each theme park. Each resort offers hotel rooms accessible to guests with disabilities including roll-in showers.

Most attractions provide access through the main queue while others have auxiliary entrances for wheelchairs and service animals along with up to five members of your party. Certain attractions require guests to transfer from their wheelchair to a ride system. For detailed information, the helpful *Guidebook for Guests with Disabilities* is available at Guest Relations at each park or at the front desk of each Walt Disney World Resort. Hand-held receivers are available to read captions at more than 20 park attractions. Each theme park offers Assistive Listening Devices, video captioning, Braille guidebooks, and audiotaped tours, all available for a refundable $25 deposit. A sign language interpreter for live shows can be made available with 1 week's notice on certain days of the week (see each individual park for details). For additional information go to **www.disneyworld.com** or call **407-824-4321(voice)** or **407-827-5141(TTY).**

Hair salons—Full-service salons are located at the Grand Floridian, Contemporary, Yacht and Beach Club, and the Dolphin as well as at the Grand Cypress Resort and Gaylord Palms Resort. An old-fashioned barber haircut can be had on Main Street in the Magic Kingdom.

International travelers—Park guides in Spanish, Japanese, French, Italian, Portuguese, and Dutch are found at Guest Relations in each theme park. Personal Translation Units in French, German, Japanese, Portuguese, and Spanish are available at each theme park for 13 of the more popular attractions. Interpreters are available by calling the **Foreign Language Center** at **407-824-7900**. Many restaurants offer menus in several foreign languages. Foreign currency may be exchanged up to $50 daily at Guest Relations at the four theme parks and up to $500 daily at any WDW resort.

Laundry and dry cleaning—Convenient coin-operated washers and dryers are located at every Disney hotel in addition to same-day dry cleaning and laundry service.

Lockers—Lockers can be found in every Disney park including the water parks, Downtown Disney, and the Ticket and Transportation Center (TTC).

Lost and found—Lost item claims may be made at each individual park's Lost and Found. The central **Lost and Found** is located at the TTC where items not claimed the previous day are sent; call **407-824-4245**.

Mail—The closest post office is located at 12541 Highway 535 at the Shoppes of Buena Vista open Mon–Fri from 9 A.M.–4 P.M. and Sat from 9 A.M.–noon. Stamps may be purchased and letters mailed at all four theme parks, Downtown Disney, and all WDW resorts. All shops at WDW offer worldwide shipping for a fee.

Medical care—First aid centers are located at all major theme parks during park hours. Twenty-four hour in-room medical care for nonemergencies is handled by **Florida Hospital Centra Care In-Room (407-238-2000)**. **Centra Care Walk-In Medical Care (407-239-6463)** has five locations open Mon–Fri 8 A.M.–midnight, and Sat–Sun 8 A.M.–10 P.M., with complimentary transportation available and most insurance plans accepted. **Emergency dental services** are available by calling **407-238-2000**. **Emergency medical** needs are met by the **Sand Lake Hospital** at I-4 Exit 74A, or at **Celebration Health** located on WDW property in the town of Celebration. WDW provides complimentary refrigeration for insulin; however, there is a $10-per-night charge for small in-room refrigerators.

Money matters—Walt Disney World accepts cash, traveler's checks, personal checks (at the resorts only with a $50 limit per day and only if drawn on a U.S. bank along with a valid driver's license and a current major credit card), Disney Dollars (available at Disney Stores, Guest Relations, and Resort Services, although I can't for the life of me understand why anyone would purchase them except as a gift), and seven types of credit cards: American Express, MasterCard, Visa, Discover, Japanese Credit Bureau, Diners Club, and the Disney Credit Card.

Guests of a Disney-owned property may charge throughout Disney by using their room key as long as a credit card imprint is given at check-in. ATM machines are readily available throughout WDW with locations at each resort, each theme park, Downtown Disney, and the TTC.

SunTrust Bank (407-828-6118), located across from Downtown Disney Marketplace, is the Official Bank of WDW offering many services including ATM machines, foreign currency exchange, emergency check cashing, cash advances on credit cards, American Express traveler's checks services, and wire transfers. Open Mon–Wed and Fri 9 A.M.–4 P.M., and Thurs 9 A.M.–6 P.M.

Pager rentals—Each Disney park and resort offers pager rentals at Guest Relations.

Parking—Parking at Disney theme parks is free to all registered guests of Walt Disney World resorts as well as for Annual Passport holders. All others pay $7 per day. Make sure you make a note of what section and aisle you have parked in; the lots are enormous. Save your receipt if you are planning on park-hopping; it allows you to park for that day only at any of the other Disney theme parks for no additional fee.

All Disney resorts now charge $6 per day for valet parking with no charge for self-parking.

Pets—Only service dogs for guests with disabilities are allowed in Disney's theme parks and resorts. Pet kennels are available at the TTC, Epcot, Disney–MGM Studios, the Animal Kingdom, and Fort Wilderness Resort and Campground. Proof of vaccination is required. Day boarding is $6. Overnight boarding, available only at the TTC, is $9 (including food) for WDW resort guests and $11 for off-site guests. Pets must be walked daily by their owners. More unusual pets such as birds, ferrets, nonvenomous snakes, and small rodents are accepted as long as they are in their own carriers. Reservations not accepted. Call **407-824-6568** for more information.

Parent/guardian switch—Parents traveling with young children who don't meet height restrictions should consider utilizing the rider switch program. One parent waits with the child while the other rides and then the second parent hands off the child and goes to the head of the line. Just speak to the cast member on duty.

Safety—Walt Disney World is generally a safe environment, but caution must still be taken. There were three late-night robbery/abductions in the parking lot of Downtown Disney in early 2002. Be alert at all times, particularly at night, and try to travel in a group. Always lock your room door and make sure you verify who is knocking before allowing them entry. Use the safe provided in your room for money and valuables. Park in well-lit areas, lock your car, and be aware of your surroundings when leaving the car. Take extra care when traveling to Orlando and places outside Walt Disney World where security is less stringent.

Security checkpoints—Since September 11, all bags are checked before entering the theme parks. Allow extra time if arriving for priority seating.

Smoking policy—Disney has a very strict smoking policy. All WDW restaurants and public areas at each resort are smoke-free environments. Tobacco products are not sold in the theme parks, where smoking is limited to designated areas; look for the cigarette symbol on the guide maps. Smoking is allowed in all lounges and all Pleasure Island clubs with the exception of the Adventurer's Club and Comedy Warehouse. Rooms are set aside for smokers on request at each WDW resort.

Strollers and wheelchair rentals—Strollers, wheelchairs, and ECVs may be rented at all major theme parks. Retain your receipt for a replacement at any other Disney theme park for that day only. Wheelchairs are also available at all Disney resorts.

Telephone calls—Orlando has a 10-digit calling system meaning you must dial the area code of 407 followed by the number when making a local call anywhere in the Orlando area.

VIP tour services—For those who want special service, Disney offers personalized tours of all four theme parks. For $75 per hour with a 5-hour minimum, a VIP guide will assist you and up to nine others with a customized day at the parks and plenty of Disney trivia along the way. Don't expect to move to the front of the line, but do expect special seating for parades, stage shows, and dining. Reservations must be made at least 48 hours in advance by calling **407-560-4033.**

ENGAGEMENTS, WEDDINGS, AND HONEYMOONS AT DISNEY

More than 15,000 couples have taken their wedding vows in the storybook atmosphere of WDW, and countless newlyweds have enjoyed their dream honeymoon. Imagine being escorted to your wedding in Cinderella's glass coach with horses and footmen in attendance or perhaps a themed wedding in Epcot's Italy Pavilion surrounded by a replica of St. Mark's Square. Everything can be arranged from the flowers to the photographer, the waiters to the music. You can even have Disney characters at the reception. To speak to a **wedding planner** call **407-828-3400. Honeymooners** should call **800-370-6009.** Check out **www.disneyweddings.com** and **www.disneyhoneymoons.com.**

Wedding locations—Although weddings are allowed just about anywhere on Disney property, here are some of the most popular sites. If you'd like your wedding at one of the theme parks, expect the price to skyrocket. The **Wedding Pavilion** at the Grand Floridian Resort, a gazebo-shaped structure nestled on the shores of the Seven Seas Lagoon with a magical view of Cinderella's Castle, is the hands-down favorite. The **Rose Garden** fronting Cinderella's Castle at the Magic Kingdom is another top pick. **Cinderella's Castle** offers a medieval-style banquet afterward.

At Epcot, there is the **Living Seas Lounge**, which has a 5.7-million-gallon aquarium as a backdrop, or any of the **World Showcase pavilions.** **Sea Breeze Point** at Disney's Boardwalk Resort offers a white gazebo on the Boardwalk overlooking Crescent Lake. There's also a wedding gazebo located in a serene rose garden at the **Yacht Club Resort.**

Sunset Pointe at the Polynesian Resort is on a grassy hill overlooking the Seven Seas Lagoon with Cinderella's Castle in the background. **Sunrise Terrace** at the Wilderness Lodge offers a 4th-floor balcony overlooking the pine trees and Bay Lake. You can also have your marriage ceremony on Disney Cruise Line's private island, **Castaway Cay**.

Wedding themes—Choices include a traditional wedding to a variety of Disney-themed weddings. Some theme ideas include an Under the Sea wedding at the Living Seas Pavilion, a Beauty and the Beast Ball Wedding, a Cinderella Wedding, or a Winter Wonderland Wedding.

Wedding/honeymoon packages—Disney's **Intimate Wedding** packages are just how they sound, small and intimate with a maximum of eight guests at your choice of one of five locations at Disney Deluxe Resorts. Included are accommodations, Ultimate Park Hoppers, an onsite wedding coordinator, wedding officiant, bouquet for the bride and boutonniere for the groom, reception including the cake, a violinist, flautist or guitarist for the ceremony as well as the reception, limousine, dinner for two, romance basket, wedding gift, and certificate. Prices for 4-night packages begin at around $3,300. Events with more than eight guests are considered **Custom Weddings**, which begin at $7,500.

Disney **Cruise Line Intimate Wedding** packages begin at around $4,000 for a 3-day cruise and include a ceremony on Castaway Cay, Disney's private island, marriage license, concierge service, services of a wedding planner, a pianist for the wedding, cake and champagne reception, seating for two at Palo (the adults-only dining room) on your wedding night, romance basket, and special wedding gift.

The **Honeymoon Grand Plan** includes accommodations at a deluxe resort, Ultimate Park Hoppers, commemorative Disney Fairy Tale Honeymoon pins and tote bag filled with treats, pre-arrival honeymoon itinerary planning, all meals, unlimited use of selected recreational facilities, admission to Cirque du Soleil, a fireworks cruise, unlimited use of selected theme park tours, a romantic spa treatment, a Leave a Legacy tile at Epcot, and a professional photography session. Prices for a 3-night package begin at around $3,000 per couple.

A 7-night **Land and Sea Honeymoon** combines a stay at WDW with a 3- or 4-night Disney cruise including the same amenities as the Honeymoon Escape Package along with champagne in your stateroom, a massage, priority seating at Palo, and his and her watches. Prices are around $2,700–4,100 per couple.

CHAPTER 3

Accommodations

Disney is rich in choices for the deluxe traveler. But what is best for you? Let's try to narrow down the field of possibilities by pinpointing your party's personality and preferences.

Those traveling with small children will find themselves spending quite a bit of time at the Magic Kingdom. Strongly consider choosing one of the Magic Kingdom Resorts where the park is just a short monorail hop away, easily accessible for a quick afternoon nap or a dip in the pool. Adults traveling without children will probably enjoy being closer to Epcot and Disney–MGM Studios, so consider one of the Epcot resorts. Here it's just a short walk or boat ride away from both parks as well as a world of possibilities in nearby dining and entertainment. Those who enjoy nature and would like to be in a quiet, more isolated hotel should opt for the Animal Kingdom Lodge, where hundreds of animals roam just 30 feet from your room balcony. If the convenience and comfort of a living area and kitchen is appealing, think about one of the home-away-from-home resorts located throughout WDW. If you plan on spending several days at Universal with perhaps a visit to SeaWorld or Discovery Cove, book 3 or 4 nights at one of the hotels near Universal and then afterward move to a Disney hotel.

Also consider room type preferences. Is a view of the water or pool important? Or would you rather pay less and have a view of the resort's gardens? Will a standard room be all that you need or should you consider one on the concierge level or perhaps even a suite? Of course budget, together with how much time will be spent in the room, are major considerations and will play a large part in your decision. If hanging out at the hotel is definitely part of your plan, the concierge rooms are a smart idea at about $100 more per day per room. These accommodations, located on a keyed-access floor, offer the use of a private lounge with complimentary continental breakfast, snacks throughout the day, before-dinner hors d'oeuvres and cocktails, and late evening cordials and desserts. This is in addition to private registration and check-out and the assistance of a concierge staff ready to assist you with priority seating, special dinner shows, or anything else within their power. Definitely a nice plus to your vacation. Suites in each of the deluxe resorts come in virtually all shapes and sizes, some as large as 2,000 or more square feet, certainly the most luxurious way to go if your pocketbook allows it.

Would you rather stay within WDW or do you prefer an off-property location? Staying on property certainly has its pluses. In addition to the many benefits (see page 31 for more details), consider the ease of transportation. Parents of teens can allow them time on their own without worrying about their every move. And teens will love the freedom of hopping aboard the monorail or a Disney bus to tour the parks without parents. I consider only a handful of off-property resorts as deluxe, all of them either within 5 or 10 minutes of Walt Disney World. Of course, always consider Universal's hotels if your plans include a few days at the Universal parks. One of the chief reasons to consider a stay off-property is if someone (particularly someone who is paying) is Mickey Mouse phobic. For them, Disney theming, though terrific, is a bit of overkill and the thought of spending the entire day in the park and then returning to more of the same is just too much.

WALT DISNEY WORLD RESORTS

Although Walt Disney World offers travelers a choice of 22 resorts, only those meeting the standard of superior first class or deluxe have been considered for review in this guidebook. All have attractive guestrooms, landscaped grounds of sheer artistry, exceptional service, top-notch recreational facilities and services, and, with the exclusion of some of the home-away-from-home properties, at least one excellent restaurant if not two or three. And all, with the exception of the off-site properties, offer Disney's special touch.

Benefits of staying at Disney

- Complimentary and convenient Disney transportation by monorail, motor coach, ferryboat, and water taxi.
- Complimentary parking at Disney theme parks.
- Easy access to the parks, making midday breaks and naps possible, plus allowing parties to effortlessly split up midday to go their independent ways.
- Charge privileges utilizing your resort identification cards (a credit card imprint must be left at the registration desk) for purchases throughout Disney.
- E-Ticket Nights when, for an additional fee, the Magic Kingdom is open only to WDW resort guests after official closing time.
- Guaranteed park admission to Disney's theme parks, particularly important during busy holiday periods when filled to capacity parks often close to non-Disney resort guests.
- Extra Magic Hour, 1 hour early opening at a different theme park each morning. The schedule is:

Sun—Magic Kingdom	Wed—Epcot
Mon—Animal Kingdom	Thurs—Magic Kingdom
Tues—Disney-MGM Studios	Fri—Animal Kingdom
	Sat—Disney–MGM Studios

- Package delivery from anywhere on property directly to your hotel.
- Preferred tee times at Disney's six golf courses.
- The Magic of Disney 24 hours a day.

Disney Resorts

Although Disney offers a nice range of resorts in every price category, we will only consider the deluxe resorts and the home-away-from-home properties. The moderate properties, though interesting and well themed, do not fit the designation of luxury and, of course, the budget properties do not even come close.

Disney's Deluxe Properties

Disney's deluxe properties are graced with impressive lobbies, painstakingly landscaped grounds, first-rate restaurants, elaborately themed pools, and gracious accommodations. These include the Grand Floridian Resort and Spa, the Polynesian Resort, the Contemporary Resort, the Wilderness Lodge, the Animal Kingdom Lodge, the Boardwalk Inn, the Yacht and Beach Club, and the Walt Disney World Swan and Dolphin.

The Wilderness Lodge as well as the Animal Kingdom Lodge are a slightly different level of deluxe. Standard rooms here are smaller than other deluxe properties; however, what they lack in room space they more than make up for in atmosphere. Opt for a deluxe room instead of a standard at these properties and you will be more than satisfied.

Those regulars of 5-star properties such as the Ritz Carlton or Four Seasons should not expect quite the same amenities at Disney. Although Disney's properties are very nice, don't look for triple-sheeted beds, soft down pillows, plush towels, deluxe toiletries, giant marble bathrooms, and butlers. And don't expect pay movies, HBO, and your choice of 100 channels. The point is to just enjoy the unparalleled theming and exceptionally friendly service in the 4-star-rated rooms at the "Happiest Place on Earth."

For those choosing to stay off-property, the deluxe properties include the Celebration Hotel, the Hyatt Regency Grand Cypress, the Villas of Grand Cypress, and the Gaylord Palms Resort. And at Universal are the Hard Rock Hotel, Portofino Bay Hotel, and the Peabody Hotel. All are excellent alternatives to the Disney resorts.

Disney's Home-Away-From-Home Properties

Old Key West, the Villas at Disney's Wilderness Lodge, the Boardwalk Villas, and the Beach Club Villas are Disney's four home-away-from-home properties. All are Disney Vacation Club timeshare properties leased out to nonmembers when rooms are available, a great way to enjoy Disney with all the conveniences of home including a full kitchen, living room, and a bath for each bedroom.

Although they come highly recommended, I am not terribly enamored of the studio rooms, whose only advantage is a mini-kitchen consisting of a microwave, small refrigerator, and sink. A better choice for just about the same price is a guestroom at one of the deluxe hotels. The Boardwalk and the Beach Club Villas have easy access to all services and recreation facilities of their adjoining hotels plus the advantage of being close to the many shops and restaurants of the Boardwalk and nearby Epcot. The Villas at Disney's Wilderness Lodge is just a hop, skip, and a jump away from the facilities of the adjoining Wilderness Lodge and a boat ride away from the Magic Kingdom. Although Old Key West is a beautiful property, it has a more remote location and lacks in restaurant facilities, offering only one moderate dining venue.

Check-In and -Out

Check-in time is 3 P.M. at all Disney resorts and 4 P.M. at all home-away-from-home resorts. If arriving early in the day, go straight to your hotel to register and have your luggage stored until check-in time, then head off to a park or spend time exploring the property. In slower seasons it's sometimes possible to check in early.

On check-in you'll receive a resort bulletin with up-to-date information on hotel services, recreation, and special events as well as a Walt Disney World Update with park hours, rehabs (what's attractions are currently closed for renovation), and special events. If you'd like a head start, ask for a copy of the park guide maps. You'll also be handed a Disney Transportation Guide, an extremely useful tool for drivers as well as those utilizing Disney's extensive transportation system.

Re-request any preferences at registration. Be sure to ask to have your room pointed out on a map of the hotel; if the location is undesirable say so before leaving the desk. And if you've booked the concierge level or a suite, remember to identify yourself as a concierge guest to the bellman on arrival. He will escort you directly to their private check-in.

On check-out, if you're taking a late plane home and plan on spending your last day in the parks, simply store your luggage with either the concierge or valet parking until your return later in the day. Remember check-out is at 11 A.M. and your Ultimate Park Hoppers are good until midnight of the same day. If you're staying at more than one Disney property, valet services will transfer your luggage free of charge with luggage arriving by 3 P.M.

Disney Discounts

Yes, this book is about a Disney deluxe vacation, but even the biggest spenders like a bargain. And bargains are as easily available at the deluxe resorts as they are at the budget ones. Better yet, opportunities to save on everything from dining to entertainment to behind-the-scenes tours abound. With the many discounts available, only in the busiest seasons should anyone pay full price for a Disney resort. Here are some of the many ways to save:

Seasonal discounts—Rooms at WDW are priced on a seasonal basis using a 4-season system that varies according to resort type. Remember, the busier the season, the more expensive the room. Approximate seasons for deluxe hotels are as follows:

- Value season—early Jan to mid-Feb, early Jul or late Aug (depending on the resort) to late Sept, and early Nov to right before Christmas
- Regular season—end of Apr to early Jul or the end of Aug (depending on the resort) and again from late Sept to early Nov
- Peak season—mid-Feb to the end of Apr
- Holiday season—just before Christmas to Dec 31

Annual Pass rates—This is one of Disney's best bargains. With the purchase of an Annual Pass, you'll not only receive unlimited park admission for 1 year but also excellent room rates. Only one person in the room need be a pass holder to obtain up to a 30% discount available throughout most of the year. Also included is a quarterly *Mickey Monitor* newsletter, a special Illuminations lagoonside viewing area in Italy, and discounted admission to Blizzard Beach, Typhoon Lagoon, Pleasure Island, and DisneyQuest as well as discounts on selected dining, merchandise, car rentals, behind-the-scenes tours, spa treatments, water sports, boat rentals, and miniature golf.

Resort discounts usually aren't available until 2 to 3 months in advance and are, of course, limited. A good strategy is to hold a room at the regular price just to be safe and continue calling periodically until the pass holder discount becomes available, at which point the reservation agent will lower your rate. With the amount saved, the additional cost of an Annual Pass over a Park Hopper could pay for itself in just 1 night.

Sunshine Getaway Package—Each year in Jan through the first half of Feb, Disney offers a Sunshine Getaway Package at a great price including accommodations and Ultimate Park Hoppers.

Fall Fantasy Package—Each year from the end of August through September, Disney offers a Fall Fantasy Package similar to the Sunshine Getaway Package above.

AAA discounts—If purchasing admission tickets or accommodations from the AAA Vacations desk, members receive not only a discounted price of 10–20% but a AAA Vacations Diamond Card for dining, behind-the-scenes tours, recreation, and merchandise discounts plus preferred viewing areas for the Magic Kingdom and Epcot fireworks and preferred parking near the entrance of the theme parks (the parking fee still applies). AAA rates are also available through Disney Central Reservations.

Entertainment publications—By purchasing either your local or the Orlando version of this discount book at a cost of around $35, members are eligible for 50% off discounts to hotels throughout the U.S. Participating deluxe hotels in Orlando are the Walt Disney World Swan and Dolphin and Universal's Hard Rock and Portofino Bay Hotel. To purchase go online at **www.entertainment.com.**

Florida residents—Residents of Florida receive great benefits, particularly in the slower times of the year. Call **407-824-4321** for special prices on hotel rooms and theme park passes.

Amusementpark.com—For discounts on park tickets go online to **www.amusementpark.com.** As an example, the savings on a 4-Day Hopper is $5 per ticket, including shipping.

Making Your Reservations

Don't call for reservations until you narrow the field down to two or three resorts that best suit your needs. Reserve as soon as you possibly can, particularly for travel during major holidays or summer, to assure that your preferred resort and room type are available. Again, decisions need to be made. Is it best to go with a package or book a "room only" reservation and treat your air, hotel, and car as separate elements? Is it wiser to make the reservations yourself or call your travel agent? How about booking your trip on the Internet? All good questions. With such a wide array of booking choices on the market, there is no substitute for a good travel agent. They can certainly save you a lot of time, headaches, and usually, money.

For those of you who like to do it yourself, here are some options.

Disney and Universal Booking Numbers

Call **Walt Disney World Central Reservations** at 407-934-7639 or go online at **www.disneyworld.com** for all on-site Disney hotels. Universal's on-site hotels may be booked online at **www.uescape.com** or by calling **888-U ESCAPE** or **800-23-LOEWS**.

Major Airlines Servicing Orlando

Major airlines servicing Orlando are **Delta** (the official airline of WDW), **American, United, Continental, Southwest, Northwest, America West, Air Canada, Canadian Airlines,** and **US Airways.** Find the lowest airfare either by calling your travel agent, each individual airline servicing your city (a lot of work), or shopping the Internet, particularly websites such as **Expedia, Orbitz,** and **Travelocity.** No one should ever pay full fare for a coach class seat unless booking at the last minute. Try to stay over a weekend for the lowest fares, and shop, shop, shop. Fares to Orlando tend to be quite a bargain.

Booking a Package or Not

Hundreds of travel packages are out there, many of which will save you money. But many won't. In my experience, both as a travel agent and as an individual traveling to Disney, many are not a bargain at all. By utilizing the above discounts and buying your airfare separately, you will usually come out ahead of the game. Remember when purchasing a package to consider if all of the included options will be used. If not, you'll almost certainly be overpaying. Paying for everything in one package is certainly convenient but it is always worth the effort to shop around. Travel agents have access to tour operators as well as the discounted offers above and can help you decide what is in your best interest. The following are worthy travel companies who market Disney:

- Walt Disney World Central Reservations: **407-934-7639** or **www.disneyworld.com**

- Walt Disney Travel Company: **800-828-0228** or **www.disneytravel. com**
- Delta Dream Vacations: **800-872-7786** or **www.deltavacations.com/ disney.html**
- American Express Vacations: **800-297-6898** or online at **www.travel. americanexpress.com**
- AAA Vacations: call your local AAA or **888-937-5523** or go online at **www.csaa.com**
- Continental Vacations: **800-634-5555** or **www.coolvacations.com**
- American Airlines Flyaway Vacations: **800-321-2121** or **www.aa vacation.com**
- Universal Studios Vacations: **888-322-5537** or **www.universal orlando.com**
- US Airways Vacations: **800-455-0123** or **www.usairways vacations.com**

Disney's Vacation Package Plans

Walt Disney World Central Reservations as well as several of the above tour operators offer Disney's special package plans. The more elaborate ones are only a good buy if you think you will use all of the additional features. Beware of purchasing a plan with elements you do not want or need. First-timers may want to stick with the basic plan and pay separately for everything else as needed during their vacation.

Disney also offers **air/sea vacations**. Those who love cruising should consider 3 or 4 nights on the *Disney Wonder* or 7 nights on the *Disney Magic* combined with several days at a Disney resort hotel, the best of both worlds (see page 471 for detailed information on the Disney Cruise Line).

Disney's package plans are as follows:

Basic plan—Includes accommodations and general admission to Disney's Wide World of Sports.

Dream Maker package—Includes accommodations, Ultimate Park Hoppers, commemorative Disney trading pins, and one complimentary feature per room including a round of miniature golf for each guest, a Leave a Legacy tile at Epcot, and a storytelling event at Epcot for each guest.

Dream Maker Silver Plan—Includes accommodations, Ultimate Park Hoppers, commemorative Disney Trading Pins, access to preferred parade viewing at the Animal Kingdom and preferred fireworks viewing in the Magic Kingdom and Epcot, and two Magical Wishes Features per person, per night, including breakfast, lunch, or dinner at your choice of selected theme park and resort restaurants, select behind-the-scenes theme park tours, selected spa treatments (counts as two wishes), up to 6 hours at a Disney Children's Activity Center, admission to Cirque du Soleil (counts as two wishes), and more.

Dream Maker Gold Plan—Includes accommodations, Ultimate Park Hoppers, breakfast, lunch, and dinner per person, per night at your choice of theme park and resort restaurants, unlimited use of select resort recreation including golf, fishing, and boating, unlimited access to select behind-the-scenes tours, unlimited access to Disney's Children's Activity Centers, a Commemorative Disney Trading Pin, access to preferred parade viewing at the Animal Kingdom and preferred fireworks viewing in the Magic Kingdom and Epcot, and admission to Cirque du Soleil.

Dream Maker Platinum Plan—Includes accommodations, Ultimate Park Hoppers, Disney Magical Moments Trading Pins, personalized pre-arrival itinerary planning, breakfast, lunch, and dinner daily at your choice of over 150 restaurants including Victoria and Albert's and in-room dining, light snacks and refreshments, unlimited use of select resort recreation, admission to Cirque du Soleil, one spa treatment per person (ages 10 and older), an exclusive Disney Grand Plan keepsake, a Fireworks Cruise, unlimited access to Disney Children's Activity Centers and in-room private childcare, two images on a Leave a Legacy tile at Epcot, reserved seating to Fantasmic at Disney–MGM Studios, access to preferred parade viewing at the Animal Kingdom and preferred fireworks viewing in the Magic Kingdom and Epcot, and unlimited access to select behind-the-scenes tours.

Great Golf Escape—Includes accommodations, one round of golf per person, per night's stay including green fees, cart rental, club cleaning and storage, a bucket of range balls, $25 same-day second round, 30-minute private golf lesson, complimentary round-trip transportation to golf courses, and preferred 120-day advance booking of tee times.

Considerations When Booking Your Vacation

When considering a concierge-level room, take into account the schedule you will more than likely keep during your vacation. If you plan on spending most of the day and into the evening at the parks or perhaps going straight to dinner from the parks, the additional price for concierge service will not be worth the expense. You'll probably only have time to take advantage of the continental breakfast and perhaps the late night cordials and dessert, with the remaining offerings wasted. If returning to the hotel to dress and relax before dinner or an afternoon swim at the pool sounds more to your liking, the concierge level can't be beat. The continuous food and beverages, the extra attentive service, and that special feeling of staying in a small hotel within a larger complex certainly goes a long way.

Inquire if any major construction will be in progress at your resort of choice during your visit. If so, book another property. No matter how nicely they try to cover up a pool reconstruction or major facelift, it most certainly will affect your overall resort experience. Take my word for it. If the reservation agent does not have adequate information on the extent of the renovation, call the front desk of the resort. They are usually candid and will advise just how you as a guest will be affected.

At the time of booking, request anything special or important to you such as a particular view, the desire to be far from the elevator or pool, a smoking or nonsmoking room, or bed type. Remember these requests are never guaranteed unless reserving a suite with an assigned room number (usually only the presidential or vice presidential suite). The only assurance Disney will make is connecting rooms when children are involved.

Don't forget to ask for special packages, especially in value season. These sometimes include accommodations, park passes, and taxes, all at a substantial savings. And remember to take advantage of any discounts such as Annual Pass holder rates or AAA rates (see pages 34-35 for more details).

Reserve tee times, childcare, or any special dinner shows at time of reservations.

If you'd like a refrigerator in your room for the additional charge of $10 per day, request one now. Refrigerators are usually included in concierge rooms and suites.

Read on for a "best of" listing.

Best resort pools
- The Yacht and Beach Club's Stormalong Bay, a 3-acre mini water park
- The Swan and Dolphin's lush grotto-style lagoon pool
- The newly renovated Volcano Pool at the Polynesian Resort with its luxuriant waterfall, smoking peak, and perfect views of Cinderella's Castle
- The boulder-strewn wonderland at the Wilderness Lodge with its very own erupting geyser
- The lush fantasyland pool at the Hyatt Regency Grand Cypress cooled by 12 waterfalls

Best deluxe resort
On Disney property it's the Grand Floridian Resort with its upscale Victorian atmosphere and lagoonside setting facing the Magic Kingdom. Off-property it's the lavish Villas of Grand Cypress overlooking one of the best golf courses around. At Universal, go for the Portofino Bay Hotel with its unsurpassed ambience of an Italian seaside resort.

Best home-away-from-home property
The Villas at Wilderness Lodge with its Bay Lake frontage and national park character or the new Beach Club Villas conveniently located next door to Epcot.

Best atmosphere
The Animal Kingdom Lodge, where more than 100 animals roam the savanna and the air is pulsating to the beat of African drums. Running a close second is Universal's Portofino Bay Hotel where guests are transported to a seaside Italian village.

Best lobby
How to choose? Three make the cut: the Wilderness Lodge, the Grand Floridian, and the Animal Kingdom Lodge, all eye-popping in their grandeur.

Best access to the parks

The Contemporary, Polynesian, and Grand Floridian with monorail access to the Magic Kingdom, Epcot, and the Ticket and Transportation Center. At Universal, the Hard Rock Hotel is just a 5-minute walk or boat ride away to Universal Studios, Islands of Adventure, and CityWalk.

Best for romance

The Polynesian Resort whose lush tiki torch-lit grounds and white-sand beaches with views of Cinderella's castle are simply dreamy, or Universal's Portofino Bay Hotel where an evening stroll along the bay with Italian arias playing in the distance can't be beat.

Best for nature-lovers

Wilderness Lodge, a nature-lover's dream of rushing water-falls, spouting geysers, and bubbly creeks, all surrounded by stately pine trees and beautiful Bay Lake.

Best for tennis

The Contemporary Resort or the Hyatt Regency Grand Cypress.

Best for golf

Hyatt Regency Grand Cypress and the Villas of Grand Cypress offering four Jack Nicklaus signature designed courses.

Best resort lounges

- California Grill Lounge—The Contemporary Resort's 15th-floor lounge with unrivaled views of the Magic Kingdom and the Seven Seas Lagoon, great for cocktails, sushi, and a view of the Fantasy in the Sky fireworks display.

- The Outer Rim—Yet another lounge in the Contemporary with stellar views of the sunset over Bay Lake.

- Mizner's Lounge—2nd-story lobby lounge at the Grand Floridian overlooking the pristine grounds of this one-of-a-kind hotel.

- The Grand Floridian's Lobby Lounge—Sip on cocktails in the magnificent lobby of the Grand Floridian to the sounds of a big band orchestra or live piano music.
- Tambu Lounge—Order a tropical drink here at the Polynesian Resort's Great Ceremonial House amid lush foliage and views of the Seven Seas Lagoon.
- Territory Lounge—Rustic lounge in the Wilderness Lodge.
- Velvet—Ultra-hip cocktail lounge at the Hard Rock Hotel.
- Bar America—Portofino Bay's sophisticated lounge overlooking the romantic piazza.
- Top of the Palace Lounge—High atop the Wyndham Palace Resort near Downtown Disney is this sophisticated bar with the best views around.

MAGIC KINGDOM AREA RESORTS

Nestled on the Seven Seas lagoon fronting the Magic Kingdom are three resorts, the Contemporary, the Polynesian, and the Grand Floridian. All are connected to each other as well as to the Magic Kingdom and Epcot (via the Ticket and Transportation Center, or TTC) by monorail. In this, the most enchanting area of Walt Disney World, are magical views of Cinderella's castle and a convenience to the Magic Kingdom that simply can't be beat. The Wilderness Lodge and the Villas of Wilderness Lodge, both considered Magic Kingdom resorts, are not connected to the monorail; however, they are accessible to the Magic Kingdom by boat with the added plus of a pristine setting smack dab in the middle of a pine tree forest fronting beautiful Bay Lake.

Those driving for the first time to the Magic Kingdom Resorts may feel confused when the signage seems to be leading straight into the Magic Kingdom parking lot. You'll need to drive up to the second turnstile on the right and advise the parking lot attendant that you are checking in and they will wave you past. Stay all the way to the right and follow the signs to your hotel.

Disney's Contemporary Resort $$ to $$$$

The 15-story A-frame Contemporary Resort is a long-familiar landmark. What used to be considered modern is now pretty darn austere with its soaring open interior, sharp edges, and angles. Love it or hate it, its accessibility to the Magic Kingdom can't be beat. And the sight of the monorail silently gliding through its core is simply magical. Bordering Bay Lake, the 1,000-room property consists of a high-rise tower, two 3-story wings, and a next-door convention center, making this resort a favorite choice for groups. On the 15th floor sits the California Grill, one of Disney's best restaurants, with a bird's-eye view of the Magic Kingdom.

Wacky trees cut in futuristic forms line the entrance leading to the somewhat sterile, marble-floored lobby. Stark but sleek, its small seating area is adorned with angular leather sofas and chairs in shades of purple, teal, and black. To feel the grandeur of this resort you'll need to head to its centerpiece, the 4th-floor Grand Canyon Concourse. This soaring space boasts 11-story windows on either end with floors of guestrooms surrounding the vast atrium on two sides. At its heart stands a charming 90-foot mosaic mural of Native American children. Here you'll find shops, restaurants, a monorail station, and a bar with fantastic views of Bay Lake, all constantly buzzing with traffic. In contrast, the exterior garden wings are a much quieter alternative to the activity of the main building. Just a short distance from the tower by covered walkway, they offer a variety of views; some with vistas of Bay Lake but sadly others within sight of a concrete parking lot. **4600 North World Drive, Lake Buena Vista, FL 32830; 407-824-1000; Fax 407- 824-3539. Check-in 3 P.M., check-out 11 A.M. For reservations call 407-W-DISNEY or your travel agent.**

Rooms

Guestrooms—Before entering your room, don your sunglasses or risk being blinded by the blazing colors and zany patterns reminiscent of a Jetson cartoon. Purple and yellow walls, kooky contemporary carpet, and multicolored Picasso-style bedspreads make this the most unsettling room in Disney's repertoire. Headboards composed of a wooden backsplash of color running the length of one wall are topped with amoeba-shaped lighting. Furnishings include an austere bureau with loads of drawers, an armless sleeper sofa fronted by a large table, and a comfy green-and-yellow checked easy chair paired with a green leather ottoman. The bathroom, the only toned-down space in the 394-square-foot room, is bedecked in rich brown marble and black granite. Divided into two areas, one offers a single sink and tub and the other a commode and additional sink. Amenities include a keyed safe, iron and ironing board, and morning newspaper.

Tower rooms, all with balconies, are the ticket here and worth the additional cost with knockout views of either the Magic Kingdom on one side or Bay Lake on the other. The higher the floor, the quieter and the better view. The lower floors can be noisy due to their suspended position over the Grand Canyon Concourse where the clamor of Chef Mickey's character breakfast begins in the wee hours of the morning.

The quieter, 3-story garden wings are certainly an alternative. Be prepared for a bit of a hike from the main building, although they come with the added convenience of being close to the pool. None contain balconies; however, if you're lucky enough to score a room on the ground floor facing Bay Lake, you'll find a nice patio outside your back door. And be sure to book a Garden View room (comes with a garden, pool, or lake view) or suffer the consequences of a standard room with a parking lot view. What the Contemporary calls a Wing Room comes with a slightly larger bath and a king bed but a non–parking lot view is not guaranteed.

Concierge rooms—Tower Club rooms located on the 12th floor have access to a limited concierge service. A lounge of sorts near the elevators is open from 7 A.M.–4 P.M. offering a continental breakfast and afternoon snacks of sweets, lemonade, coffee, tea, and sodas. Additional amenities include the services of a concierge desk and room refrigerators.

Fourteenth floor rooms and suites enjoy a separate concierge space with express check-in/check-out, a large private lounge with views of the Magic Kingdom, and the services of a concierge staff. Offerings include a continental breakfast, midday snacks, evening wine with hot and cold hors d'oeuvres (catered by the California Grill), and after-dinner cordials and dessert. Extra amenities include a refrigerator and nightly turndown service.

Suites—The two-bedroom, two-bath Presidential Suite located on the 14th floor sports two balconies with spectacular Magic Kingdom views and a spacious living room with wet bar, queen sleeper sofa, desk, and 6-person dining table. Guests love the huge king-bedded master with its large sitting area and desk as well as a whirlpool bathtub with separate walk-in shower and vanity desk.

Also on the 14th floor are one-bedroom suites with one and a half baths, two balconies, 6-person dining area, and spacious living room with a sofa sleeper and wet bar. The separate bedroom has two queen beds. Offered in both lake and Magic Kingdom views, and with the addition of another guestroom can become a Two-Bedroom, Two-and-a-Half-Bath Suite. Colors in the 14th-floor suites are a bit more subdued than the regular guestrooms.

Roomy Deluxe Garden Suites, located in the garden wings with views of Bay Lake, sleep eight and contain over 1,300 square feet with two bedrooms and two baths plus a comfortable living area, dining table, two daybeds, queen sofa sleeper, and kitchen. Junior Suites, also located in the garden wings, are a bit larger than a standard room with either one king or queen bed, a daybed, and a large bath in addition to excellent views of the lake. Suites in the garden wing do not include concierge service.

Room tip: Rooms located in the wings do require a bit of a trek to board the monorail. If you plan on walking to the Magic Kingdom (only a 10-minute walk and a smart alternative to the monorail after park closing), ask for a room close to the park in the North Garden Wing. Although tower rooms on the Magic Kingdom side have a marvelous view of the park, they also come with a not-so-marvelous view of the parking lot; however, it's worth it for front-row seats of the nighttime fireworks display.

Restaurants

California Grill—Popular 15th floor restaurant; dinner only. Innovative cuisine accompanied by sweeping views of the Magic Kingdom and the Seven Seas Lagoon • full review on page 348.

Chef Mickey's—4th floor Grand Canyon Concourse. Breakfast and dinner • dine with Chef Mickey and friends • full review on page 349.

Concourse Steakhouse—4th-floor all-day steakhouse. Grilled steaks, pastas, seafood • monorail soars overhead • full review on page 351.

Contemporary Grounds—Lobby counter service; open 7 A.M.–9 P.M. Hot tea, espresso, cappuccino, café lattes, hot chocolate, iced coffee, granitas • biscotti, muffins • beer, wine, liqueurs.

Food and Fun Center—Lobby-level 24-hour snack bar and grill. Grilled entrees available 7 A.M.–10 P.M. Breakfast: cereal, bagels, croissants, waffles, fruit, pancakes, egg platters • lunch and dinner: burgers, grilled chicken breast sandwiches, chicken strips, quiche, hot dogs, chili, nachos, pizza, cold sandwiches, fruit, salads • children's menu: hot dog, peanut butter and jelly sandwich, chicken strips, mac 'n' cheese, grilled cheese.

In-room dining—Available 24 hours.

Libations

California Grill Lounge—15th-floor lounge in the California Grill Restaurant • spectacular views of the Magic Kingdom and Seven Seas Lagoon • sophisticated wine and cocktail list • pristine sushi and sashimi • inventive appetizers.

Outer Rim—4th floor. Sweeping views of Bay Lake • specialty drinks, martinis, wine, beer, coffees • appetizers: brie and fruit, chips and black bean salsa, peel-and-eat shrimp, ginger glazed wings.

Sand Bar and Grill—Pool bar. Daiquiris, frozen lemonade, pina coladas (both alcoholic and non) • lunch: burgers, hot dogs, chicken bacon melt, turkey and tuna subs, deli salad, nachos, ice cream bars, smoothies, brownies, cookies.

Recreation and Activities

Arcade—Located in the Food and Fun Center on the lobby level; open 24 hours. Largest Disney hotel arcade.

Beach—Small white-sand beach, located near marina.

Boating—Boat on miles of Bay Lake and the adjoining Seven Seas Lagoon • WaterMouse boats • pontoons • canopy boats • sailboats • catamarans • specialty cruises.

Children's playground—Located near the North Garden Wing.

Electrical Water Pageant—On the Seven Seas Lagoon nightly at 10:05 P.M.; best viewed from the 15th-floor observation deck (at an earlier time), it first is seen on one side of hotel (observation deck) then moves around to the other side (at 10:05) bay-view tower balconies, or Bay Lake beach. Delightful 1,000-foot string of illuminated barges featuring King Neptune and his court of whales, sea serpents, and other deep-sea creatures. May be canceled due to inclement weather

Fishing—Guided 2-hour fishing excursions for up to five people include boat, guide, and gear • 1-hour kids' fishing excursion for ages 6–12. Call **407-WDW-PLAY** for reservations; catch and release only.

Swimming—Bay Lake. Two heated pools, two hot tubs • largest pool (6,500 square feet) has a 17-foot-high waterslide • smaller pool rests at the end of the dock surrounded by marvelous lake vistas • little or no theming.

Tennis—Disney Racquet Club is located near the North Wing; call **407-WDW-PLAY** for information. WDW's major tennis facility • six lighted hydrogrid clay courts • pro shop • Peter Burwash International Tennis Professionals available for lessons and clinics.

Volleyball—Sand volleyball court located on the beach.

Water-skiing and parasailing—Only Disney resort offering water-skiing, wakeboarding, jet-skiing and parasailing. For reservations call **407-WDW-PLAY** up to 90 days in advance.

Services

Childcare—At the Mouseketeer Clubhouse; open daily 4:30 P.M.– midnight for potty-trained children ages 4–12; located adjacent to the Food and Fun Center. Open to registered guests of any Disney-owned property. For reservations call **407-824-1000, ext. 3038.**

Hair salon—American Beauty Salon located on 3rd floor; open 9 A.M.–6 P.M. Hairstyling • color • facials • manicures and pedicures.

Health club—Olympiad Health Club located on 3rd floor; open 6 A.M.–9 P.M. Life Circuit machines • treadmills • fitness bicycles • Cybex machines • free weights • dry sauna • tanning facilities • personal training and massage by appointment.

Shopping

BVG—Disney merchandise and then some • Disney logo apparel and sleepwear • swimwear • home decor • confections and chocolates.

Concourse Sundries and Spirits—Snacks • sundries • film • cigars • wine • liquor • newspapers • books.

Fantasia—Disney merchandise.

Transportation

Monorail to the Magic Kingdom (or take the 10-minute walkway). Monorail to the Ticket and Transportation Center then transfer to the Epcot monorail. Buses run to Disney MGM Studios, Animal Kingdom, Blizzard Beach, Downtown Disney, and Typhoon Lagoon. The Blue Flag Launch, operating between 7:30 A.M.–10 P.M., departs from marina to Wilderness Lodge and Fort Wilderness. Monorail to the Polynesian and the Grand Floridian Resorts.

To reach other Disney resorts during park operating hours take the monorail to the Magic Kingdom and from there pick up a bus to your resort destination. After park hours, bus to Downtown Disney and transfer to your resort destination.

Disney's Grand Floridian Resort and Spa
$$ to $$$$$

Nestled on the shores of the Seven Seas Lagoon and fronting the Magic Kingdom, this world-class, exclusive resort is Disney's flagship, one that lives up nicely to its exalted reputation. Its red-gabled roofs and Victorian elegance draw inspiration from the grand Florida seaside "palace hotels" of the 19th century during America's Gilded Age.

Impeccably maintained and perfectly manicured grounds are strung with fragrant, blossom-filled lanes that meander among the 4- and 5-story buildings of gleaming white clapboard siding, red shingled roofs, fairytale turrets, and intricate latticework. Housekeepers in Victorian period costumes stroll the grounds twirling lacy parasols.

The favorite gathering spot is the exquisitely soaring, 5-story Grand Lobby topped with stained-glass cupolas and massive filigreed chandeliers. Strewn with potted palms, cushy seating, and extravagant flower arrangements, it's at its liveliest in the late afternoon and evening when entertainment rotates between a relaxing piano player and a dynamic eight-piece big band orchestra. You'll find yourself time and time again being drawn back to this elegant spot for afternoon tea or nightly cocktails. Because the resort contains a popular wedding chapel, don't be surprised to see white-gowned brides frequently roaming the lobby. If you're in luck, a Cinderella coach with coachmen and white horses will be on hand to whisk away the newly wedded couple.

Aquatic enticements include a crescent white-sand beach dotted with brightly striped, canopied lounge chairs, a large sophisticated pool in the central courtyard, a new beachside Florida springs–style pool, and a classy marina sporting a wide assortment of watercraft. A full-service health club and spa, tennis courts, five restaurants, two lounges, and sophisticated shopping round out the list of exceptional offerings. **4401 Floridian Way, Lake Buena Vista, FL 32830; 407-824-3000; Fax 407-824-3186. Check-in 3 P.M., check-out 11 A.M. For reservations call 407-W-DISNEY or your travel agent.**

Rooms

Guestrooms—Beautifully appointed and luxurious, these graciously restyled guestrooms are the most comfortable in Disney's repertoire. Decorated in a Victorian floral motif, each contains one king or two queen beds (most have queens), full-size daybed/sofa, two chairs and a table, armoire-concealed television, and minibar. At over 400 square feet, they are among the largest in the "World." Marbled baths have separate twin sinks, mounds of plush towels, an extra phone, luxury toiletries (no Mickey Mouse soaps for this hotel), and hairdryer. Beds are soft and cushy with the best pillows around, the sizable closet contains an electronic safe and bathrobes, and all rooms have daily newspaper delivery and nightly turndown service. Most rooms come with generously sized balconies and vary only in the view of either the gardens or the lagoon.

Lagoon-view rooms face either the Magic Kingdom or the Polynesian Resort (choice of views is on request only and not guaranteed). Garden views overlook the flowering grounds, the sparkling courtyard pool, or the marina. On the top floors you'll find dormer rooms with vaulted ceilings whose private balconies require standing for a view; although their high ceilings give them a more open feel, most do not offer daybeds and are actually a bit smaller than a normal guestroom.

Lodge Tower Rooms are located in turreted corners of many of the buildings. They are similar to a standard room with balcony, but with a turreted, larger sitting area as well as an additional phone and TV.

Room tip: For a lagoon-view room with the best vistas of the Magic Kingdom, ask for one in the Boca Chica building. (Magic Kingdom views are also available in Sago Cay and Conch Key.) Rooms in Sago Key are the most peaceful in the resort offering maximum quietude in a setting far from the pool, but they also require a longer walk to the main building. Sugar Loaf and Big Pine are closest to the main building and the monorail; however, both are near the courtyard pool and can be a bit noisy.

Concierge rooms—Accommodations on the concierge level vary from standard guestrooms to larger deluxe rooms to one- and two-bedroom suites to turret honeymoon suites, all offering a variety of views including marina, lagoon, and garden. Located in both the upper floors of the main building (the Royal Palm Club) and the Sugar Loaf building (the Lodge Concierge), they provide extra amenities such as VCRs, private check-in and -out, and the feel of being a special guest in a much smaller hotel.

The Royal Palm Club, located on the 4th floor of the main building, is the most upscale of the two concierge lounges. It includes the services of a concierge staff plus a continental breakfast, midday offerings of finger sandwiches, vegetables and dip, fruit, cookies, and lemonade, and late afternoon tea with scones, tarts, fruit, tea, and lemonade. In the early evening expect wine along with appetizing hors d'oeuvres from the resort's notable restaurants the likes of cheese, pate, ravioli, prosciutto and melon, marinated vegetables, and salads. Kids look forward to their own spread of chicken fingers and corn dogs. After-dinner mini-eclairs and cream puffs as well as chocolate-covered strawberries and tarts are served with a nice selection of liqueurs.

The Lodge Concierge, located in the lobby of the Sugar Loaf building, offers a scaled-down version of the Royal Palm Club minus the alcohol. And don't expect a lagoon view in this building. You'll find only garden, marina, or pool views here. Of course, the room prices are substantially lower than those in the Royal Palm Club.

Suites—Suites are over the top here and can be had in all shapes and sizes. The largest is the elegant Presidential Suite in the main building at 2,200 square feet, with two bedrooms, two and a half baths, formal living area, dining room, large screen TV, CD player, VCR, wet bar, refrigerator, even its own piano, private elevator, and five balconies. The main building's one-bedroom, one-and-a-half-bath Vice Presidential Suite at 1,083 square feet offers a huge king-bedded master with seating area, a full-size parlor, and four balconies. You'll also find a wide assortment of One- and Two-Bedroom Suites ranging from 678 to 1,792 square feet, all outfitted with at least one wet bar, a parlor, anywhere from one and a half to three baths, and most with more than one balcony.

A nice getaway is the Cape Coral Suite located in the remote Sago Cay building at the edge of the property. Situated on the ground floor it boasts two bedrooms, two baths, and a lovely patio with perfect views of Cinderella's castle and the Magic Kingdom fireworks. Honeymoon Suites are a favorite with a four-poster king bed, a large sitting room (not a separate space) with a sofa, two reading chairs, coffee table, wet bar, and entertainment center. Only some come with a balcony or a whirlpool tub, but all come with terrific views of the Magic Kingdom.

Restaurants

Citricos—Dinner only • innovative New American cuisine • world-class wine list • full review on page 350.

Garden View Tea Room—Lobby tearoom; open 2 P.M.–6 P.M.; priority seating available • English-style tea served in high style • teas • crumpets • scones • pate • fruit and cheese • trifle • pound cake • strawberries and cream • tea sandwiches • champagne.

Gasparilla Grill and Games—24-hour snack bar; grill items served 6:30 A.M.–midnight; dine inside adjacent to the arcade or outside overlooking the marina. Breakfast: fresh fruit, oatmeal, grits, warm cinnamon buns, cereal, French toast sticks, egg and bacon or sausage croissants • lunch and dinner: hot dogs, chicken strips, grilled chicken sandwich, pizza, chili, burgers • anytime items: slushes, salads, fruit, frozen yogurt, soft-serve ice cream, cookies, muffins, bagels, pastries.

Grand Floridian Café—Breakfast and lunch • casual café • garden-view setting • full review on page 352.

Narcoossee's—Dinner only. Waterside setting • fresh seafood • views of the Magic Kingdom fireworks • full review on page 355.

1900 Park Fare—Breakfast and dinner. Character buffet • Victorian charm and the sound of Big Bertha, an antique French organ • full review on page 355.

Victoria and Albert's—Dinner only. Disney's grandest dining establishment • AAA 5-Diamond Award • full review on page 360.

Private dining—24-hour room service • in-room dinner served butler-style • dine on board the Grand I yacht or in one of the many secluded and romantic venues located throughout the property.

Libations

Courtyard Pool Bar—Specialty drinks, beer, wine, beverages • cold sandwiches.

Lobby cocktails—Cocktails in the magnificent lobby beginning daily at 3 P.M. Entertainment by the Grand Floridian Society Orchestra alternating with a gifted piano player.

Mizner's Lounge—2nd-story lobby lounge. Picturesque views of the hotel courtyard and pool • cocktails, port, cognac, brandy, coffee • premium cigars • appetizers.

Citricos Lounge—Located within Citricos Restaurant. International wines, martinis, cocktails, espresso • appetizers • dessert.

Narcoossee's Lounge—Located within Narcoossee's Restaurant. Specialty drinks, wine, espresso • appetizers • dessert • step outside for views of the Magic Kingdom fireworks and the Electrical Water Pageant.

Beachside Pool Bar—Cocktails, beer, frozen drinks, beverages • spinach dip, shrimp cocktail, Cobb salad, Caesar salad, croissant sandwiches, fruit plate, turkey club sandwich, burgers, Philly cheese steak sandwich, BLT sandwich • children's menu: mini burgers, chicken strips, hot dog, grilled cheese, PB&J sandwich.

Recreation and Activities

Arcade—Located inside Gasparilla Grill.

Beach—In front of the Florida Natural Springs Pool. Lovely crescent of silky white-sand beach • canopy-covered lounge chairs • no swimming allowed in the lagoon.

Boating—Rentals at the Captain's Shipyard Marina; call 407-WDW-Play for reservations. WaterMouse boats • pontoon boats • canopy boats • sailboats • specialty cruises • 45-foot Sea Ray yacht available for charter; call 407-824-2439.

Children's Activities and Playground—Playground located near the Mouseketeer Club; reserve fee-based activities (only available for children ages 3–9) up to 120 days prior by calling 407-WDW-DINE. Pool games • arts and crafts • "Grand Kid Adventures in Cooking" offered Tues and Fri 10 A.M.–11:45 A.M. ($20) • 2-hour supervised sail to a deserted island to search for buried treasure on Mon, Wed, and Thurs at 10:00 A.M. ($25) • "Wonderland Tea Party" Mon–Fri at 1:15 P.M. ($25)

Electrical Water Pageant—On the Seven Seas Lagoon nightly at 9:15 P.M.; best viewed from the beach or the boat dock near Narcoossee's; may be canceled due to inclement weather. Delightful 1,000-foot string of illuminated barges featuring King Neptune and his court of whales, sea serpents, and other deep-sea creatures.

Fishing—2-hour guided bass fishing excursion including guide, boat, and gear for up to five guests • 1-hour kids' fishing trip for children ages 6–12. Call 407-WDW-PLAY for reservations; catch and release only.

Swimming—New Florida natural springs–style pool fronting the beach offers a waterfall, sunbathing deck, changing rooms, kiddie pool, waterslide, and pool bar • 24-hour free-form pool cools the central courtyard along with a children's wading pool and whirlpool • both pools heated.

Tennis—The Wingfield Tennis Courts offer two Har-Tru lighted clay courts • lessons available; 407-WDW-PLAY.

Tours— Complimentary floral tours with the Grand Floridian floral artists. Sign up at Guest Relations 30-minutes prior; offered each Thurs at 9 A.M.

Volleyball—Sand volleyball court located on the beach.

Services

Hair salon—The Ivy Trellis Salon open daily 9 A.M.–6 P.M.

Childcare—At the Mouseketeer Club adjacent to the Gasparilla Grill; open daily 4:30 P.M.–midnight for potty-trained children ages 4–12; call **407-WDW-DINE** for reservations; open only to guests of the Grand Floridian or those dining at the resort. Disney movies • art activities • video games.

Spa and health club—Grand Floridian Spa and Health Club; treatment hours 8 A.M.–8 P.M.; health club open 6 A.M.–9 P.M.; **407-824-2332**. 9,000 square-foot facility • spa: massage, shiatsu, reflexology, facials, water therapies and soaks, hand and foot treatments, body treatments and wraps • health club: treadmills, stair climbers, cycles, elliptical trainers, Cybex strength equipment, free weights • personal training available • locker rooms equipped with whirlpool, Turkish steam bath, Finnish sauna, robes, and slippers • full review on page 298.

Shopping

Bally of Switzerland—Leather jackets • handbags • footwear • wallets • luggage • ties • belts.

Commander Porter's—Understated Disney logo clothing • golfing attire • resort wear.

M. Mouse Mercantile—Disney merchandise store • logo clothing • watches • costumes • plush toys • souvenirs • videos • unusual items for the office.

Sandy Cove—Disney Home Collection merchandise • Limoges porcelain • chocolates • cigars • sundries • newspapers.

Summer Lace—Women's designer resort clothing • swimwear.

Transportation

Transportation choices to the Magic Kingdom include both the monorail and water taxi. To Epcot take the monorail to the Ticket and Transportation Center (TTC) and transfer to the Epcot monorail. Direct bus to Disney–MGM Studios, Animal Kingdom, Downtown Disney, Typhoon Lagoon, and Blizzard Beach. Monorail service to the Contemporary Resort and either walk, water taxi, or monorail to the Polynesian.

To reach other Disney resorts during park operating hours take the monorail to the Magic Kingdom and pick up a bus from there to your resort destination. After park hours bus to Downtown Disney and then transfer to your resort destination.

Disney's Polynesian Resort $$$ to $$$$

Along with a warm aloha and a lei greeting, guests are invited to enter the soothing South Seas environment of the Great Ceremonial House, a green oasis sheltering the front desk, shops, and restaurants of the Polynesian Resort. Some find this resort a bit hokey and old-fashioned, but it has a loyal following—and I love it.

Vines encase the rugged lava rock cataracts that cool the 2-story lobby resting below towering palm trees. Among the centerpiece garden is a profusion of flowering orchids, bromeliads, ginger, and anthurium scattered throughout banana trees, elephant ears, and rubber plants. High-backed rattan chairs sit on floors of polished flagstone while overhead brilliantly colored macaws perch in the branches of the surrounding foliage. From here, 2-story picture windows draw the eye outdoors to the lush landscaping surrounding the Volcano Pool and the Seven Seas lagoon beyond.

Located on the monorail system and within walking distance of the Ticket and Transportation Center, the Polynesian is the most convenient of the Disney resorts with direct access to both the Magic Kingdom and Epcot. Eleven tangerine- and mahogany-tinted longhouses are scattered throughout the luxuriant grounds. More than 75 species of dense vegetation have been thriving here for years, and the result is delightfully overwhelming. Ducks and ibis roam the thick grassy lawns; rabbits hop along walkways. Meandering pathways lined with volcanic rock are torch-lit in the evenings, and soft Hawaiian melodies set the mood for memorable nights. Three white-sand beaches dotted with hammocks and lounge chairs are a spectacular place to sun or, in the evening, view the Magic Kingdom fireworks. **1600 Seven Seas Drive, Lake Buena Vista, FL 32830; 407-824-2000; Fax 407-824-3174. Check-in 3 P.M., check-out 11 A.M. For reservations call 407-W-DISNEY or your travel agent.**

Rooms

Guestrooms—The largest standard rooms in Disney are here at the 847-room Polynesian; those in the newer Tokelau, Tahiti, and Rapa Nui longhouses are downright enormous. Two queen beds attractively canopied in bamboo and covered with a batik print in shades of teal, terra-cotta, and black—along with the rattan furnishings—evoke an island atmosphere. A daybed adorned with batik pillows sits below a banana leaf mirror; curtains sport the same banana leaf motif. Smallish baths are without the typical split bath configuration and double sinks found at other Disney properties, but all are handsomely festooned with rich green marble and a fun, primitive Polynesian decor. Baths in the newer buildings are a bit larger. Consider bringing your own hairdryer; those supplied in the rooms look at least 20 years old. Amenities include iron and ironing board, keyed safe and daily newspaper.

Concierge rooms—Nestled up against the beach is the Hawaii concierge building offering the services of a top-notch concierge staff as well as private check-in and -out. The bi-level Royal Polynesian Lounge is among the best in Disney's concierge repertoire and affords a fantastic view of Cinderella's Castle and the Magic Kingdom fireworks. Accommodations come with either a lagoon or garden view, but 2nd-floor rooms do not have balconies. Although the 3rd floor rooms offer the very best views, all are smoking rooms. Additional amenities include bathrobes, in-room mini refrigerator and nightly turndown service.

Open from 7 A.M.–10 P.M., the concierge service offers complimentary food and beverages, beginning with a continental breakfast. From noon–4 P.M., cookies, guava juice, lemonade, coffee, and iced tea are served. Evenings choices include hot and cold appetizers and wine with after-dinner cordials and mini desserts. This kid-friendly lounge offers children their own small sofa and chairs with continually running videos on a big screen TV—a negative point for many—and their own snack table. Barrels of iced-down sodas and bottled water make this a favorite stop for guests.

Suites—All suites are located in the small and intimate 2-story Tonga longhouse. Their only drawback is the inconvenient walk to the concierge lounge in the Hawaii building. A continental breakfast is served in the foyer of the Tonga building.

For the ultimate vacation, try the King Kamehameha, a 2-story wonder with two bedrooms, two and a half baths, parlor, and kitchen. The upstairs master offers a balcony, an enormous two-part bath with a sink, bidet, toilet, whirlpool tub, mini-TV, and walk-in closet on one side—and a bath, shower, sink, and toilet on the other. The second bedroom and bath are similar to a standard guestroom with balcony. Downstairs is a great parlor with TV, VCR, stereo, 4-person dining table, three small sofas, rattan chairs, coffee table, overhead paddle fans, half bath, and bar stools in front of the full kitchen (minus a stove). A balcony the length of the suite overlooks the marina and Cinderella's Castle in the distance.

The two-bedroom, three-bath Ambassador Suites have a master with a four-poster king bed, entertainment armoire, chaise lounge, desk, table and two chairs, large bath, and balcony. The beautifully furnished living room provides two small couches, a large TV, chaise lounge, dining table for four, pull-down bed, large garden-view balcony the length of the room, wet bar, full bath, and separate full kitchen (minus a stove). The second bedroom is the same size as a standard guestroom with a balcony.

The marina-view One-Bedroom/One-Bath Princess Suites offer two queens in the bedroom as well as a daybed in the separate parlor.

Room tip: Your best chance of receiving the perfect room (of which there are many) is to educate yourself before check-in and request exactly what you would like both at reservation time and again at the front desk before you are handed a key. The following information may sound excessive, but it could make the difference between a perfect vacation and a disappointing one. The newer longhouses of Tokelau, Tahiti, and Rapa Nui feature the largest rooms, all of which come with patios or balconies and a convenient location near the Ticket and Transportation Center. Older longhouses are closer to the Great Ceremonial House but lack 2nd-floor balconies.

The 2-story Niue and Tonga longhouses, with the Tonga being an all-suite building, are small and intimate. The Niue lacks 2nd-floor balconies. Water-view rooms in the Tahiti building front a lovely beach with great views across the lagoon but are also located very close to the Ticket and Transportation Center with noise from the ferryboat during park hours. One side of the Samoa and the Niue buildings faces the rambunctious Volcano Pool, a plus or minus depending on your personality. One side of the

Aotearoa, Tonga, and Rarotonga longhouses faces the monorail, and one side of the Rapa Nui faces the parking lot, although these are actually considered garden views.

If staying in the Fiji, Tuvalu, Tonga, and Aotearoa you had better enjoy the beat of drums because the Polynesian Luau is held nearby. The worst view is from the so-called garden-view side of the Tuvalu longhouse that stares at the next building only a few feet away.

Restaurants

Captain Cook's Snack Company—24-hour snack bar located in the Great Ceremonial House; grill closes at 11 P.M. Breakfast: French toast sticks, breakfast sandwiches, scrambled eggs, cereal, fruit, pastries • lunch and dinner: burgers, hot dogs, pizza, chicken sandwiches, pork sandwiches, chicken strips, and cold sandwiches • children's menu: hot dog, chicken strips.

Kona Café—Breakfast, lunch, and dinner. American cuisine with delicate hints of Asia • casual dining • breakfast Tonga Toast, a batter fried banana-stuffed sourdough bread rolled in cinnamon sugar—a Disney specialty • full review on page 354.

Kona Island—Near the monorail platform; open at 6:30 A.M. Express service • Kona coffee, lattes, espresso, iced mochas, hot chocolate • breakfast breads, sticky buns, pastries, cookies, muffins.

Ohana—Dinner only. All-you-care-to-eat feast prepared on an 18-foot fire pit • Mickey Mouse hosts a family-style breakfast • full review on page 356.

Polynesian Luau Dinner Show—Shows are held at the Luau Cove Tues–Sat, 5:15 P.M.–8 P.M.; subject to cancellation in inclement weather; call **407-WDW-DINE** for reservations • South Seas island party, traditional dancing and music • Polynesian-style feast served family style: roasted chicken and pork ribs along with shrimp fried rice, sauteed vegetables, pineapple upside-down cake • unlimited drinks, including beer and wine.

In-room dining—Available from 6:30 A.M.–midnight.

Libations

Barefoot Pool Bar—Under the Volcano Pool's thatched-roofed bar. Tropical alcoholic and nonalcoholic drinks • imported beer.

Tambu Lounge—Located upstairs in the Great Ceremonial House; open 1 P.M.–midnight; appetizers served 5–10 P.M. Picturesque views of the Seven Seas Lagoon • tropical drinks served in hollowed-out pineapples and coconuts • appetizers: egg rolls, chicken tenders, cheese plate, shrimp cocktail.

Recreation and Activities

Arcade—Moana Mickey's Fun Hut open 24 hours. Three rooms of game fun with the latest in video equipment.

Beaches—Three idyllic beaches feature perfect vistas of the Seven Seas Lagoon and the Magic Kingdom; swimming is prohibited in the lagoon. Lounge chairs, beach hammocks, swings • prime viewing for the Magic Kingdom fireworks • best views: beach in front of Tahiti longhouse • closest to Volcano Pool: beach in front of Hawaii longhouse • most secluded: beach on the Grand Floridian side of the property.

Bicycles—Rentable at the marina • 2- and 4-seater surrey bikes.

Boating—Boat rentals available at the Mikala Canoe Club for enjoyment of the Seven Seas Lagoon and adjoining Bay Lake • WaterMouse boats • pontoons • sailboats • water-ski excursions for up to 5 guests • fireworks boating excursion with driver.

Children's activities and playground—Playground located near Volcano Pool • arts and crafts and Disney movies daily in the Never Land Club noon–4 P.M. • pool games • hula lessons.

Electrical Water Pageant—On the Seven Seas Lagoon nightly at 9 P.M.; best viewed from the beach, Ohana, or a lagoon-view room; may be canceled due to inclement weather. Delightful 1,000-foot string of illuminated barges featuring King Neptune and his court of whales, sea serpents, and other deep-sea creatures.

Fishing—Guided 2-hour fishing excursions for up to five people including boat, guide, and gear • guided 2-hour kids' fishing excursions for children ages 6–12. Call **407-WDW-PLAY** for reservations.

Jogging—A 1½-mile scenic jogging path circles the resort. Ask for a map at Guest Relations.

Swimming—Nanea Volcano Pool features a smoking volcano slide, underwater music, and sparkling waterfall, all with a superb view of Seven Seas Lagoon—kiddie pool nearby; no whirlpool • quieter East Pool is often filled with ducks in the morning • both pools are heated.

Volleyball—Sand court located on beach in front of Volcano Pool.

Services

Childcare—At the Never Land Club, open 4 P.M.-midnight, for potty-trained children ages 4–12; cost includes buffet dinner; call **407-939-3463** for reservations. Peter Pan–themed facility with a replica of Wendy's bedroom • arcade games • arts and crafts • Disney classic movies on a giant screen • open to registered guests of any Disney-owned property.

Spa and health club—The Grand Floridian Spa is located between the Grand Floridian and the Polynesian.

Shopping

Maui Mickey—Disney merchandise.

News From Polynesia—Polynesian Resort logo merchandise • framed watercolor prints of the resort • beach towels • grass skirts • straw hats • leis • Hawaiian-print clothing • tropical-inspired gifts • newspapers • magazines • books.

Polynesian Princess—Women's resort wear • swimwear.

Robin Crusoe's—Men's resort wear.

Somoa Snacks—Liquor, beer, wine (a nice selection), sodas • snacks • sundries.

Trader Jack's—Disney merchandise.

Wyland Gallery—Environmental marine art.

Transportation

Transportation choices to the Magic Kingdom include both the monorail and water taxi. To reach Epcot, walk to the Ticket and Transportation Center (TTC) (you'll find excellent signage throughout the resort) and take a direct monorail. Direct bus to Disney–MGM Studios, Animal Kingdom, Downtown Disney, Typhoon Lagoon, and Blizzard Beach. Monorail, water taxi, or walking path to the Grand Floridian and monorail service to the Contemporary.

To reach other Disney resorts during park operating hours take the monorail to the Magic Kingdom and pick up a bus from there to your resort destination. After park hours bus to Downtown Disney and then transfer to your resort destination.

Disney's Wilderness Lodge $$ to $$$

Teddy Roosevelt would say "bully" to Disney's dramatic depiction of an early 1900s national park lodge, an atmosphere that simply can't be beat. I challenge you to keep your jaw from dropping open on your first encounter with its awesome 8-story lobby. Sheer walls of ponderosa pine logs and rugged rock surround the huge, open expanse filled with oversized leather chairs and Native American craftwork of beaded moccasins, feathered headdresses, textiles, and drums. Relax in old-fashioned rockers fronting the massive, 82-foot-tall fireplace composed of rockwork replicating the diverse strata of the Grand Canyon. Two authentic 55-foot Pacific Northwest totem poles overlook rustic stone and hardwood floors topped with Native American rugs, teepee chandeliers, and a bevy of "park ranger" staff who roam the lodge attending to guests. Quiet and seductive nooks and crannies on the floors above the lobby offer hours of privacy, and rows of back porch rockers facing the resort grounds look out to a serene scene of natural beauty.

Guestrooms extend above the lobby and then outside to two 7-story wings composed of quarry stone, chunky log walls, and green tin rooftops surrounded by a breathtaking scene of roaring waterfalls, rushing creeks, and towering pines. What begins in the lobby as a bubbling hot spring turns into Silver Creek and then widens to become a sparkling waterfall emptying into the boulder-lined, hot springs–style swimming pool, one of Disney's best. The sound of crickets is heard beneath the bridges and along the meandering pathways lined with natural grasses, junipers, sotols, and wildflowers. On the shores of Bay Lake, Wilderness Lodge's very own geyser, surrounded by a steaming expanse of geothermal activity, erupts hourly from early morning to late night.

And after dark when the waterfall is lit, it's even more wonderful. **901 Timberline Dr., Lake Buena Vista, FL 32830; 407-824-3200; Fax 407-824-3232. Check-in 3 P.M., check-out 11 A.M. For reservations call 407-W-DISNEY or your travel agent.**

Rooms

Guestrooms—Those who have experienced other deluxe Disney resorts may be surprised at the small guestrooms here measuring only 340 square feet. Though pleasant, they don't leave room for a sitting area. Bedding is either two queens, a king (handicapped accessible rooms), or a queen and a set of bunk beds (an extremely popular choice with the kids). You'll find it's a bit like staying in a nicely decorated young boy's room from the 1950s. Earthy shades of green and brown abound in the attractive carpet, plaid curtains, and Native American motif bedspreads. Prints of the American West and old territory maps bedeck the honey-colored walls.

Furnishings include a woodland scene-painted pine armoire, a small dresser in the entry hall, and a small table and two chairs. Bathrooms are a few feet smaller than other deluxe resorts with a separate vanity holding two double sinks and a hairdryer. The adjoining bathtub/commode area is embellished with white-and-gold tiles and wallpaper imprinted with old-fashioned scenes of an Indian village. Room view choices include: standard view offering a look at either the parking lot or rooftops, lodge views of either the forested area facing the Magic Kingdom (views of the park and the fireworks are mostly obscured by the trees except from some rooms on the top floors) or the adjoining Wilderness Lodge Villas and woods, or picturesque courtyard views of either the pool or Bay Lake. Amenities include a small safe, iron and ironing board, and daily newspaper.

If a larger room is more to your liking think about either the Honeymoon Rooms or the Lodge Deluxe Rooms. Standard-view Honeymoon Rooms, located on the top floor surrounding the lobby, are slightly larger than standard guestrooms with king beds as well as a marble Jacuzzi tub in a larger than normal bathroom (remember they come with dormer balconies meaning you must stand for a view). Lodge Deluxe Rooms at close to 500 square feet offer a comfortable sitting area holding a queen sleeper sofa, two easy chairs, coffee table, 2-person table and chairs, TV, wet bar, coffee maker, and refrigerator with ice maker. The bedroom, separated by curtained French doors from the parlor, has two queen beds, entertainment armoire, and another small balcony. These come with either a woods or courtyard view.

Concierge rooms—Concierge rooms on the 7th floor offer the services of a concierge desk in an informal lounge of sorts set up near the elevator overlooking the lobby. Included is continental breakfast, light snacks and beverages throughout the day, afternoon tea, evening hors d'oeuvres and wine, and after-dinner cordials and dessert. Extra amenities include bathrobes, nightly turndown service, and upgraded amenities.

Suites—The 885-square-foot Vice Presidential Suite (also known as the Yosemite) is decorated cowboy style with rawhide curtains and branding iron towel bars. It offers one bedroom with a king bed, one and a half baths, and separate parlor with sleeper sofa, mini-kitchen, desk, 4-person dining table, and wet bar. The oversized bath has a whirlpool tub.

The 1,000-square-foot Presidential Suite (also known as the Yellowstone) is a Teddy Roosevelt delight with an elk-horn chandelier and a fantastic marble bathroom with whirlpool tub. The separate living area holds a half bath, dining area, mini-kitchen, and wet bar.

Room tip: Although Disney considers this a deluxe property, the rooms cannot compare in size or amenities. However, the theming can't be beat, more than making up for the smallish rooms. The 6th and 7th floor balconies are dormers where you must stand for a view over the railing. If quiet is important, request a room away from the lobby and pool.

Restaurants

Artist Point—Dinner only. Outstanding Pacific Northwest cuisine and wines • views of Bay Lake and courtyard waterfall • full review on page 345.

Roaring Forks Snacks—Open 6 A.M.–midnight; grill items available 7 A.M.–11 P.M. Cozy atmosphere indoors and picturesque outdoor area near pool • breakfast: sausage biscuit, breakfast sandwich, scrambled eggs plate, bacon, hash browns, breakfast pizza, oatmeal, cereal, yogurt, fruit, pastries, bagels, croissants • lunch and dinner: delicious smoked turkey sandwich, pizza, Philly steak sandwich, hot dogs, burgers, chicken strips, chili, nachos, salads, ice cream, desserts.

Whispering Canyon Café—Open breakfast, lunch, and dinner. Western-style fun and hearty food • smoked meats served skillet-style • full review on page 361.

In-room dining—Available 7 A.M.–11 A.M. and 4 P.M.–midnight.

Libations

Territory Lounge—Next to Artist Point Restaurant; open 4:30–11:30 P.M. Rustic atmosphere of lodgepole pine posts, old territorial maps, prints of America's West, vintage surveyor equipment, and carved wooden bears • Pacific Northwest wine, beer, specialty drinks, coffees, all "guaranteed to prevent snakebite" • light meals: potato skins, nachos, chicken wings, pizza, buffalo burgers.

Trout Pass—Log cabin pool bar; open noon to dusk. Picturesque setting on Bay Lake fronting a babbling stream • specialty drinks, beer, smoothies, beverages • nachos, giant soft pretzels, popcorn, chips, ice cream.

Recreation and Activities

Services and recreational activities here are shared with the adjacent Villas of Wilderness Lodge.

Arcade—Buttons and Bells Game Arcade. State-of-the-art video games for all levels.

Beach—Bay Lake Beach is nestled up against tall pine trees with lounge chairs facing dazzling Bay Lake.

Bicycles—Rentable at the marina for exploration of the wilderness trails connecting to the next-door Fort Wilderness. Mongoose bicycles • 2- and 4-seater surrey bikes.

Boating—Rentals for the enjoyment of Bay Lake and the Seven Seas Lagoon at Teton Boat Rentals; call **407-WDW-PLAY** for reservations. WaterMouse boats • canopy boats • pontoon boats • sailboat • canoe adventure Tues and Sat at 3:30 P.M. and Thurs and Sun at 11:30 A.M. • 1-hour Birthday Cruise for up to four people includes a driver, birthday cake, and soda • Magic Kingdom fireworks cruise.

Children's activities and playground—Children's playground located on the beach • duck races • arts and crafts • fireside storytelling • pool activities • beach games • next-door Fort Wilderness, just a boat ride away, offers nightly hayrides and a sing-along campfire program followed by a Disney classic movie.

Electrical Water Pageant—On the Seven Seas Lagoon nightly at 9:30 P.M.; best viewed from the beach or boat dock; may be canceled due to inclement weather. Delightful 1,000-foot string of illuminated barges featuring King Neptune and his court of whales, sea serpents, and other deep-sea creatures.

Fishing—2-hour fishing excursion for up to five guests includes boat, fishing equipment, and guide. Call **407-WDW-PLAY** for reservations.

Jogging—Near the marina, jogging paths connect to Disney's Fort Wilderness where two trails, one through the forest of towering pines and one along Bay Lake, make for pleasant exercise routes.

Swimming—A top attraction at Wilderness Lodge is its boulder-lined, free-form pool featuring waterfalls, rocky overlooks, waterslide, and a nearby geyser. You'll also find a kiddie pool as well as two spas. This is one of Disney's best.

Tours—Meet in the lobby for ranger-led tours of the hotel. Check the hotel guide for times; no reservations necessary.

Volleyball—Sand volleyball court located on Bay Lake Beach; equipment at Teton Boat Rentals.

Services

Childcare—At the Cub's Den, open 4:30 P.M.-midnight, for potty-trained cubs ages 4–12; open to registered guests of any Disney-owned property; cost includes a chuck wagon dinner; call **407-WDW-DINE** for reservations. Storytelling • video games • arts and crafts • Disney movies.

Health club—Sturdy Branches Health Club located at the adjoining Villas of Wilderness Lodge; open 6 A.M.–7 P.M. Cybex equipment • Smith Machine • treadmills and stair climbers • free weights • exercise bicycles • personal training and Swedish massage, available by appointment.

Shopping

Wilderness Lodge Mercantile—Daniel Boone–style shopping. Coonskin hats • Mickey and friends miniature totem poles • Wilderness Lodge logo clothing • forest ranger hats • Disney merchandise • sundries • books • magazines • food staples • snacks • wines and liquors.

Transportation

Since the monorail does not reach this neck of the woods, Wilderness Lodge is definitely less accessible than other Magic Kingdom resorts. Take the boat leaving from the Northwest Dock and Ferry (a separate area from the marina) to the Magic Kingdom, Contemporary Resort, and Fort Wilderness. Direct bus to Epcot, Disney–MGM Studios, Animal Kingdom, Downtown Disney, Typhoon Lagoon, and Blizzard Beach.

To reach other Disney resorts during park operating hours take the boat to the Magic Kingdom and pick up a bus or monorail from there to your resort destination. After park hours bus to Downtown Disney and then transfer to the resort.

The Villas at Disney's Wilderness Lodge
$$ to $$$$$

Sharing the same lobby, check in desk, and amenities with the adjoining Wilderness Lodge (a short, covered walkway connects the two) is this 136-room Disney Vacation Club property, a tribute to the Western railroad hotels built in the early 1900s. Rooms not occupied by members are available to the many visitors who wish to stay on Disney property but would also like the convenience of a full kitchen and the extra breathing space of a full living area.

The 4- and 5-story Villa buildings, tucked away in the pine trees, are tinted with soothing earth tone shades of soft brown and green. Inside the lobby, guests are greeted by a rustic 4-story atrium of log construction adorned with detailed woodcarving and paintings of the Northwest. A rock and timber living room made snug with fireplace, leather rockers, and window seats features railroad memorabilia, some belonging to Walt Disney. Scattered seating nooks, each one more inviting than the next, encourage relaxation. Outside a small springs-style pool is surrounded by towering pine trees and natural vegetation. For additional information on the Villas' recreation, services, restaurants, libations, transportation, and shopping, see the above section on the Wilderness Lodge. **801 Timberline Drive, Lake Buena Vista, FL 32830; 407-938-4300; Fax 407-824-3232. Check-in 4 P.M., check-out 11 A.M. For reservations call 407-W-DISNEY or your travel agent.**

Rooms

Villa choices come in studios as well as one- and two-bedroom units (three-bedroom units are not offered at this property), each with a balcony or patio. Autumn colors in splashes of rich red and forest green intermingle with rustic pine furnishings. Couches upholstered in Indian print are mixed with curtains and chairs sporting a fun plaid design. Woodland scene prints decorate the cream, gold, and crimson walls and the carpet is whimsically imprinted with a pinecone motif. The full kitchens are small but efficient and bedrooms feature woodland scene-carved headboards and down-home quilt bedspreads in a leaf and pinecone print. Views from all units are of either the pool or the woods with some of the units on the higher floors offering a view of Bay Lake. Ask for a villa on the back side away from the pool for a delightfully quiet area facing the woods.

The 356-square-foot studios sleep a maximum of four people plus one child under 3 and include either two queen beds or one queen bed and a double sleeper sofa, armoire with TV, small dining table and two chairs, patio or balcony, microwave, mini-refrigerator, coffee maker, and wet bar. Baths have a single sink with a separate, small bath/commode area embellished with colorfully splashed tile. A small closet holds an iron and ironing board. Just slightly larger than the next-door Wilderness Lodge guestrooms, their advantage is the addition of a sleeper sofa and mini-kitchen but at a higher nightly rate.

The One-Bedroom Villas, at 727 square feet, sleep a maximum of four plus one child under age 3. Each unit has a small living area with a queen-size sleeper sofa, reading chair, entertainment center containing a TV/VCR, 2-person dining table, and a balcony or patio. The kitchen, open to the living area, contains a refrigerator, stove, dishwasher, coffee maker, toaster, microwave, and all utensils, dishes, and pots and pans to make a complete meal. The spacious bedroom holds a king-size bed, armoire with TV, small table, and rattan chair and adjoins a two-room bath, one holding a whirlpool tub, vanity sink, and hairdryer with the other containing a commode (in a separate enclosure), shower, and an additional freestanding sink. A nice feature is the convenient stacked washer/dryer.

Two-Bedroom Villas sleep a maximum of eight people plus one child under 3 and offer 1,080 square feet of room. This unit is exactly the same as the one-bedroom with the addition of a studio bedroom, which adds up to two bathrooms, two bedrooms, living area, kitchen, three TVs, and two balconies or porches.

Recreation and Activities

Swimming—The scent of pine perfumes the air at the peacefully quiet Hidden Springs Pool, a free-form pool with geyser bubbles. No lifeguard on duty.

Services

Health club—Sturdy Branches Health Club open 6 A.M.–7 P.M. Cybex equipment • Smith Machine • treadmills • stair climbers • free weights • exercise bicycles • Swedish massage therapy available both in the club or in-room • personal training available.

EPCOT AREA RESORTS

Those who plan to spend a large portion of their vacation at Epcot and Disney MGM Studios should strongly consider selecting one of the resorts in this terrific area. Options include the Beach Club, the Beach Club Villas, the Yacht Club, the Boardwalk Inn, the Boardwalk Villas, and the Walt Disney World Swan and Dolphin. All front Crescent Lake (with the exception of the Beach Club Villas) and all are within walking distance or a boat ride to Epcot, Disney–MGM Studios, and the Boardwalk. With such easy access to so many resorts and Epcot just a few minutes away, you'll find more restaurant and entertainment choices than you can count.

Disney's Beach Club $$ to $$$$

Blue and white 5-story Cape-Cod–style buildings fronting a sea grass–bordered white-sand beach and the 25-acre Crescent Lake exudes the feeling of a trip to early 20ᵗʰ-century Martha's Vineyard. Inviting white rockers await you on the front porch of this slightly more casual sister property of the Yacht Club, both of which are Robert A.M. Stern–designed. Inside the pink- and cream-colored lobby is an idyllic seaside ambience of bare wood floors and summery rattan chairs. You may have to suppress the desire to run and quickly throw on a bathing suit.

The casually elegant grounds surrounding the resort's 583 rooms are landscaped in a variety of crape myrtles, gardenias, and roses. Of course, the resort's highlight is the fantastic Stormalong Bay, the winding wonderland of a mini–water park shared with the Yacht Club. Since this is the closest resort to Epcot, it offers super-easy access to Epcot's International Gateway entrance, a convenience that can't be beat. **1800 Epcot Resorts Blvd., Lake Buena Vista, FL 32830; 407-934-8000; Fax 407-934-3850. Check-in 3 P.M., check-out 11 A.M. For reservations call 407-W-DISNEY or your travel agent.**

Rooms

The 380-square-foot guestrooms are bedecked with teal-and-cream checked carpeting, multicolored striped curtains, pleasing beach scene bedspreads, and metal teal headboards. A large white wooden bureau holds the television and minibar with an additional bureau found near the bathroom. In the corner sits a small combination table/desk with two summery white wicker chairs. Many rooms also offer a full-size sofa/daybed. The lively decor continues in the bath where sailing ship motif wallpaper and shower curtains adorn the separate tub and commode area. Outside is a gray and white marble vanity with two sinks, makeup mirror, and hairdryer. Amenities include a small keyed safe, iron and ironing board, and a daily newspaper.

The water-view Deluxe Rooms, at 533 square feet, offer two queen beds in an extra-large bedroom as well as a separate sitting room with daybed and reading chairs.

The only aspect of the hotel that disappoints is the scarcity of full-size room balconies, most of which are of a 1-by-3 feet, standing-room-only type. If a balcony is important to you, strongly request a full balcony (although there are very few) or a 1ˢᵗ floor patio; it might be simpler to book the adjoining Yacht Club instead.

Room tip: Request an Illuminations view when booking your room and remember that the standard-view rooms could have a view of the parking lot. Water-view rooms aren't always of Cresent Lake; many times they face Stormalong Bay, a somewhat noisy location.

Concierge rooms—The 5ᵗʰ-floor concierge-level rooms include the amenities of a small but cozy lounge (one that tends to be a bit crowded when the occupancy level is high) with complimentary food and beverages throughout the day. Expect a continental breakfast, afternoon snacks of beverages, cookies, crudites, pretzels, popcorn, fruit, and cake, early evening wine and hot and cold hors d'oeuvres the likes of stuffed mushrooms, mini corn dogs, vegetarian sandwiches, puff pastry chicken cups, and cheese, and after-dinner dessert and liqueurs. Additional amenities include the services of a friendly concierge staff, private check-in and -out, nightly turndown service, and bathrobes.

Suites—All suites regardless of floor location are part of the concierge level. For the ultimate in luxury choose the 2,200-square-foot Presidential Newport Suite. A large marble foyer leads to an enormous formal living room with two seating areas, fireplace, wet bar, dining table for eight, full kitchen (minus a stove), and half bath. In the colossal master bedroom are two queen beds topped with attractive rattan headboards, desk, two easy chairs with ottomans, a relaxing chaise, armoire, and loads of windows with everything outfitted in shades of sea foam green and pink-and-white stripes. The sensuous marble master bath holds a lavish whirlpool tub, separate toilet area with a bidet, separate walk-in shower, mini TV, and large walk-in closet. The second bedroom is actually the size of a one-bedroom suite with a separate sitting area. Three extended balconies almost encircle the entire suite.

The 5ᵗʰ floor Vice Presidential Nantucket Suite at 996 square feet is a one-bedroom, one-and-a-half-bath gem with a sizable parlor holding a sofa, coffee table, easy chairs, wet bar with microwave and small refrigerator, 4-person dining table, and balcony offering a quiet courtyard view. The airy bedroom has a canopy king bed, chaise lounge, desk, armoire, standup balcony overlooking Stormalong Bay, and a beautiful marble bath with whirlpool tub, separate shower, double sinks, and mini TV.

Restaurants

Beaches and Cream—Open breakfast, lunch, and dinner. Disney's best milkshakes and ice cream stop • burgers and sandwiches • continental breakfast served from 6:30 A.M.–10:30 A.M. • full review on page 346.

Cape May Café—Open for breakfast and dinner. Breakfast buffet with Goofy and friends • evening New England–style clambake buffet • full review on page 349.

In-room dining—24-hour room service available.

Libations

Hurricane Hanna's Grill—Poolside snack bar. Grilled chicken sandwiches, chicken strips, cheeseburgers, hot dogs, wrap sandwiches, chicken or tuna salad • children's menu: chicken strips, PB&J sandwiches, mini cheeseburgers • beverages, cocktails, beer, alcoholic and nonalcoholic frozen drinks.

Martha's Vineyard—Cocktail lounge adjoining Cape May Café. Nice selection of international and California wine and champagne, many by the glass • beer, port, single malt scotch, cognac, cordials, smoothies • light meals: steamed clams and mussels, peel 'n' eat shrimp, barbecue ribs, chicken tenders, Caesar salad, clam chowder.

Riptide Lounge—Small hideaway off the lobby offering evening cocktails.

Recreation and Activities

Arcade—Lafferty Place Arcade located next to Beaches and Cream Soda Shop.

Beaches—An enticing white-sand beach dotted with lounge chairs fronts Crescent Lake with views of the Boardwalk and the Epcot fireworks.

Boating—Rentals at Bayside Marina for touring Crescent Lake and the adjacent waterways; call **407-WDW-PLAY** for reservations. WaterMouse • canopy boats • pontoon boats • Illuminations cruise on pontoon boats or the "Breathless," a 24-foot replica of a 1930s Chris Craft Runabout (make reservations exactly 90 days ahead or risk losing out)—the viewing point from under the International Bridge is unrivaled.

Children's playground and activities—Playground located near Stormalong Bay. Pool activities include water volleyball • treasure hunts • tug o' war.

Croquet—Grass croquet court located on Beach Club side of property; complimentary equipment available at Ship Shape Health Club.

Fishing—2-hour guided fishing excursions on Crescent Lake depart both morning and afternoon from the Yacht Club marina for a maximum of five guests including gear and beverages • 1-hour fishing excursion for children ages 6–12. Call **407-WDW-PLAY** for reservations; 24-hour notice required; strictly catch and release.

Jogging—Joggers utilize the ¾-mile circular Boardwalk as their track.

Swimming—Stormalong Bay is an eye-popping free-form, mini–water park complex that meanders between the Yacht and Beach Club. The most divine pool at Disney, its 3 acres of winding, watery delight offer sandy-bottom pools, a giant "shipwreck" waterslide, a tidal whirlpool, bubbling hot tubs, a kiddie pool with its own slide next to the beach, and enough length to float lazily in inner tubes to your heart's content. Inner tubes available for rent; swimming not allowed in Crescent Lake.

Those looking for a bit of peace and quiet should try the more serene pool and whirlpool located at the Epcot end of the resort at the Beach Club, or the Dolphin end of the Yacht Club. All pools are heated.

Tennis—Complimentary and available 7 A.M.–10 P.M.; equipment available at Ship Shape Health Club (**407-WDW-PLAY**) • Lighted hard-surface court • private instruction and clinics available for a fee.

Tours—A complimentary walking Garden Tour of the Beach and Yacht Club's beautifully landscaped grounds is led by a member of Disney's horticulture team each Mon, Wed, and Fri at 8:30 A.M. and again at noon.

Volleyball—Sand court located near the beachfront walkway; pick up ball at Ship Shape Health Club.

Services

Childcare—The Sandcastle Club, open 4:30 P.M.–midnight, for potty-trained children ages 4–12; cost includes dinner; open only to registered guests of the Yacht Club, Beach Club, Beach Club Villas, and Boardwalk Inn and Villas; call **407-WDW-DINE** for reservations. Video games • board games • arts and crafts • movies • play kitchen.

Hair salon—Periwig Beauty and Barber Shop open 9 A.M.–6 P.M.; walk-ins welcome • haircuts • perms • color • manicures and pedicures.

Health club—Ship Shape Health Club open 6 A.M.–7 P.M. Hammer Strength • Cybex and Life Circuit machines • free weights • spa • steam room • sauna • personal training and massage available by appointment • tanning bed.

Shopping

Atlantic Wear and Wardrobe Emporium—Resort wear • swimwear • Disney logo clothing • souvenirs • sundries • framed Beach Club watercolor prints • small assortment of groceries.

Transportation

Watercraft taxi to Disney–MGM Studios from the Bayside Marina at the Yacht Club. Although boat transportation is available to Epcot, it's quicker to walk to the park than to walk to the marina to catch it. The Boardwalk is a 5-minute stroll around the lagoon. Bus service is offered to the Magic Kingdom, Animal Kingdom, Typhoon Lagoon, Blizzard Beach, and Downtown Disney.

To reach other Disney resorts outside of the Epcot Area Resorts you must first bus to Downtown Disney and then transfer to your resort destination.

Disney's Beach Club Villas $$ to $$$$$

Disney's newest home-away-from-home resort designed by Robert Stern reflects the architecture of the oceanfront homes in Cape May, NJ, in the early part of the 20th century. Adjoining the Beach Club Resort and within a very short walking distance to Epcot, this property shares all facilities with the Yacht and Beach Club, including its fantastic pool. Housed in Cape Cod–style villas washed in a soothing teal green with sparkling white latticework trim, all units have either a garden or pool view each with a balcony or patio. Check-in is at the Beach Club Resort. See the above Beach Club Resort for recreation, services, restaurants, libations, transportation, and shopping. The Beach Club Villas has its own quiet pool, Dunes Cove, with whirlpool, lockers, and restrooms. **1900 Epcot Resorts Blvd., Lake Buena Vista, FL 32830; 407-934-2175; Fax 407-934-3850. Check-in 4 P.M.; check-out 11 A.M. For reservations call 407-W-DISNEY or your travel agent.**

Rooms

Villa choices come in studios as well as one and two-bedroom units (three-bedroom units are not offered at this property), each with a nice balcony or patio. Soft peach walls and ocean blue and sea green furnishings and fabrics intermingle with pickled white- and blue-trimmed furnishings, rattan chairs, and seahorse, seashell, and dolphin decorative tiles. Seaside framed prints decorate the soft peach–colored walls with carpeting imprinted in a vine motif. Kitchens come with granite countertops and bedrooms feature cream-colored scrolled metal headboards and morning glory print bedspreads.

The 356-square-foot Studios sleep a maximum of four people plus one child under 3 and include a queen-size bed, double sleeper sofa, armoire with TV, small table and two cushioned rattan chairs, patio or balcony, microwave, mini-refrigerator, coffee maker, and wet bar. Baths have a single sink with hairdryer and a separate, small bath/commode area embellished with seashell motif shower curtains and whimsical seashell tile. A small closet holds an iron and ironing board. The decor is a bit different in the studios with a soft blue coral reef pattern bedspread and curtains, soft blue wooden headboards, and a pastel plaid sofa bed. Each unit contains a patio or balcony. Just slightly larger than the next-door Beach Club guestrooms, their advantage is the addition of a sleeper sofa and mini-kitchen but at a higher nightly rate. Accommodates four adults and one child under 3.

The One-Bedroom Villa, at 727 square feet, sleeps a maximum of four plus one child under age 3. Each unit has a small living area with a queen-size sleeper sofa, reading chair, entertainment center containing a TV/DVD player, 5-person booth-style dining table, and a balcony or patio. The small but adequate kitchen, open to the living area, contains a refrigerator, stove, dishwasher, coffee maker, toaster, microwave, and all utensils, dishes, and pots and pans to make a complete meal. The spacious bedroom holds a king-size bed, armoire with TV, desk, and sea green easy chair as well as an additional patio or balcony. It adjoins a two-room bath, one holding a whirlpool tub, vanity sink, and walk-in closet with a laptop-size safe, iron, and ironing board while the other contains a commode (within an enclosure), shower, and an additional freestanding sink. A nice feature is the convenient stacked washer/dryer.

Two-Bedroom Villas sleep a maximum of eight people plus one child under 3 and offer 1,080 square feet of room. This unit is exactly the same as the one-bedroom with the addition of a studio bedroom, which adds up to two bathrooms, two bedrooms, living area, kitchen, three TVs, and three balconies or porches.

Disney's Boardwalk Inn $$ to $$$$

The Boardwalk Inn's intimate charm captures the feeling of a Mid-Atlantic seacoast retreat. The lobby is a nostalgic living room scene of chintz-covered, oversized chairs, invitingly plump sofas, floral rugs, and potted palms set atop gleaming hardwood floors and plush area rugs. Walls are a soothing sea green with cream-colored trim and looming overhead is the barrel-shaped, chandeliered ceiling embellished with delicate latticework. Views from the oversized windows are of a lush courtyard green fronting a festive, old-fashioned boardwalk. Step outside to the wide verandah lined with white wicker rocking chairs, a perfect early evening spot from which to bathe in the pink glow of sunset as the Boardwalk slowly comes alive.

The resort's gleaming white 4-story buildings dotted with latticework and crowned with sea green roofs and cheerfully striped awnings are set around interior courtyards fragrant with blooming roses. Adjoining the Inn and sharing all amenities is the Boardwalk Villas, a home-away-from-home property. Both front the lighthearted 1940s-style Boardwalk overlooking Crescent Lake and are just a short walk away from Epcot's International Gateway entrance. **2101 Epcot Resorts Blvd., Lake Buena Vista, FL 32830; 407-939-5100; Fax 407-939-5150. Check-in 3 P.M.; check-out 11 A.M. For reservations call 407-W-DISNEY or your travel agent.**

Rooms

Guestrooms—Accommodations average 390 whimsical square feet, all with French doors leading to full-size balconies or patios. Cheerfully furbished in a floral decor, leaf patterned wallpaper, and rose-studded carpeting, most offer two queen beds with white iron headboards (a few come with kings), small table and two chairs, a soft blue armoire with TV, and ample closet space. Daybeds just large enough for a small child come in many of the rooms and a second clothes dresser is near the bathroom. Baths have a marble-topped vanity with double sinks, hairdryer, and makeup mirror with separate tub and toilet area. Amenities include a keyed wall safe, iron and ironing board, and a daily newspaper.

Standard-view rooms could mean either a view of the front of the hotel and perhaps a bit of the parking lot or a delightful one of the peaceful, interior courtyard and hopefully the Illuminations fireworks. Water-view rooms are pleasing but those closest to the Boardwalk or overlooking the pool could be a bit noisy. Keep in mind that ground floor rooms have open patios that afford little privacy with vistas sometimes blocked by too-tall hedging.

Deluxe Rooms offer more space with the addition of a nice seating area including a queen sleeper sofa and easy chair.

Concierge rooms—Consider upgrading to one of the 65 concierge-level rooms where the Innkeeper's Club, a relaxing lounge on the 4th floor with a splendid view of Illuminations, offers a complimentary continental breakfast, midday refreshments of chips and salsa, popcorn, pretzels, nuts, and beverages, and afternoon finger sandwiches and cookies. Early evening brings hors d'oeuvres and wine and after dinner are cordials and dessert. All this along with concierge services, nightly turndown service, private check-in and -out, and bathrobes.

Suites—A gated, white picket fence encircles the serene, two-storied Garden Suites, most with their own private yard and entrance. Downstairs is a living area with a TV, queen-size sofa bed, wet bar, small refrigerator, and half bath while upstairs is a loft bedroom with four-poster bed and a bath with whirlpool tub. Some of these suites have a private balcony instead of a yard so be sure to request your preference.

From the two balconies of the beautifully decorated two-bedroom, two-and-a-half-bath Presidential Steeplechase Suite are sweeping views of the Boardwalk and Crescent Lake. This 2,170-square-foot wonder comes with a poshly furnished, massive living room with two seating areas and 8-person dining table. The lavish master bedroom boasts a gorgeous canopied four-poster bed, and in the marble master bath is a whirlpool tub and separate shower.

Restaurants

See Disney's Boardwalk Restaurants on pages 278-279.
In-room dining—24-hour room service.

Libations

Belle Vue Lounge—Located in the Inn off the lobby; open 5 P.M.–midnight. Sentimental lounge with the music of Bennie Goodman playing from vintage radios • additional balcony seating outdoors over-looking Boardwalk • cocktails and cold appetizers.

Leaping Horse Libations—Luna Park pool bar; open 11 A.M.–dusk. Deli and tuna sandwiches, hot dogs, chicken pita, chicken Caesar salad, nachos, fruit, ice cream • children's menu: PB&J sandwich, turkey and cheese sandwich • smoothies, beverages, beer, wine, specialty drinks.

Recreation and Activities

Arcade—Sideshow Arcade just off the Village Green. The newest in video and computer games and old reliable pinball machines • larger arcade located at ESPN Club on Boardwalk.

Bicycle and surrey rentals—Found in front of the Village Green • 2-, 4-, and 6-seater surreys • single and tandem bicycles available for rent at Community Hall.

Children's activities and playground—Playground next to the pool. Arts and crafts in Community Hall • Luna Park poolside activities • complimentary Very Merry Un-Birthday Party at 2 P.M. Fri for ages 4–12 (reservations required; call **407-939-6486**).

Ferris W. Eahlers Community Hall—Open 8 A.M.–10 P.M. Croquet • badminton • shuffleboard • video games • foosball • movies • arts and crafts • ping-pong • bike, book, and video rentals.

Fireworks cruise—View Illuminations from the privacy of a pontoon boat. Call **407-WDW-PLAY** for reservations.

Fishing—Guided 2-hour fishing excursions for up to five people including boat, guide, and gear each morning • guided 1-hour kids' fishing trip for children ages 5–12 departs from Community Hall Mon–Fri at 10 A.M. Call **407-WDW-PLAY** for reservations at least 24-hours in advance; catch and release.

Jogging—Joggers utilize the circular ¾-mile Boardwalk as their track.

Swimming—190,000 gallon Luna Park Pool with 200-foot-long "Keister Coaster" waterslide, a re-creation of a 1920s wooden roller coaster • kiddie pool and whirlpool • smaller Inn Pool and whirlpool in Rose Courtyard on Epcot side of inn • quiet Villa Pool and whirlpool found next to Community Hall. All pools are heated and open 24 hours.

Tennis—Two hard-surface, lighted courts on Villa side of property • complimentary to registered guests. Make reservations at Community Hall; for private and clinic instructions call **407-WDW-PLAY**.

Shopping—See Disney's Boardwalk Shopping on page 279.

Services

Muscles and Bustles Health Club—Open 6 A.M.–7 P.M. to guests of Disney-owned resorts • free weights • Cybex strength training equipment • Smith Machine • stair climbers • exercise bicycles • LifeFitness treadmills • saunas • steam rooms • tanning bed • personal training and massage available by appointment.

Transportation

Water taxi to Epcot and Disney–MGM Studios from the Boardwalk Marina. It's a 5- to 10-minute walk to Epcot's International Gateway along the Boardwalk and a 15-minute walk to Disney–MGM Studios along the newly opened walkway found behind the hotel. Bus service to the Magic Kingdom, Animal Kingdom, Typhoon Lagoon, Blizzard Beach, and Downtown Disney.

To reach other Disney resorts outside of the Epcot Area Resorts you must first bus to Downtown Disney and then transfer to your resort destination.

Disney's Boardwalk Villas $$ to $$$$$

Sharing the same lobby, check-in desk, pool, and all amenities as the adjacent Boardwalk Inn is this Disney Vacation Club property. Villas not occupied by members are available to the many visitors who wish to stay on Disney property but would also like the convenience of a kitchen and the extra breathing space of a full living area. The pastel, 3-story buildings are decked out with yellow-striped awnings and lush lawns while inside you'll find a summer seaside cottage atmosphere in the hallways painted with white picket fences and the wooden decking motif of the carpeting. Seating areas scattered throughout sport rattan chairs topped with gingham and flower pillows. See the above Boardwalk Inn section for recreation, services, restaurants, libations, transportation, and shopping. **2101 Epcot Resorts Blvd., Lake Buena Vista, FL 32830; 407-939-5100; Fax 407-939-5150. Check-in 4 P.M., check-out 11 A.M. For reservations call 407-W-DISNEY or your travel agent.**

Rooms

Villa choices come in studios, one-bedroom, two-bedroom, and three-bedroom Grand Villas, each with balcony or patio. All are decorated in a variety of soothing shades of pastel.

Studios at 359 square feet are one-room accommodations with a queen bed and one double sleeper sofa, small table and two chairs, a mini-kitchen with microwave, sink, and small refrigerator, and balcony or patio. The bath has a single sink vanity outside the tub and toilet area.

One-Bedroom units at 712 square feet have a small living area that accommodates a chintz-covered foldout couch, several chairs, an entertainment center containing a TV/VCR, and a small balcony or patio. The cheerful kitchen is open to the living room with a breakfast bar and barstools and contains a small, but adequate refrigerator, a stove, dishwasher, coffee maker, toaster, microwave, and all utensils, dishes, pots and pans to prepare a complete meal. A 2-person dining table sits out in the living area. The bedroom holds a king-size bed and adjoins a 2-part, white-tiled bath with whirlpool tub, sink, and hairdryer. A separate area holds the commode, shower, and a freestanding sink. In the bathroom closet is a safe, iron, and ironing board. Added pluses are a stacked washer/dryer and a portable crib. Request a villa that offers an additional balcony or patio off the master bedroom (most do).

Two-bedroom units at 1,072 square feet are essentially one-bedroom villas joined with a studio.

Grand Villas, at a whopping 2,142 square feet, are three-bedroom, three-bath accommodations offering a king-bedded master with whirlpool tub and two additional bedrooms, each with two queen beds and a bath. The living area has a queen sleeper sofa, dining area, and a full-size kitchen with a large balcony overlooking Crescent Lake. Each unit contains a full-size washer and dryer.

Room tip: If you're having trouble choosing between a studio here or a hotel room at the Boardwalk Inn, opt for the more spacious hotel room for the same price; the only plus in booking a studio is its mini-kitchen.

Disney's Yacht Club $$ to $$$$

A lighthouse perched on the pier leads the way to the sophisticated ambience of an exclusive yacht club. A navy blue blazer should be in order for a stay at this Robert Stern–designed resort composed of 4- and 5-story shingle-style buildings of soft gray beaded clapboard and balconies shaded by red and white-striped awnings. Fronting Crescent Lake and a sliver of beach that stretches over to the adjoining Beach Club, its prime location within walking distance to Epcot's International Gateway entrance as well as the Boardwalk and just a short boat ride away to Disney Studios is near perfect. The polished, sleek lobby of ship-shiny hardwoods, potted palms, roped nautical railings, leather couches, and overstuffed, striped easy chairs creates an environment reminiscent of a classy Eastern seaboard hotel of the 1880s. The antique globe centering the room along with detailed ship models and oceans of gleaming brass complete the picture. The resort shares Stormalong Bay, a fantasyland pool complex, and all recreational areas and facilities with its sister property, the Beach Club. **1700 Epcot Resorts Blvd., Lake Buena Vista, FL 32830; 407-934-7000; Fax 407-934-3450. Check-in 3 P.M.; check-out 11 A.M. For reservations call 407-W-DISNEY or your travel agent.**

Rooms

Enter the casually elegant, nautical-theme guestrooms through a yacht-style door. Inside you'll find sea blue nautically themed spreads topped with a gleaming white headboard in a ship's wheel motif, brass sconce lamps, an undulating border of waves gracing the ceiling over blue-and-white striped wallpaper, and red-white-and-blue checked maritime curtains. Rooms are fairly spacious at 380 square feet with cheerful all-white furnishings including a small writing table with two chairs, a bureau on top of which sits the TV, a minibar, and an additional dresser near the bath. French doors lead to a private balcony or patio with a variety of views. Some rooms come with a daybed and all have an easy chair and spacious closet. The marble bath vanity holds double sinks, an outdated hairdryer, makeup mirror, and TV speaker below porthole-style mirrors with a separate blue-and-white tiled tub and toilet area. Amenities include an iron and ironing board, small keyed safe, and daily newspaper.

Standard rooms come with either a view of the gardens or the less desirable front of the resort with perhaps a slice of the parking lot. Try for the standard rooms on the back side near the quiet pool that look out to a grassy area with a fountain and concealed duck pond. Water views look at Crescent Lake, Stormalong Bay, or sometimes both; ask for one with a view of Illuminations. If a lot of walking is not your idea of a vacation, request a room close to the lobby; the hotel is quite spread out and long treks to your room are not uncommon.

Concierge rooms—Concierge rooms and suites located on the top floor are privy to the classy Regatta Club, one of the few Disney concierge lounges with a balcony, but alas with a view of the front of the hotel instead of Crescent Lake. In the mornings there's a continental breakfast, then a midday snack and tea consisting of cookies, cake, fruit, popcorn, and beverages. Early evening brings hot and cold hors d'oeuvres such as mini-quiches and wrapped sandwiches plus chocolate chip cookies and wine (kids feast on PB&J sandwiches), and after dinner you'll find a selection of cordials and desserts. Rooms here are basically the same as the standard guestrooms but with bathrobes, turndown service, private check-in and -out, and the additional services of an excellent concierge staff.

Suites—A variety of plush suites are available, the smallest being the 654-square-foot Junior Suite with two queen beds, an armoire, and small table and chairs in the extra-large balconied bedroom and a daybed, coffee table, and chair in a small sitting area separated by French doors.

Turret Two-Bedroom Suites offer 1,160 square feet, including two queens and a bath in each bedroom; off the master is a 6-side turreted living area with sofa, chairs, entertainment armoire, 4-person dining room, and stand-up balcony.

Exactly the same are the Commodore and the Vice Presidential Suite at 1,375 square feet. Enter through a large marble foyer to two bedrooms, two-and-a-half baths, three balconies (one a stand-up) with both pool and water views, and a parlor with sofa, chairs, entertainment center with TV, DVD player, stereo, and wet bar with small refrigerator. The incredible marble master bath has a whirlpool tub, separate shower, and TV.

Almost identical at 1,636 square feet are the two-bedroom, two-and-a-half bath Presidential and Admiral suites. Both are richly decorated and come with a marble foyer, two living areas (one turreted), fireplace, a separate 8-person dining room, small kitchen, and three balconies. The master bedroom offers a whirlpool tub in the luxurious marble bath.

The largest suite at 2,374 square feet and the best on property is the 1st floor, two-bedroom, two-and-a-half-bath Captain's Deck Suite. A marble octagonal foyer leads to a nautically decorated parlor the size of three regular guestrooms with an open sitting area, full living room, large business desk, dining room with seating for 10, full kitchen (minus a stove), and a large garden patio (with a not-so-great view of the valet parking lot through the shrubbery). Each of the bedrooms has its own private patio, and the plush master offers a canopy bed, walk-in closet, large marble bath with vanity area, TV, huge shower, and separate whirlpool tub. The second bedroom is similar to a regular resort room. All suites regardless of floor location receive concierge service and amenities.

Restaurants

Yacht Club Galley—Open for breakfast and lunch. Breakfast: buffet and à la carte items • lunch: soups, salads, sandwiches, steak, pasta.

Yachtsman Steakhouse—Dinner only • one of Disney's best for steaks • seafood • full review on page 363.

In-room dining—24-hour room service; limited menu after 10 P.M.

Libations

Crew's Cup Lounge—Next door to Yachtsman Steakhouse. Cozy atmosphere of a seaport lounge • beers from the world's great seaports, wine and champagne by the glass • light meals: crab cakes, jumbo shrimp cocktail, three-cheese spinach dip, grilled steak and portobello skewers, Caesar salad, tomato and buffalo mozzarella salad, oysters Rockefeller.

Ale and Compass Lounge—Lobby bar • specialty drinks, coffee, wine, beer.

Hurricane Hanna's Grill—Poolside snack bar • grilled chicken sandwiches, chicken strips, cheeseburgers, hot dogs, wrap sandwiches, chicken or tuna salad • children's menu: chicken strips, PB&J sandwich, mini cheeseburger • beverages, cocktails, beer, alcoholic and nonalcoholic frozen drinks.

Recreation and Activities

The Yacht Club shares all recreational activities with the adjacent Beach Club. See Beach Club Recreation and Activities on pages 71-72.

Services

The Yacht Club shares all services with the adjacent Beach Club. See Beach Club Services on page 73.

Shopping

Fittings and Fairings Clothing and Notions—Disney merchandise • Disney and Yacht Club logo clothing for all ages • golfing attire • men and women's casual wear • Yacht Club Resort watercolor prints • snacks • sundries • magazines • books • newspapers • film processing.

Transportation

Water taxi to Epcot and Disney–MGM Studios from the Bayside Marina. Allow enough time for a 5- to 10-minute interval between incoming and departing boats. It's a 10-minute walk to Epcot's International Gateway entrance and 5 minutes to the Boardwalk. Take a bus to the Magic Kingdom, Animal Kingdom, Typhoon Lagoon, Blizzard Beach, and Downtown Disney.

To reach other Disney resorts outside the Epcot Resort Area you must first bus to Downtown Disney, then transfer to your resort destination.

Walt Disney World Dolphin $$ to $$$$

Operated by Sheraton Hotels but situated within the grounds of Walt Disney World, this pyramid-shaped, Michael Graves–designed resort can certainly be described as whimsical. All eyes are immediately drawn to the pair of 5-story dolphins high atop the 27 stories of the structure and then are immediately lured to the exterior fountain composed of giant-size clamshells cascading 9 stories down to the hotel entrance. Shades of rich coral and turquoise create a cacophony of color throughout the hotel and into the imposing lobby draped with a gaily striped cabana-style tent. Underneath it sits a fanciful fountain of dolphins surrounded by a bevy of upscale shops. Outside you'll find the fantasyland Grotto Pool fronting the white-sand beach of Crescent Lake.

Extensive meeting facilities, ballrooms, and exhibit halls make this a popular choice for conventioneers, so come prepared for large groups roaming the public areas both here and at the next-door Swan, which shares all recreational and service facilities with the Dolphin.

Although this is technically not a Disney-owned hotel, guests receive the same amenities as other Disney resorts including E-ticket nights, Disney transportation to all attractions, complimentary parking, length-of-stay passes, package delivery, guaranteed park admission, and preferred tee times. However, charging privileges to your hotel account do not extend outside of the Dolphin or Swan. Dollar for dollar, still the Disney-owned deluxe properties are a better choice unless you happen to be Disney-phobic and prefer a convenient hotel that also offers a break from everything Mickey at the end of your day. **1500 Epcot Resorts Blvd., Lake Buena Vista, FL 32830; 407-934-4000; Fax 407-934-4099. Check-in 3 P.M.; check-out 11 A.M. For reservations call 407-W-DISNEY, 888-828-8850, or your travel agent. www.swandolphin.com.**

Rooms

Guestrooms—Beach-theme hallways lead to the cabana-striped doorways of the 360-square-foot guestrooms merrily decorated in a tropical motif of pineapple-adorned headboards and brightly striped bedspreads. The vivid blue painted furnishings, blue-and-cream striped drapes, mauve-and-cream striped wallpaper, and leaf-patterned mauve carpeting make for a wacky dissonance of color. Each room holds two double beds and offers either a sofa or easy chair plus a desk, an armoire/entertainment center, minibar, daily newspaper delivery, a couple of two-line telephones with dataport, in-house movies, and Nintendo. Closets hold a keyed safe, iron, and ironing board. Baths have only a single sink, but offer a separate vanity with a hairdryer and coffee maker. A nice option is a room with a balcony for which an extra charge is assessed.

Tip: The Dolphin's guestrooms are scheduled for a major re-do.

Concierge rooms—Club Level rooms, located on the 12th and 14th floors, come with the benefit of a large 12th-floor private lounge with views of Illuminations plus a complimentary continental breakfast in the morning as well as fruit, cheese, and honor bar wine and beer from 5–7 P.M. Extra amenities include the services of a concierge desk, robes, and nightly turndown service. The lack of a private check-in desk, afternoon snacks, hot hors d'oeuvres in the evening, and evening desserts and cordials as well as the additional charge for alcoholic beverages make the concierge level here not really worth the extra cash outlay.

Suites—Junior Suites offer quite a bit more room than a regular guestroom and a second bath as well. In the bedroom is a king bed and sleeper sofa, and the large, separate parlor area holds a Murphy bed, sleeper sofa, two reading chairs, desk, wet bar with icemaker, and an extra bath.

The Two-Bedroom/Three-Bath Suite sleeping 10 is designed with a bedroom and bath on either side of a sizable parlor and offers a large living room with wet bar and ice maker, a king-size Murphy bed, sofa, two easy chairs, coffee table, and an extra full bath. This can also be configured as a one-bedroom, two-bath suite.

The Dolphin has four Presidential Suites, each with a different theme. I got a peek at the Caesar Suite with its massive living area holding two seating areas, an 8-person dining table, and full bath as well as an adjoining full kitchen (minus a stove). Each of the two bedrooms are similar to the regular guestrooms but with a totally different and upgraded decor in shades of blue, coral, and mauve. Alas there is no balcony. Similar in size and layout is the Pharaoh Suite; both have 2,451 square feet.

The two other Presidential Suites are larger 2-story units and offer either a Japanese or Southwestern decor, three bedrooms, kitchen, four different sitting areas, 8-person dining table, an entertainment center in each room, and a grand piano.

Room tip: A small percentage of the rooms offer a view of the Epcot fireworks. Go ahead and request one at time of booking and again at check-in.

Restaurants

Cabana Bar and Grill—Pool grill • salads, chicken wings, chicken fingers, burgers, hot dogs, grilled chicken sandwich, tuna sandwich, steak sandwich • full bar, alcoholic and nonalcoholic frozen tropical drinks.

Coral Café—Lobby-level café open for breakfast and lunch • breakfast: buffet and à la carte items • lunch: pasta, salads, hot sandwiches • character breakfast buffet on Sun.

Dolphin Fountain—Open 11 A.M.–11 P.M. Old-fashioned 1950s soda shop atmosphere • hot dogs, burgers, vegetarian burgers, BLT sandwich, fried chicken sandwich • ice cream, banana splits, ice cream-topped strawberry shortcake, floats, sundaes, malts, homemade pies.

Tubbi's Buffeteria and Convenience Store—24-hour cafeteria with adjoining convenience store; located on the lower level • breakfast: fresh fruit, French toast, omelets, breakfast burritos, muffins, bagels, Krispy Kreme donuts • lunch and dinner: chef salad, burgers, grilled chicken sandwiches, soup, tuna and chicken salad sandwiches, pizza, vegetarian burgers, daily Blue Plate special.

Shula's Steakhouse—Dinner only • best steak on Disney property • clubby and luxurious atmosphere • full review on page 358.

In-room dining—24-hour room service.

Libations

Lobby Lounge—Morning: coffee and pastries • afternoon and evening: cocktail service.

Shula's Steakhouse Lounge—Cigar bar adjoining Shula's Steakhouse • clubby and sophisticated • full bar, cocktails, wine, champagne, port, single malt scotch • appetizer menu.

Recreation and Activities

Arcade—Located downstairs near health club.

Basketball—Courts on each side of Grotto Pool.

Boating—Swan paddleboats near Grotto Pool.

Children's playground—Playground located in pool area.

Jogging—4 miles of jogging trails surround the resort. Ask at health club or concierge desk for a map.

Swimming—Open 24 hours; lifeguards on duty 9 A.M.–9 P.M. Rambling, 3-acre Grotto Pool located between Swan and the Dolphin Hotels • waterfall • hammocks • tropical vegetation • children's pool • two whirlpools • Spring Pool • two lap pools • Grotto and Spring pools are heated.

Tennis—Four lighted tennis courts located across Epcot Resorts Boulevard.

Volleyball—Sand courts on beach.

Services

Car rental—National Car Rental desk located in lobby.

Childcare—Camp Dolphin, open daily 5:30 P.M.–midnight, for children ages 4–12; cost includes dinner; open to all guests of WDW; call 407-934-4241 for reservations • arts and crafts • video games • Disney movies • game room excursion.

Hair salon—Open 9 A.M.–6 P.M. daily • haircuts • color • styling • manicures • pedicures.

Health club—Body by Jake Health Club open 6 A.M.–9 P.M. Sprint Weight Systems • free weights • Life Rowers and Cycles • treadmills • stair machines • aerobic classes • locker rooms • dry saunas • co-ed whirlpool • personal training and massage available by appointment.

Shopping

Brittany Jewels—Fine jewelry and timepieces.

Daisy's Garden—Disney merchandise store.

Indulgences Gourmet—Homemade candies, fudge, and caramel popcorn.

Statements of Fashion—Resort wear for men and women • swimwear • accessories.

Transportation

Boat launch to Epcot's International Gateway and Disney–MGM Studios (departs every 15–20 minutes) and bus service to the Magic Kingdom, Animal Kingdom, Downtown Disney, Typhoon Lagoon, and Blizzard Beach. If you prefer to walk, it's a pleasant 10–15 minute walk to Epcot's International Gateway entrance (one that is sometimes quicker than the boat service) or to Disney–MGM Studios in 15–20 minutes via the new walkway found behind the Boardwalk Inn and Villas.

Walt Disney World Swan $$ to $$$$

If you can peel your eyes away from the massive dolphins across the way you'll soon notice the graceful 46-foot swans atop the smaller sister property of the Walt Disney World Dolphin. Also designed by Michael Graves and operated by the Westin, the Swan, composed of a 12-story main building and two 7-story wings, is a bit more subdued than the Dolphin. Linked by an awning-covered walkway (the place to catch the boat launch to Epcot and Disney–MGM Studios), they share the glorious 3-acre grotto pool. The same coral and teal colors of the Dolphin are also predominant throughout this hotel. Its low-ceilinged, minuscule lobby adorned with a sparkling swan fountain is so understated you'll feel you've somehow missed it. But if the colossal style of the Dolphin is simply not your scene, this is the place for you.

Although technically not a Disney-owned hotel, guests receive the same amenities as other Disney properties just like the Dolphin (see above).

The lobby and the grounds are extremely attractive, and the hotel is well know for its popularity with Japanese tour groups (there's even a

Japanese tour desk in the lobby) as well as with conventioneers. **1200 Epcot Resorts Blvd., Lake Buena Vista, FL 32830; 407-934-3000; Fax 407-934-4099. Check-in 3 P.M., check-out 11 a.m. For reservations call 407-W-DISNEY, 888-828-8850, or your travel agent. www.swandolphin.com.**

Rooms

Guestrooms—Newly redecorated guestrooms in soft shades of blue and beige possess a contemporary upscale luxury instead of the previously whimsical look. Now you'll find sleek maple furnishings with frosted glass accents along with slate foyers. The old mattresses have been replaced with "Heavenly Beds," Westin's signature pillow-topped mattresses, along with triple-sheeted luxe linens, down comforters and pillows, and snow white duvets. The 27-inch TVs are found in a bureau that connects to a large desk. Rooms are 360 square feet and come with either a king bed and pull-out sleeper sofa or two double beds with a lounge chair and ottoman. Baths offer two sinks, one outside the bath area with a hairdryer and coffee maker and one inside with the tub/shower and commode. Amenities include an iron and ironing board, a couple of two-line telephones, high speed internet connection, and cable with pay movies. Views from the upper floors can be impressive with panoramas of either Disney Studios or Epcot and the Grotto Pool. A nice option is a room with a balcony, for which an extra charge is assessed.

Room tip: A small percentage of the rooms offer a view of the Epcot fireworks. Go ahead and request one at time of booking and again at check-in.

Concierge rooms—Concierge rooms are located on the 11th and 12th floors (none with balconies) with access to the large 12th-floor Royal Beach Club lounge. Here guests will find the services of a concierge staff as well as a complimentary continental breakfast, and fruit, cheese, crudites with dipping sauce, and nonalcoholic beverages from 5–7 P.M. Wine and beer are an additional charge. Extra amenities include robes and nightly turndown service. As with the Dolphin, the lack of private check-in desk, afternoon snacks, hot hors d'oeuvres in the evening, and evening desserts and cordials together with the additional charge for alcoholic beverages make the concierge level here not really worth the extra cash outlay.

Suites—Swan Studios offer a bit more square footage than a regular guestroom with a king bedroom opening up to a small sitting area with a double sofa bed and 4-person dining table. Some have balconies on request only.

The one-bedroom, two-bath Grand Suites come with a regular-size bedroom and the addition of a large living area with a sofa, rattan easy chairs, 6-person dining table, large wet bar with icemaker, balcony (in some), and extra full-size bath. It can easily be made into a two-bedroom, three-bath suite if desired by the addition of a connecting bedroom on the opposite side of the living area.

The large Japanese Governor's Suite has a somewhat austere decor along with overly loud carpeting. It offers two bedrooms, 3 full baths, parlor with a grand piano, wet bar, dining room with seating for eight, and full kitchen. More to my liking was the decor in the two-bedroom, three-bath Italian Governor's Suite with balcony, 8-person dining room, grand piano, and full kitchen.

Restaurants

Garden Grove and Gulliver's Grill—Breakfast and dinner • setting reminiscent of a giant soaring birdcage • breakfast: buffet and à la carte menu items—Saturday character breakfast with Goofy and Pluto • dinner: buffet (Italian on Sun and Thurs, American on Mon, Wed, and Sat, and Seafood on Tues and Fri) and à la carte choices of steaks, seafood, and prime rib—characters each evening.

Kimonos—Dinner only • sleek sushi and sake bar • karaoke nightly beginning at 9 P.M.

Palio—Dinner only • Disney's best Italian restaurant • full review on page 358.

Splash Grill—Poolside grill; open only seasonally • pizza, burgers, sandwiches, salads • full-service bar.

In-room dining—24-hour room service.

Libations

Lobby Court Lounge—Morning: coffee and pastries • evening: cocktail service and cigar lounge with live piano music.

Recreation and Activities

The Swan shares all recreational activities with the Dolphin.

Services

Childcare—See Dolphin Childcare.

Hair salon—See Dolphin Hair salon.

Health club—Swan Health Club open daily 6 A.M.–9 P.M. LifeFitness exercise machines • free weights • Lifecycle • treadmills • stair machines • locker rooms • dry saunas • co-ed whirlpool • personal training and massage available by appointment.

Shopping

Disney Cabanas—Men and women's resort clothing • Disney merchandise • sundries.

Transportation

See Dolphin transportation.

ANIMAL KINGDOM AREA

Disney's only deluxe resort in the Animal Kingdom area is the extraordinary Animal Kingdom Lodge. Although its isolation and solitude adds to the allure, it also makes it a less convenient choice than resorts in the Magic Kingdom or Epcot area. Those choosing this property should consider renting a car to take full advantage of all WDW has to offer in the way of resort restaurants and entertainment. Nearby, of course, is the Animal Kingdom as well as Blizzard Beach, Winter Summerland miniature golf, and Disney's Wide World of Sports.

Disney's Animal Kingdom Lodge $ to $$$$

Disney's version of an African safari lodge is truly a stunner, a faithful celebration of African wildlife, culture, cuisine, and art. Opened in April 2001, its authentic architecture combined with grasslands filled with hundreds of roaming exotic animals is simply a stroke of genius. The 6-story, horseshoe-shaped structure topped with extravagant thatched rooftops is rustically surrounded by eucalyptus fencing and 33 acres of glorious savanna. The landscape is one of golden boulders, tall bamboo, yellow flame trees, pampas grass, sweet acacia, white jasmine, copperpod trees, and date palms. Though often compared to the Wilderness Lodge in design and pricing, the Animal Kingdom Lodge is a step above in terms of sophistication.

The imposing, 5-story, thatched-roofed lobby is a wonder. As at Disney's Wilderness Lodge (both designed by architect Peter Dominick), the first impression is nothing but *wow!* Massive overhead chandeliers formed by resplendent Masai shields and spears and a large mud fireplace tower over the boulder-lined lobby. Safari chic seating, perhaps some of the most striking of any Disney resort, is extraordinary with intricate hand-carved coffee tables, handsome handwoven rugs, richly tinted rattan and cane chairs, and cushy leather sofas tossed with brilliant textile pillows. A rope suspension bridge spans the lobby and draws the eye to balconies carved with graceful antelopes and the 46-ft picture window interposed with the branches of an intricate ironwork tree. The centerpiece of the lobby is the one-of-a-kind sacred Ijele, a 16-foot, brilliantly colored mask created by the Igbo tribe of Nigeria.

Out back sits a massive yellow flame tree poised atop Arusha Rock, an outcropping with panoramic views of the savanna. Nearby is the rocking chair–surrounded firepit where storytelling, hosted by the African staff, is a nightly ritual. The lobby and restaurant greeters together with the savanna guides are cultural representatives from Africa, all more than delighted to answer questions or share information and tales of their homeland.

Located within a 5-minute drive to the Animal Kingdom theme park (but not close enough to walk), the animals you'll see here are exclusively the lodge's and are not part of the theme park's menagerie. The design is one that encourages observation of the animals from both common lookouts as well as from 75% of the rooms. Several viewing platforms are staffed by guides who are helpful in identifying the wildlife as well as communicating interesting information about each animal. Each savanna holds different species and extreme patience is sometimes required to spot them.

On occasion there's not a hint of an animal, but often the savanna is brimming with an overwhelming abundance of prime viewing opportunities. You'll see playful zebra, lanky giraffe, sprite gazelle, huge ankole cattle, herds of wildebeest, flocks of exotic birds, and more, with over 200 animals in all. It all depends on the heat of the day, feeding times, etc. But shrewd placement of watering holes and truckloads of feed brought out to the savanna encourage the wildlife to spend their time in full view of hotel guests. After dark the preserves are lit with a moon-glow effect, perfect for a nighttime stroll or after-dinner entertainment from your room balcony. And if, for some strange reason, you're bored with this marvelous place, take a tour of the hotel interior to view the outstanding collection of over 200 pieces of African art, including intricate masks, amazing beadwork, artifacts dating as far back as 8,500 BC, and much, much more. **2901 Osceola Parkway, Bay Lake, FL 32830; 407-938-3000; Fax 407-938-7102. Check-in 3 P.M., check-out 11 A.M. For reservations call 407-W-DISNEY or your travel agent.**

Rooms

Guestrooms—Don't even consider booking a room without a savanna view, well worth every penny for a front row seat of the animal-filled savanna. And don't forget to bring your binoculars from home! Enter your guestroom through the shield-covered door to an attractively designed, honey-colored room outfitted with handcrafted and carved furnishings augmented by torch-shaped lamps and tribal decor of handwoven baskets and ethnic prints. Textiles in rich earth tone shades of gold, yellow, and brown cover the beds and overhead the intricately engraved headboards are draped in a gauzy fabric reminiscent of mosquito netting. Baths have a separate granite-topped vanity area boasting double sinks, hairdryers, full-length mirror, and makeup mirror. Bathroom walls are covered with maps of Africa and the vanity is topped with a wonderful hand-carved mirror.

Poor lighting in the baths (a common complaint at many Disney hotels) is due to the gold-tinted light shades; pleasant atmosphere, but not too helpful when trying to apply makeup. Amenities include an iron and ironing board, safe, and daily newspaper. All rooms have balconies with 75% of them offering savanna views. Standard rooms at 344 square feet are a bit cramped so I highly suggest an upgrade to a Deluxe Room offering that extra 40 square feet of space needed for comfortable living quarters.

Room tip: At the Animal Kingdom Lodge are three savannas, each with their own charm; however, you might want to request the large, inner savanna. Outer ones sometimes sport a not so great view of the highway, a sliver of the resort pool, or a stockade holding that just might kill any illusion you have of being in deepest, darkest Africa.

Concierge rooms—The concierge-level rooms, all of them either deluxe rooms or suites on the 5th and 6th floor, come with the use of the thatched-roofed, 6th-floor Kilimanjaro Club overlooking the lobby. Extra amenities include the services of a concierge staff, curbside check-in, turndown service, and robes in the room. In the morning there's a continental breakfast and later come afternoon snacks and beverages, late afternoon tea of scones, cookies, and biscuits, evening wine and hot and cold hors d'oeuvres, and late night desserts and cordials. You'll even find a self-service espresso machine.

A special early morning excursion on Tues and Sat is the Sunrise Safari. Departing at 6:30 A.M. and offered only to concierge guests, it includes a 30-minute, before park hours ride through the Animal Kingdom's Kilimanjaro Safaris followed by a buffet breakfast at Tusker House. The price is $50 per person and advance reservations can be made 90 days prior to arrival through the concierge desk.

Room tip: My only hesitation in booking a concierge-level room would be the disappointment in not receiving a room with a view of the savanna. Most rooms have a savanna view, but a few come with a view of the pool; you won't know until check-in which type you will be receiving. Until Disney changes its policy to separate the rooms with two different levels of pricing, I would stick with a nonconcierge Deluxe Savanna View or a Savanna View Suite.

Suites—A 777-square-foot one-bedroom suite offers a separate parlor with a queen sofa sleeper, wet bar, and powder room; the bath has a tub and separate shower. In the two-bedroom, two-and-a-half bath suite is a parlor with sofa, easy chairs, and coffee table as well as a 4-person dining table and wet bar. The king-bedded master has a large bath with a separate shower, double sinks, and a separate vanity area as well as a balcony. The second bedroom is the same as a deluxe room with a queen bed, bunk beds, daybed, and balcony.

The ultimate in suites is the two-bedroom, two-and-a-half-bath Royal Assante Suite with over 2,115 square feet of exotic luxury. Enter the rounded foyer to the circular living room with a domed thatched roof holding a queen sleeper sofa, easy chairs, dining table for eight, kitchen, armoire with extra-large TV, fireplace, and writing desk. In the king-bedded master is a sitting room, rustic four-poster bed with mosquito net draping, plenty of built-in cabinets and dresser space, oversized tub, double-sinked granite vanity area with TV, huge separate shower, and walk-in closet; there's even a treadmill. And from the wraparound balcony are sweeping views of the savanna.

The two-bedroom, two-and-a-half-bath Royal Kuba Vice Presidential Suite at 1,619 square feet is similar but with smaller rooms, a stair climber instead of treadmill, and a less extensive balcony. Both suites have lovely African-inspired furnishings.

Restaurants

An interesting array of dining choices, many with an African flair, will please even the most timid eaters. Wine connoisseurs will love the fact that the Animal Kingdom Lodge has the largest offerings of South African wines in the U.S. The hotel's only lack is a full-service restaurant open for lunch, the only Disney deluxe hotel without such a venue.

Boma—Breakfast and dinner • lively African marketplace atmosphere • African and American food buffet • full review on page 347.

Jiko—Dinner only • one of Disney's loveliest restaurants • international food with an African flair • extensive South African wine list • full review on page 353.

The Mara—Self-service snack bar; open 6:30 A.M.–11:30 P.M. • breakfast: scrambled eggs, waffles, brioche French toast, egg and bacon croissant sandwich, breakfast pizza, fruit smoothies, oatmeal, pastries, muffins • lunch and dinner: homemade soup, pizza, fish and chips, grilled chicken sandwiches, fried shrimp, burgers, sugar cane and rotisserie chicken, fresh fruit, cold sandwiches, pita wraps, salads • children's menu: hot dog, chicken strips.

In-room dining—Available 6:30 A.M.–midnight.

Libations

Capetown Lounge and Wine Bar—Jiko's eye-catching bar • largest South African wine list in the U.S.

Uzima Springs—Thatched-roofed pool bar • frozen margaritas, daiquiris, pina coladas, beer, wine, nonalcoholic smoothies.

Victoria Falls Lounge—Lounge overlooking Boma; open 4 P.M.–midnight • African bush lodge atmosphere • exotic, African-inspired cocktails, South African wine, port, beer.

Sports and Recreation

Arcade—Pumbaa's Fun and Games arcade located near the pool.

Children's playground—Hakuna Matata playground near pool • nice view of the flamingo area and savanna.

Storytelling—Each evening at 7:30 P.M. around the outdoor Arusha Firepit • African culture honored through storytelling.

Swimming—11,000 square-foot Uzima Pool, the lodge's version of a watering hole highlighted by a 67-foot waterslide • cement is darkened to create the effect of swimming out in the bush, minus the crocodiles • two secluded whirlpools • kiddie pool • heated.

Tours—Daily architecture and art collection tours. Meet at Ogun's Firepit at 3:30 P.M.

Services

Childcare—Simba's Cubhouse, open 4:30 P.M.–midnight, for potty-trained children ages 4-12; cost includes dinner; open to all registered guests of Walt Disney World resorts; call **407-WDW-DINE** for reservations • classic Disney movies • storytelling • arts and crafts.

Health club—Zahanati Massage and Fitness Center open 6 A.M.–7 P.M. Free weights • Cybex equipment • LifeFitness treadmills • stair climbers • exercise bicycles • steam rooms • saunas • personal training • select spa treatments: facials, massage, body treatments with in-room service available for an additional fee.

Shopping

Zawadi Marketplace—African woodcarvings • hand-painted ostrich eggs • pewter and wood animal napkin rings • wooden masks • woven baskets • Zimbabwe pottery • Animal Kingdom Lodge logo merchandise • coffee table books on Africa • sundries • cigars • wine • liquor.

Transportation

Bus transportation to all four Disney theme parks, Downtown Disney, Typhoon Lagoon, and Blizzard Beach. To reach other Disney resorts you must first bus to Downtown Disney and then transfer to your resort destination.

DOWNTOWN DISNEY AREA

Another exciting area is the one encompassing Downtown Disney with its profusion of restaurants, shopping, and nightlife as well as DisneyQuest, AMC Theaters, and Cirque du Soleil. Resorts nearby are Disney's Old Key West along with the off-property Hyatt Regency Grand Cypress and the Villas of Grand Cypress. Close are Typhoon Lagoon as well as the Lake Buena Vista Golf Course.

Disney's Old Key West Resort $$ to $$$$$

For a taste of a Key West–style village and the convenience of home-away-from-home condominium-style accommodations, look no more. This was the first of the Disney Vacation Club properties, and villas not occupied by members are available to the many visitors who want to stay on Disney property but would also like the added plus of a kitchen and extra breathing space of a full living area. Clustered around the registration building is a small marina area on the shores of the Trumbo Canal consisting of the main swimming pool, a restaurant, store, and bar plus a small health club and activity center. A red-and-white striped lighthouse leads the way to a 156-acre property scattered with a palette of 2- and 3-story pastel structures, each with a shiny tin roof, white gingerbread trim, and striped awnings. Peace and quiet prevails amid the tropical landscaping of palms, flowering hibiscus, and brilliantly colored bird-of-paradise. Numerous waterways and lagoons together with the Lake Buena Vista Golf Course that runs throughout the property make for soothing views from many of the villa's patios and balconies.

1510 North Cove Road, Lake Buena Vista, FL 32830; 407-827-7700; Fax 407-827-7710. Check-in 4 P.M.; check-out 11 A.M. For reservations call 407-W-DISNEY or your travel agent.

Rooms

Villas here are the largest of all the home-away-from-home properties offering plenty of room to sprawl out. Decorated in a soothing pastel color scheme of greens and mauves, furnishings are soft blond and pickled wood furniture with plaid sofas and floral bedspreads. An abundance of windows and plenty of softly turning ceiling fans make for airy, bright rooms. Each unit has a patio or balcony with varying views of either waterways, the golf course, the woodlands, or a combination of all of the above. Bathrooms are large with shiny white tiles, pickled green wood trim, and whirlpool tubs (except in the studio units). A portable crib is stored in the closet in each unit along with an iron and ironing board.

The 376-square-foot studio accommodates up to four adults plus one child under 3. It holds two queen beds, small table with two chairs, armoire with TV, and a mini-kitchen with a small refrigerator, coffee maker, sink, and microwave. There are no safes in these units, but safety deposit boxes are available at the front desk free of charge. Nice-sized baths offer two sinks with one inside the bathtub/commode area and one outside and the small stacked washer/dryers are an added plus.

One-Bedroom Villas are 942 square feet, sleeping six and one child under 3 with a separate living area, full-size kitchen, and spacious bedroom. The roomy living room is appointed with a sleeper sofa and love seat, coffee table, and easy chair in addition to a 4-person dining table and TV/VCR. The green-tiled kitchen, open to the living area, includes a microwave, coffee maker, dishwasher, toaster, sink, and full-size refrigerator and is stocked with dishes, flatware, pots and pans, even placemats and cloth napkins. The spacious tiled patio is perfect for dining al fresco and opens into the living area as well as the master bedroom. A roomy king-bedded master holds a television, armoire, dresser, and cozy sitting chair and ottoman and connects to a two-roomed bath with large whirlpool tub, separate shower, and two sinks. You'll find a wall safe in the master bathroom closet and a laundry room with full-size washer and dryer, iron, and ironing board.

Spacious 1,333 square feet Two-Bedroom Villas sleep eight and one child under 3. They're exactly the same as the one-bedrooms with the addition of a large extra bedroom with two queens, armoire with TV, a small table and chairs, and a second bath.

The gigantic Three-Bedroom/Four Bath Grand Villas sleep up to 12 people and 1 child under age 3 and offer a whopping 2,202 square feet of space. These 2-story units are luxuriously roomy with the addition of hardwood floors in the living area, lofty ceilings, rattan game table, stereo system, and a 6-person dining table. A laundry room is situated off the full-size kitchen. The master bedroom is located downstairs with the usual whirlpool tub, two sinks, and shower with a separate commode. The two other bedrooms, each with bath, are found upstairs with two queens in one and two doubles in the other. An additional bath is located in the downstairs hallway.

Room tip: There are no elevators here; if stairs are a problem, request a ground floor room.

Restaurants

Good's Food To Go—Snack bar open 7:30 A.M.–10 P.M. Breakfast: breakfast croissant sandwiches, scrambled eggs, bagels with cream cheese, pastries, cinnamon rolls, muffins, cereal, fruit • lunch and dinner: cheeseburgers, hot dogs, sandwiches of turkey, tuna, and chicken salad, chef salad, fruit plate.

Olivia's Café—Breakfast, lunch, and dinner • tasty food in a casual Key West setting • full review on page 357.

Turtle Shack—Poolside snack bar open seasonally.

Pizza delivery—Available 4 P.M.–midnight.

Libations

Gurgling Suitcase—Tiny beach-style bar adjacent to marina and main pool • specialty drinks, beer, cocktails, wine, sodas.

Recreation and Activities

Arcade—Electric Eel Arcade located next to marina.

Bicycles—Available for rent at Hank's Rent 'n' Return • mongoose bicycles • 2- and 4-seater surrey bikes • hydro bikes.

Boating—Rentable at Hank's Rent 'n' Return for a trip down the Trumbo Canal to Downtown Disney • pontoon boats • canopy boats • paddle boats • WaterMouse.

Children's activities and playground—Sandcastle-themed playground near main pool; additional playground located near quiet pool on Turtle Pond Road; activities occur daily at Conch Flats Community Hall • coloring contests • face painting • sand art • arts and crafts • complimentary Unbirthday party for children ages 5–10 on Thurs afternoon (reservations required).

Conch Flats Community Hall—Arts and crafts • family bingo • board games • foosball • ping-pong • large-screen TV • video rentals.

Jogging—3-mile path winds through the property.

Swimming—Free-form main pool surrounded by palms and luxuriant tropical plants • nearby whirlpool, sauna, and sandcastle-theme kiddie pool • three additional quiet pools spread around property • all pools are heated.

Tennis—Equipment rentable at Hank's Rent 'n' Return • three tennis courts; two lighted courts near main pool, the other more isolated court is not.

Other activities—Equipment available at Hank's Rent 'n' Return • shuffleboard • volleyball • basketball courts.

Services

Health club—R.E.S.T. Beach Recreation Department open 6:30 A.M.–midnight; club use is reserved for guests of the Disney Vacation Club Resorts only • stair climbers • treadmills • free weights • Nautilus equipment • massage, hot tub, and sauna available at the adjoining Slappy Joe's.

Shopping

Conch Flats General Store—Groceries • wine • beer • sundries • newspapers • books • souvenirs • Old Key West logo attire • toys • groceries delivered to your villa for a nominal fee.

Transportation

Bus transportation is provided to all four Disney theme parks plus Blizzard Beach, Typhoon Lagoon, and Downtown Disney with five bus stops scattered throughout the resort. To reach other Disney resorts you must first bus to Downtown Disney and then transfer to your resort destination. The Trumbo Ferry departs every 20 minutes noon–9:40 P.M. to Downtown Disney (weather permitting). A car is a definite plus here due to the large size of the property and lack of dining options.

OTHER NOTABLE RESORTS NEAR DISNEY

Celebration Hotel $ to $$

Billed as "Orlando's only luxury boutique hotel" this charmingly intimate property lives up to its name. Only minutes from Walt Disney World, its Old World Florida style is enchanting and appealing, a perfect alternative to the hustle and bustle of the Disney resorts. Within its 4-story pastel veneer are 115 alluring guestrooms outside whose windows are vistas of a picture-perfect lake and the charming town of Celebration.

The cozy living room–like lobby is dotted with small seating areas of period furnishings reminiscent of early 20th-century Florida hotels. Cushy sofas and cane easy chairs made plump with pillows are surrounded by potted palms, rich hardwood floors topped with thick area rugs, and gently turning rattan paddle fans. Out back is a gracious brick terrace with restful rocking chairs and a peaceful view of Celebration Lake. And lying just outside the front door is the town of Celebration with its delightful boutiques and excellent dining choices. Guests have privileges at the nearby Celebration Golf Course as well as at the 60,000-square-foot Celebration Fitness Center and Day Spa with complimentary transportation in the hotel's 1947 black Cadillac. **700 Bloom Street, Celebration, FL, 34747; 407-566-6000; Fax 407-566-6001. Check-in 3 P.M.; check-out 11 A.M. For reservations call 888-499-3800 or your travel agent. www.celebrationhotel.com.**

Rooms

Hallways of rich brown carpeting are painted in an eye-pleasing pistachio and near the elevators are super sitting areas of dark leather sofas and rattan chairs. Guestrooms are stylishly decorated with understated golden bedspreads, walls of soft butternut yellow, subtle tropical drapes, and rich cherry-wood furnishings. All have armoires with TV and minibar, oversized writing desks, and tall windows with charming views of either the lake or the town of Celebration. Comfortable beds are dressed in luxe linens and soft downy pillows, a welcome change from the Disney hotels. Rooms offer high-speed Internet access, three phones with data ports, on-demand movies, video games, safe, iron, ironing board, coffee maker, morning newspaper, and turndown service. Ample-sized baths offer a single sink on a spacious vanity, Yardley bath products, thick towels, makeup mirror, and hairdryer. Sixty percent of rooms have lake views although only a few have standup balconies.

King-bedded Deluxe Rooms at 320 square feet are snug but cozy with a reading chair and table in a dormer window area. Accommodates two people. Superior Rooms at 380 square feet are more comfortable with either two queens or a king, a large desk, and two pillowed rattan easy chairs. Accommodates up to four people. The 420-square-foot Junior Suites are oversized rooms with either two queens or a king and a sitting area holding a double sleeper sofa, coffee table, desk, wet bar, and small refrigerator. French doors lead to a standup balcony. Accommodates up to five people. The wonderful 700 square feet Luxury Suites offer a living area with a queen sleeper sofa, two rattan chairs, coffee table, desk, entertainment center with TV, and a wet bar with a small refrigerator and microwave. In the separate bedroom is a king-size four-poster bed and French doors leading to a standup balcony. Accommodates up to four people.

Restaurants

Plantation Dining Room—Breakfast daily; dinner Tues–Sat • plantation-style setting serving New Florida cuisine • breakfast buffet.

In-room dining—Available 6–10 A.M. and 5:30–11 P.M. from the Plantation Room.

Libations

Lobby Bar—Open 5 P.M.–midnight • full bar • live piano entertainment Fri and Sat evenings.

Recreation and Activities

Nature trails—Celebration's nature trails begin just outside the hotel.

Swimming—Small heated pool • whirlpool • delightful lake views.

Services

Health club—Lakeside views • treadmills • elliptical machines • weights stations.

Transportation

Complimentary transportation is available to WDW theme parks (must be arranged 90 minutes prior). For a change of pace, make use of the 1947 black Cadillac that transports guests to the Celebration Golf club or the Celebration Fitness Center and Day Spa just minutes away.

Gaylord Palms Resort $ to $$$

With the opening of the Gaylord Palms Resort in February 2002 came a new and distinctive luxury option to the Orlando area. The 9-story resort's claim to fame is its immensely beautiful 4½-acre glass-domed atrium representative of the fascinating and diverse Sunshine State. Conveniently located at I-4 and Osceola Parkway, it's only a 5-minute drive to Walt Disney World and just 15 minutes to Universal Studios. Beneath the stunning Grand Atrium sit the Emerald Bay and St. Augustine areas where visitors will find a Spanish fort, lush vegetation, towering palms, rushing waterfalls, and a street of shopping opportunities. The spirit of the islands comes alive in the festive, 5-story Key West wing with its blue lagoon centered with a moored 60-foot sailboat, all surrounded by piers, palm trees, and daily sunset celebrations. Everyone's favorite locale is the intimate Everglades, where wooden walkways lead to a foggy swamp filled with lofty cypress trees alive with the sound of frogs, crickets, and the growls of alligators. All of this under one giant dome.

Because this is a major convention hotel with over 400,000 square feet of meeting facilities and ballrooms, I suggest steering clear of here when any large conferences are occurring. They simply take over the hotel; plenty of fun for the conventioneers, but a bit disappointing for any outside guests not associated with the convention. **6000 W. Osceola Parkway, Kissimmee, FL 34746; 407-586-0000 Fax 407-586-1999. Check-in 3 P.M.; check-out 11 A.M. For reservations call 407-586-2000 or your travel agent. www.gaylordpalms.com.**

Rooms

Guestrooms—The 410 square feet luxurious guestrooms offer either one king or two queen beds, a desk with two chairs, and armoire with TV and mini refrigerator. Each room comes with an iron, ironing board, coffee maker, complimentary high-speed Internet access, a couple of two-line telephones (one of them cordless), in-room movies, and laptop-size safes wired for recharging. Baths are above par with Saltillo tile flooring, granite countertops, adorable palm tree wallpaper, double sinks, makeup and full-length mirrors, and hairdryers. King-bedded rooms offer large walk-in showers in place of bathtubs as well as an easy chair with ottoman. Inner rooms facing the atrium have French doors leading to a pleasant balcony or patio, but be prepared to hear the noise from below which in busy times can be a bit annoying for light sleepers; ask for a higher floor, avoid a room over one of the restaurants, or simply consider one of the Florida-view rooms that face the exterior but come without balconies. The Key West area is particularly loud with live entertainment until 10:30 P.M.

The tropical decor in the Key West area consists of white wood furnishings, bright cabana-striped bedspreads, and periwinkle-and-lime carpeting. Everglades rooms have light wood furnishings, mossy green bedspreads, and palm motif curtains. The St. Augustine guestrooms in the Grand Atrium have rich walnut furnishings along with soothing gold fabrics, map motif pillow shams, carpeting reminiscent of Spanish tile, and mosaic design chairs. Rooms in the Emerald Bay are the most expensive with butternut-colored walls, sophisticated dark walnut furnishings, and fun gold-and-blue monkey motif bedspreads along with elegant touches such as elevated beds and crown molding, accompanied by nightly turndown service.

Suites—There are plenty of choices in upscale accommodations with 106 suites on property. All are one bedroom, one bath, but many come with the option of adding standard rooms on either side to make a two- or three-bedroom suite.

Nine Presidential Suites offer 1,500–2,515 square feet with king beds, whirlpool tubs, dining areas, spacious living rooms, meeting room (except in the octagonal Presidential Suites), wet bars, and numerous balconies; three are octagonal located in the St. Augustine area with views of the front exterior of the resort, four panorama are located in the Emerald Bay area with interior views, and two standard are found in Emerald Bay or St. Augustine with exterior views.

Thirty-seven king-bedded Executive Suites located in either Key West or the Everglades with either atrium or exterior views are 625–725 square feet offering a separate living area with a 4-person dining table, wet bar, sofa, coffee table, and easy chair; nine Emerald Bay Executive Suites all view the Grand Atrium and offer king beds in a three-sided bedroom with a separate parlor holding a sofa, easy chair, desk, armoire, and a full bath.

Emerald Bay Deluxe Suites, 831–960 square feet, are located in the Emerald Bay area with separate king-bedded rooms along with a living area holding a 6-person dining table, wet bar, sofa, easy chairs, and desk.

Restaurants and Snacks

Ben and Jerry's—Hand-scooped Ben and Jerry's Ice Cream • sundaes • banana splits • fruit smoothies • milkshakes.

Old Hickory Steakhouse—Dinner only • dine above the swamps of the romantic Everglades • steaks and seafood • full review on page 373.

Planet Java—24-hour coffee shop • specialty coffees, wine, beer, sodas • pastries, muffins, salads, sandwiches.

Sunset Sam's Fish Camp—Open 11:30 A.M.–4 P.M. for lunch and 5–10 P.M. for dinner • delightful Key West–style seafood restaurant • 60-foot sailboat bar overlooking the lagoon with island-style entertainment nightly, colossal-sized drinks, and raw bar • conch and clam chowder, fish sandwiches, crab cakes, seafood pasta, potato-crusted snapper, fisherman's stew.

Villa de Flora—Breakfast, lunch, and dinner • Old World–style mansion atmosphere • Mediterranean-style buffet with chef stations.

In-room dining—24-hour room service • opt for the candlelit dinner served butler-style in your room.

Libations

Auggie's Jammin' Pianos—Open 5 P.M.–1 A.M.; piano music begins at 9 P.M. Sing along with comedic dueling pianos playing old favorites.

Lobby bar—Cocktails on the elegant terrace surrounding the lobby • live piano music.

Old Hickory Steakhouse Bar—Attractive candlelit bar adjoining the Old Hickory Steakhouse • overlooks the misty swamps of the Everglades • martinis, port, sherry, wine, beer, single malt scotch, specialty drinks, cognac • appetizers: cheese fondue, Caesar salad, onion soup, shrimp cocktail, crab cakes, raw oysters, cheese plate.

South Beach Pool Bar—Roaming servers offer tropical drinks poolside • light meals: sandwiches, pizza, salads.

Sunset Sam's Fish Camp Bar—60-foot sailboat anchored in lagoon out front of Sunset Sam's Fish Camp Restaurant • oversized island-style drinks on the *S.S. Gaylord* • raw bar • evening sunset celebration Jimmy Buffett–style with steel band, stilt walkers, and balloon animals for the kids.

Recreation and Activities

Children's playground—Sand beach playground lies next to Marine Pool.

Golfing—Golf at nearby Falcon's Fire Golf Club; complimentary transportation for registered guests • 18-hole Rees Jones signature designed course • preferred tee times.

Swimming—Zero-entry Marine Pool with delightful octopus slide, whirlpool, kiddie pool, private cabanas, and adjoining sandy beach and children's playground • more peaceful and sophisticated South Beach Pool with private cabanas and two whirlpools.

Shopping

Disney Gateway—Disney theme park tickets • Disney merchandise.

Details—Brighton merchandise • women's resort wear.

Godiva Chocolatier—Godiva chocolates.

✦ **Island Style**—Island-style housewares, handblown glass, and hand-painted furniture.

Marketplace News and Sundries—Gaylord Palm logo attire • Florida souvenirs • sundries • magazines • books.

Mel Fisher's Treasures—Authentic treasures from the shipwreck Atocha and the Santa Margarita • gold doubloons and silver reales (or pieces of eight) in jewelry settings • Atocha emeralds • gold bars.

Orlando Harley-Davidson Gear Shop—Harley-Davidson apparel and merchandise.

PGA Tour Shop—Golf apparel and merchandise • resort wear for men.

St. Augustine News and Sundries—Newspapers • candy • snacks • sundries.

Services

Car rental—Hertz Car Rental located in the lobby.

Hair salon—Canyon Ranch SpaClub Salon open 9 A.M.–8 P.M.; call **407-586-2160** for appointments • hair and nail treatments • makeup consultation • makeovers.

Health club and spa—The Canyon Ranch SpaClub; workout facility open 6 A.M.–9:30 P.M., spa open 8 A.M.–9 P.M.; call **407-586-2051** for reservations • 2,500 square feet fitness facility • LifeFitness exercise machines • treadmills • elliptical cross trainers • upright and recumbent bicycles • free weights • exercise classes including yoga, water fitness, and circuit training • 20,000 square feet spa facility • 25 treatment rooms • spa boutique • full review on page 299 • **www.canyonranch.com.**

Childcare—La Petite Kids Station, open Mon–Thurs 9 A.M.–10 P.M. and Fri–Sat 9 A.M.–11 P.M., for potty-trained children ages 3–14;

cost includes snacks; call 407-586-2505 for reservations • arts and crafts • video games • karaoke • indoor climbing • play-acting.

Transportation

Complimentary shuttle service is available to all four Walt Disney World parks departing every hour on the hour during park operating hours. Purchase tickets at the concierge desk for shuttles to other area theme parks.

Hyatt Regency Grand Cypress $$ to $$$

Located less than a mile from Walt Disney World and almost around the corner from Downtown Disney, the Grand Cypress Resort is composed of both the Hyatt Regency and the Villas of Grand Cypress who share a sprawling property and a wealth of recreational facilities. A tropical feel with an Oriental flair pervades the luxuriant 18-story atrium lobby of the Hyatt Regency where a soothing atmosphere of verdant palm trees, flowering foliage, and trickling streams intermingle with the notable art collection. A warm welcome begins on arrival with a glass of champagne punch and a congenial staff ready and waiting to assist.

Through walls and walls of glass, the luxuriant grounds quickly lure guests outside to a dazzling 1,500-acre wonderland of a lush landscape filled with over 50,000 annuals, its own private lake, and fantasyland pool. Stroll along meandering pathways through exotic tropical foliage intermingling with moss-covered boulders, trickling waterfalls, sculpture gardens, and soothing ponds. Or relax lakeside in swaying hammocks while swans glide gracefully across the waters of Lake Windsong. What's more, you'll not find a Mickey Mouse in sight.

With 65,000 square feet of meeting space, be prepared for plenty of conventioneers. Here, however, ballrooms in a separate downstairs area out of the way of the public spaces give the resort a much more inviting feel than most convention hotels. **1 Grand Cypress Blvd., Orlando, FL 32836; 407-239-1234; Fax 407-239-3800. Check-in 4 P.M., check-out noon. For reservations call 800-233-1234 or your travel agent. www.hyattgrandcypress.com.**

Rooms

Guestrooms—Glass elevators rise to 750 well-appointed guestrooms, cheerfully restyled and outfitted with green leaf wallpaper and bedspreads, jungle green carpeting, and tropical motif curtains and padded headboards. Dark green marble tops the side tables and the large desk that sports a second phone and a computer hookup. A pale wood armoire holds the TV offering cable and pay movies, minibar, safe, and coffee maker. Beds are extravagantly made with luxe linens and plush pillows. Marble baths contain only a single sink but come with luxuriously plush towels. Each 360-square-foot room offers a balcony, daily newspaper delivery, iron, ironing board, and hairdryer. And the only difference between a standard and deluxe room is simply in the view.

Room tip: Ask for an upper floor deluxe room and receive not only a view of the unbelievable pool but outward to a stunning vista of the surrounding area including literally all of Walt Disney World. Light sleepers will want a room away from the atrium in order to avoid the loud music wafting up from the lobby bar until the wee hours of the morning.

Concierge—The Regency Club, located on the privately accessed 11th and 17th floors offers an 11th-floor lounge with complimentary continental breakfast as well as afternoon cookies and lemonade. From 5–8:30 P.M. there are hors d'oeuvres, wine, and beer and from 8:30–10 P.M. guests will find wine, champagne, beer, and liqueurs. Concierge guestrooms come with bathrobes.

Suites—Executive Suites come with one or two bedrooms on either side of a parlor with each bedroom as well as the parlor the size of a standard room. The parlor holds a sleeper sofa, desk, and 4-person dining table; off the parlor is a full-size bath.

VIP Suites have the same configuration as the Executive Suites with the same one or two bedroom option but with a living area twice the size, a dining room table for six, wet bar, sofa and chairs, as well as an additional half bath. Both Executive and VIP Suites are available on the Regency Club level.

A great choice is a Bi-Level Suite offering a loft bedroom with a king bed, whirlpool tub, and the option of an additional connecting bedroom. The living area holds a 6-person dining table, a large sitting area, wet bar, half bath, and patio. These vary in size from 504 square feet and up with access to the Regency Club.

Restaurants

Cascade—Breakfast, lunch, and dinner • delightfully casual dining spot centered with a 35-foot cascading mermaid fountain and views of the lush Hyatt grounds through its almost solid wall of windows • Sunday breakfast buffet.

Hemingways—Dinner only • steaks and seafood in a Key West atmosphere • full review on page 371.

La Coquina—Dinner and Sunday brunch; closed for dinner seasonally • elegant restaurant • best Sunday brunch around • views of Lake Windsong • full review on page 372.

Palm Café and General Store—Snack bar near pool; open for breakfast, lunch, and dinner • breakfast: Krispy Kreme donuts, French toast, omelets, pancakes, waffles, oatmeal, fruit • lunch and dinner: pizza, sandwiches, salads, burgers, fried chicken, nachos, hot dogs • indoor and outdoor seating • adjoining General Store sells ice cream, beer, soda, chips, candy, cookies.

White Horse Saloon—Open Tues–Sat 6–11 P.M. Saloon atmosphere • Black Angus beef and free-range chicken • country-western music • longneck beer.

In-room dining—24-hour room service.

Libations

Hurricane Lounge—Adjoins Hemingway's; open nightly • atmospheric cocktail bar • full bar • premium cigars • food from next-door Hemingway's.

On the Rocks—Pool bar tucked away behind the grotto waterfall • tropical drinks • ice cream • snacks.

Trellises—Atrium lobby bar; open 4 P.M.–2 A.M. Live entertainment nightly • outside seating available.

White Horse Saloon—Open Tues–Sat, 5 P.M.–midnight • western-style saloon • live country-western music nightly • open to the entire family.

Recreation and Activities

Arcade—Located behind the grotto pool's waterfall • video entertainment and pinball machines.

Basketball—Court located near Racquet Club; balls available from Racquet Club attendant.

Beaches—1,000-foot beach on the shores of 21-acre Lake Windsong • hammocks and lounge chairs.

Boating—Rentable at Towel Hut next to pool for recreation on Lake Windsong; complimentary with payment of resort fee • paddleboats • sailboats • canoes • kayaks • hydrobikes • aquacycles.

Bicycling—Rentable at Towel Hut next to pool; complimentary with payment of resort fee • bike paths, one 3.2 miles and the other 4.7 miles.

Children's playground—Playground located just outside of Camp Hyatt.

Fishing—Fishing permitted on Lake Windsong for guests only; catch and release.

Fire pit—Located on the shore of Lake Windsong Fri and Sat evenings • blazing fire • storytelling • roasted marshmallows.

Golfing—See Villas of Grand Cypress.

Horseback riding—See Villas of Grand Cypress.

Jogging—Three jogging courses ranging from 1.3 miles to 4.7 miles meander through the property.

Nature area—45 acres of nature area in conjunction with the Florida Audubon Society • a mile of raised boardwalks on three different trails.

Pitch 'n' Putt Golf—Located on Lake Windsong; complimentary with payment of resort fee; no tee time required • 9-hole, par-3, pitch 'n' putt course.

Scuba—Participants must be at least 13 years old ; 24-hour notice required • 2-hour pool scuba lessons.

Swimming—Sensational 800,000-gallon, half-acre pool • 12 waterfalls • meandering grottos • 3 whirlpools • suspension bridge • 2 waterslides, one 125-foot long • main pool not heated.

Tennis—Call the Racquet Club at 407-239-1944 to reserve a court; complimentary with payment of resort fee • 12 tennis courts—8 clay (Har-Tru) and 4 hard (Deco-Turf II) • 5 lighted • 2 open-air racquetball courts • Pro Shop • instructional packages for all levels • round robins • game matching • racquet stringing • rentals • ball machines • videotape analysis.

Volleyball—Sand court located at beach; water volleyball in grotto pool.

Services

Childcare—Camp Hyatt, open daily Memorial Day to Labor Day 9 A.M.–4 P.M. and weekends only the remainder of the year, for children ages 5–12; 24-hour notice required; call 407-239-1234 for reservations.

The Childcare Center is open Sun–Thurs 8 A.M.–10 P.M. and Fri and Sat 8A.M.–11 P.M., for potty-trained children ages 3–12 • arts and crafts • outside play area • sand sculpting • volleyball • movies • pitch 'n' putt golf • magic shows • nature walks • tennis.

Hair salon—Grand Cypress Salon open daily • full range of salon services for men and women.

Health club—Located behind grotto waterfall; open 6 A.M.–10 P.M.; complimentary with the payment of resort fee • Keiser and Gravitron exercise equipment • treadmills • Lifecycles • stair climbers • cross-trainers • free weights • morning aerobics classes • men and women's sauna and steam room • lockers • personal training and massage available by appointment.

Helipad—Helipad on property open 8:30 A.M.–10 P.M. daily. Landing clearance must be arranged at least 8 hours in advance.

Shopping

Promenade Jewelers—Brighton jewelry, frames, and purses.

Racquet Club Pro Shop—Tennis attire, footwear, accessories, and equipment.

W.H. Smith—Women and men's casual resort wear • Grand Cypress Resort logo clothing • sundries • snacks • books • magazines.

Transportation

Complimentary shuttle service within the resort is available 6:30 A.M.–1 A.M. including service to the Villas of Grand Cypress and all recreational facilities. A complimentary hourly shuttle departs to Disney's four theme parks. A stay here almost demands a car rental.

Villas of Grand Cypress $$ to $$$$$

Hands down, accommodations here are the most exquisite in the Orlando area. Part of the Grand Cypress Resort, the Villas of Grand Cypress shares a golf club, racquet club, equestrian center, and all facilities with her Hyatt Regency neighbor. Named as one of the "Top 15 Golf Resorts" by readers of *Conde Nast Traveler* magazine, it sits within 1,500 acres of astonishing beauty. Posh, AAA 4-Diamond and Mobil 4-Star Mediterranean-style villas overlook overwhelmingly gorgeous undulating greens, romantic lakes, and flowering foliage. Check-in is a breeze; the guard at the gate calls ahead and after a speedy registration in the small lobby along with complimentary soda, beer, and bottled water, the staff is ready and waiting to swiftly escort you directly to your plush villa. All are clustered in a series of nicely landscaped cul-de-sacs encircled in natural grasses, flowering bougainvilleas, climbing jasmine, and swaying palm trees. This is a property not only for ardent golfers (although it is a golfer's paradise) but for discerning vacationers who wish to be near Walt Disney World but at the end of the day come home to plenty of comfort and not a trace of Mickey Mouse. **1 N. Jacaranda, Orlando, FL 32836; 407-239-4700; Fax 407-239-7219. Check-in 4 P.M.; Check-out Noon. For reservations call 800-835-7377 or your travel agent. www.grandcypress.com.**

Rooms

Villas are a haven of taste and comfortable enough to be your own. Decked out in subtle shades of golden beige mixed with rich navy blue, they are so roomy you'll be tempted to stay in for the day just to revel in the luxury. Plush bedding and enormous marble baths with whirlpool tubs are par for the course. Even though the Club Suite Villa is more luxurious than any standard room in Disney's repertoire, I suggest spending the $100 more per night to upgrade to the One-Bedroom Villa, worth every additional penny. For larger families, units are available with two, three, and four bedrooms. Each has twice daily housekeeping in addition to nightly turndown service, safes, iron and ironing board, and bathrobes. Included in the room rate is a morning newspaper, use of the villas' bicycles, health club, and sauna. Although there are no on-demand movies, you'll find cable TV and a nice selection of complimentary videos that can be delivered to the room. All rooms have a view of the golf course with 50% of them also offering a water view; be sure to request one with both.

The smallest room type available is the Club Suite Villa with 425 square feet of luxury. Similar to a Junior Suite it offers a sunken sitting room with a queen sleeper sofa open to the bedroom. No kitchen in these units, only wet bars. The lavish baths come with a large whirlpool tub with separate shower. Outside each unit is a private patio.

One-, Two-, Three-, and Four-Bedroom Villas all come with a full kitchen complete with stove, sink, full-size refrigerator, coffee maker, dishwasher, microwave, blender, toaster, and plenty of dishes, pots and pans, etc. Living rooms are spacious with striking furnishings including a queen sleeper sofa, two easy chairs, and coffee table in addition to a TV, VCR, and stereo. The separate formal dining room is a true luxury and an abundance of attractively draped windows and French doors make for a bright and airy space. Opulent marble baths have a large whirlpool tub, huge separate glassed-in shower, single sink, makeup mirror, deluxe toiletries, and hairdryer.

The One-Bedroom Villa has a luxurious separate living room with fireplace, wet bar, and queen sleeper sofa, formal dining room, full kitchen, and three terraces. The master bedroom is similar to the Club Villa Suites with a step-down sitting area off the bedroom as well as a second wet bar. Two-Bedroom Villas come in both 1- and 2-story units boasting two bedrooms (one with a sitting area exactly like the Club Villa Suite), two master-type baths, three patios, full kitchen, beautiful living room (some with a fireplace), wet bar, queen sleeper sofa, and formal dining room. The Three-Bedroom Villa, some 1-story and some 2, offers three master baths together with the same amenities as the Two-Bedroom Villa, and the 2-story Four-Bedroom Villa contains two bedrooms with seating areas, four baths, and the same amenities as the other villas.

Restaurants

Black Swan—Dinner only • AAA Four-Diamond restaurant • some of the best cuisine in the Orlando area • full review on page 369.

Fairways Restaurant—Located in the Golf Club; breakfast, lunch, and dinner • casual dining spot • greats view of the greens.

Poolside Snack Bar—Snacks and sandwiches • wine, beer, cocktails, soda.

In-room dining—Available 7 A.M.–11 P.M.

Libations

Fairways Lounge—Located in the Golf Club • casual bar • great views of the greens.

Recreation and Activities

The Villas share facilities with the Hyatt Regency Grand Cypress, but at a mile and a half away it requires a car or shuttle ride. See the Hyatt's Recreation and Activities section for more information.

Bicycles—Complimentary bicycles available at the pool area.

Golfing—Cited by *Golf* magazine as one of the Best Golf Resorts in America with North and South courses named as one of top 25 courses in America • four Jack Nicklaus–designed golf courses • Golf Club with two restaurants • Pro Shop • Golf Academy offers lessons under the guidance of PGA and LPGA certified professionals utilizing CompuSport video teaching technology.

Horseback riding—The Equestrian Center is located within the grounds of the Villas of Grand Cypress but about a mile down Jacaranda (the road fronting the property); open daily 8:30 A.M.–5 P.M. • first facility in U.S. approved by the British Horse Society • riding instruction in both western and English for all skill levels • junior lessons for ages 2–9 • pony rides • 44-stall barn • lighted and covered riding area • outdoor lighted jumping and dressage rings • cross-country course • locker rooms • Tack and Gift Shop selling equestrian equipment, attire, gifts.

Swimming—Small, beautifully landscaped free-form, heated pool • whirlpool with waterfall • locker-style restrooms with sauna.

Services

See the Hyatt Grand Cypress Services section for more information.

Childcare—Private in-room babysitters arranged with 24-hour notice.

Private spa services—Range of in-room spa and salon services • Swedish massage • body polish • manicure • pedicures.

Shopping

Golf Shop—Golf apparel, accessories, equipment.

Tack Shop—Riding equipment • equestrian gifts.

Transportation

See Hyatt Regency Transportation.

UNIVERSAL ORLANDO RESORTS

With the opening of first Portofino Bay Hotel, later the Hard Rock Hotel, and in the summer of 2002 their newest property the Royal Pacific Resort with two more in the works, Universal has established itself as a complete and self-contained vacation destination. Not only have they established a hotel foundation, their offerings include some of the most deluxe properties in all of Orlando. All are within walking distance or a short boat ride to Universal's theme parks and CityWalk, all are operated by Loews Hotels, and all are worlds apart in personality.

If rock music and contemporary rooms are your thing, Hard Rock should definitely be your choice, but if gracious accommodations with a European ambiance are more your style it is Portofino all the way. Watch out, Disney!

A weakness of all of Universal's hotels is the lack of room balconies. Disney has continued to indulge vacationers with balconies from which to enjoy the glorious Florida weather but Universal hasn't mastered this lesson. Hopefully they will realize the error of their ways as they add more hotels to their repertoire.

Why stay at a Universal on-site hotel?

On-site guests receive exceptional entitlements. Included are:

- Express Ride access each day of your stay—Simply present your hotel identification keycard and be ushered to the Universal Express line with a wait of 15 minutes or less. This is heaven in busy season. The only exceptions to this policy are the *Pteranodon Flyers* at IOA and the waterslide in *Fievel's Playland* at Universal Studios.

- Preferred seating for all seated theater shows in both Universal parks as long as you arrive a minimum of 20 minutes prior to show time.

- Dining priority seating (not available on Fri and Sat evenings) by presenting your room key at all full-service restaurants in both parks and most full-service restaurants at CityWalk—excluding Emeril's, which takes its own reservations (**407-224-2424**).

- Charge purchases to your room and pay the entire bill at checkout.

- Package delivery directly to your hotel room from select retail shops.

- Complimentary transportation by water taxi or shuttle bus to both parks and CityWalk and complimentary shuttle bus to SeaWorld and Wet 'n' Wild.

- Length-of-stay passes are available providing unlimited access to both parks and admission to CityWalk beginning at check-in and ending at midnight on the day of check-out.

Booking a Universal Vacation

Consider staying several nights at one of Universal's fantastic resorts for convenient access to the Universal theme parks, CityWalk, Wet 'n' Wild, SeaWorld, and Discovery Cove combined with a stay at Disney for one great vacation.

Packages

Call **800-711-0080** or **888-837-2273** for Universal resort packages. To book online go to **www.usevacations.com**. And always price the Universal hotels separately by calling Loews Hotels at **800-23-LOEWS**.

Carnival Cruise Lines offers a 3- or 4-day cruise combined with a Universal Orlando land package on the *Fantasy* (**888-227-6482** or **www.carnival.com**), which sails out of Port Canaveral.

Discounts

At the time of publication, both Hard Rock and Portofino Bay Hotel accept the Entertainment Card offering 50% off the published rate of many hotels nationwide. It isn't necessary to purchase the Orlando book to obtain the discount; buy your book locally in your hometown or purchase one at **www.entertainment.com**. Another way to save big is to check out Universal's Hot Deals at **www.usevacations.com**. Universal annual passholders and AAA members also receive seasonal discounts.

Hard Rock Hotel $$ to $$$

Hard Rock's motto is "love all, serve all" and serve they certainly do at the single coolest place in Florida to hang out in California-hip style. Luxury reigns from the ultraslick marble lobby to the marvelous pool complex to the stylish guestrooms. Designed to look as if it were the home of a rock star, the California mission–style architecture features a cream-colored stucco exterior, clay red-tiled roofs, shaded porches supported by arched beams, wrought-iron balconies, and imposing towers. And Hard Rock's prime location within a 5-minute walk or boat ride to Universal's theme parks is certainly a major plus.

The striking, sunken lobby will bowl you over with its panoramic views through enormous picture windows of the sparkling pool and palm-studded grounds along with a distant vista of Universal Studios. Relax in lavish seating areas of chocolate-brown leather chairs and cushy, velvet sofas scattered among towering potted palms and massive glass vases overflowing with opulent, fresh flowers. Glassed display coffee tables showcasing guitars from music legends are strewn throughout the seating areas, and walls are lined with the likes of an Elvis jumpsuit, a Jimi Hendrix guitar, the shoes of famous rockers, and scads of gold records—over $1 million worth of rock-and-roll music memorabilia. It's a mix of pure luxury and star worship.

Service is friendly and energetic although it sometimes seems as if no one over the age of 30 is employed here. The staff are allowed plenty of freedom and they take full advantage so come prepared for spiked and off-color hair and plenty of pierced body parts. I was so enamored with this hotel that I was even willing to overlook the fact that it is impossible to escape the loud rock music blasting away in every public space; over 900 speakers are scattered throughout the property, all running 7 days a week, 24 hours a day. Of course, the younger crowd loves it. But rest assured, from the moment you enter the hallways leading to your luxurious room, only beautiful silence is heard. **5800 Universal Blvd., Orlando, FL 32819; 407-503-ROCK; Fax 407-503-ROLL. Check-in 4 P.M.; check-out 11 A.M. For reservations call 888-U ES-CAPE, 800-23-LOEWS, or your travel agent. www.loewshotels.com or www.universalorlando.com.**

Rooms

Universal has certainly outdone Disney when it comes to luxurious rooms. Modern without being stark, the 650 guestrooms and suites offer a clean, contemporary motif, one that is certainly good-looking. The overall tone is stylish and sophisticated with soothing colors of soft moss green and cream complementing the gorgeous carpet shaded with the same green mixed with a robin's egg blue. White swag curtains frame lovely picture windows and soft white walls hold framed black-and-white photos of rock and roll legends. Sumptuous beds are laid with luxe linens, down duvets, and cushy pillows. Novel lighting casts a soft glow throughout. Each room features an entertainment center with CD player (each guest receives a special Hard Rock compilation CD on arrival), two dual-line telephones, large in-room safe, stocked minibar, iron and ironing board, coffee maker, ceiling fan, and writing table with two chairs. Added benefits include Internet and data port access, newspaper delivery Mon–Fri, and cable TV with HBO and on-demand movies. The addition of couches, chairs, and coffee tables varies according to room size.

Guestrooms—Standard Rooms are adequate in size at 375 square feet with closet and minibar in the entrance hall, either two queens or a king bed, table and two chairs, and a lounge chair. A separate, single sink vanity in green marble comes with super-plush towels, luxurious toiletries, hairdryer, scale, and makeup mirror while the bath/commode area contains a second sink. Views are of the gardens; a pool view comes at an additional charge.

Deluxe Rooms at 500 square feet (the king-bedded rooms are smaller) feature a larger sitting area as well as a window seat and desk, offering that extra bit of space needed to spread out. None have balconies.

Concierge rooms—The Hard Rock Club, located on the 7th floor, offers either Deluxe Rooms or King Suites with access to the Hard Rock Club Lounge featuring the services of a concierge desk along with complimentary continental breakfast, beverages throughout the day, and evening hors d'oeuvres along with beer and wine. In addition to the use of a rock and roll book and CD library, you'll receive daily turndown service, bathrobes in the rooms, and complimentary health club facilities.

Suites—Kid's Suites at 800 square feet are absolutely the greatest with two rooms: one for adults and one just perfect for the little ones. A tiled entry hall with a large, curtained closet and minibar leads to the parents' bedroom, a king bed and sitting area with loveseat, chair, ottoman, coffee table, large dresser, TV, and CD/stereo. The children's room contains two twin beds or bunk beds with brightly flowered bedspreads, a kid-size table and chairs, and armoire with TV. The convenient bath has two areas: one with a sink and commode and the other with a double-sinked vanity and shower.

King Suites at 650 square feet are especially nice with a living area featuring a full-size sleeper sofa, easy chair with ottoman, and coffee table in addition to a table and four dining chairs. In an alcove is a king bed, dresser, TV, and second closet.

The 1,000 square feet Graceland Suite is fit for a king with a flat-screen TV and fireplace in the master and a living area with hardwood floors, golden velvet furnishings, silken drapes, dining table for 10, and a baby grand piano.

Restaurants

Beach Club Bar and Grill—Poolside bar • attractive covered, outdoor grill and bar • lunch and dinner: grilled specialties, sandwiches, salads, desserts • full bar, tropical drinks.

Emack and Bolio's—Ice cream and coffee adjacent to Sunset Grill • hand-scooped ice cream • smoothies • ice cream drinks • floats • ice cream sodas • Starbucks coffee.

The Palm—Open weekdays for lunch, daily for dinner • famous New York–based steakhouse featuring prime, aged cuts of beef and jumbo Nova Scotia lobster • full review on page 377.

Sunset Grill—Open for breakfast, lunch, dinner • casual restaurant • American favorites.

In-room dining—24-hour room service.

Libations

Velvet Bar—Open 4 P.M.–2 A.M. Hip cocktail lounge • huge list of specialty martinis and drinks • premium cigars • aged port • single malt scotch • appetizers • desserts.

Lobby Lounge—Sophisticated lobby lounge • drinks • appetizers • desserts.

Sports and Recreation

Arcade—High-tech games and pinball machines.

Golf—Special rates and tee times are available for guests at Keene's Point, a Jack Nicklaus signature course located 12 minutes away.

Swimming—12,000-foot zero-entry pool • underwater sound system • several whirlpools • 250-foot long pool slide (the longest at any U.S. hotel) • surrounded by sand beach, massive boulders, lofty palm trees, and flowering, tropical plants • poolside tented white cabanas available for full- and half-day rentals equipped with lounge chairs, television, phone, fax lines, videos, refrigerator, and ceiling fan • adjoining outside game area featuring shuffleboard, ping-pong table, and life-size chess and checkers • roaming waiters serve food and drinks from Hard Rock Beach Club.

Volleyball—Sand beach court next to pool.

Services

Childcare—Camp Lil' Rock, open Sun–Thurs 4–11:30 P.M. and Fri and Sat 4 P.M.–midnight, for children ages 4–14 • face painting •

treasure hunts • movies • video games• arts and crafts • outside playground.

Spa—Greenhouse Spa located at the nearby Portofino Bay Hotel; complimentary transportation provided • in-room or in-cabana massage can be scheduled.

Health club—The Workout Room open 6 A.M.–9 P.M. Cybex cardiovascular and strength training equipment • locker rooms • steam rooms • saunas • whirlpool.

Shopping

Hard Rock Hotel Store—Hard Rock Hotel logo clothing • Hard Rock collectible pins • sundries • newspapers • magazines • snacks • express photofinishing.

Transportation

A 3-minute water taxi or a lovely, landscaped walkway transports you to Universal Studios, Islands of Adventure, and CityWalk. Boats begin service at 7:30 A.M. and depart every 30 minutes until 2:15 A.M. Security on bicycles patrol the walkway throughout the day and into the late night. Complimentary shuttle bus service to Universal, SeaWorld, and Wet 'n' Wild.

Portofino Bay Hotel $$ to $$$

For the height of luxury in a Mediterranean seaside setting head straight for this exclusive hotel. The folks at Universal have outdone themselves in designing a hotel to resemble the harbor and idyllic seaside town of Portofino, the jetsetter's paradise on the Italian Riviera. The scenery is pure postcard with colorful fishing boats bobbing in the seductively curving bay. Gentle waves lap against the shoreline of sunbleached stucco buildings with shuttered windows and trompe l'oeil decorative facades. A charming, waterside piazza, loaded with appetizing restaurants, offers plenty of outdoor seating areas and a scattering of interesting shops. The ambience of a quaint Italian village is overwhelming as you wander the cobbled, winding streets encountering tiny brick piazzas, back alleyways, sparkling fountains, lofty bell towers, and flickering iron streetlamps. And I mustn't forget the lobby, resplendent with marble floors, tiled murals, sparkling Venetian glass chandeliers, and refined furnishings. **5601 Universal Blvd., Orlando, FL 32819; 407-503-1000; Fax 407-503-1010. Check-in 4** P.M.; **check-out 11** A.M. **For reservations call 888-UESCAPE or 800-23-LOEWS. www.loewshotels.com or www.universalorlando.com.**

Rooms

Guestrooms—Standard rooms here at 462 square feet are larger than deluxe rooms at most other hotels and offer either a garden or bay view. Enter through a tiled foyer to an exquisite room of comfort and indulgence. Beautifully appointed four-poster beds sit high off the ground topped with golden duvet-covered comforters, fine sheets, and down pillows. The Italian furnishings include an easy chair, a large writing desk and two chairs, and an armoire holding a fully stocked minibar and TV. Some rooms offer French doors leading to deep balconies with wrought iron table and chairs (available only on request at check-in). The large tiled baths boast a granite-topped, double-sinked vanity over which hangs a mirror lined in gorgeous Italian tile. Amenities include bathrobes, a laptop-size wall safe, umbrella, iron and ironing board, soft, fluffy towels, hairdryer, scale, coffee maker, makeup mirror, full-length mirror, deluxe toiletries, and a morning newspaper.

Deluxe Pool View Rooms or what used to be the concierge rooms (concierge service no longer is available here) are located in the villa section of the resort. These are 490 square feet and come with a sitting area, CD player, fax machine, and VCR plus a separate shower in addition to the bathtub.

Room tip: Pay the extra $40 per night for a standard room with a bay view and beg for a balcony at check-in; the sunset views can't be beat.

Suites—Portofino Bay's Kid's Suites are similar to the Hard Rock Hotel's but smaller at 675 square feet with a separate bedroom done in kid-oriented decor.

The two-bedroom, two-bath Portofino Parlor at 930 square feet offers a parlor with sleeper sofa, or consider the two-bedroom, two-bath Villa Parlor at 1,360 square feet with a parlor over twice the size of the Portofino Parlor and the addition of a dining room and kitchenette.

The Governatore Suite at 2,700 square feet offers two bedrooms and three full baths with a living area holding two sofas, big screen TV, dining table for 10, and an office area . Extra pluses are a large balcony and a luxurious whirlpool tub in the master bath.

The fantastic Presidente Suite is much like the Governatore's Suite only with a whopping 3,220 square feet of luxury. The decor is done in soft neutrals intermixed with splashes of red. It comes with an extended balcony, a huge living room with a fireplace, a butler's pantry, dining table for 12, and a posh marble master bath with whirlpool tub and separate shower.

Restaurants

Delfino Riviera—Dinner only Tues–Sat. • Italian food in elegant surroundings • full view on page 376.

Gelateria/Caffe Espresso—Open 6 A.M.–noon and 4–10 P.M. Coffee • espresso, lattes • pastries • gelato.

In-room dining—24-hour room service.

Mama Della's Ristorante—Dinner only Tues–Sun • old-world, hearty Italian food • festive atmosphere of Mama Della's home • outdoor seating available on piazza • full review on page 376.

Sal's Market and Deli—Open 11 A.M.–11 P.M. daily • authentic and delightful Italian deli • antipasto • brick-oven pizza • panini • salads • adjoining wine shop • excellent strolling musicians entertain Fri and Sat evenings • additional seating on piazza.

Splendido Pizzaria—Adjacent to Beach Pool; open daily 11 A.M.–5 P.M. Brick-oven pizzas • salads • burgers • hot dogs • sandwiches.

Trattoria Del Porto—Breakfast and lunch daily with dinner served Thurs–Mon • family-style restaurant • character dinner on Fri • delicious banana pecan pancakes, frittatas at breakfast • outdoor seating available on piazza.

Libations

Bar America—Open 4 P.M.–midnight • one of the most elegant bars around • martinis • fine wines • grappa • single malt scotch • appetizers: smoked salmon, shrimp cocktail, flatbread pizza, beluga caviar • dessert: chocolate petite fours, chocolate-dipped strawberries, biscotti • pianist entertains on Fri and Sat evenings.

Splendido Poolside—Beach Pool bar • cocktails • smoothies • sweets • ice cream.

Thirsty Fish Bar—Open Mon–Fri 5 P.M.–2 A.M.; Sat–Sun noon–2 A.M. Family-friendly bar • food service available from Sal's Deli.

Sports and Recreation

Arcade—Located adjacent to Beach Pool.

Children's playground—Located by children's pool.

Golf—Special rates and tee times are available for guests at Keene's Point, a Jack Nicklaus signature course located 12 minutes away.

Swimming—Mediterranean-style Beach Pool with waterslide, waterfall, kiddie pool, and 2 secluded whirlpools • secluded Hillside Pool at end of the East Wing surrounded by landscaped gardens • Villa Pool encircled by tall cypress trees, tinkling fountains, and swank cabanas available for rent with TV/VCR, lounge chairs and table, and pool floats • cabanas are complimentary with a Greenhouse Spa in-cabana massage.

Services

Car rental—Alamo Rent-A-Car desk located just off main lobby.

Childcare—Campo Portofino, open Sun–Thurs 5–11:30; Fri and Sat 5 P.M.–midnight, for children ages 4–14; cost includes dinner; reserve 24 hours in advance.

Health club—The Greenhouse Spa and Fitness Center open 6 A.M.– 8 P.M. with personal services beginning at 8 A.M. Massage • facials • body treatments • hydrotherapy treatments • manicures • pedicures • salon services • scalp and hair treatments • fitness center: full gym, Cybex equipment and machines, free weights, coed whirlpool, steam room, sauna, locker facilities • full review on page 299.

Shopping

Alta Moda—Resort wear • accessories.

Galleria Portofino—Italian paintings, sculpture, glass items, and fine jewelry.

L'Ancora—Gift items • necessities.

Le Memorie di Portofino—Portofino Bay logo merchandise • resort wear • Italian pottery • gift items • sundries • magazines.

Universal Studio Store—Universal Studios merchandise.

Transportation

A walking path connects Portofino Bay with the Hard Rock Hotel, Universal Studios, Islands of Adventure, and CityWalk or take the lovely, convenient boat ride leaving from the dock located bayside. Complimentary shuttle bus service to Universal, SeaWorld, and Wet 'n' Wild.

OTHER NOTABLE RESORTS NEAR UNIVERSAL

In addition to the Peabody, a 584-room Ritz Carlton is slated to open in the Grande Lakes area (almost equal distance between Walt Disney World and Universal) in July 2003 complete with a Gregg Norman–designed 18-hole golf course and a 40,000 square feet spa with 40 treatment rooms.

The Peabody $$$

This 891-room resort (with a new tower scheduled to begin in late 2003) is certainly a luxury property worth considering, just 5 minutes from Universal Studios and 15 minutes to Walt Disney World. The striking marble lobby is a favorite meeting place for viewing the legendary ducks who spend their day in the attractive atrium lobby pool, ceremoniously marching down the red carpet each evening at 5 P.M. to board the elevator that delivers them to their 4th floor Duck Hotel. The tradition dates back to the 1930s when the manager of the Peabody Hotel in Memphis returned from a hunting trip and after a few nips of whiskey, decided it would be humorous to have live duck decoys in the hotel's fountain. Public areas are decorated in shades of neutral with sleek yet comfortable seating areas, masses of fresh, exotic orchids, and a wealth of contemporary American art.

Remember, however, that the Peabody caters specifically to the business traveler and their families. With over 57,000 square feet of meeting space and a location directly across from the Orange County Convention Center, be prepared to see plenty of conventioneers roaming the grounds. And the traffic-laden International Drive location is another minus. But the hotel and rooms are awfully attractive, and if you are primarily interested in spending time at Universal Studios and SeaWorld it certainly is an alternative to the Universal Hotels. With three superb restaurants and sophisticated lounges to choose from, it's a wonderful retreat after a day in the parks. **9801 International Drive, Orlando, FL 32819; 407-352-4000; Fax 407-351-0073. Check-in 3** P.M.**; check-out noon. For reservations call 800-PEABODY or your travel agent. www.peabodyorlando.com.**

Rooms

Guestrooms—Generous-sized guestrooms are sleek and sophisticated, smartly decorated with understated pale wood contemporary furnishings, green-and-gold toned bedspreads, and honey-colored carpeting. Each comes with a soft green chenille easy chair, a writing desk with data-port hookup, and an armoire holding the minibar and TV with cable TV, in-room movies, and video games. Handsome floor-to-ceiling drapery cover large picture windows, some with views of the surrounding lakes and far off Disney. Beds are more than comfortable with luxury linens and feather pillows. A mirrored vanity table sits outside the single-sinked marble bath filled with nice thick towels, a mini television, hairdryer, and luxe toiletries (even duck-shaped soap). Add to that the extra touches of nightly turndown service, an iron, ironing board, robes, two phone lines, and a morning newspaper delivered each day (even the *New York Times* on Sunday). Sadly, none of the guestrooms has balconies. Superior Rooms are 400 square feet and come with either two double beds or one king while Deluxe Rooms at 450 square feet are all king-bedded.

Two types of Executive Guestrooms (similar to a Junior Suite at 457 square feet) come with all the extras of a regular room but with a king bed and an open sitting area holding a sleeper sofa, easy chair, coffee and side tables, and armoire. A bargain considering they are only $40 more per night than a Superior Room.

Concierge rooms—Concierge rooms are Superior Rooms on the top three floors offering the services of the 26th-floor Peabody Club, a private lounge with a full-time concierge. Included is a continental breakfast as well as hors d'oeuvres from 5–7 P.M. followed by petit fours and coffee from 8:30–10 P.M. An honor bar is available each evening. Concierge guests also receive complimentary use of the Peabody Athletic Club, nightly turndown service, and complimentary valet parking.

Suites—The two bi-level Presidential Suites, at 1,825 square feet, are wonderful. A sleeping loft and bath with whirlpool tub is upstairs while downstairs is the living room with huge picture windows, a formal dining area, separate den with a sleeper sofa and full bath, walk-in wet bar with refrigerator, balcony, and private whirlpool.

Four VIP Suites at 1,340 square feet offer one bedroom with two full baths (one with a whirlpool bathtub), full living area with walk-in wet bar and refrigerator, and dining room; two of the suites come with a large balcony. An optional connecting bedroom is available for both the Presidential and VIP Suites.

Superior Plaza Suites at 1,159 square feet have a bedroom and bath in addition to a separate large parlor with dining area, walk-in wet bar with refrigerator, wall bed, balcony, and a second bath. Plaza Suites at 885 square feet offer a bedroom and a separate large parlor with a wall bed and extra bath, and Deluxe Plaza Suites are the same size with the addition of a wet bar with a refrigerator.

Executive Suites at 600–800 square feet have either one bedroom, two baths or two bedrooms, three baths, all with a separate living area containing a wall bed; some come with a balcony.

Restaurants

B-Line Diner—Open 24 hours • diner specializing in 1950s comfort food with a modern flair • express window offers carry-out bagels, pastries, specialty coffees, sandwiches, salads, ice cream, desserts.

Capriccio—Dinner only with Sunday afternoon brunch • Northern Italian cuisine in an upscale trattoria atmosphere • excellent Sunday champagne brunch.

Dux—Dinner only • sophisticated Mobil 4-Star, AAA 4-Diamond rated restaurant • full review on page 385.

In-room dining—24-hour room service.

Libations

Capriccio Lounge—Located just off Capriccio Restaurant • orchid-filled, black marble wine bar • quieter alternative to the bustling lobby bar.

Lobby Bar—Come around the 5 P.M. cocktail hour to watch the Peabody's famous ducks waddle down the red carpet to their evening abode on the 4th floor • afternoon tea service • evening live entertainment along with cocktails and appetizers.

Mallards Lounge—Sophisticated lounge with comfortable booths and cushy sofas • full bar • appetizers: spinach and cheese dip, quesadillas, shrimp cocktail, sampler platter.

Peabody Pool Bar—Open seasonally. • frozen drinks, beer, beverages • hot dogs, burgers, sandwiches, fruit plate.

Sports and Recreation

Arcade—Located on the 4th floor recreational level.

Golf—Captain's Choice Golf Service arranges tee-times and complimentary transportation to over 20 of the area's best private and public golf courses • pro shop located on 4th floor • for reservations call **407-352-1102.**

Jogging—Jogging map available at the Athletic Club for four routes surrounding the hotel.

Swimming—4th-floor outdoor heated, nearly Olympic-sized lap pool overlooks the massive Orange County Convention Center (not exactly the best view around) • very large children's pool with waterfall • giant-sized whirlpool • no theming or tropical landscaping here; just a study in the bare necessities.

Tennis—Complimentary to hotel guests • four lighted, hardtop courts located outside on the 4th floor recreation level • racquet rental, private instruction, and player matches available.

Services

Hair salon—Nu London Salon located on 4th floor • facials • hairstyling • perms • color • waxing • nail care.

Health club—Peabody Athletic Club located on the 4th floor • Nautilus equipment • free weights • treadmills • bicycles • stair climbers • cross-trainers • saunas • steam rooms • whirlpool • tanning bed • step aerobics and body sculpting classes • personal training and massage therapy available.

Shopping

Aqua Swimwear—Swimwear and accessories for men and women.

Golf Pro Shop—Golf attire, accessories, and equipment.

W.H. Smith—Men and women's casual attire • sundries • books • magazines.

Transportation

Regular shuttle service is available to all four Walt Disney World theme parks, Universal Studios, and SeaWorld for a nominal fee. A car rental here is a must for convenience.

CHAPTER 4

Disney Theme Parks

When people think about Walt Disney World, usually the first thing that comes to mind is the Magic Kingdom. Most never envision a complex twice the size of Manhattan with four theme parks spread out over 27,000 acres. Yes, the Magic Kingdom was the first Disney park built in Orlando, completed in 1971, but a decade later in 1982 was the debut of Epcot. Twice the size of the Magic Kingdom, it brought something quite different to Walt Disney World—an education in technology and innovation, and other lands and cultures. Disney–MGM Studios opened in 1989, and along with it came the glamour and glitz of show business and then in 1998 Disney's newest theme park opened to rave reviews. With the Animal Kingdom came a park conveying the theme of unity and harmony between all living creatures. Each park is unique and wonderful and offers its own brand of enjoyment. And who knows what we can look forward to in the future?

Disney Admission Prices

There are a variety of options when it comes to park passes. Consider exactly how many days will actually be spent in the Disney parks and if a visit to one of the water parks, DisneyQuest, Wide World of Sports, and Pleasure Island will be part of your plans. Remember, it is not necessary to use the hopper passes on consecutive days and unused days never expire; however, if you purchase an Ultimate Park Hopper it ends with your stay.

You may wish to purchase passes before leaving home by calling 407-824-4321, going to www.disneyworld.com, or visiting your nearest Disney Store to save time in line your first morning at the park. If you'd like to wait until arrival, passes may be purchased at any of the four major theme parks, the Ticket and Transportation Center (TTC), or at any of the Disney resort hotels. Call or check online for current prices.

One-day ticket—Valid for admission to one theme park, 1 day only; no park-hopping allowed.

Park Hopper—Available as either a 4- or 5-day pass. Come and go as you please to all four Disney theme parks. Does not need to be used on consecutive days and unused days have no expiration date.

Park Hopper Plus—Available as either a 5-, 6-, or 7-day pass. Come and go as you please to all four Disney theme parks along with the options of admission to Blizzard Beach, Typhoon Lagoon, Pleasure Island, and Disney's Wide World of Sports. The 5-day pass includes two options, the 6-day three, and the 7-day four. You may not hop from water park to water park as you can with the major theme parks. Does not need to be used on consecutive days and unused days have no expiration date.

Ultimate Park Hopper—Sold only to guests of WDW resort hotels and one that may only be purchased as part of a package. A length-of-stay pass good from the moment you check in until midnight the day of check-out for unlimited admission to all four Disney theme parks, Disney water parks, Pleasure Island, DisneyQuest, and Wide World of Sports. It expires at midnight on the day of check-out. If arriving at Disney either late in the evening or departing early in the morning, ask to have your Ultimate Park Hopper not include one of those days. If you are both arriving late and departing early, spending a day or two at Universal Orlando, or do not plan on visiting the water parks, DisneyQuest, or Pleasure Island, consider buying another type of pass.

Annual Pass—Unlimited access to all four Disney theme parks as well as complimentary parking and an array of discounts (see page 34) for 365 days. If your stay is more than 7 days or you plan to return within the same year, this is the way to go. You may even consider this type of pass for shorter stays simply to receive the great room discounts available for Annual Pass holders; only one person in your party must have an annual pass to obtain the discount. For those who make an annual trip to Disney, plan your return trip a few weeks shy of the expiration date of your pass and your park admission will already be paid.

Premium Annual Pass—Same as the Annual Pass but also includes Blizzard Beach, Typhoon Lagoon, Wide World of Sports, and DisneyQuest. A good buy if staying more than 10 days or returning within the same year.

Price Without Tax

	ADULT	CHILD (3–9)
1 Day/1-Park Ticket	$50	$40
4-day Park Hopper	$199	$159
5-day Park Hopper	$229	$184
5-day Park Hopper Plus	$259	$208
6-day Park Hopper Plus	$289	$232
7-day Park Hopper Plus	$319	$256
Annual Pass	$369	$314
Premium Annual Pass	$489	$416
Blizzard Beach and Typhoon Lagoon 1 day	$31	$25
Pleasure Island 1 evening	$21	–
DisneyQuest	$31	$25
Wide World of Sports	$9	$7
Cirque Du Soleil	$72–82	$44–49

Fastpass

Fastpass is a free service offered to all visitors as a way of reducing time spent waiting in line. As you approach a Fastpass attraction you'll see two time clocks on display: one estimating the wait time in the normal line, the other the return time for the Fastpass being issued at the moment. If the normal wait time is less than 30 minutes, by all means get in line. If not, just insert your park pass in one of the machines located at each individual Fastpass attraction and receive a ticket printed with a designated one-hour window in which you may return and enter a special line with little or no waiting.

Only one Fastpass at a time can be issued. Once you use your Fastpass or you have waited 2 hours, you may be issued another Fastpass. Each person must have a Fastpass to enter the line and must show it to the cast member at the beginning of the line and the cast member waiting at the boarding area. There is usually not a need to use Fastpass for the first hour or so after the park opens. Note that on the most popular attractions, particularly in the busier seasons, those seeking a Fastpass late in the afternoon may find there are none left for the remainder of the day.

Touring Advice

Much ado is made in some guidebooks of exactly how to attack each park and in what direction and order to tour. I think a bit of planning is necessary and I have outlined a suggested touring plan in each theme park section. However, it does take the fun out of your vacation if you are tied down to a ridiculous, high-speed timetable. During slow times of the year use these tours to determine which attractions are the most desirable in each park and simply see each one as you encounter them.

In the busier seasons just be at the park entrance a half hour early at which time the gates are usually open along with a few stores and breakfast stops. Be in place at rope drop and head immediately to the most popular ride in the park. In the Magic Kingdom this means Splash or Space Mountain; in Epcot it's Test Track; at the Studios the biggies are the Tower of Terror and Rock 'n' Roller Coaster, and at the Animal Kingdom move quickly to the Kilimanjaro Safaris. When you are finished with that attraction pick one or two of the most popular rides and knock them off. After that you will have lost your edge on the latecomers so simply explore each attraction as you come to it and don't forget to utilize Fastpass.

At the very least, plan a loose itinerary for each day and make priority seating for any full-service restaurants. Find out before leaving home the park hours for the days of your vacation, if there are any evening fireworks planned, and what special events might be happening during your stay by going on line at **www.disneyworld.com** or calling **407-824-4321**. The worst thing you can do is to wake up each morning and then decide what you want to do that day; that's best left for free days when you plan to just relax by the pool.

Speaking of free days, try to schedule one at some point in the middle of your trip to ease sore feet, unwind, and just enjoy. Failure to plan at least a bit could mean showing up at the Magic Kingdom expecting to stay for the parade and fireworks only to find there are none scheduled for that day. Or you might lose out on eating at that special restaurant that your friends told you about. Of course, don't plan so stringently that there's no spontaneity in your day, no time to smell the roses. This is Disney after all.

The best piece of advice I can give you is to come in the slower times of the year (see pages 6-7 for details). Avoid holiday weekends (except for maybe Labor Day and Veteran's Day), and summer. Of course, this may not be possible for those tied down to school schedules. I took my children out of school to go, worrying about the extra homework later. It was well worth it!

For Thrillseekers

Some of us crave a bit more action than Peter Pan's Flight. For that rush of adrenaline, head straight to these attractions:

Tower of Terror (Disney–MGM Studios)—Plummet 13 stories bungee-style on this stomach-dropping thrill ride.

Rock 'n Roller Coaster (Disney–MGM Studios)—Rocket from 0 to 60 mph in less than 3 seconds, immediately hit your first inversion, then loop and corkscrew in the dark through a Hollywood night with Aerosmith blaring in your ears.

Incredible Hulk Coaster (Universal's Islands of Adventure)—This green monster launches you from a near standstill to 40 mph in 2 seconds, then immediately into a zero-G dive roll. Attaining speeds up to 60 mph, loop through inversion after inversion and twice underground before finally coming to a halt on this unbelievable monster.

Dueling Dragons (Universal's Islands of Adventure)—Take a ride on the world's first inverted, dueling, near-miss coaster as your legs dangle free. At certain points you'll swear your feet almost touch those of the opposite dragon as it goes roaring by.

Adventures of Spider-Man (Universal's Islands of Adventure)—The most remarkable attraction in the Orlando area combines 3-D film, special effects, and moving vehicles to simulate a 400-foot drop that will knock your socks off.

Back to the Future (Universal Studios)—Strap into an 8-passenger DeLorean motion simulator suspended above an IMAX-size screen and get ready for the ride of your life.

Kracken (SeaWorld)—The fastest and steepest coaster in Orlando. And what's more, there's no floor! Try that one on for size.

Ride-Share Program

Disney offers this program for parents with small children at all attractions with a height restriction that prohibits little ones. Tell the cast member you wish to utilize this option when you enter a line. Your entire party will proceed through the line until the loading area when one adult will ride while the other stays behind with the child. When the first adult returns, the second adult will load without delay while the other waits with the child.

Attractions offering this program are:

Magic Kingdom—Big Thunder Mountain • ExtraTERRORestrial Alien Encounter • Space Mountain • Splash Mountain.

Epcot—Body Wars • Test Track.

Disney–MGM Studios—Rock 'n' Roller Coaster • Star Tours • Tower of Terror.

Animal Kingdom—Dinosaur • Kali River Rapids.

THE MAGIC KINGDOM

Everyone's image of Disney is encompassed in a mere 107 acres of pure enchantment. Walt Disney World's oldest theme park is a kid's fantasy of marvelous, themed lands created to charge the imagination of young and old alike. Around every corner is a vision bound to take the breath away, one that's guaranteed to draw you back time and time again. Cinderella's castle, the visual magnet of the Magic Kingdom, hits you square in the face as you walk under the train station and into a world of make-believe with all the glory of Main Street spread out before you and that fairytale castle at the end. Then get ready for the time of your life.

Park Basics

Getting There

Those driving to WDW should take Exit 64 or 67 off I-4, then follow the signs to the Magic Kingdom.

Using WDW Transportation

From the Grand Floridian, Polynesian, and Contemporary Resorts—Board the monorail at your resort and get off at the monorail station at the park's entrance or take the boat launch to the Magic Kingdom boat dock located directly in front of the park entrance. You may also walk the 10-minute path from the Contemporary.

From the Wilderness Lodge and Villas—Take the Wilderness Lodge boat launch to the Magic Kingdom boat dock located directly in front of the park entrance.

From Other Disney Resorts, Disney–MGM Studios, the Animal Kingdom, and Downtown Disney—Board bus marked Magic Kingdom.

From Epcot—Either take the bus marked Magic Kingdom or board the monorail to the Ticket and Transportation Center (TTC), then transfer to either the ferry or the direct monorail to the Magic Kingdom.

Parking

Cost is $7 per day; free to Walt Disney Resort guests and Annual Pass holders. Keep your receipt; fee also good for parking at the Animal Kingdom, Epcot, and Disney–MGM Studios on that day only.

Because of the beautiful obstacle of the Seven Seas Lagoon, parking at the Magic Kingdom is a bit different than at the other three Disney theme parks. Park in the lot, make a note of the section and aisle, and board the tram to the Transportation and Ticket Center. From there, take the ferry or the monorail for the final leg of transportation to the park entrance. If the monorail line is long, take the quicker ferry. If riding the monorail, make sure you board the one departing for the Magic Kingdom, not Epcot.

Operating Hours

Open 9 A.M.–7 P.M. with extended hours during holidays and the busy season. Call 407-824-4321 or log on to www.disneyworld.com for updated park hours along with parade and fireworks information.

During the slower times of the year, the Spectromagic parade and Fantasy in the Sky fireworks don't take place on weekdays so try to plan a weekend night at the Magic Kingdom to enjoy the evening festivities. Main Street is normally open a half hour before official park opening time. To get a jump on the crowds, arrive at least an hour early allowing plenty of time to park and ride the monorail or ferry, buy tickets, purchase a snack or cup of coffee, and be one of the first to hit the big attractions. I recommend heading straight to Splash or Space Mountain.

Fastpass Attractions

See page 133 for Fastpass details. Buzz Lightyear's Space Ranger Spin • Space Mountain • Splash Mountain • The Many Adventures of Winnie the Pooh • Peter Pan's Flight • The Haunted Mansion • Big Thunder Mountain Railroad • Jungle Cruise.

Services

ATM machines—Three ATM machines are located in the park: next to the locker rentals under the Main Street Railroad Station, near the Frontier Shootin' Arcade, and in the Tomorrowland Arcade. An additional machine is located outside the park at the TTC.

Baby care center—An infant facility located next to the Crystal Palace at the castle end of Main Street is outfitted with changing tables, highchairs, and a room for nursing mothers. Formula, baby food, suntan lotion, diapers, milk, and over-the-counter children's medications may be purchased. All restrooms throughout the park are outfitted with changing tables.

Cameras and film processing—The Camera Center located in the Main Street Exposition Hall sells cameras, film, videotapes, and batteries. Two-hour film processing is available here and anywhere else the Photo Express sign is displayed.

First aid—For minor medical problems head to the First Aid Center at the end of Main Street next to Crystal Palace.

Guest relations—City Hall, just inside the park entrance on the left, houses Guest Relations where a knowledgeable staff is ready to assist you with priority seating, lost children, purchase of annual passes and upgrades, stamps, messages for separated parties, information for guests with disabilities, foreign currency exchange, sign language services, complimentary battery charging, fax services, international phone cards, VIP tour information, behind-the-scenes programs, resort reservations, and character greeting information. A smaller Guest Relations is located on the right before entering the park.

Guests with disabilities—A guidebook for guests with disabilities is available at Guest Relations (see The Basics on page 22 for more information). Guests with mobility disabilities should park adjacent to the Entrance Complex (ask at the Auto Plaza for directions). Wheelchairs and ECVs are available for rent. Most restaurants and shops in the Magic Kingdom are accessible to guests with disabilities although some counter-service locations have narrow queues with railings (ask a host or hostess for assistance). Companion assisted restrooms are located at First Aid and four other locations.

Over half of the attractions provide access through the main queue while others have auxiliary entrances for wheelchairs and service animals along with up to five members of your party. Certain attractions require guests to transfer from their wheelchair to a ride system.

Braille guidebooks, assistive listening devices, video captioning, and audiotape guides are available at City Hall for a $25 refundable deposit. With 7-day notice, a sign language interpreter will be provided at live shows on Mon and Thurs. Many theater-type attractions have reflective captioning. For more information call **407-824-4321.**

Lockers—Lockers are located at the **TTC**, as well as under the Main Street Railroad Station and are available for $7 per day including a $2 refundable key deposit. If you're park-hopping, keep your receipt for another locker at the three other Disney theme parks for no extra charge.

Lost and found—Located at City Hall near the entrance or call **407-824-4245.**

Lost children—Locate lost children at the Baby Care Center located next to the Crystal Palace at the castle end of Main Street. Go to City Hall after operating hours.

Package pickup—Purchases may be sent to the Town Square Exposition Hall for pickup at the end of the day. Allow 3 hours for delivery. Disney resort guests may send their packages directly to their hotel for next-day arrival.

Pet kennel—A kennel is located next to the **TTC**. Daily rate is $6. For information call **407-824-6568**. Proof of vaccination is required.

Readmission—If you plan to leave the Magic Kingdom and reenter the same day, make sure to retain your ticket and have your hand stamped before departing.

Strollers and wheelchairs—Rentals are located on the right as you enter the turnstiles. Single strollers are $8 per day, double strollers $15, wheelchairs $8, and electric convenience vehicles $40 per day including a $10 refundable deposit. If you are park-hopping, keep your receipt for a replacement at the three other Disney parks.

The Lay of the Land

The compact Magic Kingdom consists of seven bewitching lands accessed by five bridges leading from a central hub in front of Cinderella's Castle. Travel down Main Street to reach the hub from the front entrance. Traveling clockwise around the hub you first encounter the bridge to Adventureland, then the bridge to Liberty Square and Frontierland, the third crosses under the castle to Fantasyland, the fourth drops you close to Toontown, and the fifth into Tomorrowland.

Magic Kingdom–Lovers

If much of your time will be spent at the Magic Kingdom, choose one of the monorail-serviced hotels (Contemporary, Grand Floridian, and Polynesian). From these you're at the park in just a matter of minutes. Boat transportation is also available from the Grand Floridian and the Polynesian. Although the Wilderness Lodge and Villas are not serviced by the monorail, there is boat service to the Magic Kingdom.

Magic Kingdom

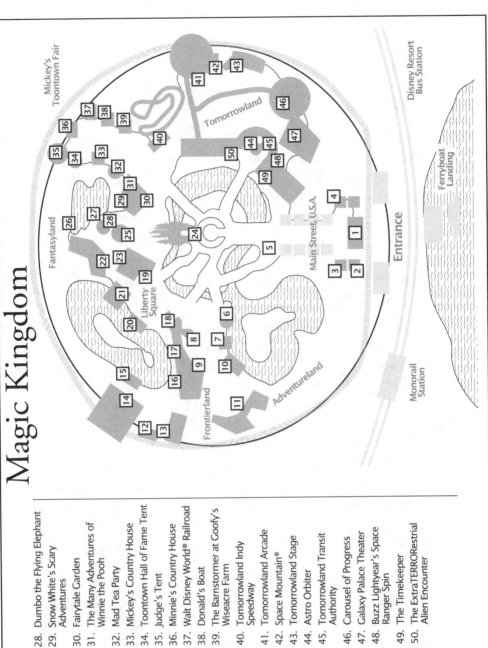

1. Walt Disney World® Railroad
2. City Hall
3. Main Street Vehicles
4. Town Square Exposition Hall
5. Guest Information Board
6. Swiss Family Treehouse
7. Shrunken Ned's Junior Jungle Boats
8. The Magic Carpets of Aladdin
9. The Enchanted Tiki Room –Under New Management
10. Jungle Cruise
11. Pirates of the Caribbean
12. Walt Disney World® Railroad
13. Splash Mountain®
14. Big Thunder Mountain Railroad
15. Tom Sawyer Island
16. Country Bear Jamboree
17. Frontierland Shootin' Arcade
18. Country Character Roundup
19. The Hall of Presidents
20. Liberty Square Riverboat
21. The Haunted Mansion
22. "it's a small world"
23. Peter Pan's Flight
24. Cinderella's Surprise Celebration
25. Cinderella's Golden Carousel
26. Ariel's Grotto
27. Fantasyland Character Festival
28. Dumbo the Flying Elephant
29. Snow White's Scary Adventures
30. Fairytale Garden
31. The Many Adventures of Winnie the Pooh
32. Mad Tea Party
33. Mickey's Country House
34. Toontown Hall of Fame Tent
35. Judge's Tent
36. Minnie's Country House
37. Walt Disney World® Railroad
38. Donald's Boat
39. The Barnstormer at Goofy's Wiseacre Farm
40. Tomorrowland Indy Speedway
41. Tomorrowland Arcade
42. Space Mountain®
43. Tomorrowland Stage
44. Astro Orbiter
45. Tomorrowland Transit Authority
46. Carousel of Progress
47. Galaxy Palace Theater
48. Buzz Lightyear's Space Ranger Spin
49. The Timekeeper
50. The ExtraTERRORestrial Alien Encounter

Breakfast choices at the Magic Kingdom

- Cinderella's Royal Table's character breakfast.
- Crystal Palace's character breakfast.
- Main Street Bake Shop for pastries.
- Caffe Italiano, a kiosk in Main Street Square for pastries and coffee.
- Scuttle's Landing in Fantasyland for muffins and bagels.

Suggested 1-day itinerary at the Magic Kingdom for adults with young children

Although this is a suggested 1-day itinerary, those with young children may want to plan for 2 days at the Magic Kingdom. With so many attractions for the little ones, 2 days spent at a relaxing pace is certainly preferable over a 1-day mad dash through the park, allowing time to head back to the hotel for a midday nap or dip in the pool. If a second day can't be spared, get a good rest the night before and see as much as you can without overtiring the kids.

- Make a before–park opening priority seating (call exactly 60 days prior at 7 A.M. Orlando time) for breakfast at Cinderella's Royal Table. Get the earliest seating possible to be finished close to park opening time.

- Head straight to Fantasyland, pick up a Fastpass for Winnie the Pooh, then ride Dumbo and Peter Pan's Flight until your Fastpass time. Afterward take in Cinderella's Golden Carousel, Mickey's PhilharMagic Show (opening in 2003), It's a Small World, Ariel's Grotto, and Snow White's Scary Adventure.

- Head to Mickey's Toontown Fair. First visit the Hall of Fame and the Judge's Tent for a visit with the Disney characters. Afterward take in both Mickey and Minnie's Homes as well as the Barnstormer and then have a splashing good time at Donald's Boat.

- Time for a late lunch. Eat at one of the many counter-service joints—my favorite is Pecos Bill Cafe.

- Pick up a Fastpass for the Haunted Mansion before finding a place for the Share a Dream Come True Parade.
- Return to the Haunted Mansion before moving on to the Pirates of the Caribbean in Adventureland. Pick up a Fastpass at the Jungle Cruise before getting in line for the Magic Carpets of Aladdin and if you are making good time see the Swiss Family Treehouse and Country Bear Jamboree; if not skip them for another trip.
- Move on to Tomorrowland, pick up a Fastpass for Buzz Lightyear and take in the racecars at Tomorrowland Speedway.
- If your kids (or you) are not totally exhausted by now and there is an evening parade and fireworks, have dinner at either the Crystal Palace or the Liberty Tree Tavern (both character meals so be sure to plan ahead with priority reservations) and a shopping spree at the Emporium before the evening's festivities.

Suggested 1-day itinerary at the Magic Kingdom for adults and older children

- Have breakfast at your hotel or pick up a quick treat at the Main Street Bakery. Whatever, try to be finished with your meal and in line for the rope drop at park opening time.
- Head straight to Splash Mountain in Frontierland, then take in Big Thunder Mountain next door.
- Cut back through the hub to Tomorrowland, pick up a Fastpass for Space Mountain (if necessary) and during your wait see Alien Encounter.
- If anyone in your party is interested in the attractions in Fantasyland (as I usually am) go there now. It will probably be necessary to pick up a Fastpass for either Peter Pan's Flight or Winnie the Pooh, so check that out first before your tour of this land begins. Ride Peter Pan's Flight, Snow White's Scary Adventure, the Many Adventures of Winnie the Pooh, and, if you really like torture, It's a Small World.
- After Fantasyland have a relaxing lunch at either the Liberty Tree Tavern or Tony's Town Square Restaurant.

- Pick up a Fastpass at the Haunted Mansion in Liberty Square before settling down for the afternoon Share a Dream Come True Parade at 3 P.M.
- After the parade head to the Haunted Mansion and then see the Pirates of the Caribbean in Adventureland.
- Afterward pick up anything of interest to you that you missed during the day. Good choices would be Buzz Lightyear, the Jungle Cruise, or the Magic Carpets of Aladdin.
- Before leaving take a stroll down Main Street for shopping and a late afternoon snack.
- If there are evening parades and fireworks either make priority seating at Cinderella's Royal Table for dinner (a noncharacter meal) and enjoy the park until the evening's festivities begin or head back to your hotel (easy to do if you are staying at a monorail-serviced property), freshen up, and have an early dinner before returning for the parade and fireworks.

Magic Kingdom don't-miss attractions

Space Mountain • ExtraTERRORestrial Alien Encounter • Peter Pan's Flight • The Haunted Mansion • Splash Mountain • Big Thunder Mountain Railroad • Pirates of the Caribbean • both parades as well as the Fantasy in the Sky fireworks.

Magic Kingdom's top dining spots

The Crystal Palace • Liberty Tree Tavern at lunch • Tony's Town Square Restaurant.

Main Street U.S.A.

Stroll down one of the most significant streets in America, a turn-of-the-century town where once upon a time life was simple and enchanting. Main Street, representative of small-town USA, is the epitome of an exemplary lifestyle that was optimistic, uncomplicated, and aboveboard. It tends to put a smile on your face and a song in your heart and sets the mood for the entire wonderful day in this magical park. Here you'll find barbershop quartets singing on street corners, jitneys honking as they make their way to the central hub, marching brass bands, Dixieland jazz, and the delicious aroma of freshly baked cookies, all surrounded by quaint Victorian-style buildings with gingerbread trim. Most people speed down Main Street to move on to the "real" attractions; resist the urge or save time for a visit before leaving.

Photo op: Stop in the Town Square for a great snapshot with a bronze of Roy Disney and Minnie Mouse. They're sitting on a park bench with all of Main Street and the castle in the background.

WALT DISNEY WORLD RAILROAD**

Genuine 1928 steam-powered trains puff around the perimeter of the Magic Kingdom with stops in Frontierland, Mickey's Toontown Fair, and Main Street USA. Entire loop takes **approximately 20 minutes.** Trains depart each station about 7 minutes apart.

MAIN STREET VEHICLES**

Hop on a variety of old-time vehicles putting and honking their way down Main Street to Cinderella's Castle. Enjoy horseless carriages, jitneys, and shiny red fire engines or the nonmotorized horse-drawn trolleys pulled by handsome Belgian and Percheron draft horses.

TOWN SQUARE EXPOSITION HALL/CAMERA STORE*

More than a camera and film store, it's also a bit of an attraction. Here you'll also find a nostalgic display of vintage Kodak cameras and the 40-seat Milestones in Animation theater where Disney's first animated films are continually showing. If you've had your photo taken by a Disney photographer during the day, pick it up here.

Tip: Sit on the front porch in comfy rockers and watch the action on Main Street while the rest of your party shops at the Emporium across the street. For a great photo opportunity, cozy up to the bronze Goofy on the park bench; don't be surprised if he lets out a giggle or two.

Shopping on Main Street

The Chapeau—Loads of Disney toppers • monogramming available.

Crystal Arts—Glassblower at work • crystal Disney figurines • cut-glass bowls, vases, and paperweights • don't forget to check out the $25,000 crystal Cinderella castle.

Disney Clothiers—Disney logo clothing for all ages.

Emporium—Just about everything Disney under the sun on the corner of Town Square at this true landmark, the granddaddy of Disney merchandise stores.

Firehouse Gift Station—101 Dalmatians plush toys • children's fire hats • personalized fire department badges • firemen figurines • "God Bless America" bumper stickers.

Harmony Barbershop—Old-fashioned barbershop waxes nostalgic with vintage barber chairs and cash register • don't look for it in the old spot; it's moved around the corner next door to the Car Barn.

Main Street Athletic Club—Athletic merchandise • Disney jerseys • ESPN clothing • baseball caps • tennis merchandise • sports-related plush animals • golfing staples.

Main Street Cinema—Disney costumes, videos, and CDs • plush toys.

Main Street Confectionery—Freshly made individual chocolates, fudge, and peanut brittle • Rice Crispies treats • jellybeans • lollipops • rock candy.

Main Street Gallery—Disney collectibles • animation cells • collector plates • Limoges hand painted boxes • Lenox porcelain character figurines • books • lamps • postcards.

Main Street Market House—Disney merchandise for the home • Winnie the Pooh dinnerware • Mickey logo blankets • Chef Mickey aprons • character teapots and cookie jars.

Uptown Jewelers—Huge assortment of Disney watches and jewelry • globe music boxes • handsome clocks both fun and formal • porcelain figurines • charms • money clips • cufflinks • create your own one-of-a-kind customized and personalized watch fashioned by a Disney artist who will hand draw a character to place on the face of your timepiece.

Fun tip: Turn off Main Street between Uptown Jewelers and Main Street Market House and hang out on one of the benches below the 2nd-story window on the left advertising music, dance, ballet, and tap lessons. Soon you'll hear the sound of piano practice, voice lessons, and tap dancing.

Information Board

Located at the end of Main Street is a board filled with wait times for attractions along with parade and special entertainment information. Use these leads to head in the direction of least resistance.

E-Ride Nights

Disney has a special offer for those who just can't get enough of the Magic Kingdom. On exclusive nights for $12 per adult or $10 per child, Disney resort guests holding a multi-day pass may purchase a ticket add-on to that day's admission for a 3-hour extension after the park officially closes. Open are 9 of the most popular rides in the park including Space Mountain, Alien Encounter, Buzz Lightyear, Astro Orbiter, Tomorrowland Transit, the Haunted Mansion, Splash Mountain, Big Thunder Mountain, and Country Bear Jamboree. Tickets are limited to 5,000 people, translating into virtually no waits in line, and must be purchased from Guest Relations at your resort or the day of at the Magic Kingdom ticket window. It's essential to enter the park before official closing time and take your voucher after 4 P.M. to either City Hall, Splash Down Photo at Splash Mountain, or the Tomorrowland Arcade and receive a wristband allowing you to stay in the park past closing.

Tomorrowland

The future envisioned by Jules Verne and A. G. Wells never quite came to pass. But in Tomorrowland that dream still exists. It's as if you've been plunked down into a Jetson cartoon within a metallic, futuristic city of unbending metal palm trees, bizarre stainless steel towers straight out of Flash Gordon, ultra-modern seating topped with colorful but stiff umbrellas, and angled store fronts blazing with neon lighting. Populated by robots and aliens, here is a place where time travel certainly seems possible.

ASTRO OBITER**

A lift transports you to a rocket platform where you'll board toy-like, Buck Rogers–style space vehicles circling high above Tomorrowland. This is probably a ride only children will enjoy; however, some adults think it comes with the best views of the park. **2 minutes.**

Tip: This is a very slow loading ride; if lines are long, skip it.

BUZZ LIGHTYEAR SPACE RANGER SPIN***

Buzz Lightyear is recruiting Junior Space Rangers to seek out and eliminate the Evil Emperor Zurg. Board 2-seater, Martian-green Star Cruisers and be ready to blast away at all Z-marked targets with your laser beam while spinning your spacecraft in all directions. Scoreboards in the vehicle keep track of your success as you slowly move through a neon galaxy jam-packed with robots and green aliens. Although really just an updated, glorified shooting gallery/video game that should only appeal to children, tons of adults who stand in line over and over again to play it think of it as the challenge of a lifetime. **Fastpass. 4-minute ride.**

CAROUSEL OF PROGRESS**

Technological progress from the beginning of the 20th century and into the future is seen from the perspective of an audio-animatronic family. Visitors seated in the original theater, first seen at New York's 1964–65 World's Fair, revolve through four different scenes of American life where each succeeding generation marvels at the new timesaving devices of their era. Particularly enjoyable for adults who can remember the past and a fun look at the past for those who are too young to remember. **20-minute show. Open only in the busiest times of the year.**

THE EXTRATERRORESTRIAL ALIEN ENCOUNTER***

X-S Tech, the galaxy's largest development company, would like to demonstrate their newest product to visiting Earthlings. Have a seat in a circular room with a intergalactic teletransport unit looming in the center. During the presentation something goes terribly wrong. A fearsome alien creature is mistakenly transported as the theater plummets into total darkness. He breaks through the transporter accompanied by shattering glass, billows of smoke, and a blast of cold air. Your imagination quickly works overtime as he crashes, snorts, and tromps round and round in the pitch dark. At times you can feel his hot breath on your neck and your seat jerking as he lurches past, and boy how he loves to slime you with his lizard-like tongue. All in all, it's a creepy riot, though some find it simply terrifying. **20-minute show. Minimum height 44 inches.**

Tip: This is definitely too frightening for small children. For others, the totally dark room, earsplitting noise, and hot breath on the neck can be a bit horrifying. I love it, although I usually tend to be quite squeamish.

SPACE MOUNTAIN****

In this 180-foot, conical-shaped "mountain" of white space needles is one of the most popular attractions in the park, a cosmic roller coaster shooting through the darkest depths of the solar system. Load into 6-person shuttle transporters and blast into orbit, plunging through a dark interior of sparkling comets, shooting stars, and glowing planets. Look closely to spot the other coaster ripping around on the second track. The somewhat slow (28 mph) coaster holds only small drops and no loops or twists: it's just the darkness that makes it such a thrill. **2½-minute ride. Minimum height 44 inches. Not recommended for expectant mothers, those with back or neck problems, or those prone to motion sickness.**

Tip: This is the second most popular ride in the park (Splash Mountain being the first) and lines can sometimes be extremely long. Come first thing in the morning or before park closing. And hang onto your valuables or risk losing them in the deep, dark vastness of space.

THE TIMEKEEPER***

H. G. Well's vision of a time machine comes to pass in this 360-degree standing-room-only theater. The Timekeeper, an audio-animatronic, comedic robot with the voice of Robin Williams, is the time machine's controller and your guide on this zany voyage. 9-Eye, a flying robotic camera with the voice of Rhea Perlman, returns to the past with the help of CircleVision and IMAX footage. Visit the dinosaurs, find yourself in the middle of a medieval Scottish battlefield, see DaVinci's workroom, and watch Mozart perform as a youthful prodigy. At the 1900 Paris Exposition, 9-Eye encounters H. G. Wells who comes along on a trip to the future he once envisioned of high-speed trains, racecars, automobiles, underwater exploration, airplanes, helicopters, spaceships, and even rap music. The continuing and hilarious banter between Timekeeper and 9-Eye on your journey will keep you in stitches. **20-minute ride. Open only during the busier times of the year.**

TOMORROWLAND ARCADE*

With so many other things to do in this marvelous park, I'm simply amazed that kids still want to shove money into games they can play anywhere. But play they do in this monster arcade extremely popular with the adolescent set.

TOMORROWLAND INDY SPEEDWAY*

Putt along on tracks in brightly colored racecars at barely 7 mph on a ride that has been a favorite of children since its inception at California's Disneyland. Kids love the thrill of grownup driving while adults hate the long lines, the noise, and the acrid smell of gas fumes. **5-minute ride. Minimum height 52 inches if unaccompanied by an adult.**

Tip: Be prepared for excruciatingly long waits. Teens and adults should probably skip this attraction except for perhaps reasons of nostalgia. Since the ride itself is not covered, your little spin could be extremely hot and steamy on warm days. Behind the raceway is a pleasant shortcut to Toontown.

TOMORROWLAND TRANSIT AUTHORITY*

Walt Disney planned to use this pollution-free form of transportation run entirely on electromagnets in his perfectly planned community of EPCOT. Its gently gliding cars quietly skim above the throngs of Tomorrowland, circling the Astro Orbiter and cruising through a bit of the interior of Space Mountain and the Buzz Lightyear ride. Although it's the most docile ride in the park, the bird's-eye view of the castle can't be beat and there's never a wait in line. **10-minute ride.**

Tip: If you're a fan of low-key rides, this is for you; if not, skip it or save it for your second trip to the park. Hop on the moving sidewalk behind the Lunching Pad at Rockettower Plaza to board.

Another tip: Don't miss the talking trash can usually found in front of Micky's Star Traders in Tomorrowland. Somehow it knows an awful lot about the way you look. I wouldn't dare tell its secret and spoil the fun.

Shopping in Tomorrowland

Merchant of Venus—Futuristic toys and clothing • merchandise popular with the adolescent set • wacky clocks • dazzling backpacks • lava lamps • feather boas • wigs in bright colors.

Geiger's Counter—Zany Disney souvenir hats • on-the-spot monogramming.

Mickey's Star Traders—Disney clothing and merchandise.

Mickey's Toontown Fair

What child would not want to visit the home of Mickey Mouse? Visit they can in the Magic Kingdom's special area for children. What's more you'll find Minnie's house, a roller coaster for the little ones, and a place to splash at Donald's boat. Wander through what looks a cartoon setting reminiscent of *Who Framed Roger Rabbit?*, a bright, colorful fantasy world overflowing with exaggerated sizes, nice surprises, and nary a straight line with every structure tilting and bulging at its seams. It's always country fair time and here you'll have an opportunity to meet Mickey in the Judge's Tent or a variety of other characters at Toontown Hall of Fame. **This area of the park doesn't usually open until 10 A.M.; check your guide map for times.**

THE BARNSTORMER AT GOOFY'S WISEACRE FARM**

Take a quick spin on miniature versions of Goofy's vintage crop dusting biplane. A crazy ride through Goofy's Wiseacre Farm has riders crashing through the barn (much to the dismay of the chickens) and back to the starting point so quickly they won't quite know what hit them. **1-minute ride. Minimum height 35 inches.**

Tip: Although this is a pretty tame ride, very small children may feel it is just a little too zippy.

DONALD'S BOAT**

On hot, steamy days, kids flock here in droves to cool off. Floating on the Duck Pond, a soft, cushy play area famous for its spouting water, is Donald Duck's leaky boat, the *Miss Daisy*, where mate wanna-bes can ring bells, peek out portholes, and chart their course on a map of the Quack Sea. For a nice dousing of water just pull the whistle.

MICKEY'S COUNTRY HOUSE AND JUDGE'S TENT***

An assortment of wild and zany colors assaults you on approach to Mickey's joint in the country beginning with the askew front porch of fat, yellow posts and Mickey-eared shaped windows. Peek inside Mickey's bedroom, den, rec room, and somewhat messy kitchen in this walk-through attraction. Out back is his thriving, mouse-eared vegetable garden and in the garage are recycling cans stacked high with trash (he even recycles his gloves). Most importantly, don't forget to stop at the adjacent Judge's Tent to meet and greet the mouse himself. He's there all day, but come early to avoid a lengthy wait in line.

MINNIE'S COUNTRY HOUSE***

Children love Minnie's feminine world of fat, floral furnishings and Laura Ashley–style decorations, especially because here they are free to touch and explore. Relax on her oversized, chintz sofa and look around at the cheery fireplace and framed photos of the gang. Listen to the latest messages on her answering machine and peek in the cheese-filled refrigerator, bake a cake in the oven, or pop corn in the microwave. Out back is the wacky, plant-filled sunporch and a heart-shaped gazebo where Minnie sometimes makes an appearance.

TOONTOWN HALL OF FAME***

Join the gang at the tented Hall of Fame where characters wait to meet and greet their adoring fans from shortly after park opening to closing time.

Tip: If meeting characters is a big priority with your children, come here when the Hall of Fame first opens (check your guide map for times). Later in the day lines can be overwhelming and way too much of your touring day will be spent waiting.

Shopping at Toontown

County Bounty—Disney merchandise and toys.

Toontown Farmers Market—Open-air kiosk • hats • plush toys.

Magic Kingdom's best snacks

- Cinnamon sugar pretzels in Fantasyland at a kiosk in front of Pinocchio Village Haus.
- Cinnamon-glazed almonds on the streets of Fantasyland and Adventureland.
- Dole Whip, a delicious concoction of pineapple sherbet swirled with soft-serve ice cream sold at Aloha Isle Refreshments in Adventureland.
- Anything from Main Street Bake Shop.
- Epic-sized turkey legs found at a kiosk on the streets of Frontierland and the Lunching Pad in Tomorrowland.
- Lemonade slush at the Enchanted Grove in Fantasyland.
- Citrus Swirl at Sunshine Tree Terrace in Adventureland, frozen orange juice swirled with nonfat frozen vanilla yogurt.
- Rice Crispies treats at the Main Street Confectionary.
- Chocolate-covered Mickey ice cream bars from street vendors.

Fantasyland

Cross under the towering spires of Cinderella's castle and step into a storybook setting of whimsical gingerbread cottages and glinting turreted rooftops. It's the favorite land of the young as well as the young at heart, a Bavarian-style village where the fanciful attractions housed in multicolored, tent-like structures are a tribute to Disney's most cherished, animated films. Be sure to enter Fantasyland through Cinderella's Castle (as opposed to through Tomorrowland or Liberty Square), a perfect start to your adventure.

ARIEL'S GROTTO**

When the kids are hot and restless, seek out this water play area. Before leaving, visit the copper-headed Ariel in her rocky grotto home; she signs autographs for young visitors.

Magic Kingdom character greeting spots

Check your guide map for specific greeting times. The pointing Mickey gloves on your guide map will help you find the following locations:

- In the morning on Main Street Square.
- The Character Festival in Fantasyland.
- Near the Mad Tea Party attraction in Fantasyland you'll find Alice in Wonderland characters.
- In Fantasyland at Ariel's Grotto the mermaid herself is on hand for photos and autographs.
- In Mickey's Toontown Fair meet Mickey Mouse at the Judge's Tent, a bevy of characters at the Toontown Hall of Fame, and Mickey's pals at Minnie's Gazebo behind her Country House.
- Buzz Lightyear and Jim Hawkins with B.E.N. in Tomorrowland.
- Aladdin characters near the Magic Carpets of Aladdin ride.
- Captain Hook and Mr. Smee near the Pirates of the Caribbean.
- In front of the Castle Forecourt Stage, a variety of characters can be found intermittently throughout the day.

CINDERELLA'S CASTLE***

Designers studied famous European palaces and castles before devising this 189-foot gateway to Fantasyland and symbol of Walt Disney World. Though not a ride, walk beneath it to gaze at the elaborate and glittering glass, silver, and 14-karat gold mosaic murals (over 1 million pieces in 500 different colors) lining the walkway depicting the magical story of Cinderella. At the top of the tower is Cinderella's Royal Table where visitors dine high above Fantasyland, a calm oasis above the throngs. Walk around the castle to enjoy the Bavarian-style landscaping and moat-like waterway.

Tip: A small, peaceful sitting area on the waterside walkway to Liberty Square offers a perfect view of the castle.

CINDERELLA'S GOLDEN CARROUSEL***

This 1917 carousel has been lovingly restored by Disney. Splendid scenes from *Cinderella* were painted on each of its panels and the horse's saddles and bridles were hand-tinted with brilliant hues. While circling, all the mirrors twinkle, and a band organ pumps out classic Disney themes. This is an attraction you'll be able to enjoy just by looking. **2-minute ride.**

Tip: Lines can be long during the day; return at night when the children have left and the carousel is beautifully lit.

DUMBO THE FLYING ELEPHANT**

What can be said about Dumbo except that it's a child's most anticipated ride in the Magic Kingdom as well as possibly the longest wait for the shortest ride anywhere. But there is no getting around it if little ones are in tow. Gray Dumbos with giant, flopping ears fly round and round through the air with small children and their adoring parents as companions. Buttons gently raise and lower the elephant according to the whims of tiny passengers. What more can I say? **2-minute ride.**

Tip: Because of the slow loading factor and relatively few people this ride can hold, this should be your choice for the very first ride, first thing in the morning if you're traveling with small children. If you're not an early bird, try again during the parade. You'll know your little one is all grown up when they would rather run toward Splash Mountain at rope drop.

"IT'S A SMALL WORLD"**

Originally produced for the 1964–65 World's Fair in New York, this is an attraction you either love or hate. The mind-numbing song "It's a Small World" is played over and over again in many different languages as you sail through each colorful country of darling dolls representing over 100 cultures round the world, all singing and dancing in native costume. The theme is a beautiful one of international camaraderie and friendship, but I challenge you to get a male over the age of 10 on this ride more than once. **10-minute ride.**

MAD TEA PARTY*

Whirl and twirl in huge pastel teacups inspired by Alice in Wonderland's Mad Hatter Tea Party. You're able to control the speed of the spin and it can be, depending on who's doing the spinning, a bit nauseating. Just time your lunch appropriately. The dizzy mouse you see twirling in the center teapot is probably feeling just about the same as you will after stepping off this giddy ride. **1½-minute ride. Not recommended for those prone to motion sickness.**

THE MANY ADVENTURES OF WINNIE THE POOH***

Board giant "hunny" pots to travel through the Hundred Acre Wood with Pooh and his friends, Piglet, Tigger, and Eeyore, Owl, Kanga, and Roo. Giant storybook pages relay the tale of a blustery day while sailing and bouncing through a Pooh dream sequence, rain and more rain, and at last a celebration. "Hurray." Adults and children alike will be lulled into the delights of A. A. Milne's captivating stories accompanied by delightful music. **Fastpass. 3½-minute ride.**

Tip: Expect long lines and don't forget to use Fastpass if necessary. Take time to smell the honey as you exit the ride and enter the Pooh gift shop.

MICKEY'S PHILHARMAGIC SHOW

Replacing the Legend of the Lion King and set to debut in 2003 is the next generation of 3-D technology starring Donald Duck with classic Disney characters like Mickey Mouse, Ariel, Simba, and many more. The show will be presented on a 150-foot wide screen complete with in-theater effects allowing guests to become part of the action.

PETER PAN'S FLIGHT***

This is one of the most endearing attractions in Fantasyland, sure to steal your heart. Though old-fashioned and certainly not a thrill a minute, you'll find it hard to resist flying with Peter Pan, Wendy, and the boys to Never Never Land. Take off in gently soaring Pirate ships where your adventure begins in the Darling nursery "and off we go," flying over the twinkling lights of nighttime London with Big Ben and the London Bridge standing out against a starry, moonlit city (definitely the best part of the ride). The next stop is Never Never Land, where far below are glistening waterfalls and glowing volcanoes, lovely mermaids sunning on the rocks, the Indian Village, and our first glimpse of the Lost Boys and Captain Hook's ship. All the while the movie's theme song tells us " you can fly." The sight of Wendy walking the plank with the ticking crocodile waiting below is a bit nerve-racking, but of course, Peter Pan saves the day. This ride is nothing but a charmer; perfect for all ages. **Fastpass. 3-minute ride.**

Tip: This is now a Fastpass ride, one that really doesn't work very well. Unless you ride first thing in the morning, use Fastpass or be prepared to wait for an unbelievable amount of time.

SNOW WHITE'S SCARY ADVENTURES**

Be whisked off in 6-seater mining cars to sail through both happy and dismal scenes from the Walt Disney classic movie *Snow White and the Seven Dwarfs*. You'll see Snow White singing with the birds, the wicked Queen disguised as an old peddler with her poisoned apple, the merry cottage of the Seven Dwarfs, Snow White in her glass coffin in the woods, and "love's first kiss" given by the handsome prince. The evil spell is broken as she rides off with her love into the sunset. What I'd like to know is why we don't hear more heigh-ho-ing along the way. **2-minute ride.**

Tip: This ride has been revamped, replacing many of the gloomier aspects of the previous incarnation with more pleasant scenes of Snow White and her adorable dwarfs; however, the old witch remains and could possibly scare young children.

Entertainment in Fantasyland

Storytime with Belle at Fairytale Garden—In a small nook of a theater, Belle of *Beauty and the Beast* fame tells her story with the help of children from the audience. Check your guide map for show times.

Sword in the Stone—Performed in front of the Golden Carrousel; check your guide map for show times. Join Merlin in recreating the story of Arthur who pulled the magical sword from the stone to become king. A young member of the audience is chosen to extract Excaliber and parade around in robe and crown in celebration of his miraculous feat.

Shopping in Fantasyland

Fantasy Faire—Personalized Mickey-eared hats • children's Magic Kingdom logo clothing • infant Mickey apparel.

The King's Gallery—Tucked under Cinderella's castle • medieval merchandise • velvet table runners • embroidered pillows • steins • crowns • wands • jewelry • crystal figurines • swords and shields • real find: unusual medieval costumes for children.

Pooh's Thotful Shop—Pooh paraphernalia • fun find: precious writing tablets and frames covered with the furry faces of Pooh characters.

Seven Dwarfs' Mine—Precious nightshirts embossed with sleepy dwarfs • Snow White costume • Seven Dwarf plush toys.

Sir Mickey's—Disney logo attire • hats • plush toys • Sorcerer Mickey merchandise • children's jewelry.

Tinker Bell's Treasures—A must stop for all little girls • one of the most delightful shops in all of Disney • sparkling character costumes • Tinker Bell merchandise • princess wigs and footwear • vanity sets • jewelry boxes • pajamas • watch for Tinker Bell dust frequently scattering the walls and ceiling.

Quiet spots in the Magic Kingdom

- Out the back door of Ye Olde Christmas Shop, a shady area with benches and views of the moat surrounding Cinderella's Castle.

- Aunt Polly's Dockside Inn on Tom Sawyer's Island, a great place for a snack and a chance to rest beside the Rivers of America.

- Pathway leading from behind Cinderella's Castle to Liberty Square along the moat with benches and views of the castle.

- On the side of Aloha Terrace sits a picturesque verandah overlooking the river.

- Shady sitting area next to the river before crossing the bridge into Adventureland from the hub.

- Pathway between Tomorrowland and the front of Cinderella's Castle with a quiet seating area and Cinderella's wishing well.

Magic Kingdom Behind-the-Scenes Tours

Discounts available to Annual Pass and AAA Diamond Card holders. Call **407-WDW-TOUR** for reservations.

Welcome to the Magic Kingdom—A 90-minute walking tour for Magic Kingdom first-timers designed to introduce guests to the park. Learn about services, dining, entertainment, and, of course, the attractions. **$20 plus park admission. Sun, Mon,**

Tues, Wed, and Fri at 8:30 A.M. Children under 10 complimentary.

Keys to the Kingdom—One of the best behind-the-scenes tours offered in all of Disney. Meet at City Hall for a 5-hour trip around the park to learn the hidden secrets and history of the Magic Kingdom. Visit three attractions, the Production Center where floats line up for the daily parade, and the Utilidors, the tunnels below the park. **$58 plus park admission including lunch. Tours depart daily at 8:30, 9:30, and 10 A.M., and again at 1:30 P.M. Guests must be 16 years or older.**

The Magic Behind Our Steam Trains—Join the Disney crew early in the morning for 2 hours as they prepare the trains for operation. Check out the engine cab, see the roundhouse where the trains are stored overnight, and learn about Walt Disney's fascination with steam trains. **$30 plus park admission. Mon, Thurs, and Sat at 7:30 A.M. Guests must be 10 years or older.**

Disney's Family Magic Tour—A 2-hour interactive tour through the Magic Kingdom in search of clues ending in a surprise character greeting. **$25 plus park admission. Daily at 9:45 and 11:30 A.M.**

Backstage Magic—This 7-hour tour not only includes the Magic Kingdom but Disney–MGM Studios and Epcot as well. In the Magic Kingdom visit the Utilidors, at Epcot see what goes on behind-the scenes at the Living Seas, then see an animator at work at the Studios. **$199 including lunch. Park admission not required. Mon–Sat at 9 A.M. Guests must be 16 years or older.**

Liberty Square

Celebrate a time when 13 colonies banded together to declare their independence, a time of revolution, a time when simple men became heroes. Colonial America has been re-created here in the delightful cobblestone streets lined with stately Georgian brick mansions and simple clapboard buildings. In the center of the square is a replica of the famous Liberty Bell (crack and all), a pillory popular for picture taking (who can resist crime and punishment), and a breathtaking, 138-year-old live oak Liberty Tree with 13 lanterns hanging from the branches, a traditional colonial symbol of the American freedom of speech and assembly.

HALL OF PRESIDENTS**

This all-American, patriotic show in a 700-seat theater, tells the story of the U.S. and the roles our Presidents have played in its history. The highlight is an official role call of 42 audio-animatronic presidents beginning with George Washington and ending with George W. Bush, who personally recorded an inspiring speech to add to this attraction. All nod as their names are called and realistically fidget and whisper between themselves. At the end Abraham Lincoln rises from his chair and delivers a poignant closing speech followed by the rousing "Battle Hymn of the Republic." Though some think this attraction is a bit ho-hum, the unbelievably realistic presidents, each dressed accurately right down to the braces on Franklin Roosevelt's legs, is worth the time and effort. **23-minute show every 30 minutes on the hour and half hour.**

THE HAUNTED MANSION****

Eerie sounds, toppled fountains, unkempt grounds, and not even a hint of a smile on the faces of the creepy cast member servants cause a definite sense of foreboding on approach to this Tudor-style, red brick mansion. Enter an 8-sided, gargoyle-guarded Stretch Room where your "ghost host" asks everyone to gather tightly in the "dead" center of the room and warns that "there is no turning back." Then on to board a "doom buggy," your conveyance through this dust dripping, ghostly retreat where many terrific special effects and hair-raising sounds up the ante. You may have to ride several times to notice even half of the terrific details. If this sounds frightening, it's not. It's nothing but fun and only the smallest of children will become alarmed. **Fastpass. 9-minute ride.**

Tip: If crowds seem abnormally large, it's probably because of the arrival of the Liberty Belle *riverboat or the conclusion of the Hall of Presidents show; try again at a later time. And if you're prone to allergies, don't worry; the dust used here is a manmade, nonallergenic material.*

LIBERTY BELLE RIVERBOAT**

Journey back to the days of riverboat travel on this triple-decker steamboat for a serene and relaxing cruise round the Rivers of America surrounding Tom Sawyer Island. This slow moving attraction passes numerous frontier scenes along the way including an Indian village, a burning settler's cabin, and even a rowdy inn where partying river pirates hang out. Don't worry if you don't see a pilot; this boat is attached to an underwater track. **17-minute ride departing on the hour and the half hour.**

Tip: Make your way upstairs and to the front of the covered 2ⁿᵈ-story deck for plenty of shade and a view of both sides of the river.

MIKE FINK KEELBOATS*

Although these small boats ply the same route as the Liberty Belle Riverboat, they move at a slower pace and come with a longer wait. Sit upstairs in the open or inside; either way it's a pretty tight fit. **Open only in the busier times of the year.**

Tip: Lines move slowly due to a very limited capacity on each of the two boats. If the wait is too long, hop on the immense Liberty Belle for exactly the same view.

Shopping in Liberty Square

Heritage House—Americana merchandise • USA and flag-covered clothing • Uncle Sam hats • tax money banks • books on America and the colonies • favorite find: red-white-and-blue underwear.

Liberty Square Portrait Gallery—Hand-drawn portraits and caricatures.

The Yankee Trader—Disney kitchen items • character aprons and cookie jars • kitchen magnets • WDW cookbooks • Mickey-shaped waffle iron.

Ye Olde Christmas Shoppe—Glorious assortment of Disney ornaments • toy monorail (even a model of the Contemporary Resort and Spaceship Earth to go with it) • Walt Disney World Toy Railroad sets • character stockings • merchandise personalized on the spot.

Frontierland

Every young boy's dream of the Old West is here in Frontierland, a regular Wild West settlement (or a movie version of one), complete with a saloon, trading post, general store, and hotel with plenty of hitching posts out front for the horses. "Home on the Range" plays while cast members decked out in ten-gallon hats and jangling spurs walk the planked decking and oftentimes have a shoot-out or two. There's even a border town area with plenty of cactus, mesquite, and adobe buildings topped with red-tiled roofs. Throughout the day spontaneous entertainment erupts in the form of hoedowns and washboard music with plenty of dancing cowboys and cowgirls. And when you're tired of the frontier, take a raft over to Tom Sawyer's Island for a bit of relaxation or sit yourself down for a quick game of checkers.

BIG THUNDER MOUNTAIN RAILROAD****

Inside the 200-foot, rocky outcropping resembling the scenery in Monument Valley is a zippy coaster ride offering visitors a peek at the mining country of the Old West. Disney has rounded up an amazing assortment of old mining equipment, giving a taste of the Gold Rush to this blast of an attraction. Board a 15-car, runaway mining train led by a puffing and chugging engine for a wild journey through creepy bat caves, steaming geysers, bubbling mud pots, hazardous rockslides, rumbling earthquakes, and collapsing mine shafts. The details whip by so quickly you'll have a difficult time absorbing them all. For those who like speed but not big drops, this is your coaster. There are plenty of curves and small dips but all in all you'll find it fairly tame and loads of rip roarin' fun. **Fastpass. 4-minute ride. Minimum height 40 inches. Not recommended for expectant mothers or those with back or neck problems. Children under 7 must be accompanied by an adult.**

COUNTRY BEAR JAMBOREE**

At Grizzly Hall a toe-tapping show is on the agenda featuring audio-animatronic bears who cornball joke, sing, and strum to the beat of down-home country music. From behind the red velvet curtain pops an assortment of hillbilly bears who aim to please with a medley of songs accompanied by piano pickin', guitar strummin', bottle blowin', washboard scrapin', and fiddle playin' creatures. A few of them look like they're shy a few teeth if not a few brains (probably too much inbreeding). Although cute, I would put this one in the Enchanted Tiki Birds category, meaning see it after you've done everything else you wish to do and you still aren't ready to leave. But remember, small kids adore these irresistible bears. **17-minute show.**

Tip: Enter the door on the left in the waiting area to sit in one of the front rows. Even though most adults would rather go to the dentist than sit through this show again, crowds can be sizable in busy season.

FRONTIERLAND SHOOTIN' ARCADE*

Old-fashioned shooting gallery with a reacting Old West town of targets. You'll get a chuckle out of the crazy sound effects. Unload the buffalo rifle for 50¢.

SPLASH MOUNTAIN****

This is one ride guaranteed to put a smile on your face. Who can resist the charms of Brer Rabbit, Brer Fox, Brer Bear, and the rest of the gang, even if it culminates in one heck of a plunge? Board a hollowed-out log to float through audio-animatronic scenes from Disney's classic film *Song of the South,* splashing and dropping through Brer Rabbit's Laughin' Place. Drift round the briar patch while toe-tapping music plays among the cabbages and carrots, jugs of moonshine, chirpin' birds, and croakin' frogs as you relax and bob your head to the beat. Inside the mountain Brer Fox and Brer Bear cause plenty of commotion along the way as Brer Rabbit outwits them at every turn. As you float through bayous, marshes, and caverns, all a delight to the eye with loads of colorful detail and too-cute cavorting characters, the addictive theme song "Time to Be Moving Along" plays. As the ride creeps upward, heed the doomsday warning of a gloomy pair of buzzards ("It's turning back time" and "We'll show *you* a laughing place") just before the final doozy of a splashdown over a 5-story waterfall and into an oversized briar patch. It's pretty tough to keep your eyes open (at least for first-timers) but try to grab at least a peek of the park from the top. And don't think you missed the cherished "Zip-A-Dee-Doo-Da" tune; you'll hear it on the way out. **Fastpass. 11-minute ride. Minimum height 40 inches. Not recommended for expectant mothers or those with back or neck problems.**

Tip: If you'd like to stay somewhat dry, ask the attendant for a seat in the last row and sit on the left-hand side of the log (although this really doesn't guarantee a completely dry ride). The drop's really not as bad as it looks so don't let it keep you from experiencing one of the best rides Disney has to offer.

TOM SAWYER ISLAND**

Take a raft from Frontierland to the wilderness of Tom Sawyer's Island, a great getaway from the hubbub of the Magic Kingdom. Although it's not one of the park's most popular attractions, young kids and nostalgic adults will love exploring its meandering and somewhat disorienting pathways. Encounter a gristmill with a working waterwheel, a bouncy barrel bridge, a nifty cave (complete with bat sounds), a dark mineshaft, and a frontier fort with a blacksmith, guard house, cannons, even an escape tunnel. Guide maps along the way help you get your bearings with all paths leading back to the dock. **Walk-through attraction. Closes at dusk.**

Tip: From behind the fort catch a great view of Big Thunder Mountain and its periodically erupting geyser.

Shopping in Frontierland

Briar Patch—Brer Rabbit as well as all his friends and enemies in the form of plush character toys • Splash Mountain t-shirts, mugs, and hats • Winnie the Pooh merchandise.

Frontier Trading Post—Wild West shopping • coonskin toppers • cowboy hats • leather goods • bandanas • horse blankets • copper jewelry • lariats • personalized sheriff badges • Country Bear Jamboree merchandise • finds: kids' cowboy and Indian costumes.

Prairie Outpost and Supply—Jelly beans • lollipops • rock crystal candy • cotton candy • taffy • chocolates.

Adventureland

Tiki gods greet you on the bridge spanning the river into the wilds of Adventureland. Here you'll find a hodgepodge of the South Seas, the Caribbean, Africa, and the Middle East, all of it adding up to a sense of exploration. Adventureland's latest addition is one reminiscent of the Middle East where the Magic Kingdom's newest attraction brings Aladdin and his flying carpet to life.

"THE ENCHANTED TIKI ROOM
UNDER NEW MANAGEMENT"**

For years everyone avoided this attraction. No one could bear yet another showing of the 200 audio-animatronic birds singing and chirping on and on about their wonderful Tiki Room. In its new incarnation, making fun of the old, boring routine is yet another ingenious twist of Disney humor. The show's new owners, unsophisticated Iago of *Aladdin* fame and the sensible Zazu from *The Lion King*, have decided to teach the old birds new tricks. After much ado, the birds help update the program by replacing the tired former songs with hip new renditions of "In the Still of the Night" and "Do the Conga." Although it's still pretty darn hokey, this is a more humorous and entertaining version of the same old song. **9-minute show.**

Tip: Although most adults would rather dance with a hula skirt on than see this show, the small fry love it. Try it again if you've seen only the older version of the show or if you thankfully have no recollection of it all.

JUNGLE CRUISE***

Ludicrous safari outfitters are ready and waiting on their African Queen–style boats to take a load of tourists into the wilds on a wacky tour of the world's rivers. It's a hokey yet entertaining trip teeming with audio-animatronic animals and plenty of cornball jokes and silly puns certain to keep you laughing. **Fastpass. 10-minute ride.**

Tip: Fastpass here definitely can come in handy when lengthy late morning and afternoon crowds are merciless. Kids love this attraction.

MAGIC CARPETS OF ALADDIN**

Experience the marvel of flying carpets, powerful genies, and magic lamps on the Magic Kingdom's newest attraction, one patterned after the renowned Dumbo ride. Circle a jumbo genie's bottle in 4-passenger carpets that move up and down, forward and back (helpful in dodging the water-spitting camels) at your command accompanied by music from the movie. **2-minute ride.**

PIRATES OF THE CARIBBEAN***

The tune "Yo Ho, Yo Ho, a Pirate's Life for Me" will ring in your ears for hours after departing this likable ride. Float through dripping caves and into a darkened bombardment of a Caribbean town at the merciless hands of scurvy pirates. Hundreds of shouting, singing, and grunting audio-animatronic buccaneers chase women (some women chase the men), pillage and burn the town, and party through the night. It may sound a bit rough, but it's quite a charmer and executed in nothing but good humor. **10-minute ride.**

Tip: As you enter this attraction, look up at the zany, one-eyed, talking parrot perched over the doorway.

SWISS FAMILY TREEHOUSE**

This walk-through attraction takes its inspiration from the Disney movie *Swiss Family Robinson* and the John Wyss classic novel. The home of a family of shipwreck survivors built in the branches of a tree makes for a visually super time. What fun to relive the story and experience your childhood dream of the ideal tree house. Cross over the rustic bridge to reach the enormous, moss-dripping Banyan tree and begin your ascent up handmade stairwells and rope bridges to encounter room after room balanced on the tree limbs. Look down at the Jungle Lookout; you'll be amazed at how high you've climbed.

Tip: It's a bit hard to enjoy this attraction when there are hoards of people attempting to enjoy it with you. Come early or pay the consequences. Remember that quite a bit of stair climbing is required; make sure you're in shape to scale the heights.

Tiki God Fun

Near the Jungle Cruise is a circle of tiki gods who love to play with tourists. Step on the footprints embedded in the cement and play drums with your feet. Each footprint makes a different sound so it's even more fun when more than one person participates. But beware, the tiki gods spit at gullible guests.

Shopping in Adventureland

Agrabah Bazaar—Middle Eastern, open-air marketplace next to the new Aladdin ride • fez hats • leather goods • Moroccan robes • Indian rugs • brass items • straw baskets • Aladdin costumes and toys.

Bwana Bobs—Kiosk marketing safari hats and sunglasses.

Crow's Nest—Kodak products • Disney videos and CDs.

Island Supply Co.—Hula skirts • leis • island-print attire • Roxy and Quiksilver clothing and footwear.

La Princesa de Crystal—Kiosk stocked with handblown crystal figurines.

Pirate's Bazaar—Collection of island merchandise with a Caribbean flair • beach bags • straw purses and hats • beachwear • grass hula skirts • batik clothing • swashbuckling pirate-themed merchandise • eye patches • toy swords and guns • skulls • Jolly Roger flags • pirate costumes • one-eyed Mickey Mouse pirate plush toys.

Zanzibar Trading Co.—Plush toys in safari dress • toy monkeys • rubber snakes • African-style souvenirs.

Best places from which to view the Fantasy in the Sky fireworks

- Bridge to Tomorrowland, for a prime view of Tinker Bell on her flight from the top of the castle.
- The 15th-floor California Grill observation deck at the Contemporary Resort (for this you must have dining reservations).
- The romantic beach at the Polynesian.
- The marina, or Narcoossee's Restaurant, at the Grand Floridian.
- The balcony of a tower guestroom on the Magic Kingdom side of the Contemporary Resort.
- Lagoon-view room at the Polynesian.
- Magic Kingdom lagoon-view room at the Grand Floridian.

Magic Kingdom Dining
Main Street U.S.A. Dining

Caffe Italiano—Kiosk in Main Street Square • coffee • breakfast pastries • ice cream • beverages.

Casey's Corner—Plump hot dogs loaded with your favorite condiments • eat outside on bustling verandah where a ragtime piano player entertains or inside on bleachers in front of big screen TV.

Center Street Marketplace—Kiosk serving fruit, foot-long hot dogs, chips, beverages.

The Crystal Palace—Breakfast, lunch, and dinner • Winnie the Pooh character buffet • full review on page 328.

Main Street Bake Shop—Freshly baked goodies, gourmet pastries, homemade cookies, bear claws, macaroons, giant hot cinnamon rolls dripping with icing, banana bread pudding, mini lemon meringue tarts, cheesecake • quiche, roasted vegetable sandwiches, tomato and buffalo mozzarella sandwiches, deli sandwiches, fresh fruit • juice, specialty coffees, frozen Nescafe smoothies, beverages.

Plaza Ice Cream Parlor—Hand-dipped ice cream • sit outside on a delightful covered verandah for a prime view of the castle.

The Plaza Restaurant—Lunch and dinner • deli sandwiches • ice cream delights • full review on page 329.

Tony's Town Square Restaurant—Lunch and dinner • New York–style Italian restaurant • full review on page 329.

Tomorrowland Dining

Auntie Gravity's Galactic Goodies—Soft-serve ice cream, floats, sundaes • smoothies, juice, beverages.

Cosmic Ray's Starlight Café—Three cafes in one at the largest fast-food spot in the park • robotic Las Vegas–style lounge lizard Sonny E. Clipse croons for the crowd • Cosmic Chicken: rotisserie chicken, chicken strips, grilled chicken sandwich, mashed potatoes, fries • Blast-Off Burgers: burgers, hot dogs, vegetarian burgers, toppings bar • Starlight Soup, Salad, and Sandwich: country vegetable and cream of chicken soup, chicken Caesar salad, stacked deli sandwiches, cheese steak subs • children's menu: corn dog nuggets.

The Lunching Pad at Rockettower Plaza—Snack bar under the Astro Orbiter • epic-size turkey legs • frozen Coca-Cola and Minute Maid drinks.

The Plaza Pavilion—Futuristic fast-food dining • umbrella-covered tables alongside the water offer perfect views of Cinderella's Castle • fried chicken strips, chicken garden salad, Italian "stack" sandwiches, pizza • no-sugar brownie, ice cream bars • children's menu: PB&J sandwich.

Mickey's Toontown Fair Dining

Toontown Farmers Market—Hot dogs • fresh fruit • beverages.

Fantasyland Dining

Cinderella's Royal Table—Breakfast, lunch, and dinner • dine high above Fantasyland in the towers of Cinderella's Castle • full review on page 327.

Enchanted Grove—Minute Maid lemonade and orange juice • strawberry swirl of vanilla ice cream and strawberry sherbet • lemonade or raspberry slushes • coffee • espresso • cappuccino • latte.

Mrs. Pott's Cupboard—Fudge brownie, strawberry shortcake, and hot fudge sundaes • floats, milkshakes • chocolate chunk cookies • beverages.

The Pinocchio Village Haus—Jolly German tunes fill the air amid the rustic ambience of Geppetto's village • a few tables offer peek of It's a Small World attraction • on pleasant days sit outside for prime view of Fantasyland • quarter- and half-pound cheeseburgers, quarter-pound hot dogs, topping bar, chicken garden salad (fresh mixed greens, seasoned chicken, peaches, blue cheese, and toasted walnuts tossed with a vinaigrette), turkey sandwich, vegetable garden salad, Figaro fries topped with bacon, cheddar cheese, lettuce, and tomato • brownie, frozen, no-sugar added dessert • children's menu: PB&J sandwich, hot dog.

Scuttle's Landing—Adjacent to Ariel's Grotto • breakfast: muffins, bagels, milk • caramel corn, frozen Coca-Cola and Minute Maid drinks.

Liberty Square Dining

Columbia Harbour House—Chicken strips, fried fish, tuna sandwich, clam chowder, vegetarian sandwich with hummus and broccoli slaw, vegetarian chili in a bread bowl, mixed green salad topped with chicken, pecans, pineapple, and feta (ask for lighter dressing), sandwich of ham, tomato, broccoli slaw, and cheese • apple pie • children's menu: mac 'n' cheese, bologna and cheese sandwich.

Liberty Tree Tavern—Lunch and dinner • colonial tavern serving good old American fare • lunch à la carte • colonial-dressed characters host the evening meal • full review on page 328.

Sleepy Hollow Refreshments—Seating beside moat with perfect views of Cinderella's Castle • caramel corn, brownies, cobbler à la mode, ice cream cookie sandwich • root beer float, iced cappuccino, specialty coffees, hot tea, milk, soft drinks.

Frontierland Dining

Aunt Polly's Dockside Inn—Waterside snack bar on Tom Sawyer Island • apple pie, fudge brownie or strawberry shortcake sundaes, floats, soft-serve ice cream.

Frontierland Fries—Kiosk serving McDonald's fries and beverages.

Pecos Bill Café—Best counter-service spot in the Magic Kingdom • unbelievably good chargrilled burgers and such in an Old West atmosphere • quarter- and half-pound cheeseburger, chicken wrap, quarter-pound hot dogs, grilled chicken salad, chili, chili cheese fries, great fixings bar • chocolate cream pie, root beer float • child's meal: hot dog.

Westward Ho Refreshments—Kiosk offering pink lemonade, coffee, hot cocoa, hot tea, chips • next door is the ever-popular giant turkey leg kiosk.

Adventureland Dining

Aloha Isle—Home of the famous Dole Whip, a delicious concoction of pineapple sherbet swirled with either vanilla or chocolate soft-serve ice cream • floats in pineapple, coke, or root beer • fresh pineapple • pineapple juice • picturesque verandah hangs over the river surrounding Adventureland.

El Pirata y el Perico—Mexican fast food • umbrella-covered eating verandah on the festive Caribbean Plaza • nachos, taco salad, crispy beef tacos, beef empanadas with black beans and rice, chili topped with cheese • churros, Nestle's Crunch bar • children's menu: tacos.

Sunshine Tree Terrace—Tasty Citrus Swirl, frozen orange juice swirled with nonfat frozen vanilla yogurt • nonfat frozen yogurt in vanilla and chocolate • floats, orange slush, coffee, smoothies, orange juice, cappuccino, espresso, café mocha, iced cappuccino.

Entertainment
CASTLE FORECOURT STAGE***

Cinderella's Surprise Celebration, performed throughout the day in front of Cinderella's Castle, is a new musical stage show featuring none other than Cinderella who opens the presents of laughter, courage, romance, and friendship with her friends the Fairy Godmother, Mickey and Minnie, Goofy, Donald Duck, Mulan, and Peter Pan, just to name a few. A few villains show up, but they don't succeed in spoiling the fun. A special scene presents Cinderella, Snow White, and Belle, each dancing with her prince. Children have an opportunity afterward to meet the characters. **15-minute show. See guide map for show times.**

SHARE A DREAM COME TRUE PARADE****

The new 3 P.M. parade is a huge hit with all ages. Giant floats topped with rotating globes of swirling snow, twinkling lights, and live Disney characters are accompanied by over 100 walking characters and a medley of classic Disney songs. **15-minute parade.**

Tip: Those not interested in the parade will find that this is a great time to ride the big name attractions—when all the crowds are elsewhere.

SPECTROMAGIC****

A glittering sorcerer Mickey leads the parade of dazzling Disney characters aglow with fiber optics, holographic images, and twinkling lights (over 600,000 of them), all accompanied by Disney classic songs. **Held every night in summer and peak times, but only weekends off-season.**

FANTASY IN THE SKY****

What a way to end your day at this magical park! It all begins with Tinker Bell's flight from the heights of Cinderella Castle down to the rooftops of Tomorrowland. Then before your dazzled eyes there suddenly appears a breathtaking shower of sparkling fireworks accompanied by Disney classic tunes. If you're traveling in off-season, make sure to plan an evening at the Magic Kingdom when the evening parade and fireworks are on the agenda. **Held every night in summer and peak times but only weekends off-season.**

Tip: Don't stand too close to the castle. It blocks your view of the fireworks that come from behind it.

Special Events

Night of Joy—On 2 weekend nights in early September some of the biggest names in contemporary Christian music perform at the Magic Kingdom. $35 in advance or $38 at the gate; call **407-W-DISNEY** for ticketing.

Mickey's Not-So-Scary Halloween—For 5 nights at the end of October, Halloween is celebrated at a special after-hours party featuring trick-or-treating and costumed characters. The park's most popular attractions are open accompanied by face painting, storytelling, a complimentary family photo, and a spooky evening parade and fireworks display. A special dinner at Liberty Tree Tavern with characters in Halloween costumes is available by calling **407-WDW-DINE**. $28 for adults, $23 for children ages 3–9 plus park admission; add $2 at the gate. Call **407-W-DISNEY** for ticketing.

Mickey's Very Merry Christmas Party—Snow falls on the magically decorated streets of the Magic Kingdom on select nights in December. The park's most popular attractions are open along with special parades and stage shows, evening fireworks, family photographs, Christmas-themed characters, carolers, hot chocolate, and cookies. $34 for adults, $24 for children ages 3–9 plus park admission; add $5 at the gate. Call **407-W-DISNEY** for ticketing.

EPCOT

On October 1, 1982, Walt Disney's dream of an experimental prototype community of tomorrow came true. Although he died in 1966, the Walt Disney Company brought his conception in a much broader fashion to reality and created a theme park dedicated to the resourcefulness and imagination of America's free enterprise system. Certainly not your typical theme park, it's a continual showcase of imagination, instruction, research, and invention, an education in technology and innovation, other lands and cultures.

Comprising 260 acres (over twice the size of the Magic Kingdom) and divided into two parts, Future World and World Showcase, it will take almost 2 full days and a good pair of walking shoes to truly explore its full scope. While there are plenty of attractions and activities for the little ones, Epcot's appeal is mainly to older children and adults. The draw is a huge variety of dining choices, loads of exciting entertainment, magnificent gardens, round-the-world shopping, and attractions that simultaneously entertain and educate. The grounds alone are worth the price of admission, a fact well known to horticulturists round the world. Mature, fabulous gardens abound throughout with each pavilion and country offering a distinct, native landscaping. The most important thing is just to enjoy, and with so many diverse attractions it certainly won't be difficult.

Park Basics

Getting There

Those driving to WDW should take Exit 67 off I-4 and follow the signs to Epcot's main entrance.

Using WDW transportation

From the Grand Floridian, Polynesian, Contemporary, and the Magic Kingdom—Board the monorail at either your hotel or the Magic Kingdom, disembark at the Ticket and Transportation Center (TTC), and make a transfer to the Epcot monorail.

From the Yacht Club, Beach Club, Beach Club Villas, Boardwalk Inn and Villas, and the Walt Disney World Dolphin and Swan—Walk or take a boat to the International Gateway entrance in World Showcase. Although World Showcase does not open until 11 A.M., entrance is allowed here anytime after Future World opens. Park passes may be purchased at the International Gateway.

From all other Disney resorts, Disney–MGM Studios, and the Animal Kingdom—Board bus marked Epcot.

Parking

Cost is $7 per day; free to Walt Disney Resort guests and Annual Pass holders. Keep your receipt; fee is good for parking at the Magic Kingdom, Disney–MGM Studios, and Animal Kingdom on that day only.

Parking is conveniently located in front of the park. Trams circulate throughout the parking area for easy transportation to the entry gate. Be sure to make a note of your aisle and section.

Operating Hours

Open 9 A.M.–7 P.M. in Future World (Honey, I Shrunk the Audience, Test Track and Spaceship Earth open to 9 P.M.) and 11 A.M.–9 P.M. in World Showcase with extended hours during holidays and busy season. Call 407-824-4321 or log on to **www.disneyworld.com** for updated park hours.

Entrance Plaza along with Spaceship Earth normally opens a half hour before official park opening time. To get a jump on the crowds, arrive at least 30 minutes early to allow time to park, buy tickets, purchase a snack or cup of coffee, and be one of the first to hit the big attractions. I recommend heading straight to Test Track.

Entry Gates

Epcot has two entrances: the main entrance in front of Spaceship Earth and the International Gateway Entrance in World Showcase between the United Kingdom and France. Visitors staying at the Epcot resorts should use the International Gateway entrance that opens at the same time as Future World. Park passes may be purchased at both entrances.

Fastpass Attractions

See pages 133-134 for Fastpass details. Honey, I Shrunk the Audience • Living with the Land • Test Track • Maelstrom.

Services

ATM machines—There are three in the park: next to the stroller rentals at Entrance Plaza, on the center walkway between Future World and World Showcase, and at the America pavilion in World Showcase.

Baby care center—An infant facility is located in the Odyssey Center between Test Track and the Mexico Pavilion on the east side of the park outfitted with changing tables, highchairs, and a room for nursing mothers. Formula, baby food, suntan lotion, diapers, milk, and over-the-counter children's medications may be purchased. All restrooms throughout the park are outfitted with changing tables.

Cameras and film processing—The Camera Center on your right as you enter the park and Cameras and Film next to Journey Into Your Imagination sell cameras, film, camcorder tapes, and batteries. Two-hour film processing is available here and anywhere else the Photo Express sign is displayed.

First aid—For minor medical problems head to the First Aid Center in the Odyssey Center located between Test Track and the Mexico Pavilion on the east side of the park.

Guest relations—On the east side of Spaceship Earth is Guest Relations where a knowledgeable staff is ready to assist you with priority seating, lost children, lost and found, purchase of annual passes and upgrades, information for guests with disabilities, taped narration for visitors with sight impairment, assisted listening devices, foreign currency exchange, personal translator units in Spanish, French, and German, sign language services, VIP tour information, behind-the-scenes programs, character greeting information, and resort reservations.

Guests with disabilities—A guidebook for guests with disabilities is available at Guest Relations (see The Basics on page 22 for more information). Guests with mobility disabilities should park adjacent to the Entrance Complex (ask at the Auto Plaza for directions). Wheelchairs and ECVs are available for rent. Most restaurants and shops at Epcot are accessible to guests with disabilities although some counter-service locations have narrow queues with railings (ask a host or hostess for assistance). Companion assisted restrooms are located at First Aid and five other locations.

Most attractions in Future World and the ride in Norway at World Showcase provide access through the main queue while others have auxiliary entrances for wheelchairs and service animals along with up to five members of your party. Certain attractions require guests to transfer from their wheelchair to a ride system.

Braille guidebooks, assistive listening devices, video captioning, and audiotape guides are available at Guest Relations with a $25 refundable deposit. Many theater-type attractions have reflective or video captioning and with a 7-day notice, a sign language interpreter will be provided at live shows on Tues and Fri. Call **407-824-4321** with any questions.

Information Central—Check the up-to-the-minute tip board here for wait times and parade and special event information. Located between Innovations East and West in front of the Fountain of Nations.

Lockers—Locker rentals, available for $7 per day including a $2 refundable key deposit, are next door to the Camera Center in Entrance Plaza and just outside the International Gateway entrance. If you're park-hopping, keep your receipt for another locker at the three other Disney theme parks for no extra charge.

Lost and found—Located at Guest Relations or call **407-824-4245**.

Lost children—Locate lost children at the Baby Care Center or Guest Relations.

Package pickup—Purchases may be sent to the Gift Stop located just outside the main entrance as well the International Gateway next to the stroller rentals for pick-up at the end of the day; allow 3 hours for delivery. Disney resort guests may send their packages directly to their hotel for next-day arrival.

Pet kennel—A kennel is located on the left before entering the park. Daily rate is $6. For information call **407-824-6568**. Proof of vaccination is required.

Readmission—If you plan to leave Epcot and reenter the same day, be sure to retain your ticket and have your hand stamped before departing.

Stroller and wheelchair rentals—Rentals are located on your left as you enter the park's main entrance and at International Gateway. Wheelchairs are available at the above stroller locations as well as just outside the main entrance at the Gift Stop. ECVs are available at the inside Entrance Plaza location only. Single strollers are $8 per day, double strollers $15, wheelchairs $8, and electric convenience vehicles $40 including a $10 refundable deposit. If you are park-hopping, keep your receipt for a same-day replacement at the three other Disney theme parks.

Vacation station—Just before the park's turnstiles is this stop for Walt Disney World information, dining, and resort reservations.

The Lay of the Land

Epcot looks a bit like a figure 8 with Future World being the northern region (shown on the guide map at the bottom; think "upside down") and World Showcase the southern region. Future World is composed of two concentric rings with Spaceship Earth and Innoventions forming the inner circle and the six pavilions (soon to be seven) the outer. The Universe of Energy, Wonders of Life, and Test Track are located on the

Epcot

Germany

Italy

U.S.A.

Japan

Morocco

France

American Garden Theatre

China

World Showcase Lagoon

Int. Gateway

Norway

United Kingdom

Showcase Plaza

Mexico

Canada

World Showcase

Future World

Test Track

Imagination!

World Showcase

Future World

Future Site of Mission Space

Innoventions

The Land

Wonders of Life

Universe of Energy

Spaceship Earth

The Living Seas

Entrance

east side of Spaceship Earth and the Living Seas, the Land, and Imagination on the west side. Walkways connect Future World to World Showcase made up of 11 pavilions fronted by a 1.3-mile promenade surrounding the 40-acre World Showcase Lagoon.

Suggested 1-day itinerary for touring Epcot

For optimum enjoyment, Epcot really needs to be seen in 1½ to 2 days; however, the following itinerary does hit all the highlights. This may be difficult if not impossible to accomplish in busy season but entirely possible in the slower times of the year. Come prepared with plenty of energy and a good pair of walking shoes:

- Have breakfast and be at the park a half hour before opening.
- Ride Test Track first and then move over to the west side of Future World to see *Honey, I Shrunk the Audience* at the Imagination pavilion.
- Hop next door to the Land pavilion where you'll want to ride the Living With the Land attraction.
- If lines are fairly short at Spaceship Earth, ride it now (if not, make it back here sometime before Illuminations).
- Move on to the Universe of Energy.
- Next the Wonders of Life pavilion where you will want to take in Body Wars and Cranium Command.
- Move to World Showcase and pick up a late lunch at one of the many fast-food spots.
- Work your way around World Showcase for the remainder of the afternoon, making time between stops for shopping as you try to take in most of the highlights including Maelstrom in Norway, the *Wonders of China* film, *The American Adventure* show, *Impressions de France*, and *O Canada*.
- Make priority seating at one of the World Showcase restaurants for 7 P.M., have dinner, and then roam or pick up anything you missed until about a half hour prior to Illuminations when it's time to search for a nice viewing spot for the show.
- Go back to your hotel room and collapse.

Suggested 2-day itinerary for touring Epcot

Now this is more like it, a relaxing 2 days at this massive park:

First day

- Your first day will take in all of Future World. Begin by riding Test Track and Mission Space then move across to the west side and see *Honey, I Shrunk the Audience.*

- Move over to the Land pavilions and begin by picking up a Fastpass (if necessary) to the Living with the Land attraction. During your wait take in Food Rocks and *The Circle of Life.*

- On to the Living Seas. Afterward have lunch at the Coral Reef Restaurant located at the same pavilion. Make you priority seating reservations for around 1 P.M.

- After lunch tour Innovations and then ride Spaceship Earth.

- See the Universe of Energy next and then on to the Wonders of Life pavilion to experience Body Wars (your food should be sufficiently settled by now), Cranium Command, and *The Making of Me.*

- Head for your 7 P.M. priority seating at one of the World Showcase restaurants or the Flying Fish at the Boardwalk.

- Tomorrow night you'll be staying for Illuminations so head home for a good night's sleep.

Second day

- Your second day will be a complete tour of World Showcase. Sleep in today because this area of Epcot doesn't open until 11 A.M. Begin your tour in Canada where shopping and the *O Canada* film are in order.

- Next tour the United Kingdom's cutesy shops and perhaps have a pint at the pub.

- Break for lunch at either Chefs de France or the Marrakesh Restaurant in Morocco. Make your priority seating for around 1:15 P.M. Then see the *Impressions de France* show and do a bit of perfume shopping.

- Visit Morocco to shop the interesting bazaars and alleyways.
- Japan is next with its serene gardens and the Mitsukoshi Department Store brimming with all kinds of goodies.
- Next is the American Adventure attraction, a must on every patriotic citizen's list.
- After America head to Italy for soft Italian leather and a glass of Chianti.
- Take in Germany and its jolly village and then on to the *Wonders of China* film.
- Next Norway and the Maelstrom attraction before your priority seating time of 7 P.M. at the San Angel Inn in the Mexico pavilion. Ride El Rio del Tiempo either before or after dinner and stake out a place for Illuminations at least a half hour before the show.
- See Illuminations and then head for home.

Best of Epcot

Future World—Spaceship Earth • Universe of Energy • Cranium Command • Test Track • Honey, I Shrunk the Audience • Living With the Land.

World Showcase—Impressions de France • The American Adventure • Wonders of China • Maelstrom • Illuminations.

Future World

At Future World visitors encounter shining glass pyramids, robotic fountains, shimmering steel, and unconventional landscaping. Towering high above it is Epcot's symbol, Spaceship Earth, now topped with a massive, white-gloved Mickey hand sporting a sparkling magic wand. Here visitors learn about communications, energy, health, agriculture, transportation, the oceans, and even explore their imaginations. If it sounds a bit like school, don't worry. Disney always manages to add their special style to the learning process transforming it into sheer fun.

Entrance Plaza and Leave a Legacy

Upon entering Epcot you'll first encounter Entrance Plaza where Guest Relations and stroller, wheelchair, and locker rentals are located. Immediately the eye is drawn to the immense Spaceship Earth towering overhead as you stand among granite monoliths from the Leave a Legacy program. Each is covered in one-inch square, metallic tiles digitally etched with photographs of the thousands of visitors who participated in this program during the Millennium Celebration at Epcot, one that is probably still available given the many empty monoliths.

Shopping at Entrance Plaza

Camera Center—Film • camcorder tapes • batteries • cameras • camera bags • two-hour processing • minor camera repairs • photo albums • frames • Disney software, videos, DVDs, and mouse pads • purchase pictures taken during the day by Disney photographers here.

Gateway Gifts—Disney logo clothing • plush toys • souvenirs.

Spaceship Earth***

Visible for miles, this symbol of Epcot comprises over 2 million cubic feet of expanse, a silver geosphere 180 feet tall and 164 feet in diameter composed of 954 glowing panels of different shapes and sizes. Inside you'll find an attraction chronicling the story of human communications beginning with the dawn of recorded time and ending with today's impressive network of global contact. The slow journey to the top takes visitors through marvelous, audio-animatronic scenes of man's quest for more efficient means of communication. See Cro-Magnon man storytellers, Egyptian papyrus scroll readers, ancient Greek actors, Roman couriers, Islamic scholars, and Michelangelo painting the Sistine Chapel.

Following in swift succession come the new tools and technologies of the teletype, telephone, radio, moving pictures, and television. Finally the communication super network of today conveying information at the speed of light. The most captivating scene is at the top of the sphere where in the middle of a sky thick with stars sits the earth suspended in space.

On departure, stop and experience the future at AT&T's New Global Neighborhood, an interactive exhibit of the most up-to-the-minute communication technology. **15-minute ride.**

Tip: Lines move quickly and efficiently on this continually loading ride. Because this is the first attraction visitors encounter, lines can get lengthy in the morning. If the wait looks reasonable, go for it; if not, come back in the afternoon when most people are touring World Showcase. This attraction is usually up and running a half hour before official park opening time.

INNOVENTIONS**

At Innoventions you'll find many demonstrations of the latest in technological advancements soon to be put to use in everyday life. Located in two buildings on either side of Spaceship Earth, plan on investing plenty of time to explore the numerous hands-on attractions. If possible, come in the afternoon when crowds are touring World Showcase.

Innoventions East—Segway Human Transporter, an electrical powered transportation device that weighs only 80 pounds and travels at 12 mph • an interactive forest • Internet Zone where guests can play the latest in Disney online games • House of Innoventions, a tour of a "smart home" of tomorrow where your tour guide will demonstrate three rooms of ingenious new products for the home • Tom Morrow's Playground, a children's play area including an interactive Jungle Book Rhythm and Groove and Mouse House Junior for preschool video games.

Innoventions West—Ultimate Home Theater • video car race at IBM's Networked Living • biotechnology at Beautiful Science where among other things you'll crawl through a Bug Tunnel • Disney Interactive Net for the latest in video games.

Character Connection

Next to MouseGear facing Innovations Plaza is a set of doors leading to a great character opportunity. From 9 A.M.–8:45 P.M., Mickey and Goofy visit with youngsters in a quiet, almost hidden setting. Exit conveniently into MouseGear, a whopper of a Disney merchandise store.

Entertainment Near Innovations

The JaMMitors—Young percussionists bang out rhythms on trashcans.

Kristos—Alien-looking, modern 3-person dance troupe performing strength ballet out of this world.

Shopping Near Innoventions

The Art of Disney Epcot Gallery—Disney animation artist at work • animation cells (some as high as $4,000) • Disney Classic collectable figurines in bronze and porcelain • lithographs • animation books • posters • fun find: Mickey ear-etched Waterford crystal goblets.

MouseGear—19,000-square-foot Disney merchandise emporium • kids' favorite: Spaceship Earth drinking bottle.

Ice Station Cool—Located on the west side of the Fountain of Nations. In the dead heat of summer, crowds vie for the chance to line up in a deliciously snowy, 32-degree icy igloo. At the end of the trail you'll find complimentary tastes of Coca-Cola's assortment of products from around the world and, of course, Coca-Cola souvenirs for sale.

Universe of Energy
ELLEN'S ENERGY ADVENTURE***

The massive pyramid-shaped structure that is the Universe of Energy pavilion has a roof composed of 2 acres of solar panels producing enough energy to help power the pavilion. Inside join Ellen DeGeneres on her journey to become an energy expert as she travels back to the age of the dinosaurs with Bill Nye, the Science Guy. What used to be a long, dull show has been revamped to become a humorous and informative one.

During the preshow, Ellen dreams she's a contestant on the Jeopardy show. She fails miserably, sorely lacking in energy knowledge. She calls on Bill Nye to take her back billions of years to the "Big Bang," where it all began at the birth of the universe.

Transfer to a huge traveling theater that begins to move through a dark and misty forest brimming with swamps and volcanic activity, towering prehistoric trees and plant life. The air is thick with a steamy, damp feel and the smell of sulfur and the sounds of the night only add to the thrill. Towering overhead are roaring lifelike audio-animatronic dinosaurs, the most astounding aspect of this attraction.

In the final theater Ellen and Bill review the history of man's use of energy, where energy comes from, and how to use it more conservatively. From wide-open aerial shots you'll view the world's ever expanding energy requirements, the latest technologies of solar and wind energy, and new ways of finding more oil and clean-burning natural gas. Of course Ellen, the energy expert now, returns to beat her competitors in *Jeopardy*. All the while Ellen's humor and wisecracking helps keep the informative aspect of this ride entertaining. This is one of the better attractions in Future World and worth your time simply to see the dinosaurs. **45-minute show beginning every 17 minutes.**

Tip: The theater holds almost 600 people; go ahead and wait even though lines seem long. Enter the door to the theater on the left and make a beeline to the front row of the far-left section for the best unobstructed views. Young, sensitive children may be bothered by the darkness and the huge, roaring dinosaurs.

The Fountain of Nations

The dancing fountain located in Innovations Plaza is one of the best shows in the park and, most importantly, one not requiring a wait in line. **Every 15 minutes** it explodes with jets of water, choreographed geysers shooting increasingly skyward in rhythmic movement, dancing to stirring, magnificent music. Quite a sight to see and even better after dark with added lighting effects.

Epcot's best restaurants

Coral Reef • Bistro de Paris • Restaurant Marrakesh • San Angel Inn.

Wonders of Life

Walk past the towering, colorful DNA double helix and into an expansive gold-domed structure to explore the joy of life, fitness, and well-being. Housing a ride that takes visitors through the human body, a touching film on the facts of life, and a comical attraction explaining the workings of the brain, this bright, colorful pavilion also includes a fitness zone, a film on health led by Goofy, and interactive stations emphasizing health, nutrition, and the senses. Stop in on a rainy day for plenty to see and experience under one cozy roof.

BODY WARS**

Take a voyage through the human body on a flight simulator similar to the Star Tours attraction at Disney Studios. On a rescue mission to save an immunologist lost on a routine repair, guests are miniaturized and inserted into the artery of a living human being by use of a body probe. Of course, Disney never does anything routine. Before you know it you're off on a turbulent excursion through the body, tilted and jerked backward, forward, up, and down with your only guarantee being one heck of a queasy stomach. This is not my favorite simulator ride; it's a bit boring and is easily skippable unless you are a huge fan of this type of attraction. **5-minute ride. Minimum height 40 inches. Not recommended for expectant mothers, those with heart, back, or neck problems, or those prone to motion sickness.**

Tip: Be sure to try this attraction before a meal!

CRANIUM COMMAND***

Nestled in the back of the Wonders of Life pavilion is one of the funniest shows at Epcot. Buzzy, an unpolished, new recruit straight out of Brain College, is assigned to "pilot" the most unstable brain imaginable, that of an adolescent 12-year old boy named Bobby. Witness life through Bobby's eyes as Buzzy directs him through a frantic but hilarious day while at the same time explaining how the brain functions. **Continuous shows every 18 minutes.**

Tip: Do not miss the funny preshow. The only wait is usually for the last show to end.

THE MAKING OF ME**

A touching and sensitive facts-of-life film hosted by Martin Short. If your child is at that certain, pre-adolescent age, don't miss this. The actual footage of the growing embryo and birth are excellent, but they are a bit explicit for young children. Adults might find themselves with a lump in their throat while their children may have further questions in mind; be prepared. **Continuous shows every 15 minutes.**

GOOFY ABOUT HEALTH*

Goofy (of all unlikely characters) extols the virtues of good health in this short film.

FITNESS FAIRGROUND*

Take a computerized lifestyle examination, ride a video exercise bicycle, and analyze your sport's swing.

FRONTIERS OF MEDICINE*

Interactive videos highlighting research and innovations in medicine.

SENSORY FUNHOUSE*

Test your five senses with a variety of hands-on exhibits.

Shopping at Wonders of Life

Well and Goods Limited—Golf clothing and accessories • sports-oriented t-shirts • ESPN merchandise • Minnie and Mickey plush toys dressed for sporting activities.

Mission: Space

Set to launch in mid 2003, this new pavilion in Future World, developed with the help of former NASA consultants, will replace the old Horizons. On the way to a futuristic International Space Training Center, visitors will experience, by the use of a flight simulator, the sensation of a super liftoff and weightlessness, those same sensations encountered by real astronauts.

Test Track****

Board your 6-passenger car to move through a series of rigorous tests normally used on prototype cars. Begin your journey with a hill climb, then a rough road test, two brake tests (one without and one with anti-lock brakes), subjection to extremes of hot and cold temperatures, and finally the long-awaited handling run. Speed through hairpin turns and then barrel outside onto the high-speed banking loop at speeds of over 60 mph. The last is quite a ride, not really scary but very fast and loads of fun. **Fastpass. 5-minutes ride with a short preshow. Minimum height 40 inches. An adult must accompany children under 7. Not recommended for expectant mothers or those with back, heart, or neck problems. Closed in inclement weather.**

Tip: This ride is notorious for breakdowns so prepare for long waits, some of which don't necessarily come with a ride at the end. If you want to utilize Fastpass (which is a great idea), don't wait until the end of the day; passes are sometimes gone by the afternoon. If you are willing to ride without other members of your party, the single-rider's line is a much quicker alternative; simply ask for directions at the entrance.

Shopping at Test Track

Test Track Shop—General Motors merchandise • Test Track clothing and souvenirs • for the ultimate in silly head wear, check out the bright orange traffic cone hats.

Tip: Don't miss the peaceful flowering garden between the MouseGear store and Test Track, a great place for a quiet rest.

Imagination

Under the angled pyramids of glass is the Imagination pavilion with its reverse fountain of water leaping upward in an incredible, massive stream. Inside explore the many aspects of your imagination with a ride intended to stretch your senses and creativity, as well as one of Epcot's most popular attractions, the 3-D extravaganza, *Honey, I Shrunk the Audience.*

HONEY, I SHRUNK THE AUDIENCE****

One of Epcot's most popular attractions is this full of surprises 3-D film. Professor Wayne Szalinski of *Honey, I Shrunk the Kids* fame manages to cause plenty of chaos with a series of mishaps involving his quirky inventions. Thanks to his out-of-control machines and great special effects, guests involuntarily become casualties to hundreds of scampering mice, a colossal-sized dog, and a very large python loose in a very small theater. Get out your handkerchief for the final surprise. A not-to-be-missed show. **Fastpass. Continuous shows every 20 minutes.**

Tip: Although the dark theater combined with the slapping of numerous mouse tails and a snake in the face will probably scare small children, older kids and adults will love it. Remember to use Fastpass when lines are long.

JOURNEY INTO IMAGINATION WITH FIGMENT**

In June of 2002 this revamped Imagination attraction debuted. Once again guests explore the Imagination Institute Labs, one designed to challenge the imagination. But this time the renowned Figment, some of the old audio-animatronics, and the song "One Little Spark" have returned from the original ride. And this time Figment has decided to rearrange the tour his way, allowing the imagination to run free. I think those who rode the previously boring reincarnation will be a bit more pleased with the new attraction. **5-minute ride.**

IMAGE WORKS: KODAK "WHAT IF ?" LABS*

Stop at this hands-on spot where a variety of activities are intended to charge the imagination. Perhaps the favorite enticement is the Kodak Picture Playground where guests can take their picture, insert it into the center of an animal, flower, or favorite cartoon character, and e-mail it to family or friends.

Shopping at Imagination

ImageWorks Shop—Cameras • film • frames • photo postcards with your face in a variety of background choices • images engraved in crystal paperweights or cubes • Figment merchandise.

Kodak Cameras and Film—Cameras • film • batteries • photo albums.

The Land

Food, nutrition, farming, and a healthy shot of environmental education is the agenda at one of Future World's most interesting pavilions. Here ongoing agricultural experiments are carried out in an arrangement with NASA and the Department of Agriculture, much of which can be seen in the greenhouses of the captivating Living with the Land attraction. Other stops include an excellent environmental film featuring the stars of *The Lion King* and a rocking show touting good nutrition. Visitors can dine with Farmer Mickey while revolving through the Land's ecosystems or head to the very popular food court.

Daily in the Sunshine Season Food Fair, children ages 4–8 bake Toll House cookies with a Disney chef. It's necessary to sign up early for this complimentary but limited program happening every hour on the half hour from 11:30 A.M.–3:30 P.M.

THE CIRCLE OF LIFE***

In a combination of animation and live footage the creatures of *The Lion King* convey the message of all things existing together in a delicate balance, a great circle of life. The dazzling scenes of animals and nature will make all who see this excellent film leave with a desire to do their part in preserving the beauty of the world in which we live. **20-minute show.**

FOOD ROCKS*

At an "All-Star Musical Benefit for Good Nutrition," audio-animatronic food stars rock and roll while teaching the basics of a nutritious diet. A cute show, but certainly not a must-see. **15-minute show.**

LIVING WITH THE LAND***

Explore the past, present, and future of farming on a boat tour through three diverse ecosystems: a cool, stormy rain forest, a harsh, arid desert landscape, and the rolling American prairie complete with an early 19th-century family farm. Proceed to immense greenhouses where more efficient ways of producing food are researched and developed. You'll see plants grown hydroponically without soil (check out the trees with 9-pound lemons) and aeroponically; there's even a fish farm. All of the harvest is used in Epcot's restaurants. A remarkably absorbing attraction for all ages. **Fastpass. 13-minute ride.**

Tip: At lunchtime the overflow from the food court produces extremely long waits. Plan for early morning or late afternoon.

Another tip: Check out Epcot's talking water fountains. Three (that I know of): next to the restrooms between The Land and Imagination, outside the MouseGear shop, and near the play fountain on the walkway between Future World and World Showcase. You try and figure it out!

Shopping at the Land

Green Thumb Emporium—Located downstairs in the Sunshine Season Food Fair • delightful shop laden with items for the garden • Mickey tin-roofed birdhouses • pre-planted topiaries in delightful animal shapes • bug garden stakes • garden books and hats • Florida jam • sign up here for the Behind the Seeds tour, a 1-hour guided walk through the Land's greenhouses. Reservations may be made in person or ahead by calling **407-WDW-TOURS.**

Breakfast stops in Epcot

- Fountain View Espresso and Bakery for baked goods and specialty coffees.
- Sunshine Season Food Fair in the Land for pastries, fruit, and coffee.
- The Electric Umbrella for bagel breakfast sandwiches, blueberry muffins, French toast, fruit, and cereal.
- Pure and Simple in the Wonders of Life pavilion for muffins and smoothies.
- Character breakfast at Restaurant Akershus in Norway.

Future World's Behind-the-Scenes Tours

Discounts are available to Annual Pass and AAA Diamond Card holders. Call **407-WDW-TOUR** for reservations.

Undiscovered Future World—On the 4½ hour tour, visitors will learn about the vision and history of Epcot, hear in-depth information on each pavilion (even some backstage glimpses), and take a look at Cast Services plus the Epcot marina where the Illuminations show is put together. **$49 plus park admission. Mon, Tues, Fri and Sat at 9:15 A.M. Guests must be 16 years or older.**

Epcot Dive Quest—This 2½-hour program includes a 30-minute dive in the 6 million-gallon aquarium at the Living Seas. **$140 with park admission not required but also not included. Offered daily at 4:30 and 5:30 P.M. to all certified divers; those 10-14 years old must dive with a parent or guardian. Dive equipment provided.**

Epcot Seas Aqua Tour—A 2½ hour program in the backstage area of the Living Seas with a chance to explore the aquarium using a supplied air snorkel system. **Daily at 12:30 P.M.; includes gear, t-shirt, and group photo. Park admission not required but not included. Bring a bathing suit. $100.**

Dolphins in Depth—A look at dolphin behavior and training with a chance to enter the water and get up close to these astonishing creatures. The 3-hour program includes a videotape and t-shirt. Be sure to bring a bathing suit. No swimming required. **$140 plus park admission. Mon–Fri at 8:45 A.M. Guests must be 16 years or older to participate; those ages 16–17 must have a signed waiver by a parent or guardian to enter the water.**

Behind the Seeds—A one-hour, in-depth walking tour of the Land's greenhouses led by a Disney researcher. **$6 for adults and $4 for children (3–9) plus park admission. Departing several times a day from 10:30 A.M. until 4:30 P.M. Reservations may be made same day at the Green Thumb Emporium located downstairs in the Land or ahead by calling 407-WDW-TOURS.**

The Living Seas***

A pavilion dedicated to mankind's important connection to the ocean. Begin by watching an informative, short film on the formation of the seas (those who would like to skip the film should walk through the doors signed "Hydrolator" instead of into the theater). Afterward board the "hydrolator," a simulated elevator ride designed to create the illusion of descending under the sea (an illusion that doesn't even seem to fool the kids) that takes you to the aquarium at Sea Base Alpha. Don't make the mistake of hightailing it out of this informative and engaging portion of the pavilion as many do; this is where the fun begins. Examine over 2,000 sea creatures swimming among the coral reefs in the amazing 6 million-gallon saltwater aquarium, the largest man-made ocean environment in the world. Other attractions include a twice-daily fish feed, dolphin presentations, educational talks by marine biologists, and the fascinating Marine Mammal Research Center where manatees can be observed (a schedule of activities is posted on the second level). **20-minute presentation and then however long you wish to explore Sea Base Alpha.**

Tip: This is one attraction that can be absolutely fascinating when crowds are low and pretty darn unimpressive with hoards of people. Try for first thing in the morning or in late afternoon or evening.

Shopping at the Living Seas

Aquatic Gift Shop in Sea Base Alpha—Sea animals • ocean-related books and puzzles • Dive Mickey merchandise.

World Showcase

At 11 stops around the World Showcase Lagoon, visitors discover the captivating worlds of Canada, the United Kingdom, France, Morocco, Japan, the U.S., Italy, Germany, China, Norway, and Mexico. The spirit and customs of each is portrayed through authentic-looking replicas of famous landmarks and buildings, typical streets overflowing with marvelous architectural detail, shops presenting the best of the world's merchandise, world-class cuisine and wines, and captivating entertainment. Without leaving the country, or the park for that matter, view the Eiffel Tower, walk through a Japanese garden, see Venice's St. Mark's Square, or visit a Mexican *mercado*. Plan an evening here when the countries are lit with shimmering lights and the true romance of this wonderful area of the park shines through.

For children who may not enjoy this trip around the world quite as much as their parents, there are Kidcot Fun Stops where cast members supervise art and craft projects. As an added incentive, each shop in World Showcase sells a Passport Kit containing a blank passport, an "I'm a World Showcase Traveler" button, and stamps for each country. On their visit to each of the pavilions, kids will delight in having the pages of their passport stamped and personalized. And be sure to ask for the new kids' guide to Epcot, perfect for pointing out all the fun things in store for them.

Those who weary of walking can utilize the Friendship water taxis that ply the World Showcase Lagoon, conveniently located at strategic points: two on each side of Showcase Plaza, one in front of Morocco, and another in front of Germany. Though a bit slow, they will save your weary feet quite a bit of plodding around the 1.3 miles of World Showcase walkway.

Canada

The spirit of nature is overwhelming at the remarkable Canada pavilion. Standing tall and proud is the majestic Hotel du Canada, a combination of several famous chateau-style Canadian Pacific Hotels. Walk up thick stone steps past 30-foot totem poles on your way to rugged mountains, rocky gorges, a sparkling waterfall, rushing streams, and towering evergreens. There's even a small version of the famous flowering Butchart Gardens of Victoria, British Columbia.

O CANADA***

You'll be chomping at the bit to book a trip north after seeing this awe-inspiring film shot in Circle-Vision, a splendid portrayal of the Canadian people and their spectacular land. Facilitated by the wonder of 360-degree photography, you'll feel as if you're in the center of the action. Sled along the St. Lawrence River in romantic Quebec City, sail on the Bluenose along the coast of Nova Scotia, walk the cobblestone streets of Montreal, ride the Trans-Canadian railroad, soar above the majestic mountains of Banff, stroll the Butchart Gardens in Victoria, and leave with just a small sense of the grandeur of Canada. **Shows every 20 minutes.**

Shopping

La Boutique Des Provinces—Anne of Green Gables dolls and merchandise • glass and pewter objects • great find: Linda Edgington collectable ceramics.

Northwest Mercantile—Hiking footwear (which might come in handy after a few days of park trekking) • books on Canada • maple candy and syrup • souvenir totem poles • Canada sweatshirts • rugged Roots sportswear • plush Canadian Mountie bears and moose critters • coonskin hats.

Entertainment

Off Kilter—Celtic music with a rocking twist.

United Kingdom

Where else could you find such a hodgepodge of English architectural style? Quaint, thatched-roofed cottages straight out of the Cotswolds, Queen Anne–style dwellings, lofty red brick castles, even sophisticated Georgian brick townhouses, all lining the same street. Bright red phone booths sit beside a proper English park square where a cheerful garden gazebo almost insists you linger a bit and enjoy. Stroll the street and pop in a variety of shops or consider visiting the neighborhood pub for a pint at the bar.

Tip: Don't miss the hidden butterfly garden nesting behind the Tea Caddy Shop. It can be reached out the back door of the shop, via a walkway leading from the square, or from under a vine-covered archway directly off the World Showcase walkway.

Shopping

The Crown and Crest—Scottish clan staples including kilts, ties, books, and family crests • remarkable chess sets sporting Alice in Wonderland, Sherlock Holmes, Winnie the Pooh, and Robin Hood themes • Beatles merchandise.

The Magic of Wales—All things Welsh from crystal to books and CDs to Celtic jewelry, kitchen items, and tartans.

The Queen's Table—Potpourri of fragrant soaps, fragrances, and bath crystals.

Pringle's of Scotland—Wimbledon tennis clothing • Old Course St. Andrews golf attire and memorabilia.

The Tea Caddy—English tea • fine bone china teapots and cups and the biscuits to go along with it • walk out the back door and relax in the hidden butterfly garden.

The Toy Soldier—Winnie the Pooh, Bob the Builder, and Paddington Bear merchandise.

Entertainment

The British Invasion—Performing in the gazebo in Britannia Square is a faux Beatles group (one who looks remarkably like Paul) playing all the old familiar songs.

World Showcase Players—By utilizing the audience, this troop livens up a comedic skit of King Arthur and the Holy Grail.

Pam Brody—Zany pub pianist entertains and interacts with guests in the Rose and Crown Pub.

France

Fleur-de-lis topiary and Belle Époque buildings are towered over by a 74-foot replica (1/10 the size of the original) of the Eiffel Tower in the charming France pavilion. Shining copper mansard roofs and curtained casement windows top off Parisian-style buildings overlooking a cobblestone street bustling with shops and a sidewalk café. Of course you'll find world-class cuisine; what could be more French? And if you can't stroll the banks of the Seine, you can certainly walk along the banks of the lagoon where quintessential French accordion music plays while artists sketch away. Pick up a glass of wine at the waterside kiosk and enjoy.

Tip: Beauty and the Beast as well as Hunchback of Notre Dame characters can be found in the Plume et Palette Shop.

IMPRESSIONS DE FRANCE***

Captivating images of France fill the 200-degree screen in this impressive film. Image after image appear including dazzling aerial views of the Loire chalets, mouthwatering pastry shops, grape fields in harvest, the island of Mont St. Michel, the gardens of Versailles, and the spectacular French Alps, all accompanied by stirring French classical music. If you're a lover of visual beauty, don't miss this opportunity to witness the splendor of France. **Show every 30 minutes.**

Shopping

Galerie des Halles—Miniature Eiffel Towers • diminutive replicas of Notre Dame's gargoyles • French travel posters and books • scads of paraphernalia imprinted with the paintings of the French Impressionists • French berets.

Guerlain of Paris—Guerlain fragrances and cosmetics.

Aux Vins De France—French wine, champagne, cognac, and Pernod • also sold by the glass.

L'Esprit de la Provence—South of France earthenware, cookbooks, linens, lavender-scented sachets • great find: delightful hand-painted Quimper pottery.

Parasol Kiosk—Precocious young mademoiselles will delight in these frilly parasols sold lagoonside.

Plume et Palette—Impressive abundance of French perfumes and soaps • hand-painted Limoges boxes.

Entertainment

A Chair Act—Balancing duo.

World Showcase Players—Live comedy show.

Le Mime Roland—Mime comedy.

World Showcase Behind-the-Scenes Tours

Discounts available to Annual Pass and AAA Diamond Card holders. Call **407-WDW-TOUR** for reservations.

Gardens of the World Showcase—A 3-hour tour of Epcot's World Showcase gardens led by a Disney horticulturist who offers tips for your own little plot at home. **$59 plus park admission. Tues and Thurs at 9:30 A.M. Participants must be 16 years or older.**

Hidden Treasures of World Showcase—Explore the history, architecture, and culture of the World Showcase pavilions on this 3½-hour tour. **$59 plus park admission. Tues, Thurs, and Sat 10 A.M. Participants must be 16 years or older.**

Morocco

The Casbah awaits you inside the fortress-like, sandstone walls of the Morocco pavilion. The Koutoubia Minaret, a replica of the famous 12th-century prayer tower of Marrakesh, rises above the lace-like edifices dotted with keyhole windows and vibrant hand-cut mosaic tiles. A courtyard graced by four massive tangerine trees leads the way through the Bab Boujouloud gate to the *Medina*, or old city, to its *souk* where animated alleyways filled with bazaars are humming with life and exotic Arabic music.

GALLERY OF ARTS AND HISTORY**

A museum of changing exhibits features Moroccan pottery, art, costumes, weapons, and artifacts. Look up at the marvelous hand-painted ceiling, a museum in itself.

Moroccan National Tourist Office

If a trip to Morocco sounds enticing after seeing this alluring pavilion, stop here for tourist information or to sign up for one of the free 35-minute Treasures of Morocco Tours offered several times each afternoon.

Tip: Disney Characters in the form of Aladdin and Jasmine meet daily in Morocco for photos and autographs. See your guide map for times.

Shopping

The Brass Bazaar—Decorative brass • straw items • the perfect place to pick up that Aladdin's lamp you've always wanted.

Marketplace in the Medina—Multicolored straw items • leather goods.

Souk Al Magreb—Located alongside the lagoon • fez hats • drums • blouses • jewelry • purses • safari hats • straw and brass items.

Tangier Traders—Beautiful, reasonably priced vividly colored dresses, caftans, shawls, and blouses • leather footwear.

Entertainment

Mo'Rockin—Performing modernized Arabic music on a lagoonside stage are some of the most entertaining musicians in Epcot. *20-minute show.*

Best snacks in World Showcase

- Beaver tails, a flat, deep-fried pastry served with a variety of toppings sold on the walkway in Canada.
- Cheddar cheese soup sold in the winter from a stand in Canada.
- Anything from the Boulangerie Patisserie in France.
- Baklava at the Tangierine Café in Morocco.
- Khaki gori, shaved ice topped with fruit syrups found on the walkway in front of Japan.
- Red bean ice cream from the Lotus Blossom Café in China.
- Giant soft pretzels and bratwurst at Sommerfest in Germany.
- Funnel cakes at the kiosk in America.
- Italian ice or gelato in Italy.
- Sweet pretzels at the Kringla Bakeri in Norway.
- Churros from the Cantina de San Angel in Mexico.

Even More Restaurants

Have your hand stamped before embarking on the 10-minute stroll outside the International Gateway Entrance to Disney's Boardwalk and the Epcot resorts where numerous restaurants offer a wide variety of first-rate cuisine choices. On the Boardwalk you'll find Spoodles and the Flying Fish, and across the lagoon is the Yacht and Beach Club where Cape May Café, Beaches and Cream Soda Shop, and the Yachtsman Steakhouse are good choices. A bit further on are two excellent restaurants, Palios at the Swan and Shula's at the Dolphin.

Japan

Towering over the Japan pavilion is a five-tiered pagoda representing the elements from which Buddhists believe all things in the universe are produced—the elements of earth, water, fire, wind, and sky. This is only the introduction to a serene and simplistic world of gorgeous pathways meandering through an elegant landscape of manicured Japanese gardens. Arched bridges curve over crystal-clear ponds filled with lazily swimming golden koi, and soothing music plays amid the gentle tinkling of wind chimes. A replica of the great Hall of Ceremonies in the Gosho Imperial Palace of Kyoto houses an immense retail shop downstairs owned by the three-centuries-old Mitsukoshi firm of Japan. Upstairs are two restaurants and a tranquil lounge that affords a stellar view of the lagoon where a flaming red *torii* gate stands guard, authentic-looking in every aspect, even down to the clinging oysters and barnacles at its base.

BIJUTSU-KAN GALLERY**

Cross the bridge over a moat in the rear of the pavilion and enter this gallery housed in a Japanese fortress. At press time is "Diamond Warriors: Traditions and Japanese Baseball," featuring vintage uniforms, old photos, mementos, and a collection of trading cards from the 1940s.

Shopping

Mitsukoshi Department Store—Immense store brimming with everything under the Rising Sun • kimonos • fans • slippers • porcelain • tea sets • wall hangings • paper lanterns • children's toys • Japanese liquors • pearls • geisha and samurai dolls • food items • books on Japanese cooking and gardening • bonsai tree and bamboo garden kits.

Entertainment

Matsuriza—Traditional Taiko drummers delight audiences with their exotic rhythms at the base of the pagoda.

America

Smack dab in the center of the World Showcase is the red-white-and-blue America pavilion overflowing with the spirit of 1776 colonial America. Amid the sound of fife and drum sits a stately Georgian, red brick building reminiscent of Philadelphia's Independence Hall where inside a patriotic attraction lures all loyal Americans. And out on the brick streets are kiosks selling the all-American treats of funnel cakes, popcorn, ice cream, and giant turkey legs.

THE AMERICAN ADVENTURE SHOW***

A show guaranteed to make you proud to be an American. The amazing audio-animatronic figures of Benjamin Franklin and Mark Twain combine with momentous film, inspiring music, and more than 35 lifelike, talking, gesturing, and walking audio-animatronic characters to weave the impressive tale of our nation. The grand finale film montage featuring the voices and faces of well-known and loved Americans is a real tear-jerker. Some love this show while others sleep right through it. Personally, I'm one of its greatest fans. **Shows every 35 minutes.**

Tip: It's fairly easy to get a seat in this huge theater. Try to time it when the a cappella Voices of Liberty are performing inside the waiting area and just feel your patriotism shoot up a few notches.

AMERICA GARDENS THEATER

An always-changing variety of live entertainment takes place in this lagoonside, open-air amphitheater. Check your guide map for current shows during your stay. During the Christmas holidays the moving Candlelight Procession and Mass Choir performance should be tops on your list.

Shopping

Heritage Manor Gifts—Americana gifts • tax money banks in the shape of milk bottles • red-white-and-blue underwear • giant Uncle Sam hats • American and USA memorabilia.

Entertainment
America Vybe—Contemporary singing group performing 20th-century popular music.

Spirit of America Fife and Drum Corps—Experience the energy of the American Revolution when this fife and drum quartet performs in white wigs and tricorn hats marching in buckled footwear.

Voices of Liberty—Moving a cappella choir group singing early American folk and patriotic songs in the lobby of the American Adventure Show.

Italy
The romance of Venice's St. Mark's Square, reflected in replicas of the 14th-century pink-tinted Doge's Palace and its neighboring 83-foot Campanile bell tower, is a scene almost begging for surrounding canals. All that's missing are the pigeons and a frosty bellini. Atop soaring columns are the statues of the Lion of St. Mark and St. Theodore who look down on the flower-filled balconies of the terra-cotta houses almost perfect enough for Juliet and her Romeo. And out in the lagoon gondolas moored to barbershop-striped poles lie in wait for their gondoliers.

Shopping
Il Bel Cristallo—Perfume • silk scarves and ties • soft leather wallets and handbags • Guiseppe Armani figurines.

Vinoteca—Italian wine by the glass or bottle • fine chocolates • cookies.

La Bottega Italiana—Traditional Venetian masks • Milano glass • Italian cookbooks • stationery.

Entertainment
Masquerade—Masked performers dressed in Venetian costumes stroll the pavilion while silently interacting with visitors.

Imaginum-A Statue Act—Perfectly still, white-robed statues come to life in silent interaction with visitors.

Beers From Around the World

Create your own beer festival while walking from country to country in World Showcase. Featured beers include Labatts, Molson, and Moosehead in Canada • Harp, Bass, Guinness, and Tennants in the United Kingdom • Fischer La Belle in France • Casablanca in Morocco • Kirin in Japan • Samuel Adams and Budweiser in America • Peroni in Italy • Becks in Germany • Tsing Tao in China • Ringnes in Norway • Dos Equis in Mexico.

Specialty Drinks at World Showcase

French wine and champagne from a kiosk on the walkway in front of France • sake martini at Matsu No Ma Lounge in Japan • wine tasting at La Bottega Italiana in Italy • Viking coffee spiked with Bailey's Irish Cream at Kringla Bakery in Norway • margaritas at Cantina de San Angel in Mexico.

Germany

This festive and picturesque Bavarian-style village of rustic beamed balconies brimming with multicolored flower boxes, storybook gingerbread buildings, and a towering castle is a World Showcase favorite. Around the cobblestone platz are quaint shops, lederhosen-clad hosts, a glockenspiel clock tower, and toe-tapping polka music. Of course there is a mandatory Biergarten where oompah-pah bands, yodelers, and dancers entertain while colossal beer steins are passed. And just around the corner is a delightful toy-train village with a horn-tooting caboose, miniature tunnels and bridges, tiny evergreen trees, and precious Lilliputian buildings.

Shopping

Das Kaufhaus—Geise pottery • hand-painted eggs, a process dating back 2,000 years.

Der Teddybar—Lovely porcelain Engel Puppe dolls; create your own doll for $120–$130 • Steiff teddy bears • railroad toys.

Die Weihnachts Ecke—Gorgeous assortment of German-manufactured ornaments • sparkling table runners • nutcrackers.

Glas und Porzellan—Goebel-Hummel cherubic figurines • demonstrations by Goebel master painters.

Kunstarbeit In Kristall—Sparkling crystal in a variety of opulent colors • Swarovski jewelry and crystal figurines.

Schmitt Sohnew Weinkeller—German wine and beer • wine sold by the glass and bottle.

Sussigkeiten Sweets and Cookies—Flaky German cookies • Haribo Gummy Bears • milk chocolate candy bars.

Volkskunst—Cuckoo and anniversary clocks • handmade music boxes • watches • German beer steins, many of which are limited editions.

Entertainment

Octoberfest Musikanten—An Oktoberfest-style celebration of oompah-pah singing and dancing, all accompanied by traditional folk instruments. *Daily in the Biergarten Restaurant.*

China

Sparkling in the sunlight as visitors pass under the resplendent Gate of the Golden Sun is an extravagant re-creation of Beijing's Temple of Heaven. Below delicate bridges float blooming lotus in carp-filled reflecting pools, and tinkling music soothes as you stroll amid tranquil Chinese rose gardens, willow and mulberry trees, and delicate waterfalls. It's a setting of serenity and mystery not found at most stops on the World Showcase.

WONDERS OF CHINA***

"Hearing something one hundred times is not as good as seeing it once" is the so-true quotation in the waiting area for this remarkable 360-degree film presentation of China. Your host is Li Bai, an 8th-century poet, who introduces you to his marvelously diverse country with the help of Circle-Vision. Walk atop the Great Wall, enter the Forbidden City, stand in the middle of Tiananmen Square, and cruise down the mighty Yangtze River. There are stunning views of rice terraces, the bustling streets of Shanghai, and the extraordinary Terra Cotta Warriors at the Qin Shi Huang Tomb. Perhaps the most astonishing panoramas are of the misty Huangshan Mountains and the haunting landscape of Guey Ling, the subject of artists for generations. The show's only shortcoming is its propaganda-style presentation considering the country's political shortcomings and the plight of Tibetan people. Be prepared to stand throughout the presentation. **20-minute show.**

Tip: A new movie, "Reflections of China," debuts Summer 2003.

HOUSE OF WHISPERING WILLOWS**

This ever-changing gallery of ethnic art in the form of costumes and artifacts allow visitors a glimpse of China's many-faceted culture and diverse way of life.

Shopping

Yong Feng Shangdian Shopping Gallery—Every Chinese object imaginable • Suzie Wong–style dresses • jade • puppets • lanterns • rice hats • jewelry • fans • dolls • teapots • silk garments • silk paintings • rugs • furniture.

Entertainment

Dragon Legends Acrobats—Young, limber acrobats flip, contort, and perform unbelievable feats of gymnastics.

Si Xian—Chinese silk music demonstrations in the waiting area for the *Wonders of China* show. Get there a bit ahead of time if you'd like to be chosen to play along with the musicians.

Norway

Soaring over a cobblestone courtyard is a castle modeled after Akershus, Oslo's 14th-century stronghold still standing above its picturesque harbor. Below Epcot's version is a quaint mixture of structures representing a variety of Scandinavian architecture including a wooden Stave church and a variety of red-roofed rock dwellings centered around a quaint town square. Here you'll find an entertaining boat ride through Norway's history and folklore as well as a can't-resist Norwegian bakery. The sound of children's laughter can always be heard coming from the Age of the Viking Ship, a rollicking children's playground. If all this creates a desire to travel to this enchanting country, stop at the Norwegian Tourist Board for brochures and maps.

MAELSTROM***

A favorite of World Showcase visitors is this watery boat ride through both real and mythical scenes of Norway's history. In your dragon-headed longboat, drift past a 10th-century Viking village then on to a dark, mysterious forest where a hairy, three-headed troll casts a spell on your vessel causing it to drop backward down a soggy cataract. Sail past glacier-bound polar bears, narrowly miss a plunge off the edge of a waterfall, and finally drop into a stormy North Sea. Your voyage ends in a quaint village for a pleasant, short film on Norway. **Fastpass. 10 minutes including the film.**

Tip: Although it could scare small children, drops are fairly small and of no consequence on this tame ride. If you would rather not see the film, walk into the theater and then immediately out the doors on the opposite side.

STAVE CHURCH GALLERY

A re-creation of the 13th-century wooden Gol Stave Church in Hallingdal where inside an exhibit traces the history of this almost extinct form of architecture.

Entertainment

Spelmanns Gledge—Delightful Norwegian folk music quartet.

Shopping

The Puffin's Roost—Warm jackets • Dale of Norway woolen sweaters and hats (not a lot of use for these in Florida, but they're certainly attractive) • hiking shorts • all-weather gear • sweatshirts • woolen rugs • beautiful Norwegian Christmas ornaments • Laila perfume • sweets • jewelry • toys • delightful menagerie of shaggy trolls • Viking helmets with long flaxen braids • great find: troll and Viking napkin rings and corkscrews made of pewter.

Mexico

The sight of a colossal pyramid enveloped in lush jungle foliage is an immediate draw when visitors turn the bend into World Showcase from Future World. Inside is another place and time, a magical, night-lit village surrounding the Plaza de los Amigos. The air is filled with the exhilarating strain of mariachi music in this bustling, gaslit square brimming with lively shops loaded down with tempting south-of-the-border wares. The indoor, inky-blue El Rio del Tiempo (the River of Time) floats lazily beneath a rumbling volcano beside the romantic candlelit restaurant, the San Angel Inn. On your way out view the rotating art exhibit now featuring Animales Fantasticos, original folk art woodcarving from Oaxaca, Mexico.

EL RIO DEL TIEMPO**

This lighthearted boat ride down the River of Time is a journey through the history of Mexico. Float past a smoking, darkened volcano and through pre-Columbian Mexico, glimpses of alluring beach resorts and boisterously entertaining market vendors, and a village fiesta replete with simulated fireworks and visions of present-day Mexico City. **6-minute ride.**

Tip: Although this attraction is relaxing and fairly enjoyable, it lacks the typical Disney excitement. If the line is short, by all means take the ride. If it's crowded and you're short on time, skip it.

Shopping

El Ranchito del Norte—Outdoor lagoonside shopping • ponchos • blankets • sombreros • colorful papier-mache parrots • pinatas.

La Familia Fashions—Lovely silver jewelry from Taxco • brightly painted Oaxacan animal woodcarvings • leather handbags • Talavera pottery.

La Princesa de Crystal—Glassblower at work • delicate crystal figurines.

Plaza de Los Amigos—Exotic Mexican market merchandise displayed around the plaza's trickling fountain • multicolored paper flowers • straw baskets • ponchos • blankets • sombreros • pinatas • cool, white cotton dresses • hot sauce • cookbooks.

Entertainment

Mariachi Cobre—Make it a point to be around when this outstanding performance group is playing. For those not familiar with mariachi music, it is the soul of Mexico and these musicians represent it marvelously.

Places for Romance

In Future World—The butterfly garden between MouseGear and Test Track.

In World Showcase—Hidden garden behind the Tea Caddy Shop in the United Kingdom • the charming Bistro de Paris Restaurant • the candlelit San Angel Inn Restaurant in Mexico • an Illuminations cruise • the Butchart-style gardens in Canada • garden on the canal side of France • benches overlooking the carp-filled reflecting pool in China.

Dining in Epcot

Innoventions Dining

Electric Umbrella—Futuristic eastside eatery • breakfast: breakfast bagel sandwiches, French toast sticks, breakfast burrito (flour tortilla filled with eggs, sausage, onions, and cheese), fruit, cereal, sausage, bacon • lunch and dinner: burgers, bacon and provolone–topped grilled chicken sandwich, pizza, chicken strips, hot dogs, veggie burger, chicken Caesar salad • chocolate cream pie, Toll House cookies, apple pie • children's menu: hot dog, chicken strips.

Fountainview Espresso and Bakery—Coffee and pastry shop with great views of the Fountain of Nations • chocolate croissants, pastries, muffins, bagels, chocolate mousse, creme brulee, coconut flan, Boston creme pie, Black Forest cake, Snicker's cheesecake, sugar-free cheesecake • juice, smoothies, specialty coffees (add liqueur if you wish), cordials.

Wonders of Life Dining

Pure and Simple—Counter-service restaurant dedicated to healthy food (never mind the hot dogs) • foot-long hot dogs with cheese and chili, turkey wrap, beef and bean chili, Greek salad, seasonal soup • nonfat yogurt shakes and floats, sugar-free brownies and mousse, delicious fruit smoothies, chocolate chip and blueberry muffins.

The Land Dining

Sunshine Season Food Fair—Dine below whimsical hot air balloons beside the bubbling, overflowing fountain at the food court in the Land. A variety of options sold from several counters helps to solve the problem of diverse appetites.

Bakery—Dark chocolate cake • giant cookies • cheesecake • brownies • muffins • cupcakes • key lime pie • fresh fruit cups • yogurt • cappuccino.

Barbecue—Barbecue pork and chicken sandwiches, barbecue chicken and ribs, chicken strips • apple cobbler, giant Toll House cookies • children's menu: corn dog.

Ice cream—Ice cream bars • frozen yogurt • hand-dipped ice cream • sundaes • floats • specialty coffees.

Pasta and Potato—Vegetable lasagna, linguini marinara, linguini with meatballs, chicken Parmesan, baked potatoes smothered in fajita chicken or cheese and bacon • Toll House cookies • children's menu: Mick-e-roni 'n' cheese, spaghetti marinara.

Soup, Salad, and Sandwich—Vegetable wrap, Italian sub, tuna salad, turkey and Gouda • green salad, chicken Caesar salad • seasonal soup • giant Toll House cookie, brownie, giant sugar cookie • children's menu: PB&J sandwich.

The Garden Grill—Dine with Farmer Mickey and Friends on homestyle cooking • rotate through views of the ecosystems found in the Living with the Land attraction • full review on page 331.

The Living Seas Dining

Coral Reef—Lunch and dinner • dine on delicious seafood in front of the Living Sea's massive aquarium • full review on page 330.

Showcase Plaza Dining

Refreshment Port—McDonald's french fries • Chicken McNuggets • McFlurry's in Nestle Crunch, Butterfinger, and Hi-C orange flavors.

Canada Dining

Beaver Tails—One of the most popular snacks in the World Showcase • flat beaver tail–shaped deep-fried pastries served with toppings • in cooler months, fantastic Canadian cheese soup from Le Cellier.

Le Cellier—Lunch and dinner • steakhouse in a cellar setting • full review on page 334.

United Kingdom Dining

Rose and Crown Pub and Dining Room—Lunch and dinner • traditional pub fare served with pints of lager • full review on page 337.

Harry Ramsden Fish and Chips—Typical Fish and Chips stand • super seating area on the World Showcase Lagoon • Bass Ale, Guinness, cider, sodas • shortbread • children's menu: hot dog.

France Dining

Bistro de Paris—Dinner only • 2nd-floor dining room offering gourmet French food in an upscale atmosphere • beautiful views of the World Showcase lagoon • full review on page 332.

Boulangerie Patisserie—Eye-popping French bakery • limited seating available both inside in the adjoining gift shop or outside in the charming alleyway • croissants, baguettes, cookies, meringues, eclairs, napoleons, coconut pyramids, cheesecake, tarts • cheese plates, ham and cheese croissants, quiche • cappuccino, soda, French wine and beer, juice.

Chefs de France—Lunch and dinner • lively French bistro • full review on page 333.

Crepes des Chefs de France—Lagoonside crepe kiosk • chocolate, strawberry marmalade, and orange marmalade crepes • ice cream • Fischer La Belle French beer, espresso, cappuccino, sodas.

Les Vins des Chefs de France—Kiosk serving French wine and champagne by the glass.

Morocco Dining

Restaurant Marrakesh—Lunch and dinner • exotic Moroccan cuisine • picture-perfect surroundings with bellydancer entertainment • full review on page 337.

Tangierine Café—Exotic, counter-service café • eat inside or during pleasant months outside on the tree-shaded verandah • shwarma sandwiches and platters (marinated, rotisserie-roasted sliced chicken and lamb), rotisserie chicken, roast leg of lamb, Mediterranean wraps of seafood, chicken, or tabbouleh (a south Mediterranean salad), vegetarian plate (couscous, hummus, and tabbouleh) • freshly baked Moroccan pastries • Turkish coffees, Moroccan wine, Casablanca beer, Moroccan mint tea, mimosas made with champagne and orange juice • children's menu: hamburger, pizza.

Japan Dining

Tempura Kiku—Lunch and dinner • eat batter-fried delicacies in this cozy, counter dining spot • full review on page 339.

Teppanyaki—Lunch and dinner • dine around a teppan grill with your very own chef chopping, slicing, and dicing with lightning-quick speed, preparing your meal before your very eyes • full review on page 339.

Yakitori House—Fast-food restaurant with a definite twist • dine inside in a soothing atmosphere of screen doors, kimono-clad servers, and Japanese simplicity or outdoors on the serene patio surrounded by bamboo trees, paper lanterns, and a soothing waterfall • beef curry, kushi-yaki (broiled skewers of chicken, beef, and lamb with teriyaki sauce), shrimp tempura udon or beef udon (a clear soup served over noodles), yakitori (broiled skewers of chicken and rice with teriyaki sauce), seafood salad, sushi • ginger tofu pudding, ginger, green tea, or red bean ice cream • Kirin beer, plum wine, sake • children's menu: fried chicken with vegetables, rice, and teriyaki sauce or chicken and beef teriyaki.

America Dining

The All-American Funnel Cakes—Quintessential American treat.

Liberty Inn—Tribute to all-American food (or at least what the rest of the world thinks of it) • hamburgers, hot dogs, chicken strips, vegetarian burger, turkey club sandwich, grilled chicken sandwich with bacon and provolone, chicken Caesar salad • apple pie, Toll House cookies • Budweiser and Samuel Adams beer • children's menu: hot dog, chicken nuggets.

Italy Dining

L'Originale Alfredo di Roma Ristorante—Lunch and dinner • elegant Italian restaurant • signature dish: fettuccine Alfredo • full review on page 334.

Pasticceria Italia—Kiosk offering scrumptious Italian pastries and desserts • chocolate mousse, Italian cheesecake, biscotti, toscani, cannoli, tiramisu • cappuccino, hot chocolate, espresso, caffe lattes, Peroni beer, Italian wine, granitas.

Germany Dining

Biergarten—Lunch and dinner • Oktoberfest-style German biergarten featuring buffet fare and live entertainment • full review on page 332.

Bier Stand—Beck's beer • cordials • giant soft pretzels.

Sommerfest—Located in the rear of the German pavilion • festive counter-service spot with both indoor and outdoor seating • chicken schnitzel, bratwurst and frankfurters with sauerkraut, smoked ham sandwiches, soup, soft pretzels • Black Forest cake, apple strudel • Liebfraumilch wine, Beck's beer.

China Dining

Lotus Blossom Café—Counter-service, pagoda-style eatery • open-air covered tables • Shanghai grilled chicken, sweet and sour chicken, twice-cooked beef, scallion-flavored vegetarian noodles, cold sesame noodle and marinated vegetable salad, egg rolls, pork fried rice, hot and sour soup • almond and fortune cookies, ginger and red bean ice cream • smoothies, Chinese wine and beer • children's menu: sweet and sour chicken, egg roll and fried rice.

Nine Dragons—Lunch and dinner • cuisine from five Chinese provinces are featured in this elegant World Showcase restaurant • full review on page 335.

Norway Dining

Restaurant Akershus—Breakfast, lunch, and dinner • Norwegian buffet in a medieval castle setting • Disney Princesses character breakfast • full review on page 336.

Kringla Bakeri og Kafe—Wonderful Scandinavian bakery • fantastic sweet pretzels topped with cream icing and slivered almonds • waffles topped with strawberry preserves, Lefse (traditional potato bread with butter and cinnamon sugar), cinnamon rolls, rice cream, berry tarts, sugar-free chocolate mousse, Viking helmet cookies • light open-faced sandwiches of smoked ham and cheese, smoked turkey breast, or smoked salmon and scrambled eggs • sodas, Viking coffee (with the option of a shot of Bailey's Irish Cream), wine, Ringnes beer.

Mexico Dining

Cantina de San Angel—Lagoonside fast food perfect for sipping margaritas or ice-cold Dos Equis beer • food offerings are not up to the same standards as Mexico's full-service restaurant, the San Angel Inn • tacos al carbon filled with grilled chicken, onions, and peppers, ensalada Mexicana with grilled chicken or beef, wet burrito (black beans, beef, lettuce, tomatoes, cheese, sour cream, and adobo sauce wrapped in a soft flour tortilla), combination plate (taco, burrito, and a quesadilla), nachos • churros, flan • child's plate: beef burrito, tortilla chips, churro.

Tip: Come early (and I mean early) for dinner or a drink and save a table for a seated viewpoint of Illuminations. The umbrellas tend to block the view of the higher fireworks so try for a spot on the edge of the lagoon.

San Angel Inn—Lunch and dinner • unquestionably Epcot's most romantic restaurant • spicy, traditional Mexican dishes in a candlelit riverside setting • full review on page 338.

Lounges

Matsu No Ma Lounge—2nd-story Japanese lounge with stellar view of World Showcase Lagoon and Spaceship Earth • kimono-clad waitresses • good place to watch Illuminations, not a perfect view, but a darn good one • pristine sushi, sashimi, and crispy tempura • exotic alcoholic and nonalcoholic drinks, sake, sake martinis, plum wine, Kirin beer.

Rose and Crown Pub—Cozy up to the bar for a Black and Tan at this authentic-looking English pub • one of Epcot's most popular spots in the evening hours, always jammed-packed with revelers • ales, lager, and stout by the pint or half yard in your choice of Bass, Caffrey's, Harp, Tennents, and Guinness • bar menu: fish and chips, sandwiches, fruit and cheese plate.

Sommerfest—Outdoor Biergarten-style bar • Liebfraumilch wine, Beck's beer • light meals.

Special Entertainment
ILLUMINATIONS 2000: REFLECTIONS OF EARTH****

Each evening at closing time, crowds begin to gather around the World Showcase Lagoon to witness Walt Disney World's most spectacular nighttime extravaganza. The story of the planet Earth is told in a combination of unbelievable pyrotechnic displays, amazing lasers, stirring music, and fanciful water movement. Each show takes 480 man-hours to perform and it's worth every penny. **13-minute show.**

Tip: To avoid smoke from the fireworks, check which direction the flames in the torches are pointed and avoid that side of the lagoon. Illuminations is never cancelled, even during inclement weather.

Best places from which to view Illuminations

Staking out a good spot for viewing Illuminations seems to be an obsession with some, meaning the nonobsessed will have to be content to watch the show from behind someone else's head. If a prime spot is important to you, find a place at least 30 minutes prior to show time in slow season and up to an hour in busier times. If you'd like to snag a table at one of the seated areas below you'll certainly need to think ahead. Here are my suggestions for the best views:

- An outdoor lagoon-facing table at the Rose and Crown Pub (make priority seating 1 hour prior to show time and request a lagoonside table).
- Cantina de San Angel in Mexico (find a lagoonside table or the fireworks will be partially obstructed by the table umbrellas).
- Deck outside the Matsu No Ma Lounge in Japan (not the best view but a decent, quiet one).
- From an Illuminations Cruise boat (see page 300 for details).
- Bridge between United Kingdom and France (great view, but one of the most popular spots).
- Promenade in front of Canada.
- Between Mexico and Norway.
- In front of Italy by the gondola dock (this area is sometimes reserved for private parties).
- Between Germany and China.

Special Events

Epcot Flower and Garden Festival—Six weeks each spring, Epcot is covered in more than 30 million blooms with over 100 extravagant topiaries, a rose walkway, a floating wonderland in East Lake, and an array of amazing gardens throughout World Showcase. Special appearances by nationally recognized gardeners and how-to presentations by Disney horticulturists as well as daily demonstrations, kid-friendly activities, and a nightly Flower Power concert series add to the festivities. Entrance included in the price of admission.

Epcot Summer Series—Top-notch entertainment at the America Gardens Theater for 10 weeks in the summer featuring in past years such names as Riverdance and the 56-member troupe "Blast." Entrance included in the price of admission.

International Food and Wine Festival—This month-long festival taking place each fall is the most heavily visited food festival in the world. Booths representing the cuisine of over 30 countries line the World Showcase walkway, each one selling small samples of food, wine, and beer. Events include daily cooking demonstrations presented by some of the countries' top chefs, a Junior Chef program, and wine tasting seminars. Entrance is included in the price of admission.

Special themed dinners are sold out months in advance including the Signature Dinner Series offering five delicious courses, each with a different wine, and Reserve Themed Dinners hosted by Disney chefs, a six-course affair accompanied by reserve wines (jackets requested for men). Call **407-WDW-DINE** for reservations.

Holidays Around the World—Christmas is a special time at Epcot with loads of decorations and international celebrations in many of the World Showcase pavilions. There is a nightly tree-lighting ceremony and a dazzling "Canopy of Lights" between Future World and World Showcase.

The Candlelight Processional, a nightly event staged from late Nov until the end of Dec at the America Gardens Theater, features a celebrity narrator, a 45-voice choir, and a 50-piece orchestra working together to retell the story of Christmas. Entrance is included in the price of admission. To insure seats to this performance, book a Candlelight Processional Dinner Package that includes free parking, dinner at one of several World Showcase restaurants, and a guaranteed seat to the show. For reservations call **407-WDW-DINE.**

DISNEY–MGM STUDIOS

"Welcome to the glamour and glitz of show business." Although Disney's version of the great movie era of the 1930s and 1940s is certainly a rose-colored one, its entertainment value can't be beat. On the boulevards of Hollywood and Sunset, legendary Los Angeles buildings, re-created in romanticized and appealing art-deco forms, literally scream excitement. It's as if the whole park is on the brink of breaking into a zany show at any minute.

The park is actually a working film and television studio with three production soundstages, an animation studio, and an extensive Backlot. Visitors are allowed a sample of the mystery at the Magic of Disney Animation and the Backlot Tour attraction where they are invited to watch the artistic and technical processes involved in the creation of movies, television, and animated films.

This is a small park, one that can be seen in a full day. Since many of the shows are scheduled, check your guide map on arrival for show times and plan your day accordingly.

Park Basics

Getting There

Those driving to WDW should take Exit 64 off I-4 and follow the signs to Disney–MGM Studios.

Using WDW Transportation

From the Yacht and Beach Club, the Boardwalk Inn and Villas, the Beach Club Villas, and the Walt Disney World Swan and Dolphin—Take the boat or walk the 20-minute path located behind the Boardwalk Inn.

From all other Disney resorts, Epcot, and the Animal Kingdom—Board bus marked Disney–MGM Studios.

From the Magic Kingdom—Take the monorail to the Ticket and Transportation Center (TTC) then board bus marked Disney–MGM Studios.

Parking

Cost is $7 per day; free to Walt Disney Resort guests and Annual Pass holders. Keep your receipt; fee also good for parking at Epcot, Magic Kingdom, and Animal Kingdom on that day only.

Parking is conveniently located in front of the park. Trams circulate throughout the parking area for easy transportation to the entry gate. Make a note of what aisle and section you've parked in. If you're lucky, the *Toy Story* toy soldiers will be in the lot to direct you; they are a show in themselves.

Hours

Open 9 A.M. until an hour or so after dark. Call **407-824-4321** or log on to **www.disneyworld.com** for updated park hours.

Hollywood Boulevard is usually open a half hour prior to official opening time. Arrive at least 30 minutes early, allowing time to park, buy tickets, purchase a snack or cup of coffee, and be one of the first to hit the big attractions. I recommend heading straight to Tower of Terror or Rock 'n' Roller Coaster.

Fastpass Attractions

See page 133-134 for Fastpass details • Rock 'n' Roller Coaster • Star Tours • Indiana Jones Epic Stunt Spectacular • Tower of Terror • Who Wants to Be a Millionaire—Play It! • Voyage of the Little Mermaid.

Park Services

ATM machines—Two ATM machines are located at the park: just outside the entrance and inside the Toy Story Pizza Planet Arcade.

Baby care center—At the Guest Relations Center is an infant facility outfitted with changing tables, highchairs, a companion restroom, and chairs for nursing mothers. Formula, baby food, suntan lotion, diapers, milk, and over-the-counter children's medications may be purchased. All restrooms throughout the park are outfitted with changing tables.

Cameras and film processing—Stop at the Darkroom located on Hollywood Boulevard for cameras, film, camcorder tapes, and batteries. Two-hour film processing is available here and anywhere else the Photo Express sign is displayed.

First aid—For minor medical problems head to the First Aid Center located next to Guest Relations.

Guest relations—Located just inside the park on the left is Guest Relations where a knowledgeable staff is ready to assist you with ticket upgrades, priority seating, messages for separated parties, information for guests with disabilities, taped narration for visitors with sight impairment, assisted listening devices, foreign currency exchange, VIP tour information, behind-the-scenes programs, and resort reservations.

Guests with disabilities—A guidebook for guests with disabilities is available at Guest Relations (see The Basics on page 22 for more information). Guests with mobility disabilities should park adjacent to the Entrance Complex (ask at the Auto Plaza for directions). Wheelchairs and ECVs are available for rent. Most restaurants and shops at Disney–MGM Studios are accessible to guests with disabilities although some counter-service locations have narrow queues with railings (ask a host or hostess for assistance). Companion assisted restrooms are located at First Aid and four other locations.

Most attractions provide access through the main queue while others have auxiliary entrances for wheelchairs and service animals along with up to five members of your party. Certain attractions require guests to transfer from their wheelchair to a ride system. Braille guidebooks, assistive listening devices, video captioning, and audiotape guides are available at Guest Relations for a $25 refundable deposit. Many theater-type attractions have reflective or video captioning. And with a 7-day notice a sign language interpreter will be provided at live shows on Sundays and Wednesdays. Call **407-824-4321** with any questions.

Lockers—Lockers are located at **Oscar's Service Station** on the right as you enter the park and are available for $7 per day including a $2 refundable key deposit. If you're park-hopping, keep your receipt for another locker at no additional charge at the three other Disney theme parks.

Lost and found—Located next to Oscar's Gas Station just before leaving the park or call **407-824-4245**.

Lost children—Locate lost children at Guest Relations.

Package pickup—Purchases may be sent via Package Pickup to Oscar's Gas Station near the entrance for pickup at the end of the day. Allow 3 hours for delivery. Disney resort guests may send their packages directly to their hotel for next-day arrival.

Pet kennel—A kennel is located just outside the park entrance. Daily rate is $6. For information call **407-824-6568**. Proof of vaccination is required.

Readmission—If you plan to leave Disney Studios and reenter the same day, be sure to retain your ticket and have your hand stamped before departing.

Strollers and wheelchairs—Rentals are located at Oscar's Service Station on the right as you enter the park. Single strollers are $8 per day, doubles $15, wheelchairs $8, and ECV's $40 per day including a $10 refundable deposit. Replacements are available at the Writer's Stop. If you are park-hopping, keep your receipt for a replacement at the other three Disney theme parks.

The Lay of the Land

Disney–MGM Studio's main street, Hollywood Boulevard, leads directly to the main plaza, where you'll find a 122-foot Sorcerer Mickey hat, the park's focal point. If you are facing the hat from Hollywood Boulevard, to the right are two walkways: one branching to Sunset Boulevard and the other to Animation Courtyard. On the left is the Echo Lake area of the park that leads to the New York Street section. Mickey Avenue, the park's working area, sits behind the Chinese theater and may be accessed via Animation Courtyard or New York Street. A bit more confusing than the Magic Kingdom, but fairly easy to maneuver.

Disney - MGM Studios

Washington Square

New York Street

Mickey Avenue

Animation Courtyard

7

8

9

10

11

6

1

5

Commissary Lane

2

15

4

12

3

13

Sunset Boulevard

16

Hollywood Boulevard

14

17

Entrance

1. The Great Movie Ride
2. Sounds Dangerous – Starring Drew Carey
3. Indiana Jones™ Epic Stunt Spectacular
4. Star Tours
5. Jim Henson's Muppet ★ Vision 3-D
6. Honey, I Shrunk the Kids Movie Set Adventure

7. The Disney – MGM Studios Backlot Tour
8. Who Wants to Be a Millioinaire – Play It!
9. Walt Disney: One Man's Dream
10. Voyage of The Little Mermaid
11. The Magic of Disney Animation
12. Playhouse Disney – Live on Stage!

13. Guest Information Board at Hollywood Junction
14. Beauty and the Beast – Live on Stage
15. Rock'n'Roller Coaster Starring Aerosmith
16. The Twilight Zone Tower of Terror
17. Fantasmic!

Breakfast Choices at the Studios

- The Coffee Cart at Entrance Plaza for fresh pastries, coffee, and espresso.
- Starring Rolls Bakery at the corner of Hollywood and Sunset Boulevard.
- Anaheim Produce for fresh fruit and coffee.
- ABC Commissary for scrambled eggs, French toast, and pancakes.

Suggested 1-day itinerary for touring Disney–MGM Studios

Arrive 30 minutes before park opening. Since this park offers scheduled live shows, you'll need to work in the Indiana Jones Epic Stunt Spectacular, Beauty and the Beast, and Who Wants to Be a Millionnaire—Play It! when your schedule allows during the course of the day. If you're traveling with toddlers you will certainly need to find time to see Playhouse Disney. Hopefully you've already made your priority seating arrangements for the Fantasmic Dinner Package (see pages 321-322 for full details) when you first arrived at your resort. If not, do so first thing at the corner of Hollywood and Sunset boulevards.

- Thrill junkies should immediately head down Sunset Boulevard to the Tower of Terror and Rock 'n' Roller Coaster.
- If touring with young children or if thrill rides aren't your cup of tea, skip the scary rides and see the Voyage of the Little Mermaid then head to the Great Movie Ride. Afterward take the Magic of Disney Animation tour.
- By now it should by around 1:30 and time for a snack or light lunch. Good choices are the Sunset Ranch Market or the ABC Commissary. Priority seating for the Fantasmic Dinner Package can be startlingly early (sometimes as early as 4 P.M.) so you won't want to stuff yourselves with a big lunch.
- Take the Backlot Tour and then head over to MuppetVision 3-D.

- Before the afternoon parade pick up a Fastpass for Who Wants to Be a Millionaire—Play It! and then stake out a place for the Stars and Motorcars afternoon parade.
- Swing over to Who Wants to Be a Millionaire—Play It!
- By now it is time for your priority Fantasmic Dinner Package reservations and if you are smart you will make them for the Hollywood Brown Derby.
- After dinner there should be plenty of time to ride Star Tours and see Sounds Dangerous before heading over to Fantasmic 30 minutes before show time.

Disney–MGM Studios don't-miss attractions

- Tower of Terror
- Rock 'n' Roller Coaster
- Indiana Jones Epic Stunt Spectacular
- Jim Henson's MuppetVision 3-D
- Backlot Tour
- Who Wants to Be a Millionaire—Play It!
- The Magic of Disney Animation
- Star Tours
- Fantasmic

Disney–MGM Studios best dining bets

- Hollywood Brown Derby
- 50s Prime Time Café
- Sci-Fi Dine-In Theater (for the atmosphere)

Hollywood Boulevard

Hollywood Boulevard sets the mood of the park, just as Main Street does in the Magic Kingdom, with a backward step in time to Tinseltown in its glory days. The strains of old movie tunes fill the air as you make your way down the palm-lined avenue of pastel art-deco–style buildings. Look for nutty "streetmosphere" characters (actually actors) arrayed in 1930s and 1940s attire, hilariously interacting with visitors. And at the end of all this is the park's newest icon, a sparkling, 12-story sorcerer Mickey hat.

THE GREAT MOVIE RIDE***

Journey through the magical world of the movies inside a replica of Hollywood's Grauman's Chinese Theater. Board your tram for a trip through audio-animatronic re-creations of classic movie scenes featuring such musical greats as Gene Kelly under his New York street lamppost in the scene from *Singin' in the Rain* and Mary Poppins singing "Chim-Chim-Cher-ee" with Bert on the rooftops of London. Meet head-on with the slimy creature from *Alien* and see the farewell scene in *Casablanca*. Witness the ancient burial chamber from *Raiders of the Lost Ark* and catch a jolly glimpse of Munchkinland from *The Wizard of Oz*. Your final stop is a film collage of memorable moments from movie history, a trip so nostalgic you'll want to do it all over again. **22-minute ride.**

Tip: The creature from Alien *may startle young children. Out front throughout the day characters often congregate for autographs and pictures.*

Shopping on Hollywood Boulevard

Celebrity 5 and 10—Personalized souvenirs • key rings • hats • robes • honorary Oscars • towels • sweatshirts.

Crossroads of the World—A revolving Mickey tops this souvenir kiosk and information booth set smack in the middle of Entrance Plaza • candy • name pins • film • autograph books.

The Darkroom—Film • camcorder tapes • cameras • batteries • disposable cameras • photo books • frames • 2-hour photo processing • photos taken by a park photographer are picked up here.

Keystone Clothiers—Men and women's apparel store • unusual variety of Disney logo clothing • sleepwear • luggage • designer sunglasses • watches • backpacks • socks • golf accessories • jackets • dress shirts • ties.

L.A. Cinema Storage—Menagerie of stuffed animals • Disney toys • darling children and infant's apparel.

Mickey's of Hollywood—Disney Studio's small version of the Magic Kingdom's Emporium • every Disney-related souvenir under the sun.

Movieland Memorabilia—Disney Studios t-shirts • plush toys • film • sunglasses.

Oscar's Classic Car Souvenirs—Film • baby products • sundries.

Sid Cahuenga's One-of-a-Kind—Dream of a store for movie star fans • variety of collectibles • original movie posters (both classic and modern) • star-signed photographs (some as high as $1,900) • animated cells.

Sorcerer Hat Shop—Found underneath Mickey's giant sorcerer hat at the end of Hollywood Boulevard • Sorcerer Mickey merchandise • trading pins.

Sunset Boulevard

Hollywood Boulevard intersects with Sunset where the fun continues. Stop here for a look at the Tip Board offering up-to-the-minute wait times for all attractions. Make your priority seating for any of the park's full-service restaurants at the Guest Relations booth at this corner before embarking down the palm-filled street lined with sleek 1940s cars, a farmer's market–style eatery, and art-deco movie facades. Vintage luggage sits at the bus stop, and nostalgic WWII tunes blare over the loudspeaker. Lying in wait at the far end of the street is the imminent and looming Tower of Terror.

BEAUTY AND THE BEAST LIVE ON STAGE***

In the 1,500 seat Theater of the Stars, a covered amphitheater reminiscent of the Hollywood Bowl, the animated characters from Disney's Beauty and the Beast come alive. It's an impressive production complete with extravagant costuming and sets, delightful song and dance numbers, and, of course, the lovely Belle, muscled, handsome Gaston, and the Beast. Favorite songs include "Be Our Guest," "Something There," and the show's theme song "Beauty and the Beast." Belle and the Beast's fairytale ending is followed by the release of a flock of doves, a finale sure to soften the heart of even the most hard-hearted. **30 minutes.**

Tip: Check your guide map for show times and plan accordingly for this popular attraction. Arrive early to assure yourself a seat and enjoy the entertaining preshow. Seating begins 30 minutes prior to show time.

ROCK ' N' ROLLER COASTER****

You've nabbed a special invitation to an Aerosmith concert, but it's clear across town and you're late! Disney's wildest roller coaster ride takes place seated inside a 24-passenger "stretch limo" speeding down a Los Angeles freeway amid blasting Aerosmith music. Zooming past, through, and around neon Hollywood landmarks you'll loop and corkscrew in the dark. And that's after you have accelerated to a speed of 60 mph in just under 3 seconds. Hold on to your hat (or anything else you might treasure) because this is pure Disney fun. **Fastpass. 10-minute ride. Minimum height 48 inches. Not recommended for expectant mothers, those with back, heart, or neck problems, or those prone to motion sickness.**

Tip: Move straight to this attraction when the park opens; you'll find it's one popular ride and certainly the biggest thrill at any Disney theme park. Then immediately go to the next-door Tower of Terror. If you'd like to sit in the front seat, just ask, but be prepared for a wait since every other daredevil in the park has the same idea. A note to the chicken-hearted: Although there are three inversions on the ride, you won't encounter any steep drops.

THE TWILIGHT ZONE TOWER OF TERROR****

On this free-falling adventure, you'll certainly feel you've entered the Twilight Zone or at the very least a brand new dimension of fright. The waiting line snakes through the crumbling grounds of the deserted, 13-story Hollywood Tower Hotel with its rusty grillwork, dry cracking fountains, and overgrown and unkempt foliage before proceeding through the spooky, abandoned lobby of dusty concierge desks, forgotten luggage, and dead flower arrangements. Step into the gloomy hotel library for a message from Rod Serling (on a black-and-white television, of course) who relays the tale of a stormy night in 1939 when an elevator filled with people was struck by lightning and disappeared. A bellhop then invites you into the boiler room where an old, rusty service elevator awaits you. It ascends and moves horizontally through several remarkable special effects and then, in the pitch black without warning, plummets 13 stories to the bottom. Up you go again, and down, and up, and down, between which you'll have dazzling views of the park. If you can stand the thrill don't miss this one—just don't try it on a full stomach. **Fastpass. 10-minute ride. Minimum height 40 inches. Not recommended for expectant mothers, those with back, heart, or neck problems, or those prone to motion sickness.**

Tip: If you chicken out, an escape route is located immediately before entering the elevator; just ask a bellhop to show you the way out.

Shopping on Sunset Boulevard

The Beverly Sunset—Sorcerer Mickey and Disney villain merchandise, costumes, posters • homemade fudge, chocolates, caramel apples, chocolate pretzels, cotton candy, Rice Crispies treats, granita frozen drinks.

Legends of Hollywood—Winnie the Pooh clothing, accessories, and toys.

Mouse About Town—Sports-oriented shop for men • Disney golfing accessories and clothing • ESPN merchandise • sunglasses • Disney jerseys.

Once Upon a Time—Disney kitchen and bath products • character aprons and towels • Pooh and Tigger dinnerware and cookie jars • Disney cookbooks • Mickey-fied soaps, candles, soap dispensers, toothbrush holders, and teakettles.

Pin Station—Disney collectible pins sold from a vintage gold Cadillac.

Planet Hollywood Super Store—Planet Hollywood's flashy logo merchandise.

Rock Around the Shop—Aerosmith memorabilia • Rock 'n' Roller Coaster stock.

Sunset Club Couture—Disney watches, jewelry, figurines, and clocks.

Sunset Ranch Souvenirs and Gifts—Open-air shop selling hats, backpacks, and souvenirs.

Tower Hotel Gifts—Tower of Terror gift shop • *I Survived the Hollywood Tower of Terror* t-shirts • Hollywood Tower Hotel logo items • horror books.

Echo Lake

The attractions at Echo Lake nestle around a small lagoon encircled with art-deco restaurants, fast-food stands, and Gertie the Dinosaur in the guise of an ice cream stand. Here you'll find the park's most popular live show, the Indiana Jones Epic Stunt Spectacular, as well as Star Tours and Drew Carey's Sounds Dangerous.

INDIANA JONES EPIC STUNT SPECTACULAR***

Enter this open-air, covered theater through thickets of bamboo and rooftops of camouflage netting. Inside is a breathtaking stunt show allowing the audience to observe the choreography of safely performed stunts and special effects—maybe even co-star. See Indiana flee a 12-foot rolling ball and a Cairo street scene in which audience volunteers play along with the professionals performing a variety of flips, drops, bullwhipping, and fist fighting. The grand finale finds Indiana making a dangerous escape through a wall of flames, a barrage of gunfire, a large dousing of water, and one very massive explosion; prepare to feel the heat. **Fastpass. 30-minute show; see your guide map for times.**

Tip: Sit lower in the audience and act very enthusiastic if you'd like a chance to participate in the program (adults only). Sit higher up if you want to be the first one out.

SOUNDS DANGEROUS**

The wonder of sound is explored in this entertaining, often underappreciated attraction. In a theater-style room, the audience dons dual audio personal headsets and follows the bumbling detective Drew in his attempt to solve a smuggling case. While trying to ensnare a bad guy, Drew, in his panic, puts his tiny tie tack camera in his mouth causing it to short circuit. Whoops! No more video, only audio. As the show continues in amazing 3-D sound, Drew keeps up his detective work while the audience squirms in the darkened theater to a variety of bizarre and unnerving sounds. **12-minute show.**

Tip: Be aware that most of the show is in a pitch-dark theater, a scenario that could be too much for small children.

STAR TOURS***

During your wait at the Transport Station, the boarding point for R2-D2 and C-3PO's intergalactic travel service, you learn that a pilot shortage has forced the company to use inexperienced trainee droids for the short shuttle service to the Moon of Endor. Nevertheless, boarding continues on the 40-passenger StarSpeeder, a flight simulator with a movie screen and pitching, jerking, and lunging seats. Buckle up and get ready for complete bedlam while hurling through space at light speed encountering death-defying plunges and interspace fighter pilots laser-blasting away with you smack dab in the middle of it. Come to a screeching halt when your incompetent aviator crookedly lands the space-craft and brings you safely back and on to the next thrilling attraction. **Fastpass. 10-minute ride. Minimum height 40 inches. Not recommended for expectant mothers, those with back or neck problems, or those prone to motion sickness.**

Tip: Consider riding this one on an empty stomach. Avoid arriving just after the Indiana Jones attraction next door lets out when long lines form.

Shopping in Echo Lake

Golden Age Souvenirs—Souvenirs • film • sunglasses • hats • t-shirts.

Indiana Jones Adventure Outpost—Hidden behind the Indiana Jones show • adventurer's staples • Mickey-eared safari hats • Indiana Jones logo t-shirts, vests, and hats • R. L. Stine books • rugged leather jackets • khaki shorts • essential rubber snakes.

Tatooine Traders—Star Tours memorabilia and collectibles t-shirts • action figures • Jedi gear • sabers • plush Ewok toys • Lego sets • Star Wars books and games • Darth Vader masks.

New York Street

Visitors love the New York Street's faux backdrop of skyscrapers, brownstone stoops, broken fire hydrants, and—what else, but traffic noise. It's like a day in the Big Apple. Take your picture under a *Singin' in the Rain* umbrella and don't miss the whimsical fountain in front of MuppetVision with Miss Piggy dressed as the Statue of Liberty twirling and spewing water above lesser Muppets at her feet.

HONEY, I SHRUNK THE KIDS MOVIE SET ADVENTURE**

In an oversized, backyard playground setting from *Honey, I Shrunk the Kids*, 30-foot blades of grass loom over a creative romping ground for kids. The sound of giant buzzing insects add to the fun and frolicking amid massive squishy Fruit Loops, giant Lego blocks, ant tunnels, net crawls, an immense film canister utilizing a dangling film strip for sliding, and a colossal leaking garden hose.

Tip: In busy season arriving early or during the parade allows your children to play without the throngs that invariably appear later in the day.

JIM HENSON'S MUPPETVISION 3-D***

Another hoot of a 3-D movie and then some! Put on your special glasses and sit back to watch your host Kermit and the bumbling, fumbling Muppets. Miss Piggy's production number, accompanied by a barrage of flying cream pies, fiber-optic fireworks, blasting cannons, floating bubbles, and squirting water, is simply a hoot. The grand finale winds up to be a major disaster that seemingly damages the theater in another example of Disney wizardry. Perhaps the wittiest segments are from Statler and Waldorf, grumpy old geezers perching in a box seat balcony offering comical commentary throughout the wacky show. **25-minute show including the preshow.**

Disney–MGM Studios character greeting spots

Check your guide map for specific greeting times. The Mickey gloves on your guide map will point you in the right direction.

- *Toy Story* friends Woody, Buzz Lightyear, and Jessie near Mama Melrose's Ristorante at Al's Toy Barn.
- Lilo and Stitch in Animation Courtyard.
- Goofy in his paint clothes at Goofy's Prop Stop just off Washington Square.
- Sorcerer Mickey in the Soundstage 1 lobby on Mickey Avenue.

Shopping on New York Street

It's a Wonderful Shop—Year-round Christmas store • Disney-inspired holiday gifts and ornaments.

Stage 1 Company Store—Muppet and Bear in the Big Blue House products • Disney clothing • souvenirs • costumes.

The Writer's Stop—Next to the Sci-Fi Dine-In Theater • combination coffee shop, sweetshop, and bookshop • giant cookies, Rice Crispies treats, muffins, pastries, candy • specialty coffees, lattes, cappuccino • Disney books, coffee mugs, CDs, games, and videos • bestseller books and paperbacks • occasional celebrity book signings.

Youse Guys Moychindice—Disney sports-related store on the New York Street • Mickey Mouse jerseys • Disney logo footballs • character plush toys dressed as sports figures.

Mickey Avenue

Head down Mickey Avenue, the park's back street, to reach the Backlot Tour where guests can view the working area of the studio. Here you'll also find the park's newest attraction, Who Wants to Be a Millionaire—Play It!

DISNEY–MGM STUDIOS BACKLOT TOUR***

Begin your tour at a newly revised special effects water tank where unsuspecting, slicker-clad volunteers are dumped with 800 gallons of water and blasted with bullets and torpedoes. It's all simply a demonstration of how special effects were produced in the attack scene from *Pearl Harbor*. Sound effects, dialog, and a musical score are added before the audience sees the overall presentation on video monitors.

Wind through the Prop Warehouse before boarding a tram to tour Disney's Backlot, the actual working area of the Studios. Pass by the giant Mickey-eared water tower, the wardrobe department, the scene shop where sets are constructed, and on to a residential street where you'll view the exteriors of the TV homes of *The Golden Girls* and *Empty Nest*. Oversized props from various movies line the road on your way to Catastrophe Canyon where the tram narrowly escapes a tanker explosion and a flash flood of 70,000 gallons of water. As you exit the tram, walk-through the American Film Institute Showcase, a changing ex-hibit of film props and memorabilia. **35-minute tour. Closes at 7 P.M.**

Tip: This is an efficiently moving ride so don't be discouraged by long lines. And sit on the right-hand side of the tram if you'd like to stay dry.

WALT DISNEY: ONE MAN'S DREAM**

Presented as part of the "100 Years of Magic" celebration, this two-part, multi-media attraction showcases the exceptional life of an exceptional man. Begin with a walk-through exhibit of movie props and posters, vintage animation cameras, interesting scale models of park attractions, collectible merchandise, photos, historical audio and video recordings, and conceptual park planning art. Special exhibits include the one full-size and seven dwarf-sized Oscars given to Walt for the movie *Snow White and the Seven Dwarfs,* a full-size prototype of Walt's office from 1940–66, and even his boyhood school desk with Walt's initials firmly carved in the tabletop.

Move into the Walt Disney theater for a 15-minute film of rare archival footage of Walt's life from his early boyhood in Marceline, Missouri, through the establishment of Walt Disney Studios to the cre-ation of his amazing theme parks, all narrated by Walt himself. And remember it all started with a mouse. **Walk-through attraction with a 15-minute movie.**

WHO WANTS TO BE A MILLIONAIRE—PLAY IT!***

Housed in a replica of the *Who Wants to be a Millionaire*'s New York studio is a re-creation of Regis Philbin's now defunct ABC show. Dur-ing a fun-filled 25 minutes, a Philbinesque host leads contestants in vying for points that will earn them small prizes (no cash awarded here) while the audience plays along on individual keypads for a chance to be next to fill the "hot seat" (the trick is to correctly answer the questions and be quick about it). Contestants may ask for help in the form of "50–50," "Ask the Audience," even "Lifelines" from complete strangers waiting in line for the next show. Don't miss it. **Fastpass. 25-minute show occurs once each hour; see your guide map for times.**

Shopping on Mickey Avenue

AFI Showcase Shop—Found on departure from the Backlot Tour and American Film Institute Showcase • MGM merchandise • small honorary Oscars • movie reference books • *Wizard of Oz* memorabilia • movie-related postcards.

The Prop Shop—Plush toys • special edition Disney dolls • Disney action figure play sets • toys • souvenirs.

Animation Courtyard

Head through the archway to the right of the giant Mickey Sorcerer hat and enter Animation Courtyard. Here you'll find the popular Magic of Disney Animation where guests can enter the world of a Disney animator. You'll also find two great shows for kids, Voyage of the Little Mermaid and Playhouse Disney.

THE MAGIC OF DISNEY ANIMATION****

One of Disney Studio's best attractions, amusing yet educational, with each stop along the way better than the last. Begin with a short and witty film hosted by none other than Walter Cronkite and the crazy Robin Williams who enlighten the audience with the rudiments of exactly how Disney animated films are created in *Back to Neverland*. Afterward, a Disney artist draws a character for the audience (it takes 850,000 separate drawings for a full-length animated film) and answers questions.

Proceed to the actual working studio where, through glass walls, visitors view the artists at work planning and sketching on a Disney film in progress. Then enjoy a humorous, informative film featuring actual Disney artists, creators, and directors who convey what it is really like to put together an animated film.

The grand finale is a collage of clips gathered from the many enchanting moments of Disney's classical animated films. On the way out is a chance to examine some of Disney's many Oscar statuettes along with an interesting exhibit of rare and classical Disney artwork in the Animation Gallery. **35-minute guided tours with a new show beginning every 15 minutes.**

Tip: Come during the week before 5 P.M. when the animators are working. It makes for a far more interesting tour.

PLAYHOUSE DISNEY—LIVE ON STAGE**

This live musical presentation features the gang of *Bear in the Big Blue House* with their friends from the Disney Channel programs of *Rolie Polie Olie, Stanley*, and *The Book of Pooh*, all performing a delightful musical revue about friendship geared to preschoolers. The audience sits on the carpeted floor with many opportunities to sing, dance, and play along. **20-minute show occurring about six times a day; check your guide map for times.**

Tip: Don't miss this if you have small children; if not, skip it.

VOYAGE OF THE LITTLE MERMAID***

Journey under the sea at one of the most beloved of attractions at Disney Studios. This tribute to the raven-haired mermaid Ariel combines puppetry, live actors, animated film, and delightful music with the help of Ariel, Flounder, and Sebastian along with the not so adorable figure of the despicable Ursula. Some of the movie's favorite songs such as "Under the Sea," "Part of Your World," and "Poor Unfortunate Souls" are combined with superb special effects utilizing black lights, lasers, rain showers, loads of bubbles, and a realistic lightning storm. How often do you have the opportunity to behold a seemingly live mermaid with a flopping tail? **Fastpass. 7-minute show.**

Tip: Don't skip this beautifully done attraction simply because you don't have small children in tow. If you would like a center seat, stand back a bit when the doors open into the theater from the preshow holding room and allow about half the crowd to enter before you. And plan on using a Fastpass; your chances of getting in without one are a bit slim.

Shopping at Animation Courtyard

In Character Disney's Costume Shop—Sparkling Disney costumes for children.

Disney Studio Store—Plush toys • kids' clothing • children's watches.

Animation Gallery—One of the most interesting stores in the park • Disney animation cell artist demonstrations • Disney collectibles • animated cells • figurines • how-to-draw books and animation books • Disney videos and CDs • postcards • greeting cards.

Dining at Disney-MGM Studios
Dining on Hollywood Boulevard

Coffee Cart—Stainless steel cart just inside the entrance gate • pastries and cookies • coffee, cappuccino, espresso, juice, lemonade, hot chocolate, frozen coffee, sodas.

The Hollywood Brown Derby—Lunch and dinner • re-creation of the famous Hollywood dining spot • best food and most sophisticated atmosphere in the park • full review on page 340.

Dining on Sunset Boulevard

Starring Rolls Bakery—Bakery and coffee stop at the corner of Hollywood and Sunset • cookies, croissants, muffins, bagels, brownies, pie, cake, strudel, cinnamon rolls, Rice Crispies treats, moon pies, sugar-free apple and cherry pie • juice, specialty coffees, hot chocolate, sodas.

Sunset Ranch Market—A miniature version of Hollywood's Farmer's Market loaded with snacks and light counter-service meals at various stands. Plentiful open-air covered seating.

Anaheim Produce—Fresh fruits and vegetables • hot pretzels • frozen lemonade • juice • sodas.

Catalina Eddie's—Cheese, pepperoni, and vegetarian pizza • garden salad • apple pie and chocolate cake • beverages.

Fairfax Fries—McDonald's french fries • beverages.

Hollywood Scoops—Hand-scooped ice cream.

Rosie's All-American Café—Burgers, vegetarian burgers, chicken strips, soup, salad, fries • apple pie and chocolate cake • children's menu: chicken strips.

Toluca Legs Turkey Co.—Giant turkey legs • Polish sausage • baked potatoes • foot-long hot dogs and chili dogs • Budweiser beer.

Dining at Echo Lake

50s Prime Time Café—Lunch and dinner • dine in a 1950s sitcom where mom is your waitress and all vegetables must be consumed • full review on page 340.

ABC Commissary—Air-conditioning and passably good food makes this one of the better counter-service restaurants in the park • entertainment in the form of ABC trailers on raised TV monitors scattered throughout the palm tree-filled dining room • breakfast: scrambled eggs, French toast, pancakes, hash browns, cereal • lunch and dinner: fish and chips, burgers, chicken yakitori (skewered and grilled in a teriyaki sauce), feijoada (Brazil's national dish, a stew served over rice), tabbouleh wrap, vegetable noodle stir-fry • cheesecake, lemon meringue pie, chocolate cream pie • children's menu: chicken nuggets, mac 'n' cheese.

Backlot Express—Found between Indiana Jones attraction and Star Tours • tin-roofed, rusty-looking warehouse overflowing with old props • abundance of multilevel seating both indoors and out • burgers, hot dogs, chicken strips, tuna subs, chicken Caesar salad • carrot cake, chocolate cake • children's menu: chicken nuggets.

The Dip Site—Trailer next to Indiana Jones entrance • strawberry and banana smoothies • chocolate or peanut butter-dipped frozen fruit bars • funnel cakes • shaved ice in a variety of flavors • giant pretzels • juice • lemonade.

Dinosaur Gertie's Ice Cream of Extinction—On the shores of Echo Lake • soft-serve ice cream • Nestle Toll House cookies • ice cream sandwiches.

Hollywood and Vine—Breakfast, lunch, and dinner • 1940s art-deco–style diner • character breakfast and lunch buffet • noncharacter dinner buffet • full review on page 341.

Min and Bill's Dockside Diner—Docked steamer in Echo Lake • milkshakes • malts • cookies • brownies • beverages • beer.

Peevy's Polar Pipeline—Frozen slurpees in Coca-Cola, Minute Maid blueberry, or raspberry lemonade flavors.

Sci-Fi Dine-In Theater Restaurant—Relive the drive-in of your youth at this most unusual restaurant • full review on page 343.

Dining on New York Street

Mama Melrose's Ristorante Italiano—New York–style Italian restaurant • best pizzas around • full review on page 342.

Toy Story Pizza Planet Arcade—Counter-service pizza • downstairs arcade • seating upstairs or outdoors on patio with views of the Muppet fountain • cheese, pepperoni, or vegetarian personal-sized pizza • Greek or tossed salad • Rice Crispies treats; chocolate chip, sugar, and oatmeal raisin cookies.

The Writer's Stop—Combination coffee shop, sweetshop, and bookshop • sit and sip coffee while watching videos on vintage television • giant cookies, Rice Crispies treats, candy • coffee specialties, sodas.

Mickey Avenue Dining

Studio Catering Co.—Adjoins **Honey, I Shrunk the Kids Playground** • covered open-air seating • popcorn • fruit cups • chips • cookies • brownies • churros • ice cream bars • beverages • Minute Maid frozen strawberry lemonade • around the corner is the **Ice Cream Fountain**, serving soft-serve ice cream, root beer floats, hot fudge sundaes.

Libations

Tune-In Lounge—Tucked into a corner of the **50s Prime Time Café** • tacky 1950s family den setting • specialty drinks from Dad's liquor cabinet, beer, and wine • appetizers • possible to order off menu from next-door 50s Prime Time Café on slow days.

Special Entertainment

DISNEY STARS AND MOTOR CARS PARADE***

Held each afternoon is this parade reminiscent of the glamorous days of Hollywood when stars arrived at movie premiers in fabulous automobiles. Over 100 characters in 15 customized vintage cars based on Disney films are led by the wail of a police motorcycle escort. The tail end of the character cavalcade is Mickey and Minnie chauffeured by Goofy and Donald Duck in a 1929 Cadillac. **15-minute parade.**

FANTASMIC***

Sorcerer Mickey's fantasies soar to new heights in the 7,000-seat Hollywood Hills Amphitheater (with standing room for another 3,000). The mouse himself orchestrates this extravaganza of fireworks held each evening with stirring music, choreographed laser effects, projecting flames, and heaving fountains combined with a gathering of Disney characters and live performers. The show, set on a lagoon-bound island topped off with a 40-foot mountain, occurs at park closing each day (twice during busy season). While Mickey struggles with the forces of good and evil in a series of lavish dreams and wild nightmares, water dances in a multitude of color, fireworks explode, storms brew, and strong wind blows. A favorite segment is the procession of floats representing the best of Disney happy endings quickly followed by a bevy of Disney villains. Of course, Mickey wins out and, to the delight of the audience, a steamboat stuffed with Disney characters sails past in anticipation of the grand finale of water, lasers, and fireworks. Plan on saving a seat way ahead of show time or be prepared to stand.

For Fantasmic seating with no waiting, book a Fantasmic Dinner Package available at Hollywood Brown Derby, Mama Melrose's, and Hollywood and Vine. Reservations can be made no earlier than 7 days in advance at the Guest Relations desk of all Walt Disney World Resorts, at the restaurant itself, or at the Studio's Guest Information at the corner of Hollywood and Sunset. There is no charge for the package, and food is ordered from the restaurant's regular menu. After your meal you'll receive a seat ticket in a special reserved area on the far right of the theater. The separate entrance located next to Oscar's Service Station on Hollywood Boulevard makes it possible to arrive only 30 minutes or so prior to show time. Reservations fill up quickly so book as early as possible. **25-minute show.**

Tip: On windy or rainy nights the show is sometimes canceled. I know it sounds tedious, but it's necessary to arrive about 1 hour prior to show time for a good seat; once the theater is full you're out of luck. If you wait until 20 minutes prior you have a good chance of a standing room only spot whose only advantage is a quick dash out once the show is over. A counter-service spot inside the theater offers hot dogs, caramel corn, ice cream sandwiches, sodas, and beer. In busy season when there are two shows, opt for the less crowded, final performance. If you'd like to be among the first out of the theater, take a seat in one of the back rows (really some of the better seats; the front rows can be a bit soggy).

Special Events

Star Wars Weekend—Each weekend in May the Studio is filled with celebrities from the *Star Wars* movies. Events include parades, pictures, talk sessions, autographs, trivia contests, and street parties. Included in regular park admission.

ABC Super Soap Weekend—Over 30 stars from favorite ABC soaps are on hand the first weekend in November to sign autographs and take pictures as well as participate in live musical performances, special editions of the Who Wants To Be A Millionaire—Play It! game show, star motorcades, and talk shows. If you're not a soap enthusiast, strongly consider steering clear of the park on this very crazy weekend when streets are jam-packed with fans running from one event to another. Included in regular park admission.

The Osborne Family Spectacle of Lights—After dark from late November until early January, snow falls on the Studio's Backlot residential street lit by over 5 million colorful bulbs. Included in regular park admission.

DISNEY'S ANIMAL KINGDOM

"We inherited this earth from our parents and are borrowing it from our children." This is the important message Disney strives to convey in this environmentally conscious theme park. It's difficult to believe the park has only been open since 1998. The 4,300,000 plants in the park are so lush and towering it's as if they've been there forever. Along with the main attractions are hidden nooks and mysterious trails just waiting to be discovered. If you see a path leading off the main walkway by all means follow it; it may just take you to a place of sheer enchantment.

The Animal Kingdom, laid out much like the Magic Kingdom, holds four lands converging into its central hub, Discovery Island. And like Cinderella's Castle, it has a central focus, in this case the massive Tree of Life, composed of 8,000 limbs, over 100,000 leaves, and a trunk covered with 325 glorious animal carvings. Although the park itself is five times the space of the Magic Kingdom, don't panic; it won't take two days to see it. Remember that much of the land is an enclave for the animals; the park itself is easily conquered in a day. Take time to explore and discover the many marvelous natural settings and experiences scattered throughout or risk leaving a bit disappointed when you haven't grasped the true significance of this magnificent theme park.

Park Basics

Getting There

Those driving to WDW should take Exit 64 off I-4 and follow the signs to the Animal Kingdom.

Using WDW transportation

From all Disney Resorts, Disney–MGM Studios, and Epcot, board bus marked Animal Kingdom. From the Magic Kingdom—take the monorail or ferry to the Ticket and Transportation Center (TTC) then transfer to bus marked Animal Kingdom.

Parking

Cost is $7 per day; free to Walt Disney Resort guests and Annual Pass holders. Keep your receipt; fee also good for parking at the Magic Kingdom, Epcot, and Disney–MGM Studios on that day only. Parking is conveniently located in front of the park. Trams circulate throughout the parking area for easy transportation to the entry gate. Make a note of what aisle and section you have parked in.

Operating Hours

Open from 8 or 9 A.M. until around dusk. Call **407-824-4321** or log on to **www.disneyworld.com** for updated park hours.

The Oasis and Discovery Island normally opens a half hour earlier than official park opening. Arrive at least 30 to 45 minutes early allowing time to park, buy tickets, purchase a snack or cup of coffee, and be one of the first to hit the big attractions. I recommend heading straight to Kilimanjaro Safaris.

Fastpass Attractions

See pages 133-134 for Fastpass details. It's Tough to Be a Bug! • Kilimanjaro Safaris • Kali River Rapids • DINOSAUR • Primeval Whirl.

What to Wear

This is the only Disney park that requires a bit of forethought in clothing. If you plan on riding the Kali River Rapids ride, be sure to wear fast-drying clothes and bring water footwear of some sort. You will more than likely become thoroughly soaked, and if you haven't dressed properly, you will feel soggy for hours afterward.

Park Services

ATM machines—An ATM machine is located just outside the park entrance.

Baby care center—An infant facility located behind the Creature Comforts shop on Discovery Island is outfitted with changing tables, highchairs, and a room for nursing mothers. Formula, baby food, suntan lotion, diapers, milk, and over-the-counter children's medications may be purchased here. All restrooms throughout the park are outfitted with changing tables.

Cameras and film processing—Look for cameras, film, camcorder tapes, and batteries at Garden Gate Gifts; 2-hour film processing is available here as well as anywhere the Photo Express sign is displayed.

First aid—For minor medical problems head to the First Aid Center located behind Creature Comforts on Discovery Island.

Guest relations—Located just inside the park on the left is Guest Relations where a knowledgeable staff is ready to assist you with priority seating, resort reservations, messages for separated parties, purchase of annual passes and upgrades, foreign currency exchange, information for guests with disabilities, sign language services, VIP tour information, and behind-the-scenes programs.

Guests with disabilities—A guidebook for Guests with Disabilities is available at Guest Relations (see The Basics on page 22 for more information). Guests with mobility disabilities should park adjacent to the Entrance Complex (ask at the Auto Plaza for directions). Wheelchairs and ECVs are available for rent. Most restaurants and shops at the Animal Kingdom are accessible to guests with disabilities although some counter-service locations have narrow queues with railings (ask a host or hostess for assistance). Companion assisted restrooms are located at First Aid and three other locations. Most attractions provide access through the main queue while others have auxiliary entrances for wheelchairs and service animals along with up to five members of your party. Certain attractions require guests to transfer from their wheelchair to a ride system.

Braille guidebooks, assistive listening devices, video captioning, and audiotape guides are available at Guest Relations for a $25 refundable deposit. It's Tough to Be a Bug has reflective captioning. With a 7-day notice a sign language interpreter will be provided at live shows on Saturdays. Call **407-824-4321** with questions.

Lockers—Lockers are located just outside the park entrance and just inside on the left for $7 per day including a $2 refundable key deposit. If you're park-hopping, keep your receipt for another locker at the three other Disney theme parks for no extra charge.

Lost and found—Located at Guest Relations or call **407-824-4245**.

Lost children—Locate lost children at the Baby Care Center or Guest Relations.

Package pickup—Purchases may be sent to Garden Gate Gifts for pickup at the end of the day. Allow 3 hours for delivery. Disney resort guests may send their packages directly to their hotel for next-day arrival.

Pet kennel—A kennel is located just outside the park entrance. Daily rate is $6. Call **407-824-6568** for information. Proof of vaccination is required.

Readmission—If you plan to leave the park and reenter the same day, be sure to retain your ticket and have your hand stamped before departing.

Stroller and wheelchair rentals—Rentals are located next to Garden Gate Gifts on your right as you enter the park. Single strollers are $8 per day, double strollers $15, wheelchairs $8, and ECVs $40 per day including a $10 refundable deposit. If you are park-hopping, keep your receipt for a replacement stroller at the three other Disney theme parks.

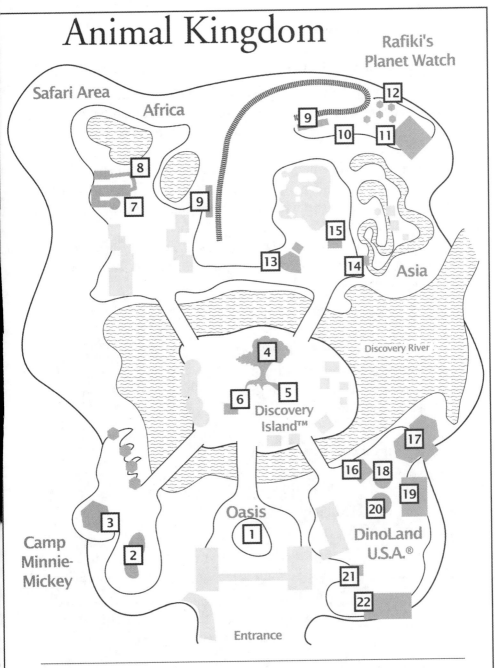

Animal Kingdom

Rafiki's Planet Watch

Safari Area

Africa

Asia

Discovery River

Discovery Island™

Oasis

Camp Minnie-Mickey

DinoLand U.S.A.®

Entrance

1. The Oasis Exhibits
2. Pocahontas and Her Forest Friends
3. Festival of the Lion King
4. The Tree of Life
5. It's Tough to be a Bug®
6. Discovery Island™ Trails
7. Kilimanjaro Safaris®

8. Pangani Forest Exploration Trail
9. Wildlife Express Train
10. Habitat Habit!
11. Conservation station®
12. Affection Section
13. Flights of Wonder
14. Kali River Rapids®
15. Maharajah Jungle Trek

16. The Boneyard®
17. Tarzan™ Rocks!
18. Fossil Fun Games
19. Primeval Whirl
20. Triceratop Spin
21. Dino-Sue
22. Dinosaur

The Lay of the Land

The Animal Kingdom's Main Street of sorts is the Oasis, a winding series of pathways leading to the hub, Discovery Island, whose focal point is the Tree of Life. Each of the Animal Kingdom's four lands—Asia, Africa, Dinoland, and Camp Minnie-Mickey—is accessed from Discovery Island. To enter each land, cross one of the bridges spanning the Discovery River that encircles Discovery Island. Only Africa and Asia can access each other without first returning to Discovery Island. A very simple layout.

Tip: A great time to visit the park is in the late afternoon when many of the hoards of people have left for the day and lines at the main attractions are at a minimum.

Suggested 1-day itinerary for touring

- Be at the park gates a half hour before opening using the time before rope drop to walk the paths of the Oasis. Those with children may want to take in the character breakfast at Restaurantosaurus before the park opens.

- At rope drop head straight to Kilimanjaro Safaris and then walk the Pangani Forest Exploration Trail.

- Explore Africa before backtracking to Discovery Island to take in the It's Tough to Be a Bug attraction. Walk the Discovery Island Trails before heading to Camp Minnie-Mickey.

- Work in the Festival of the Lion King at Camp Minnie-Mickey sometime in the morning and, if you have young children, see Pocahontas and Her Forest Friends and stop for a visit at the Character Greeting Trails.

- Head to your noon priority seating at the Rainforest Café or pick up great fast food at the Tusker House.

- After lunch it's time for Dinoland. Pick up a Fastpass to Dinosaur. During the wait take in the new rides at Chester and Hester's Dino-Rama and see Tarzan Rocks if possible. If you have children in tow make a stop at the Boneyard for playtime.

- It's now time for the afternoon Mickey's Jammin' Jungle Parade (in slower seasons, the parade is sometimes the last event of the day in which case it would be necessary to take in Kali River Rapids and the Maharaja Jungle Trek before it begins).

- Move on to Asia, pick up a Fastpass to Kali River Rapids and while you are waiting walk the Maharaja Jungle Trek and see Flights of Wonder.

- After Kali River Rapids you will be soaked. Either head out to Rafiki's Planet Watch and Conservation Station to see the exhibits or head home for a hot shower and dinner at your hotel.

Animal Kingdom don't-miss attractions

- It's Tough to Be a Bug!
- Festival of the Lion King
- Kilimanjaro Safaris
- Pangani Forest Exploration Trail
- Kali River Rapids
- Maharaja Jungle Trek
- DINOSAUR

Animal Kingdom best dining bets

- Restaurantosaurus' morning character breakfast.
- Rainforest Café.
- Tusker House.

The Oasis

The beauty of the Oasis hits you square in the face as you enter the park, a fantastic, tropical jungle of flowering plants, cooling waterfalls, and overgrown plant life thriving with a menagerie of fascinating creatures. A cool mist pervades the air amid a cacophony of chattering birds and the smell of fragrant trees and flowers. Pathways meander around the sides and through the center leading to hidden grottos, rushing streams, dripping vines, and towering vegetation. Hidden critters housed in replicas of their natural habitats—including macaws, iguanas, exotic boars, anteaters, sloths, pig-deer, and swan—are surrounded by giant banana trees, swaying palms, massive bamboo, and flowering orchids.

Most visitors have a tendency to dash through this area with alarming speed to quickly reach the "real" part of the park. In doing so they're missing one of the most beautiful places in the Animal Kingdom, an area that should be savored in preparation for all there is to come. At the very least, take a bit of time at the end of the day to fully explore this lovely place of tranquility.

Shopping at the Oasis

Garden Gate Gifts—Cameras • film • 2-hour processing • pick up photos taken by park photographers here.

Discovery Island

After making your way through the Oasis, cross the bridge over the Discovery River and into the park's central hub, Discovery Island. Here visitors congregate to wander its streets of folk art–style animal carved lampposts, benches, and vibrant storefront facades. And here, all eyes are immediately drawn to the focal point of the park, the awesome Tree of Life.

THE TREE OF LIFE

Dominating the skyline and the centerpiece of the park is the amazing Tree of Life. Looming 14 stories above Discovery Island, the 50-foot wide trunk and 170-foot wide roots of this man-made tree are carved with hundreds of absolutely amazing, twisting forms of a diversity of animals ascending from its gnarly base then up and around the mesmerizing structure. It's possible to spend hours just identifying and discovering its intricate and sometimes almost hidden designs while strolling the many pathways encircling the tree. What a remarkable symbol of the mutual reliance of all living creatures. Inside its trunk is the 3-D attraction It's Tough to be a Bug.

Tip: Think of this as an attraction all of itself instead of a way to get to the 3-D movie. Stop to relax on one of the numerous benches, perfect for observing the tree's grandeur. The best spots for picture taking are actually from the lookout points found between Asia and Africa on the opposite

*banks of the Discovery River. Just duck down one of the many paths leading
to the river.*

IT'S TOUGH TO BE A BUG!****

Hands down, this is Disney's very best 3-D movie. But the winding
walkway leading from the entrance to the theater is half the attraction.
It passes a menagerie of wildlife (even a Giant Galapagos Tortoise), lush
foliage, waterfalls, caves, and most importantly, an up-close view of the
marvelous animal carvings that make up the roots and trunk of the Tree
of Life.

It's always twilight in the low-ceilinged waiting area underneath the
Tree where chirping crickets sing Broadway tunes from such insect shows
as *The Dung and I* (featuring the hit song "Hello Dung Lovers"), *Beauty
and the Bees,* and *A Cockroach Line.* Flik (the star of *A Bug's Life)* is the
host of this creepy-crawly act of assorted bugs who only want humans
to understand them. However, much to the glee of the audience, they
just can't help misbehaving. A favorite opening act is the stinkbug that
accidentally lets his smelly, gaseous fumes rip right into the audience.
As the show progresses you'll be doused with bug spray, stung sharply in
the back, and showered with termite acid, all innocently achieved through
special effects. You'll receive one final surprise as the beetles, maggots,
and cockroaches exit safely ahead of you. **Fastpass. 8-minute show.**

*Tip: Definitely one attraction too intense for young children, particu-
larly when Hopper, the despicable grasshopper from* A Bug's Life, *scares the
dickens out of every child under 5. If you would like to sit in the center of the
auditorium, hang back a little in the waiting area and allow some of the
audience to enter ahead of you.*

DISCOVERY ISLAND CHARACTER LANDING

Just before crossing over the bridge from Discovery Island to
Dinoland U.S.A., a pathway on the right leads to a boat dock on the
Discovery River where characters from the Hundred Acre Wood sign
autographs and pose for pictures.

DISCOVERY ISLAND TRAILS

Find time to walk these trails that encircle the remarkable Tree of
Life. You'll find cascading waterfalls, verdant gardens, animal habitats,

and quiet resting spots among the many pathways meandering along the Discovery River.

Shopping at Discovery Island

Beastly Bazaar—Near the bridge to Asia • Disney home decor shop.

Creature Comforts—Next to the bridge leading to Africa • dedicated to young visitors • children's Disney logo attire • Winnie the Pooh infant wear • stuffed toys • hats • costumes • Disney videos and CDs.

Island Mercantile—Large and extensive store featuring Disney merchandise galore • jungle animal plush toys • pith helmets • Disney and Animal Kingdom logo clothing • Pin Station just outside • open half hour after park closing time for last-minute shopping.

Disney Outfitters—Safari-outfitted plush toys • Disney and Animal Kingdom logo clothing and sleepwear • nature CDs • watches • animal woodcarvings • hand-painted ostrich eggs • woven baskets.

Animal Kingdom breakfast choices

- Rainforest Café at the park's entrance for a full breakfast menu or its Magic Mushroom Bar for fruit smoothies, juice, and coffee.
- Restaurantosaurus in Dinoland for a character buffet with Donald Duck and friends.
- Tusker House in Africa for hearty breakfast croissants and biscuit sandwiches.
- Kusafiri Coffee Shop and Bakery in Africa for giant cinnamon rolls and pastries.
- Safari Coffee kiosk on Discovery Island for coffee, breakfast breads, and pastries.
- Muffins and coffee cake at Dino Bite Snacks in Dinoland.

Camp Minnie-Mickey

Although this is the home of the captivating Festival of the Lion King, you won't find a jungle here. Only the woods where it's summer camp year-round complete with Adirondack-style log cabins, split-rail fences, sparkling waterfalls, and a deliciously cool babbling brook. Although it's geared primarily to kids who love the super character greeting spot tucked away in the back, adults should still stop in, at the very least, to see the Lion King show. And those who have time to hang out on the bridge over Discovery River should watch the rocky cave in the distance for a hidden fire-breathing dragon that, on occasion, moans and shoots his hot, fiery breath out of his lair.

CHARACTER GREETING TRAILS***

At the end of four different trails are twig huts where children will find the gang from *The Lion King*, Mickey and Minnie in safari outfits, Winnie the Pooh and his friends from the Hundred Acre Wood, or woodsman Goofy.

FESTIVAL OF THE LION KING***

The all-important message of the continuing "circle of life" is wonderfully portrayed in this sensational stage extravaganza of Broadway-caliber song and dance. The story of the Lion King is told through a combination of elaborate costumes, wild acrobatic tumble monkeys, daring fire-twirlers, and massive audio-animatronic animal floats accompanied by the beat of tribal drumming and jungle noise. Don't worry if you're not acquainted with the music; you'll be an expert by the time you leave. Plan your day around this don't-you-dare-miss show. **30-minute show. Check your guide map for times.**

Tip: All 1,400 seats are great in this circular, open-air theater; however, arrive early in busy season to guarantee your party a spot. The first show of the day has the least attendance and requires less of an advance arrival. Children who would like to be chosen to participate in the closing parade should try sitting on the bottom section of the bleachers.

POCAHONTAS AND HER FOREST FRIENDS**

Pocahontas tells nature's tales in a simply delightful show. With lots of "oohs" and "aahs," her live forest friends come trotting out one by one: a turkey, a mouse, a possum, a porcupine, even a skunk. As the wind blows autumn leaves into the audience, the raven-haired Pocahontas sings "Colors of the Wind" and conveys the message of the importance of protecting and respecting the forest and its clever creatures for us and future generations. Grandmother Willow, a fascinating face in a tree trunk, speaks her words of wisdom to Pocahontas while the mischievous Twig delights the audience with his silliness. **15-minute show.**

Tip: If seats are full, standing room is allowed, but come early to be assured of a place in this small theater.

Special places in the Animal Kingdom

Discovery Island:

- The pathways surrounding the base of the Tree of Life.
- Shady seating area behind Flame Tree Barbecue where visitors can dine among waterfalls and lotus-filled ponds with prime views of the Discovery River.

Asia:

Asia has some of the best hidden paths and secret places, all leading off the walkway in both directions. Just follow anything that looks like a pathway and see where it takes you.

- Follow the path across the walkway from Flights of Wonder to a peaceful pagoda where there's always a cooling breeze accompanied by prime views of the Discovery River and the Tree of Life.
- Look for the secret path paralleling the main walkway between Asia and Africa with waterfalls and lush foliage.
- Follow the path next to Mandala Gifts leading toward the river to a ruined temple inhabited with monkeys.
- Look behind the multicolored ice cream truck for a cool and lovely pagoda.
- Take the first right after leaving Africa on your way to Asia where a short pathway leads to the banks of the Discovery River and the best views of the Tree of Life.

Africa:

- Behind Dawa Bar and Tusker House is a courtyard filled with covered tables perfect for a cooling drink.
- Behind Tamu Tamu Refreshments is a delightfully shady patio.

Lobby of Disney's Contemporary Resort

Pristine Beach at Disney's Polynesian Resort

Disney's Grand Floridian Resort's soaring lobby

Atmospheric Pool at Disney's Wilderness Lodge

Disney's Beach Club Villas

Lobby of Disney's Boardwalk Inn

Luna Park Pool at Disney's Boardwalk Inn and Villas

The Everglades of the Gaylord Palms Resort

Tomorrowland at the Magic Kingdom

Crystal Palace Character Meal at the Magic Kingdom

Epcot's Universe of Energy

Epcot's Imagination Pavilion at dusk

The Living Seas Pavilion at Epcot

United Kingdom Pavilion at Epcot

Character Meal at Epcot's Garden Grill

Twilight Zone Tower of Terror at Disney-MGM Studios

Disney's Ultra-Lush Animal Kingdom

Kilimanjaro Safaris at Disney's Animal Kingdom

Pangani Forest Exploration Trail in the Animal Kingdom

Along the Animal Kingdom's Maharaja Jungle Trek

Dino-Rama at the Animal Kingdom

Gateway to Universal Studios

San Francisco at Universal Studios

Islands of Adventure's Toon Lagoon

The Lost Continent at Universal's Islands of Adventure

Zany Seuss Landing at Universal's Islands of Adventure

SeaWorld's Anheuser-Busch Hospitality Center

SeaWorld's Shamu Stadium

Africa

Disney outdid themselves in the re-creation of a modern-day East African coastal village. A massive baobab tree looms over the town of Harambe where drums play amid the peeling, whitewashed buildings and dusty streets. Rusty overhead fans, thatched-roofed huts, and reed fences create a genuineness that's hard to beat. Take the pathway through the village to the hop-on point for the Animal Kingdom's oh-so favorite attraction, the Kilimanjaro Safaris.

KILIMANJARO SAFARIS****

You'll quickly discover the Animal Kingdom's most popular attraction when almost every visitor makes a beeline straight to Africa at park opening. Load onto covered, open-sided safari vehicles for your trip around the 110-acre African savanna brimming with baobab trees, waterfalls, rivers, watering holes, and rickety bridges. Each excursion is different and depends entirely on what animals decide to make an appearance. As you rumble across the authentic-looking landscape, your guide/driver will assist you in locating the wide assortment of animals including lions, cheetahs, warthogs, elephants, gazelles, crocodiles, wildebeests, exotic birds, giraffes, and even white rhinos. Those with luck might encounter a male lion, rare because they sleep around 18 hours a day. Some animals may come close to your vehicle while the predators and more perilous species only look as if they could behind their seemingly invisible barriers. The calm, soothing part of the ride ends when the group stumbles upon ivory poachers. In the quest to overtake them, your driver takes you on a crazy chase and in Disney fashion, the bad guy has to pay. **Fastpass. 20-minute ride. Expectant mothers and those with heart, back, or neck problems may want to sit out this bumpy ride.**

Tip: At park opening, Disney cast members will try to divert you to other areas of the park by advising you of no wait times for other attractions and a long wait for the safari. If you're in line at park opening, go straight to the safari regardless. Usually the wait is minimal, and lines are still the shortest until late afternoon. On hot days, the animals are out in full force in the morning and looking for cooler spots elsewhere in the afternoon. And don't run for cover if there is an afternoon thundershower. Head straight here for prime animal viewing, a favored time to come out for a rain bath.

Behind the Scenes Tours

Call 407-WDW-TOUR for reservations. Discounts are available to Annual Pass and AAA Diamond Card holders.

Backstage Safari—On this 3-hour tour, guests explore the animal housing areas, meet the keepers, and learn how the animals are cared for. Visit the nutrition center where the food is prepared and see the veterinary care hospital as well as participate in a discussion of conservation issues and animal behavior. **$65 plus park admission. Mon, Wed, and Fri at 8:15 A.M. Guests must be 16 years or older to participate.**

Wild By Design—Learn about the design and construction of this fascinating theme park along with a bit about the animals and their habitats. **$58 plus park admission. Tues, Thurs, and Fri. Guests must be 14 years or older to participate.**

PANGANI FOREST EXPLORATION TRAIL***

Many people walk right past this shady, self-guided trail and only when it's too late find out what they've missed. Begin at the Endangered Animal Rehabilitation Center holding Colobus monkeys and yellow-backed duikers (a species of antelope) and then on to the Research Center where naked mole rats are observed in their underground habitats. A wonderful aviary holds birds native to Africa, a cooling waterfall (complete with faux mist), and an aquarium overflowing with kaleidoscopic fish. All are drawn to the terrific underwater observation tank of swimming hippos and then on to the real highlight—a family of lowland gorillas. Take time to search for them; it can be difficult to spot them in the profuse vegetation. Experts are scattered throughout to answer questions and give short, informative talks about each exhibit.

Tip: Go early after the safari or late in the afternoon when crowds are low. It can be difficult to spot wildlife from behind rows of human heads.

Shopping in Africa

Duka la Filimu—Film kiosk near entrance to Kilimanjaro Safaris.

Mombasa Marketplace/Ziwani Traders—Animal Kingdom's best shop • interesting wooden animal sculptures • straw hats • African masks

• Nigerian clothing • Raku pottery • hand-painted bowls from Zimbabwe • beaded jewelry • Nigerian and Zulu woven baskets • Disney plush characters in safari dress • zebra flip-flops • wild animal plush toys.

RAFIKI'S PLANET WATCH**

At this self-paced education center guests are encouraged to open their eyes to the world around them and protect the earth's precious wildlife. Take a primitive train, the Wildlife Express, from the interesting Harambe Station for a 5-minute trip to Conservation Station with a behind-the-scenes peek along the way of the park's animal habitats. After disembarking, make your way up a pathway past Habitat Habit encouraging wildlife habitats in your own backyard. (Did you know that a single bat can eat up to 6,000 mosquitoes in 1 night?).

At Conservation Station, numerous exhibits promote environmental awareness and volunteerism, many of them hands on. Don't miss the Song of the Rainforest where the marvelous natural sounds of the rainforest are heard along with the trucks, chainsaws, and fires that are rapidly destroying it. Animalcam is a self-controlled camera allowing visitors an up-close view of the park's animal habitats, and interactive computers such as EcoWeb direct visitors to conservation efforts in their own community. Mermaid Tales Theater, a puppet show combined with film, focuses on environmental responsibility for children.

Move on to the Animal Health and Care Lab where scientists track wild animals with harmless transmitters for useful information geared toward preservation, the Hatchery for young birds, reptiles, and amphibians, the Veterinarian Treatment Lab allowing guests a peek into the world of the veterinarian, and the Neonatal Unit where infant animals have their health and vital signs monitored. Animal experts lead presentations designed to educate visitors while encouraging questions. Outside at the Affection Section children may pet and groom some of their favorite barnyard creatures.

Tip: If enough things are happening during your visit in the way of animal surgeries or an interesting demonstration, your time here will be extremely enjoyable. Regardless, the trip is worth the effort to learn a bit more about conservation and our role in assuring the continuation of global efforts to save the planet.

Shopping at Rafiki's Planet Watch

Out of the Wild—Open-air shop in Rafiki's Planet Watch • children's books on animals • plush animals • Animal Kingdom logo clothing • nature CDs.

Asia

The allure of Asia is irresistible at Anandapur Village where you'll find the crumbling ruins of stone temples, swinging monkeys, perfumed gardens, stalking tigers, and charming pagodas. The bustle and cacophony of the village is interspersed with gaily painted buses holding food concessions, bicycle carts filled with bottles of Coca-Cola, overflowing rickshaws, trickling fountains, bare electric lightbulbs strung across pathways, and prayer flags flapping in the breeze. It's Disney's best land yet in terms of authenticity and fascination.

FLIGHTS OF WONDER***

Set in an open-air theater, this show features beautiful birds from around the world as they fly and soar on cue from their trainer, oftentimes involving volunteers from the audience in their antics. Don't expect any birds riding bicycles here with the exception of a parrot named Groucho who sings an entire song (a little off-key); the idea is to allow spectators to see their natural behaviors. Throughout, Bwana Joe, the so-called explorer and tour guide, keeps the show moving along with a bit of comic relief. **30-minute show.**

Tip: Because it's not a thrill-a-minute show, you'll find it is fairly easy to be seated. Save it for a time when your feet need a rest.

KALI RIVER RAPIDS***

Take a white-water rafting escapade down the churning waters of the Chakranadi River in the kingdom of Anandapur. Board your 12-seater circular raft and begin by peacefully floating through a misty bamboo rainforest past crumbling temples, cascading waterfalls, and the shocking devastation of old-growth rain forests destroyed by loggers. Soon your raft is speeding along through rapid water until everyone is thoroughly drenched. Watch out for the elephants that love to squirt water on unsuspecting travelers. **Fastpass. 7-minute ride. Height re-**

quirement 38 inches. **Not recommended for expectant mothers or those with heart, back, or neck problems.**

Tip: Don't miss this ride just because you don't like getting wet. Wear a rain poncho or lightweight, fast-drying clothing and footwear. On hot summer days you'll welcome the soaking. If you like water play, look for a button in the center of the bridge as you exit the attraction; push it to spray unwary rapid riders with a stream of water shot from two stone elephants.

MAHARAJA JUNGLE TREK***

Once again Disney has outdone itself with this sensational self-guided trail. Wander through the ruins of an overgrown palace on the grounds of the Anandapur Royal Forest to encounter spectacular animal species beginning with the Komodo dragon (look hard because he's in there somewhere). In their cave are Dracula-like Malaysian fruit bats with 6-foot wingspans and behind glass enclosures are Bengal tigers roaming luxurious grasslands surrounded by gentle deer and black buck antelope. End this remarkable journey in the Asian bird sanctuary filled with the most exotic varieties imaginable.

Tip: This attraction can sometimes be astonishingly uncrowded. Come at your leisure and enjoy. Take time to gaze at the marvelous details along the trail such as broken walls of fading plaster resplendent with Indian murals, Tibetan prayer flags flapping from trees, abandoned rickshaws, and authentic-looking pagodas.

Shopping in Asia

Mandala Gifts—Tiny shop displaying Asian-inspired gifts • wind chimes • brass incense burners • sarongs • Bonsai tree kits • colorful paper umbrellas • dragon kites.

Dinoland U.S.A.

Smack in the middle of the Animal Kingdom is the archeological dig site of the Dino Institute. Cross beneath the skeleton of a 50-foot Brachiosaurus to enter this land of roadside America with its rusty camping trailers, crude souvenir stands, lofty ferns, and comfort food diners. Here you will discover the world of dinosaurs with a visit to a paleontological dig site, an attraction that will take you back to a time when dinosaurs roamed the world, and a 1950s-style roadside amusement park with rides for the entire family. You'll also find a replica of Sue, who at 40 feet long and 13 feet tall, is the largest T-Rex ever discovered.

THE BONEYARD***

This fossil fun site just for kids is a winner. Its "active" archeological dig site, an imaginative and discovery-filled playground, is the perfect place for small fry (ages 10 and under) to learn more about dinosaurs. Among massive fossilized bones, skeletal dinosaur remains, shipping crates, wheelbarrows, and piles of discarded dig material are slides, net climbs, caves, and water play areas protected from the elements by draped canvas. Cross the OldenGate Bridge, made from the bones of a 50-foot Brachiosaurus, to the Dig Site, where barefoot kids delve in the sand excavating the remains of a 10,000-year-old mammoth; the only catch is they won't be allowed to drag home what they find.

CHESTER AND HESTER'S DINO-RAMA***

This new mini-land inside Dinoland, a wacky 1950s-style roadside carnival with rides geared for the family, adds a fun touch to this area of the park.

TRICERATOP SPIN

A Dumbo-style ride where the little ones go up, down, and around in hefty 4-person dinosaurs that whirl about an enormous spinning toy top. **2-minute ride.**

PRIMEVAL WHIRL

A wacky but easygoing spinning coaster of tea cup–shaped "time machines" that whiz and twirl around a maze of tight curves, small hills, and easy plummets. The final drop is through the jaws of a huge dino fossil. **Fastpass. 3-minute ride. Minimum height 48 inches. Not recommended for expectant mothers and those with back, heart, or neck problems.**

FOSSIL FUN GAMES

Dinosaur-inspired, old-fashioned arcade games that allows users to redeem points for prizes. **Additional charge required.**

DINOSAUR***

Guests of the Dino Institute are taken on a breathtaking journey to face fiery meteors and voracious predators. The premise is a trip back 65 million years in time to retrieve an extra-large passenger, a live 16-foot, plant-eating dinosaur, and return it before the big asteroid hits the earth. Travel through a dense, dark, prehistoric forest teeming with shrieking dinosaurs, giant lizards, and massive insects in 12-passenger, all-terrain Time Rovers that rock, tilt, twist, and turn as you move along. When a hail of meteors strike your vehicle, you're off on a wild ride dodging nostril-flaring, heavy-breathing, and shrieking audio-animatronic dinosaurs until the big scream encounter with a huge Carnotaurus (the only meat-eating dinosaur) who'd like you for his dinner. **Fastpass. 4-minute ride. Minimum height 40 inches. Not recommended for expectant mothers or those with heart, back, or neck problems.**

Tip: This ride is pretty intense for children not only because of the massive, screaming dinosaurs but the scary anticipation in this very dark attraction.

TARZAN ROCKS**

The King of the Jungle gets his wild friends hopping in the high-intensity 1,500-seat Theater in the Wild. High-decibel, live rock musicians belt out the hit songs from Disney's *Tarzan* on a multilevel stage of ramps where wild, jungle gymnasts fly through the air performing acrobatics and stunt extreme Roller Blading. A well-muscled Tarzan swings in on his vine and, along with Jane, performs an aerial ballet segment. Of course Terk, Tarzan's right-hand ape, shows up to hip-hop along with the crowd. Don't miss the opening segment, the very best part of the show. **30-minute show.**

Shopping in Dinoland U.S.A.

The Dino Institute Shop—Soft, rubbery dinosaurs • dinosaur backpacks and books • toy time rovers • Dinosaur logo clothing.

Chester and Hester's Dinosaur Treasures—Zany roadside souvenir stand • toys for kids • glow-in-the-dark merchandise • Disney souvenirs • Dinosaur merchandise.

Dining in the Animal Kingdom

What the Animal Kingdom lacks in full-service restaurants, it more than makes up for in some of the most visually delightful dining spots in all of WDW. Favorites are the **Flame Tree Barbecue** for its amazing and extensive, terraced seating overlooking the Discovery River and the **Tusker House** with its yummy food and themed safari dining rooms. The park's only full-service restaurants are the **Rainforest Café** with access from both outside and inside the park and **Restaurantosaurus** offering a character buffet for breakfast only; the rest of the day it turns into a fast-food spot with **McDonald's** fare.

The Oasis

Rainforest Café—Breakfast, lunch, and dinner • enter through the thundering waterfall gracing the entrance to the Animal Kingdom • dine among screeching and roaring jungle animals • fun merchandise store • priority reservations advised • full review on page 344.

Discovery Island

Flame Tree Barbecue—Disney's most amazing outdoor eating area on level after tropical level of terraces overlooking Discovery River and the shores of Asia • barbecue chicken, slabs of ribs, green salad with chicken, smoked pork shoulder sandwich, smoked chicken breast sandwich, chicken salad sandwich, cole slaw, fries, onion rings, baked beans • key lime pie • Budweiser and Safari Amber beer • children's menu: PB&J sandwich, mini hotdog.

Pizzafari—Brilliant bug-carved shutters, glorious jungle murals on every wall, molded bugs and beasts hanging from the ceilings—the most delightful counter-service spot in the park • hidden wrap-around porch with views of the woods • adjacent gazebo-shaped screened porch offering a quiet getaway • pizza topped with either pepperoni or cheese, mesquite grilled chicken Caesar salad, hot Italian deli sandwich • chocolate mousse cake • Budweiser draft and Safari Amber • children's menu: PB&J sandwich, cheese pizza.

Safari Coffee—Early morning coffee and pastry stop just past the Oasis • espresso, cappuccino, coffee, milk, sodas, hot chocolate, juice • pastries, bagels, muffins, coffee cake.

Safari Pretzel—Nachos • pretzels • beer • beverages.

Safari Popcorn—Popcorn • cotton candy • beer • frozen lemonade • fruit punch.

Turkey Leg Kiosk—Giant turkey legs • chips • beer • beverages • brain freezes, half strawberry and half blueberry frozen slushes.

Camp Minnie-Mickey

Chip 'n' Dale's Cookie Cabin—Freshly baked sugar, oatmeal, and chocolate chip cookies • ice cream cookie sandwiches, ice cream bars • S'mores, brownies • juice, beverages.

Ice Cream Cabin—Soft-serve ice cream • floats • fresh fruit • beverages.

Africa

Harambe Fruit Market—Fruit stand near entrance to Kilimanjaro Safaris • fresh fruit, chips, giant pretzels • beer, juice, beverages.

Harambe Popcorn—Popcorn • coffee • beer, beverages.

Kusafiri Coffee Shop and Bakery—Inside Tusker House (with an additional outside window) • perfect for a quick breakfast before boarding the Kilimanjaro Safaris • tables out back along the Discovery River • pastries, cookies, cake, brownies, muffins, giant iced cinnamon rolls • coffee, hot tea, espresso, cappuccino, hot cocoa, sodas, juice.

Munch Wagon—At Rafiki's Planet Watch • beverages • pretzels • hot dogs.

Tamu Tamu Refreshments—Soft-serve ice cream, sundaes, floats, smoothies (sugar-free or with ice cream) • seating out back on a delightful patio.

Tusker House—By far the best counter-service food in the park • dine in the Safari Orientation Centre, whose whitewashed walls are covered in African handicrafts or out back where tables are set up for atmospheric dining along the Discovery River (too bad a wall blocks the view) under thatched umbrellas • breakfast: ham, egg, and cheese croissant, sausage or bacon and egg biscuit, fruit plate, cereal, muffins, giant cinnamon rolls, pastries • lunch and dinner: grilled chicken sandwich topped with Swiss cheese and ham, vegetable wrap, grilled chicken salad, smoked turkey wrapped in a flour tortilla with slaw, rotisserie and fried chicken served with lovely mashed potatoes, savory gravy, and fresh green beans • cheesecake, chocolate cake, carrot cake • Budweiser and Safari Amber beer • children's menu: mac 'n' cheese.

Asia

Anandapur Ice Cream—Soft-serve ice cream and floats served from a brightly painted bus.

Chakranadi Chicken Shop—Rotisserie chicken in a blanket (an herbed flour tortilla), pork pot stickers with spicy Asian sauce, chicken fried rice, roasted corn • beverages, beer • eat on the umbrella-covered tables nestled behind the shop.

Sunaulo Toran Fries—McDonald's fries • beverages.

Dinoland U.S.A.

Dino-Bite Snacks—Breakfast: muffins, coffee cake • hand-scooped ice cream served in a waffle cone, root beer floats • churros, popcorn • Safari Amber beer, beverages.

Dino Diner—Soft-serve ice cream • warm chocolate chip cookies • caramel apples • ice cream floats • beverages.

PetriFries—McDonald's fries • beverages.

Restaurantosaurus—Summer camp lodge cafeteria for resident students of the Dino Institute with mounted dinosaur heads, rustic twig chairs, and rock fireplaces • on balmy days head for the nifty screened-in porch for a quiet meal • breakfast: Donald's Breakfastosaurus, a character breakfast buffet hosted by Donald himself (full review on page 343) • lunch and dinner: Chicken McNuggets, Happy Meals, hot dogs, grilled chicken salad, fixings bar • chocolate chip cookies, peanut butter brownies, McDonald's cookies • Budweiser and Safari Amber beer.

Libations

Dawa Bar—Open-air bar in Harambe Village straight out of a movie set • whitewashed posts advertising cold beer and rusting, rugged bar • a pity that a solid wall blocks the views of Discovery River • full bar • several beers on tap including Disney's special brew Safari Amber plus Casablanca and Zambezi, frozen margaritas, specialty drinks.

Magic Mushroom—Wacky bar inside Rainforest Café topped with a towering toadstool • seating on bar stools (complete with tails) carved and painted to resemble the bottom half of jungle animals • outside entrance • great way to see Rainforest Café without eating a full meal • specialty drinks, smoothies, juice, coffee.

Special Entertainment: Mickey's Jammin' Jungle Parade

This island street party parade carouses around the Tree of Life each afternoon. It features Mickey and his gang riding in zany safari vehicles and a bevy of giant rolling animal sculpture drums sounding out an energetic world beat. Look for cars filled with Mickey, Minnie, Goofy, Donald, and the gang from *The Lion King,* each overloaded with their idea of exactly what should be taken on an extended vacation. Interspersed in the parade are lofty animal puppets on stilts along with rickshaws filled with lucky visitors chosen from the crowd, all frolicking along the route with cheerleaders and tour guides in one wacky parade. **15-minute parade.**

CHAPTER 5

Beyond the Theme Parks

DISNEY'S BOARDWALK

Inspired by the Mid-Atlantic wooden seaboard attractions of the 1940s, Disney's Boardwalk, just a short walk from Epcot, offers dining, shopping, and entertainment on the shores of Crescent Lake. Situated in front of the Boardwalk Inn and Villas, it's a perfect destination for an after-Illuminations dinner at Spoodles or the Flying Fish or perhaps a late night excursion to one of its nightclubs, Jellyrolls and Atlantic Dance. The Boardwalk is at its best in the evening hours when all restaurants are open and entertainment in the form of arcades, midway games, musical performers, magicians, fortune tellers, sword swallowers, and more is in high gear; don't bother during the daytime when many of the restaurants are closed and entertainment is nil. Although Jellyrolls charges a small cover, there is no admission to walk the Boardwalk. For up-to-date information call **407-939-3492**.

Getting There

The Boardwalk is a 5-minute walk from Epcot's International Gateway, a short stroll away from the Yacht and Beach Club or the Walt Disney World Swan and Dolphin, and a boat ride away from Disney–MGM Studios. If traveling from a Disney resort during park hours, take transportation to the closest theme park and then bus to the Board-walk Inn. After park hours it becomes a bit more complicated requiring a trip to Downtown Disney's Pleasure Island and then a transfer to the Boardwalk Inn; much less frustrating is to either drive a car and park it at the Boardwalk Inn or simply cab it.

Parking

Park in the complimentary self-park lot in front of the Boardwalk Inn. Valet parking is available for $6.

Hours

Dining hours vary with some spots opening as early as 7 A.M. for breakfast and others not closing until 2 A.M. Shop from 10 A.M.–10 P.M. with the exception of the Screen Door General Store, open from 8 A.M.–midnight.

Restaurants and Snacks

Big River Grille and Brewing Works—Brewery and restaurant • neither food nor the atmosphere is recommended but the brew and the view from the boardwalk tables is worth a stop • sandwiches, salads, grilled entrees. Open 11:30 A.M.–midnight; bar open until 1:30 A.M.

Boardwalk Bakery—Watch luscious pastries being prepared through glass windows from the Boardwalk • cakes, muffins, cupcakes, cookies, pastries, donuts • specialty coffees, beverages, smoothies • deli sandwiches of roast beef, chicken salad, and turkey, Italian subs.

Boardwalk Joe's—Kiosk in front of General Store • coffee, lattes, hot chocolate, coffee coolers, smoothies, juice • cookies, pastries.

Boardwalk Pizza—Spoodles pizza, calzones, salads • beer, wine, beverages.

Boardwalk to Go—Hot dogs (including foot-long, chili, and cheese dogs), onion rings, curly fries, nachos • frozen drinks.

Crepe-On-a-Stick—Kiosk serving crepes-on-a-stick: fresh strawberry and powdered sugar, apple and cinnamon-spice, Swiss milk chocolate, banana and cinnamon sugar, smoked turkey and cheddar, ham and cheese • ice cream, floats, lemonade.

ESPN Club—Dine under 90 monitors with 25 satellite feeds • live hosts • surprise appearances by sports personalities • prize-winning trivia games • salads, burgers, sandwiches, steaks, pasta, fish • drinks and light snacks in the Side Lines Bar, where each table is wired with up-to-the-minute sports action • ESPN merchandise shop • arcade. Open Sun–Thurs 11:30 A.M.–1 A.M.; Fri and Sat 11:30 A.M.–2 A.M.; appetizers only after 11:30 P.M.

Flying Fish—Dinner only • Disney's best seafood restaurant • full review on page 352.

Seashore Sweets—Ice cream and sweets shop • extremely popular after Epcot fireworks • hand-dipped ice cream, soft-serve frozen yogurt, ice cream sodas • cotton candy, cookies, confections, saltwater taffy • coffee.

Spoodles—Breakfast and dinner • Mediterranean inspired cuisine served in a family atmosphere • convenient walk-up pizza window perfect for take-out meal • full review on page 359.

Shopping

Disney's Character Carnival—Disney merchandise store.

Screen Door General Store—Small variety of grocery staples, wine, liquor.

Thimbles and Threads—Disney logo clothing for children and adults • sleepwear • watches • hats.

Wyland Galleries—Marine environmental art.

Nightclubs

Atlantic Dance—Open 9 P.M.–2 A.M.; guests must be at least 21 years old for admittance; closed Sun and Mon • newly revamped club now serving up Latin music with live entertainment each Fri and Sat night • Tues, Wed, and Thurs is DJ-driven Top 40s plus hits from the 80s and 90s • arrive at opening time and make a quick dash upstairs to the outdoor terrace for an excellent view of the Illuminations fireworks.

Jellyrolls—Open nightly 7 P.M.–2 A.M.; $5 cover charge; guests must be 21 or older for admittance • sing, clap, and laugh along with comedians at dueling pianos.

DOWNTOWN DISNEY

The addition of the West Side and Pleasure Island to Disney Marketplace created what is now known as the wildly successful Downtown Disney, a combination of over 70 scene-setting restaurants, shops, and nightclubs. During the day it's a perfect getaway from the parks, but at night after the parks close, Downtown Disney comes alive.

At Disney Marketplace you'll find the largest Disney Store in the world along with the volcano-smoking Rainforest Café. Pleasure Island is a nighttime mecca with eight clubs and a nightly New Year's Eve celebration. And then there's the West Side, loaded with dining and entertainment venues including Wolfgang Puck Café, House of Blues, Gloria Estefan's Bongos, Cirque du Soleil, and Disney Quest. This is a large complex, so utilize the boat transportation or shuttle bus between the Marketplace on one end and the West Side on the other.

Getting There

Those driving should take I-4 to Exit 67 or 68 and follow the signs to Downtown Disney. Direct buses from all Disney resort hotels and additional boat service from Old Key West. Buses stop first at the Marketplace and then between Pleasure Island and the West Side.

Parking

Parking here can be difficult, particularly during busy season and weekend evenings when both locals and visitors alike jam Downtown Disney. If you're a guest of a Disney resort, consider using Disney transportation to avoid the hassle of parking. Self-parking is complimentary with valet parking available for $6 (complimentary for guests with disabilities) Thurs–Mon after 5:30 P.M. at two locations: between the Marketplace and Pleasure Island near McDonald's and in front of Cirque du Soleil at the West Side.

Hours

Shops at Downtown Disney Marketplace are open 9:30 A.M.–11 P.M. Pleasure Island clubs are open 7 P.M.–2 A.M., shops from 10:30 A.M.–1 A.M. Downtown Disney's West Side shops are open 10:30 A.M.–11 P.M. Restaurant hours vary; see specific restaurants for exact times.

Guest Relations

Stop here for priority seating, lost and found, wheelchair and stroller rental, park passes, and services for guests with disabilities along with general information. Located at both the West Side and at the Marketplace.

ATM machines

Located near Guest Relations and next to the House of Blues on the West Side, under the Rock N Roll Beach Club at Pleasure Island, and at the World of Disney as well as Guest Relations in the Marketplace.

Downtown Disney's best dining bets

- Wolfgang Puck Café
- Portobello Yacht Club
- Rainforest Café
- Bongos
- House of Blues

Downtown Disney Marketplace

Shopaholics should head here first. With its own marina offering boat rentals and fishing trips to a wide variety of shopping (including the largest Disney Store in the world) along with the ever-popular Rainforest Café and its rumbling volcano, this is one popular spot.

Captain Jack's Marina—WaterMouse boats • canopy and pontoon boats • cane pole rentals • morning 2-hour guided fishing trip for up to five people includes boat, guide, and equipment • specialty cruises for up to 12 people. Call **407-WDW-PLAY** for reservations.

Shopping at the Marketplace

The Art of Disney—Disney collectibles • animation cells • figurines • specialty merchandise.

Discover Garden Shop—Unique plants including Disney character topiaries • fun gardening accessories • Mickey garden stakes.

Disney at Home—Unusual collection of Disney bed and bath items • vinyl shower curtains with character hooks • Mickey and Pooh logo bath towels • Tigger plush pillows • character-shaped drawer pulls • Mickey-fied chair and ottoman • Mickey-etched martini shaker and glasses.

Disney's Days of Christmas—Whopper of a Disney Christmas store • character ornaments and plush toys • stockings • tree skirts and toppers.

Disney's Pin Trader—Giant pin-trading store. Build-A-Pin station.

EUROPSPAIN by Arribas Brothers—Crystal art in the form of vases, bowls, and other sparkling items • Swarovski crystal • Guiseppe Armani figurines • Lladros • on-the-spot engraving.

Basin—Handmade, natural soaps and shampoo.

Gourmet Pantry—Gourmet food store perfect for a quick snack or take-home • pastries, cookies, croissants, cake, brownies, chocolates • sandwiches, deli meats, soup, salads • gourmet coffee, wine, liquor • small assortment of groceries and staples • gifts for cooks: character cookie jars, salt and pepper shakers, refrigerator magnets, Mickey and Minnie bride and groom wedding cake toppers.

Lego Imagination Center—Giant Lego sculptures • 3,000-square-foot outdoor play area • store with every Lego set imaginable.

Once Upon a Toy—Downtown Disney's newest store • 16,000 square feet of Disney and Hasbro toys, many of them exclusive • bulk Lincoln Logs and Tinker Toys • build-your-own Mr. Potato Head station.

Pooh Corner—Winnie the Pooh merchandise.

Rainforest Café Retail Store—Popular shop adjoining the restaurant • Rainforest Café logo merchandise and attire • plush animal toys • glow-in-the-dark t-shirts and sleepwear.

Studio M—Have your picture taken with Mickey • camera shop • personalized mouse pads and t-shirts.

Team Mickey Athletic Club—Huge assortment of sports-related merchandise, clothing, and equipment.

Summer Sands—Swimwear for all ages.

Disney's Wonderful World of Memories—Scrapbooking materials • Disney stationery and office supplies.

World of Disney—Largest Disney merchandise store in the world • 50,000 square feet filled with just about every Disney item imaginable • elaborate displays in 12 theme rooms.

Dining at Downtown Disney Marketplace

Cap'n Jack's Restaurant—Lunch and dinner • not one of Disney's best dining spots, but decent, reasonable seafood • outdoor lagoonside tables for sipping tasty frozen margaritas.

Ghirardelli Soda Fountain and Chocolate Shop—Open 10:30 A.M.–midnight • San Francisco–based chocolate stop • great assortment of chocolate delights • steaming coffee, lattes, espresso • soda shop • premium ice cream, banana splits, ice cream sundaes, hand-scooped shakes and malts, ice cream sodas, floats.

Forty Thirst Street Express—Kiosk offering specialty coffees, cold coffee drinks, smoothies, cookies.

Fulton's Crab House—Lunch and dinner. Stone Crab Lounge open until 2 A.M. Dine inside a replica of a Mississippi riverboat on some of the freshest seafood around • popular Stone Crab Lounge is one of Disney's best • full review on page 364.

McDonald's—Open 8 A.M.–1 A.M.

Rainforest Café—Lunch and dinner • follow the rumbling sound and the smell of volcanic ash to this extremely popular hot spot • dine amid waterfalls and exotic audio-animatronic jungle animals • full review on page 344.

Wolfgang Puck Express—Breakfast, lunch, and dinner • counter-service taste of Wolfgang Puck's inventive cuisine that's easier on the pocketbook • pizza, Caesar and chinoise salads, rotisserie chicken, pasta, sandwiches.

Pleasure Island

It's New Year's every night of the week at this 6-acre playground for adults. Wall-to-wall clubs and a nightly street party with live entertainment and midnight fireworks make this the party-lover's choice for nighttime entertainment. After 7 P.M. a cover charge of $21 includes entrance into all eight clubs (admission is included with an Ultimate Park Hopper); a small discount is available for Annual Pass holders. Children are welcome here; however, only those 18 years or older may enter unless accompanied by a parent or legal guardian and only those 21 years or older are allowed in Mannequins Dance Palace and BET Soundstage Club, Thurs–Sat. Clubs are open until 2 A.M.

Nightclubs at Pleasure Island

If you like partying with a crowd, plan your trip here on weekend nights when things are really hopping. Weekdays, particularly in slow season, tend to be a bit dead.

8 Trax—Disco to the hits of the 1970s • gaudy revolving disco ball and music à la *Saturday Night Fever* • 1980s night on Thurs.

Adventurer's Club—Eccentric explorers relay tales of their unbelievable escapades, inviting guests to participate in their club activities • British hunting club atmosphere • rooms adorned with funky artifacts, silly photos, and quirky trophies and treasures circa 1930, some of which come to life when you least expect it • continuous entertainment, each a bit more off-the-wall than the last • nonsmoking club.

BET Soundstage Club—The latest in rap, Hip-Hop, RandB, and Reggae • DJs and live performers • must be 21 or older for admission Thurs–Sat • karaoke on Thurs 9–11 P.M.

The Comedy Warehouse—Improv comedy delivered by the Who, What, and Warehouse players • several 30-minute shows occur nightly with no two ever alike • arrive early for a seat, particularly on weekends • nonsmoking club.

Mannequins Dance Palace—Newly renovated, award-winning dance club sporting the latest in DJ-driven modern dance music • dramatic state-of-the-art lighting and super sound system • revolving dance floor • 3 stories of contemporary furnishings and sleek bars • performances by the Pleasure Island Explosion Dancers • Open to those 18 or older Sun–Wed and those 21 or older Thurs–Sat.

Motion—Top-40 music club • two levels of DJ-driven music, blue lighting, and wide screen music videos.

The Pleasure Island Jazz Company—Sophisticated club with a New Orleans feel • live jazz and blues performers nightly • long list of cocktails, specialty coffees, wine by the glass, fine cigars • four shows nightly beginning at 8:15 P.M.

Rock N Roll Beach Club—Three-level club • live bands and DJs playing rock and roll.

Shopping at Pleasure Island

Changing Attitudes—Another trendy teen store specializing in Tommy Hilfiger, Quiksilver, and Roxy merchandise.

DTV—Disney staples store • videos and CDs • plush toys • character clothing • souvenirs.

Mouse House—All things Mickey and friends • t-shirts • sweatshirts • golf accessories • nightshirts • backpacks • luggage • silly hats.

Reel Finds—Movie-theme t-shirts and mugs • autographed star pictures • celebrity memorabilia.

Superstar Studios—Record a CD, cassette, or music video in which you are the star.

Suspended Animation—Disney collectibles • animation cells • porcelain figurines.

Dining on Pleasure Island

D'Zertz—Cake • cookies • cheesecake • ice cream • frozen yogurt • specialty coffees.

Gyros Express—Gyros • shish kebabs.

The Missing Link—Fast-food window • chicken strips, cheese steak subs, barbeque pork sandwiches, grilled chicken sandwiches, sausage subs, hot dogs, burgers, nachos • Toll House cookies • margaritas, beer, beverages.

Portobello Yacht Club—Dinner only. Pleasure Island admission not required to dine • Italian food in a nautical atmosphere • full review on page 366.

Stage Pizza—Individual pepperoni and cheese pizza.

Disney's West Side

The newest area of Downtown Disney and perhaps the most popular is Disney's West Side. Here you'll find some big names including the House of Blues, Wolfgang Puck Café, and Gloria Estefan's Bongos together with big entertainment in the form of Cirque du Soleil, an AMC 24-screen theater, and DisneyQuest. It's always hopping but those preferring a bit of peace and quiet can opt for a quiet stroll along the pleasant promenade running beside the Buena Vista Lagoon. It's definitely the most happening place around and the perfect place to allow teens to assert their independence with an evening out on the town minus the parents.

AMC Theaters

Watch newly released flicks in this state-of-the-art, 24-screen theater. Call **407-827-1308** for movie listings and show times.

Cirque du Soleil

The tent-shaped building overpowering the West Side of Downtown Disney is none other than Cirque du Soleil, the most talked about entertainment venue in town. Although it's a bit like a circus—not one you've ever seen or even imagined—it's more a mixture of circus, dance, drama, and street entertainment, more than worth the hefty price of admission. And because of its immense popularity, think about booking your seats as early 6 months in advance.

How to explain this extraordinary event? The show, entitled *La Nouba,* has over 60 mesmerizing performers in outrageous costumes entertaining in the midst of fantastical live music (not one syllable is uttered throughout the show) and surrealistic choreography. Witness daring, gravity-defying acts, each one more outlandish and bizarre than the next. Two showstoppers are the young Chinese girls performing a routine with a diabolo, a Chinese yo-yo (You won't believe it!) and a trampoline finale with power men literally running up the sides of a wall. The sheer physical strength of these performers is absolutely amazing and quite a sight to see. For tickets call **407-939-7600** or go online to **www.cirquedusoleil.com;** two shows Tues–Sat at 6 P.M. and 9 P.M.; no shows on Sun and Mon; 90-minute performances.

Tip: Although some seats are better than others, there really isn't a bad seat in the house. You may want to avoid the first row of the highest tier; the handicapped accessible seats in front block your view a bit.

DisneyQuest

With five floors of virtual games and adventures diverse enough to entertain the entire family, it's an indoor interactive theme park with a multitude of attractions that can be played over and over for the single cost of admission. Upstairs are 2 stories of food choices including an Internet café and an exciting food court of sorts. Open Sun–Thurs 11:30 A.M.–11 P.M.; Fri. and Sat 11:30 A.M.–midnight; same-day reentry allowed with ticket and hand stamp; Annual Pass holders receive a discount; guests under 10 must be accompanied by a parent or legal guardian.

Tip: Come during the daytime on weekdays and avoid rainy days. Although DisneyQuest is mainly geared to kids and adolescents, it's a great place for quality family time. Adults traveling alone may want to pass unless they really love games or want to try a virtual reality situation.

Four zones offer different types of action. These include:

The Explore Zone

Worth the price of admission alone • most of the popular rides are here including the best attraction of all, Pirates of the Caribbean.

Aladdin's Magic Carpet Ride—Don virtual reality head coverings while boarding a motorcycle-like contraption that controls your speed and altitude. Fly through the ancient city of Agrabah on your magic carpet in search of precious jewels.

Pirates of the Caribbean—Battle for Buccaneer Gold—Become a swashbuckling pirate in a fierce battle for treasure at this virtual, 3-D adventure. A crew of four do battle on a 20 square-foot motion platform with six gun stations poised for a skirmish. One person steers while the others man the cannons, shooting at hostile ships and sea serpents as the ship rocks and pitches as if on a stormy ocean. Your final objective is to blow up Jolly Roger and his ghost ship. It's a blast (no pun intended)! **Minimum height 35 inches.**

Treasure of the Incas—Direct a tiny remote-controlled vehicle in search of Incan treasure. By using the monitors and steering wheels mounted on the wall, steer a miniature car with the help of others in your party through the maze found under a glass-enclosed floor.

Virtual Jungle Cruise—Board a life-size rubber raft and with the motion sensor oars control the direction and speed of your white-water adventure. The rafts, which inflate and deflate, together with the large projection screen simulate water motion while paddling and splashing through a prehistoric world of dinosaurs.

Create Zone

Animation Academy—Take a mini-course in Disney animation on digital sketchpads to create your own cartoon character. If you're happy with your creation it may be purchased at the Guest Gallery.

Cyberspace Mountain—One of the most popular attractions here is this design-your-own roller coaster ride. Create the coaster of your dreams with the aid of a computer and Bill Nye, the Science Guy, and then actually ride your idea of the perfect coaster. Guests may control speed, drops, loops, and corkscrews before trying it all out in a 360-degree pitch-and-roll simulator. Afterward watch a video of your upside-down self . Up to two people may ride the simulator together. **Minimum height 51 inches.**

Living Easels—Frustrated artists can make a creation with a choice of backgrounds and then enhance it with a variety of creatures, characters, and plants. Of course, you may purchase a copy of your artwork at the Guest Gallery.

Magic Mirror—Perfect for those who would like a makeover, even if it is only virtual. Have your picture taken in front of a mirror and then proceed to change as many aspects of your face as you desire. Pictures of your creation may be purchased at Guest Gallery.

Radio Disney Songmaker—Create your own original song inside a sound booth by choosing the music, title, lyrics, and singer. A CD of your masterpiece may be purchased at the Guest Gallery.

Sid's Create-A-Toy—If you loved that creepy kid from *Toy Story*, you'll love creating a computerized monster toy from the parts of various creatures strewn throughout Sid's room. You can actually purchase the twisted creature from Guest Gallery.

Replay Zone

Buzz Lightyear's AstroBlaster—It's space-age bumper cars! Be either the driver or the gunner in your two-seat "astroblaster" vehicle. The driver vacuums up as many of the asteroid balls that roll around on the floor as possible while the gunner proceeds to shoot them from cannons. A direct hit causes the cars to spin wildly. **Minimum height 51 inches.**

Midway on the Moon—Play arcade-type games for prizes. These require an additional fee to participate.

Classic Games—Some of the old favorites from arcades of the past.

Score Zone

Daytona USA—Racecar driver Sega game; up to 12 can compete in a race to the finish.

Invasion! An ExtraTERRORestrial Encounter—Played in front of a 360-degree screen with one person acting as a pilot of a space walker and up to three others as gunners. The goal is to rescue as many stranded colonists as possible and obliterate all aliens. Don't waste your time; this game seems to go on forever.

Mighty Ducks Pinball Slam—Become a human pinball! Up to 12 people stand on 5-foot-tall joysticks that move with body action in relation to a 25-foot screen representing a pinball game. Then score, score, score. **Minimum height 48 inches.**

Ride the Comix—Soar through a 3-D comic book to fight villains sword-to-sword in a virtual reality game. You may have to wait in line a bit for this one.

The Underground—Walls of the latest video games along with some of the old favorites including air hockey and pinball machines.

Eating at DisneyQuest

Wonderland Café—Coffee/dessert bar with a twist • booths and chairs shaped like spades, hearts, and clubs with a play station at each booth featuring Wonderland Web Adventures • specialty coffees, lemonade, smoothies • cheesecake, mud pie, hot fudge brownie sundaes, ice cream.

Food Quest—Mini Cheesecake Factory • Soup, Salad, and Sandwich: chicken salad, pulled barbeque chicken, grilled chicken breast, cheese steak sandwiches, rotisserie chicken, Caesar salad, Chinese chicken salad, chicken quesadillas, homemade soup, nachos • Burgers, Dogs, and Wraps: wrap sandwiches (Chinese chicken, chicken Caesar, teriyaki chicken), burgers, chili, cheese dog, Polish sausage • Pizza, Pasta, and Panini: grilled sandwiches (grilled chicken, smoked turkey, or chicken and mushrooms), pizza (cheese, pepperoni, vegetarian, and barbeque chicken), pasta (meat sauce, chicken Bolognese, or marinara), brownies, cupcakes, chocolate mousse cup, apple cobbler.

Shopping at Disney's West Side

Candy Cauldron—Scrumptious candy made on the spot • candy and caramel apples • chocolates • homemade fudge • cotton candy • lollipops • Rice Crispies treats • chocolate-covered pretzels.

Celebrity Eyeworks Studio—The latest in designer sunglasses.

Cirque du Soleil Store—Cirque du Soleil videos, CDs, logo t-shirts, and related merchandise.

DisneyQuest Emporium—DisneyQuest logo clothing and merchandise • Disney souvenirs.

Guitar Gallery—Selection of electric and acoustical guitars • rare collector instruments (some as high as $24,000) • Fender, Gibson, and Martin logo hats, jackets, and t-shirts • guitar accessories.

House of Blues Retail Store—House of Blues logo merchandise • folk art from the Delta region of the South • hot sauce • Cajun seasoning • DVDs • HOB collectibles.

HoyPoloi—Beautiful glass items for the home • sculpture in glass, metal, and wood • gift items • scented candles • whimsical lamps • indoor water sculptures • unusual jewelry.

Magic Master—Small magic emporium filled with all the trappings needed for hocus-pocus fun • magic tricks and kits • reproductions of vintage magic books and posters • continuous demonstrations, many of which are explained behind the store's bookcase.

Magnetron—Every refrigerator magnet imaginable.

Mickey's Groove—Everything Mickey Mouse, including clothing, hats, and merchandise.

Planet Hollywood on Location—Planet Hollywood merchandise.

Sosa Family Cigars—Fine cigars • smoking accessories from around the world • master cigar roller in action Thurs–Sat evenings.

Starabilias—Nostalgic star memorabilia • movie props • star clothing • autographed LPs • signed movie posters • huge assortment of collectibles • vintage pinball machine • CD jukebox.

Virgin Megastore—2-story store home to a mammoth selection of music • extraordinary World Music selection • preview CDs at the many listening stations located throughout the store before you buy • books • magazines • software • videos • great children's section • small café serving coffee, beverages, and pastries with an outdoor patio high above the West Side.

Dining at Downtown Disney's West Side

Bongos—Cuban theme restaurant and entertainment spot owned by Gloria Estefan • full review on page 363.

Café Cubano—Bongo's walk-up window sidewalk café • café Cubano, café leche, café Americano • Cuban sandwiches, black bean soup, ham croquettes, empanadas filled with chicken or beef, papas rellena (breaded potato stuffed with ground beef Creole) • tres leches cake (absolutely delicious sponge cake topped with a mixture of three types of milk), flan (traditional, cheese, or chocolate). Open 10:30 A.M.– at least 11:30 P.M.

House of Blues—Lunch, dinner, and Sunday Gospel Brunch • great Mississippi Delta–style dishes • popular Sunday Gospel Brunch • live blues Thurs–Sat nights • 2,000-person capacity music hall • full review on page 365. Call 407-934-BLUE or go online at www.hob.com for information and reservations.; tickets also available at Ticketmaster.

Wetzel's Pretzels—Handmade pretzels in a variety of flavors.

Planet Hollywood—Lunch and dinner. Popular chain restaurant with a funky "out-of-this-world" atmosphere • barrage of movie memorabilia • giant video screens running a constant stream of movie clips •

just passable food but teens think it's the greatest. Open 11 A.M.–1 A.M.; bar closes at 2 A.M.

Wolfgang Puck Grand Café—Four separate dining concepts in one facility: café with both indoor and patio seating, upscale dining room on 2nd floor, B's Lounge and Sushi Bar, express patio dining • full review on page 367.

WATER PARKS

At Walt Disney World visitors can choose from two different water parks, each with its own brand of entertainment. At Blizzard Beach you'll find the 120-foot Summit Plummet slide and at the tropical Typhoon Lagoon is a whopper of a surf pool. Both are beautifully themed and landscaped and each offers something for just about everyone. A third water park, River Country, did not reopen for the summer of 2002 and there is no word on it reopening in 2003.

Locker and towel rentals are available at both parks and life jackets are complimentary with an ID required for rental. Coolers are allowed as long as they don't contain alcoholic beverages or glass containers (alcoholic drinks may be purchased within the parks). An adult must accompany children under age 10 and all swim attire must be free of rivets, buckles, or exposed metal. Parking is free.

Arrive early in the morning to avoid the long lines that start forming at almost every attraction by midday. During the summer months parks are sometimes filled to capacity by mid-morning and new guests are kept from entering until late in the afternoon. Weekends are the very worst when the locals add to the swell. And during the sizzling days of summer don't forget to bring water footwear to protect tender feet on the scorching hot pavements. Both parks are on a rotating schedule of refurbishment in the winter months so call ahead before heading out for the day.

Tip: In the busy summer months when the water parks are open until 8 P.M., think about arriving mid to late afternoon when the morning guests are beginning to depart. It's the best time to enjoy the attractions minus the crowds.

Blizzard Beach

Disney's newest and largest water park has a very strange theme of a melting alpine ski resort in the middle of the hot Florida sunshine. The thaw has created a watery "winter" wonderland where chairlifts carry swimmers instead of skiers up to slalom and bobsled runs that are now thrilling waterslides. Although you'll find quite a few tame attractions here, this is Disney's water park for daredevils with wild, rushing water and death-defying slides. Upon arrival head straight for Summit Plummet to avoid huge lines later in the day.

Hours vary according to the season but are usually 10 A.M.–5 P.M. with extended hours until 8 P.M. in the summer months. For several months each winter Blizzard Beach closes for refurbishment. In the cooler months the park is closed on Fri and Sat. Call **407-560-3400** for up-to-date information. Admission prices are $31 for adults and $25 for children ages 3–9.

Getting There

Blizzard Beach is located in the Animal Kingdom area on West Buena Vista Drive. If using Disney transportation, direct buses depart from all resorts, the Animal Kingdom, and the Ticket and Transportation Center (TTC).

Attractions
CHAIRLIFT

A one-way chairlift ride to the top of 90-foot Mt. Gushmore for access to the daredevil slides. If the wait is too long, walk the 138 stairs of the Summit Trail to the top. **Minimum height 32 inches.**

CROSS COUNTRY CREEK

Seven different entrances access this slow-moving creek encircling the park, perfect for those who want to lazily tube away the afternoon.

DOWNHILL DOUBLE DIPPER

Partially enclosed, side-by-side tube slides great for a competitive downhill race. **Minimum height 48 inches.**

MELTAWAY BAY

One-acre wave pool with "melting snow" waterfalls. The swells here are not as intense as those at Typhoon Lagoon.

RUNOFF RAPIDS

Those wanting a thrill but not a scare will love this attraction. Tube down your choice of three runs (one is enclosed, the others are open) for a blast of a ride. The enclosed slide is not as dark as it seems with tiny pinholes of light peeking through as you zip along. To reach this attraction go behind Mt. Gushmore, pick up a tube at the bottom of a tall flight of stairs, and start climbing.

SKI PATROL TRAINING CAMP

The preteen set beeline it here for tame water attractions including easy slides, a T-bar drop, and a floating iceberg walk.

SLUSHER GUSHER

Double-humped, 90-foot speed slide through a snowbanked gully. **Minimum height 48 inches.**

SNOW STORMERS

Set of three slides allow guests to race headfirst through slalom-style switchbacks.

SUMMIT PLUMMET

The king of all water park attractions. From the top is a 120-foot plunge at speeds of 60 mph down the tallest, fastest waterslide in the U.S. The slide itself is a 350-foot speed trap where daredevils body slide so fast they won't even know what hit them as they plummet to the bottom. **Minimum height 48 inches.**

TEAMBOAT SPRINGS

One of the most popular rides in the park, this 1,200-foot white-water raft ride is the longest in the world. Accommodating from three to five people per raft, it twists and turns through a fun-filled succession of waterfalls.

TIKE'S PEAK

Designed for those under 4 feet tall, there's sand play, wading pools, a squirting ice pond, igloo forts, and tiny waterslides perfect for small fry.

TOBOGGAN RACERS

Eight-lane mat slide where a challenge means headfirst down a steep slope.

Eating

Avalunch—Foot-long hot dogs, honey mustard chicken sandwich, deli club wrap, grilled chicken Caesar salad • ice cream • beverages.

Lottawatta Lodge—Ski lodge–style eatery, the largest in the park • burgers, pizza, barbeque chicken sandwich, broiled chicken sandwich, chicken Caesar salad, chicken strips, chicken or deli wraps, foot-long hot dogs, turkey legs • children's menu: mac 'n' cheese, chicken strips, hot dog.

Warming Hut—At the base of the Downhill Double Dippers • foot-long hot dogs, smoked barbecue pork sandwich, grilled chicken Caesar salad, smoked turkey leg • ice cream • beverages.

Shopping

Beach Haus—Swimsuits • coverups • water footwear.

Typhoon Lagoon

This 56-acre tropical fantasyland is a beauty. The premise is that of a great storm sweeping everything in its path to a once sleepy resort town that became Typhoon Lagoon. The shrimp boat "Miss Tilly" perched high atop the 95-foot summit of Mount Mayday creates a ruckus every half hour when it tries in vain to dislodge itself by spewing a geyser of water high above the park. Geared toward a bit tamer crowd than Blizzard Beach, only one waterslide here is a daredevil's delight. The park's main draw is the 2¾-million-gallon wave pool that boasts the tallest simulated waves in the world (some as high as 6-feet tall).

Hours vary according to the season but are usually 10 A.M.–5 P.M. with extended hours until 8 P.M. in the summer months. For several months each fall Typhoon Lagoon closes for refurbishment. In cooler months the park is closed on Sun and Mon. Call **407-560-4141** for up-to-date information. Admission prices are $31 for adults and $25 for children ages 3–9.

Getting There

Typhoon Lagoon is located across Buena Vista Drive from Downtown Disney's West Side just off I-4. If using Disney transportation the bus to catch is marked Downtown Disney which stops at Typhoon Lagoon.

Attractions

BAY SLIDES

Tame body slides ending in the calm side of the Surf Pool.

CASTAWAY CREEK

Those who prefer the lazy way of life relax in inner tubes carried along by the gentle currents of Castaway Creek. Jump in at one of five entrances along the creek and encounter waterfalls, caves, and rain forests as you drift along.

GANGPLANK FALLS

Family raft ride accommodating up to 4 or 5 people per raft, twists and turns through waterfalls and past rocky landscaping.

HUMUNGA KOWABUNGA

Trio of speed slides for the most daring. Fly along down 214-foot slides at speeds of around 30 mph, a feat for those with strong hearts. Lines can be excruciatingly long, so aim for this attraction first thing in the morning. **Minimum height 48 inches.**

KETCHAKIDDEE CREEK

Only those youngsters under 4 feet tall are allowed to play in this children's area of water sprays, wading pools, water cannons, mini-slides, climbing caves, and waterfalls.

MAYDAY AND KEELHAUL FALLS

Side-by-side easygoing slides for single raft riders. Mayday is a bit rougher than Keelhaul with quite a few bumps that bruise the rear.

SHARK REEF

Pick up your snorkeling gear and prepare yourself for the bracingly cold saltwater of Shark Reef. Instructors are on hand to guide inexperienced snorkelers as they swim through a short but sweet pool of tropical fish, stingrays, and harmless sharks, all assembled around a sunken tanker. This is an excellent way to introduce children to snorkeling in a non-threatening manner and for those nonswimmers in the group an underwater viewing room in the hold of the ship offers a peek through its portholes. To alleviate panic, remind children (and for that matter some adults) that the leopard and bonnethead sharks here are harmless.

STORM SLIDES

Though quite a bit tamer than Humunga Kowabunga, this trio of body slides are for those with a bit more daring. Visitors corkscrew down 300 feet through caves and waterfalls at speeds of about 20 mph. Try all three with a bit different experience offered on each.

TYPHOON LAGOON SURF POOL

The main attraction here is Florida's largest inland surfing lagoon. What you may think is a typhoon warning is the foghorn announcing the impending wave that is soon to follow, some as high as 6 feet. A separate but nearby lagoon for children is perfect for those too small for a wave in the face. The surrounding beach is loaded with lounge chairs and thatched-roofed coverings for your relaxation (if that's possible considering the crowds of people and the constant shrieking from the pool). If something quieter is more to your liking, intimate lounging areas can be found on the Shark Reef side of the park or at the super-secluded Out of the Way Cay, a beach where only adults long to be.

SURFING LESSONS

Before park opening on Tues and Fri is your chance to take surfing lessons in the huge wave pool. Surfboards are provided. $125. Participants must be at least 8 years old. Call **407-WDW-SURF** for reservations.

Eating

Leaning Palms—Hot dogs, chili dogs, cheeseburgers, hot deli sandwich, fried chicken sandwich, cheese and pepperoni pizza, grilled chicken

Caesar salad • milkshakes, virgin strawberry coladas, wine coolers, beer • children's menu: grilled cheese pretzel, hot dog, PB&J sandwich.

Typhoon Tilly's—Fish and chips, chicken wrap, fried chicken, Philly cheese steak sub, meatball sub, foot-long hot dogs • children's menu: grilled cheese pretzel, hot dog.

Shopping

Singapore Sal's—Swimwear • resort clothing • beach towels • hats • water footwear • sandals • sunglasses • sunscreen • Typhoon Lagoon logo merchandise.

SPAS

When your muscles are aching and your body is screaming for rest after days at the parks, sooth your jangled nerves at a spa. Immerse yourself in luxury with one or two of these feel-good treatments guaranteed to rejuvenate and swiftly get you back on your feet and ready for another long day of walking.

The Grand Floridian Spa

This luxurious 9,000-square-foot spa and health club offers a broad range of treatments and packages along with an adjoining health club. Open 6 A.M.–9 P.M. Guests ages 10 and older are welcome in the spa although an adult must accompany those under 18. Call **407-824-2332** for further information and reservations. Treatments include:

Massage therapies: Swedish massage • sports massage • shiatsu • mother-to-be massage • reflexology.

Skin care treatments: Gentlemen's facial • my first facial for ages 4–12 • aromatherapy facial • stress recovery facial.

Water therapies and soaks: Aromatherapy bath • sports bath with deep heat • peaceful nights bath with candlelight, essential oils, and bubbling jets.

Body treatments: Aromatic herbal body scrub • aromatherapy massage and body wrap • paraffin body masque to soothe muscles and joints • marine algae body masque.

Hand and foot treatments: Spa manicure or pedicure • my first manicure or pedicure for children • paraffin treatments for dry hands and feet • soothing tired legs treatment.

Couples treatments: Grand Romantic Evening in a candlelit couples room with each person receiving an aromatherapy massage • 3-hour couples instructional massage with step-by-step instruction in massage therapy.

Canyon Ranch SpaClub at Gaylord Palms Resort

The 20,000-square-foot spa facility at the new Gaylord Palms Resort is the largest one in Central Florida. Certainly the most expensive spa around, they offer an array of treatments available in 25 treatment rooms. The adjoining spa boutique offers makeup and skin care products to take home. There is an adjoining fitness club as well as a full-service salon. A full menu of services is available online at **www.canyonranch.com.** Open 8 A.M.–9 P.M. Call **407-586-2051** for spa reservations.

Facials: Delicate antioxidant facial • deep cleansing/purifying facial • aqua lift replenishing facial.

Massage: Stone massage using heated, round basalt stones • sports massage • shiatsu • reflexology • euphoria (aromatherapy scalp massage followed by a warm botanical body mask and a soaking tub, then a light, relaxing massage).

Body scrubs: Mango sugar glo scrub • seaweed, moor mud, or grape seed mud cocoon • grape seed scrub.

Body treatments: Revitalizing hydrotherapy • contouring hydrotherapy.

The Greenhouse Spa at Portofino Bay Hotel

Spoil yourself at Portofino Bay Hotel's luxurious facility offering 14 treatment rooms. The adjoining fitness center, complimentary with a spa treatment, has a full gym with sauna and locker facilities. In-room and in-cabana massage offered as well.

Open 6 A.M.–8 P.M. with personal services beginning at 8 A.M. and salon hours of 9 A.M.–7 P.M. Call **407-503-1244** for an appointment. Complimentary transportation provided from the Hard Rock Hotel.

Massage therapies: Well-being massage • aroma stone therapy • well-being back massage.

Face treatments: Herbal cleansing • aromapure facial • oxygen facial • pro-collagen facial • vitamin C facial.

Anti-aging treatments: Microdermabrasion treatment • clinical face peel • intensif facial • intensif eye saver.

Body treatments: Hydromassage • exotic lime and ginger salt glow • cellutox aroma spa ocean wrap • total glow self-tanning treatment.

Hand and foot treatments: Ultimate spa manicure and pedicure • men's manicure • reflexology pedicure • reflexology foot massage.

SPECIAL EXCURSIONS

Although everything at Walt Disney World seems special, several offerings really take the cake. Plan on at least one of the following excursions to make your stay extra unique, a memory to last a lifetime.

Birthday cruises

Celebrate that special occasion with a pontoon birthday cruise complete with driver, birthday cake, and nonalcoholic beverages. Offered at the Yacht Club, Contemporary, and the Wilderness Lodge. $220 for up to 12 people.

Children's tea party

There is a **Wonderland Tea Party** Mon–Fri at 1:15 P.M. at **1900 Park Fare** in the Grand Floridian. Hosted by characters from *Alice in Wonderland,* the children play games, listen to stories, and drink apple "tea." Strictly for children ages 3–10. $25. Call **407-WDW-DINE** for reservations.

Fireworks cruise

Each evening from the docks of the Boardwalk, Yacht Club, and all of the Magic Kingdom Resorts, boatloads of visitors depart for a special viewing of either the Fantasy in the Sky display at the Magic Kingdom or Illuminations at Epcot. From the privacy of your own piloted boat, cruise around before anchoring at a prime viewing spot from which to view the fireworks show.

Illumination cruises are offered nightly with your choice of either a 24-foot pontoon boat seating 10 or a beautiful 24-foot reproduction of a 1930s Chris Craft, the Breathless, accommodating 6 to 7 people. Reservations can be made up to 90 days in advance and sometimes sell out on the first day. Starting at $120. Call **407-WDW-PLAY**.

Hayrides and horseback riding

Disney's Fort Wilderness offers several opportunities for the frustrated cowboy. Hayrides depart each evening from Pioneer Hall for a 45-minute trip at a cost of $8 per adult and $4 per child. No reservations are taken; the wagon departs when full. Or consider a very tame, cowboy-guided trail ride for a cost of $30 per person with a minimum age of 9 and 48-inches tall and a maximum weight of 250 pounds. Reservations are required and may be made up to 2 weeks in advance by calling **407-WDW-PLAY**. Younger children can opt for a $2 pony ride at the Fort Wilderness Petting Farm.

The Villas of Grand Cypress Equestrian Center

Open to the public, offers trails rides along with private lessons (see the individual resort listing for details). For more information call **407-239-4700**.

Parasailing and water-skiing

For water-ski and parasailing action head to the **Contemporary Resort**. Water-ski, wakeboard, and tube for $140 per hour including the boat, driver, and instruction. Regular parasailing packages begin at $85 per flight for a single and $135 for a tandem including 8–10 minutes in the air and 450 feet of line. Premium packages begin at $105 for a single and $155 for a tandem with 10–12 minutes in the air and 600 feet of line. Participants must weigh at least a total of 100 pounds and no more than 300 pounds. For reservations call **407-WDW-PLAY** up to 90 days in advance.

302 ᘓThe Luxury Guide to Walt Disney World

Picnic cruises

Book a picnic cruise from the Wilderness Lodge for an afternoon on Bay Lake and the Seven Seas Lagoon.

Pirate's cruise—Children ages 3–10 sail from the dock of the Grand Floridian on a 2-hour supervised trip to a deserted island in search of buried treasure. The $25 fee includes snacks, bandanas, and treasure. Call **407-WDW-DINE** for reservations. Mon, Wed, and Thurs at 10 A.M.

Rent a yacht

For the ultimate in luxury, charter a 45-foot Sea Ray yacht, the Grand I, departing from the **Grand Floridian Resort.** Accommodating up to 12 people, it includes a captain and a deckhand. Food and cocktails are an additional charge. Cost is $350 per hour. Call **407-824-2439** for reservations.

Surfing lessons

Before **Typhoon Lagoon** opens on Tues and Fri, surfing lessons are offered, plus a chance to catch 10 waves in the huge wave pool. Surfboards are provided. Guests must furnish their own transportation to the park since buses are not up and running that early in the morning. Participants must be at least 8 years old and strong swimmers. $125. Call **407-939-7529** for reservations up to 60 days in advance. Minimum of 13 people per class.

CHAPTER 6

Sporting Diversions

If it's the outdoors you like, Disney and the surrounding area is definitely the place to head. Along with an overabundance of theme parks there is also a wealth of sporting activities. Miles of waterways insure plenty of boating and fishing, golf courses abound, tennis courts are located at just about every property, and plenty of pathways insure room for bicycles and joggers. The sunny Florida weather almost guarantees year-round access with the exception of an occasional cold snap or two. And if spectator sports are your thing, there's the Wide World of Sports located right on Disney property.

GOLF

Disney Golf

With four out of six of Disney's golf courses a tradition on the PGA Tour, there is certainly no lack of choice when it comes to playing a round while visiting Mickey Mouse. In fact, some have been known to never quite make it to the parks, so intent are they on trying to play all of Disney's 99 holes. At each are full-service clubhouse facilities including pro shops, driving ranges, locker rooms, on-course beverage service, and a snack bar or restaurant. Guests of all Disney resorts receive complimentary taxi transportation, preferred tee times, and special rates. Golf clubs and shoes are available for rent. For more information visit the Disney golf website at **www.golf.disneyworld.com**.

Fees—There are three rate seasons with each course charging slightly different rates (Eagle Pines and Osprey Ridge are the most expensive). During high season (mid-Jan–end of Apr) rates are $129–174, May–Sept $95–115, and Oct–mid-Jan $110–145. Day guests pay $5 more and twilight specials are offered for about half the price. The 9-hole, walking Oak Trail is $38 for adults and $20 for juniors.

Instruction—Available from the PGA Professional Staff at any course. Half-hour private lessons are $50 per adult and $30 for juniors age 17 and under.

Tee times—To book tee times or for golf information call 407-WDW-GOLF. Reservations may be made up to 90 days ahead for Disney resort guests, 30 days ahead for day guests, and must be guaranteed with a major credit card.

Osprey Ridge and Eagle Pines

Disney's newest courses both play from the Bonnet Creek Golf Club located between the Magic Kingdom and Downtown Disney. Osprey Ridge, recognized as one of the top 10 resort courses in America by *Golf* magazine, offers the peaceful remoteness of a gorgeous woodland and wetland setting. Dramatically raised greens and tees, 70 bunkers, and 9 water holes make this Tom Fazio–designed course Disney's most challenging. *7,101 yards. Slope: 135.*

Eagle Pines, quite a contrast to Osprey, offers a different type of challenge with its low profile and vast sand beds. In its nature preserve setting, this Pete Dye–designed course boasts low, dish-shaped fairways separated by sand and native grasses, 16 holes with water, and strategically placed bunkers. Back at the clubhouse the Sand Trap Bar and Grill offers light choices for breakfast and lunch with indoor and outdoor dining along with a full bar. *6,772 yards. Slope: 131.*

Palm and Magnolia

Located near the Magic Kingdom within the grounds of the Shades of Green Resort (an armed forces resort on Disney property) are the first courses ever opened at Walt Disney World, both designed by Joe Lee. Here the National Car Rental Golf Classic is held each October and here the 18th hole of the Palm is rated as the 4th toughest on the PGA Tour.

The heavily wooded Palm is one of Disney's most difficult courses with fairways cinched by tall trees and lovely, elevated greens, nine water holes, and 94 bunkers *(6,957 yards. Slope: 133)*. At Magnolia, the longest of all Disney's courses, wide fairways are framed magnificently by over 1500 magnolia trees. It too doesn't lack for challenge with 12 holes of water and 98 bunkers in the midst of large, undulating greens. Check out the 6th hole hazard in the shape of Mickey Mouse *(7,190 yards. Slope: 133)*.

Oak Trail

In a corner of the Magnolia Course, this 9-hole, par 36 walking course is a good choice for family fun. With its small, rolling greens it's an ideal course for beginners; however, it does pose a few challenges for the serious golfer or a quick round of golf for those who want to get on to the parks. *2,913 yards.*

Lake Buena Vista Course

Located in the Downtown Disney area within the grounds of the soon-to-open Saratoga Springs Resort and the Old Key West Resort is this country club setting, Joe Lee–designed course having the rare distinction of having hosted a PGA, LPGA, and a USGA event. Wandering through pine forests and weaving its way through the resorts, this shortest of Disney's 18-hole courses sports small, elevated greens with plenty of bunkers, narrow fairways, and an island green on the 7th hole. This is a great place for beginners, but challenging enough for the more experienced. Bird-lovers will appreciate that it's also designated a certified Audubon Cooperative Sanctuary. *6,819 yards. Slope: 128.*

Golfing Beyond Disney

The Orlando area is bursting at the seams with many excellent golf courses. Here are several close to Walt Disney World:

Celebration Golf Club

Call **407-566-GOLF** or **888-2PLAY18** for tee time reservations.

Just 10 minutes away from Walt Disney World in the town of Celebration is a Robert Trent Jones, Sr. and Jr.–designed course running amid a park-like setting in a natural wetland environment. Rated number 12 in the state of Florida by Florida Golf News, its rolling terrain winds through picturesque lakes and a landscape of native oak, pine, and magnolia. Featuring demanding greens along with strategic hazards, it also sports five sets of tees on every hole. The Nike Golf Learning Center is perfect for new golfers and the pro shop offers golf accessories and name brand attire. A full-service restaurant, the Windmill Tavern, serves breakfast and lunch daily. *6,772 yards. Slope: 135.*

Falcon's Fire Golf Club

For information, call **407-239-5445** or toll free at **877-878-FIRE** or go online at **www.falconsfire.com.**

This Rees Jones–designed, 18-hole course offers beautiful scenery and plenty of challenges with loads of bunkers and deceptive greens. Located close by in Kissimmee, you'll find a well-stocked pro shop, the Falcon's Nest Restaurant, even complimentary valet parking. Carts come with the Pro Shot Digital Caddy System where monitors give distances to the pin and suggestions on each hole. *6,901 yards. Slope: 138.*

Grand Cypress Golf Club

Call **800-835-7377** or **407-239-1909** for information and reservations.

Cited by *Golf* magazine as one of the Best Golf Resorts in America with the North and South courses named among the top 25 courses in America, the Grand Cypress Resort, consisting of the Hyatt Regency Grand Cypress and the Villas of Grand Cypress, boasts four Jack Nicklaus–designed golf courses: the 9-hole North, the 9-hole South, the 9-hole East, and the 18-hole St. Andrews–style New Course. At the Golf Club, located on the grounds of the Villas of Grand Cypress, the Golf Academy offers lessons under the guidance of PGA and LPGA certified professionals in a 21-acre practice facility. Also available is CompuSport, which uses video teaching technology in an innovative way to perfect your game.

MINIATURE GOLF

Miniature golf fans have four courses to play at Disney, each sporting 18 fun-filled holes.

Charge to play is $10 for adults and $8 for children ages 3–9; receive a 50% discount on a second round played the same day. Hours are 10 A.M.–11 P.M. subject to weather and seasonal changes. For more information call 407-WDW-PLAY.

Fantasia Park

Two 18-hole miniature golf courses, Fantasia Gardens and Fantasia Fairways, are located across Buena Vista Drive from the Swan Hotel near Epcot, Disney MGM Studios, and the Boardwalk. Play amid tutu-clothed hippos, silly alligators, and cavorting fountains ending with Sorcerer Mickey splashing guests with his mop and buckets at the *Fantasia*-inspired Fantasia Gardens course.

The more challenging Fantasia Fairways was designed as a miniature golf course and is great for those who like a more traditional round amid sand traps, water hazards, doglegs, roughs, and lush putting greens. A limited snack bar with small arcade is on-site.

Winter Summerland

Designed for Santa and his elves as an off-season vacation spot, this hot and cold, sand and snow miniature golf course is a kick. Sitting adjacent to Blizzard Beach, guests play either the Snow course amid Christmas music, ice hockey rings, snowmen, ice castles, and igloos or the Sand course where Caribbean music plays while Santa grills turkey outside his mobile home surrounded by sandcastles and surfboards. A limited snack bar is on the premises.

TENNIS

For Disney court information call **407-WDW-PLAY**, for the courts at the Swan and Dolphin **407-824-3578**. Courts are complimentary and are on a first-come, first-served basis.

All of Disney's deluxe hotels with the exception of the Polynesian, Animal Kingdom Lodge, and the Wilderness Lodge, offer tennis courts. The tennis program is run by Peter Burwash International whose professional staff will travel to any resort court for lessons. Courts are found at the Contemporary (6 Hydrogrid Clay), the Grand Floridian (2 Har-Tru Clay), Yacht and Beach Club (1 Hard), Old Key West (3 Hard), Boardwalk Inn and Villas (2 Hard), and the Swan and Dolphin (4 Hard). Lighted courts are available everywhere. Bring your own racquet, no rentals are available.

Serious tennis players may want to consider staying at the Contemporary Resort where Disney's Racquet Club at the Contemporary Resort boasts the best facilities around with six Hydrogrid clay courts. Its pro shop offers a player-matching program along with clinics, private lessons, tennis togs, and restringing services. Open from 7 A.M.–7 P.M. daily.

Outside of Walt Disney World consider the excellent tennis facility at the Hyatt Regency Grand Cypress Racquet Club with 8 Har-Tru and 4 Deco-Turf II courts along with clinics, private and semi-private lessons. The Grand Cypress Tennis Academy offers 5 hours of instruction with videotaped analysis, match strategy, and play, along with a written evaluation and a guaranteed game match service. For information and reservations call **407-239-1234**.

BIKING

An assortment of bicycles for adults and children may be rented at the Boardwalk Inn and Villas, Wilderness Lodge and Villas, the Polynesian, and Old Key West, and off-property at the Hyatt Grand Regency Cypress and the Villas of Grand Cypress. At the Boardwalk Inn, bikers can pedal their way around the walkway surrounding the ¾-mile Crescent Lake, while those at the Wilderness Lodge can take advantage of the beauty of the adjoining Fort Wilderness and its miles of pine forests. At the Polynesian take a spin around the property on a surrey and at Old Key West you'll find trails running throughout the property.

Mongoose bicycles rent for approximately $6 per hour or $19 per day with surreys renting for $15 per half hour for a 2-seater and $17–19 for a 4-seater. Helmets are provided free of charge. Children under the age of 18 must have a signed waiver from a parent or legal guardian.

BOATING AND WATERWAYS

With miles and miles of waterways, boating is a major pastime at Walt Disney World. And with some of the most incredible weather in the nation, water sports are an important draw. Most resorts as well as Downtown Disney have their own marina with a variety of boats available for hire (see individual resort listings for specific details). Boating is offered on the following waterways:

- The Seven Seas Lagoon, accessed from the Grand Floridian and the Polynesian and connected to Bay Lake.
- Bay Lake accessed from the Contemporary Resort and the Wilderness Lodge and connected to the Seven Seas Lagoon.
- Crescent Lake around whose shores sit the Epcot Resorts of the Yacht and Beach Club, the Beach Club Villas, the Boardwalk Inn and Villas, and the Swan and Dolphin.
- Buena Vista Lagoon at Downtown Disney leads to the waterways of Old Key West.

Boating choices include:

Canoes

Only the Polynesian and the Wilderness Lodge rent canoes. A canoe adventure is available Tues and Sat at 3:30 P.M. and Thurs and Sun at 11:30 A.M. for $5 per person at the Wilderness Lodge (call marina for reservations).

Canopy Boats

These 16-foot canopy-covered, motorized boats can accommodate up to eight adults. Available at the Grand Floridian, Contemporary, Yacht and Beach Club and the Beach Club Villas, Wilderness Lodge, Old Key West, and Downtown Disney. Approximately $25 per half hour.

Luxury Yacht

For the ultimate in luxury, charter the 45-foot Sea Ray, the Grand I, docked at the Grand Floridian. Accommodating 10–12 people, it includes a captain and deckhand with food and cocktails at an additional charge. $350 per hour. For reservations call **407-824-2439**.

Pedal Boats

Available at the Swan and Dolphin (swan pedal boats) and Old Key West. $6–13 per half hour.

Pontoon Boats

Motorized 24-foot canopied pontoon boats holding up to 10 people are perfect for those who want a non-thrill ride around the Disney waterways. Available at the Grand Floridian, Contemporary, the Polynesian, Yacht and Beach Club and the Beach Club Villas, Old Key West, Wilderness Lodge, and Downtown Disney. Approximately $33 per half hour.

Sailboats

The Grand Floridian, Polynesian, Contemporary, and the Wilderness Lodge rent sailboats in various sizes accommodating from two to six people. Catamarans are available at the Grand Floridian, Polynesian, and the Contemporary, but they do require a bit of sailing experience. Approximately $20–24 per hour.

WaterMouse Boats

The boats that immediately catch the eye are these 2-seater mini-power boats zipping around Disney's lakes at an average of 22 miles per hour. Kids love them, particularly because children 12 years or older and at least 5 feet tall may drive one without adult supervision (although they must have a signed waiver from a parent or guardian). Available at the Contemporary, Polynesian, Grand Floridian, the Yacht and Beach Club and the Beach Club Villas, Downtown Disney, Old Key West, and the Wilderness Lodge. Approximately $21 per half hour.

WATER-SKIING AND PARASAILING

Head to the Contemporary Resort for water-ski and parasailing action. Run by Sammy Duvall Water Sports. See page 301 for pricing and information.

FISHING

Walt Disney World's stocked fishing lakes are filled with plenty of bass, perfect for the amateur as well as the seasoned fisherman. From the marinas of the Contemporary, Polynesian, Grand Floridian, and Wilderness Lodge and Villas is fishing on Bay Lake and the Seven Seas Lagoon. The waterways surrounding Epcot and Disney Studios are your fishing holes from boats departing the Yacht and Beach Club, Beach Club Villas, and the Boardwalk Inn and Villas. And from Cap'n Jack's Marina at Downtown Disney angle for bass on Lake Buena Vista. No fishing license is required and it's strictly catch and release.

Two-hour guided bass fishing trips (maximum of five people) are $156–184 per boat. Included is a guide, Zebco equipment, and beverages. Excursions may be prearranged up to 60 days in advance by calling 407-WDW-PLAY and must be made at least 24 hours in advance.

Special 1-hour excursions for children ages 6–12 leave the marinas of the Contemporary, Polynesian, Grand Floridian, and the Boardwalk Inn and Villas. For miles of shore fishing head over to Fort Wilderness where cane poles and rods and reels may be rented at the Bike Barn in the Meadow Recreation Area.

Guests of the Hyatt Regency Grand Cypress Resort and the Villas of Grand Cypress can fish from the shores of Lake Windsong.

JOGGING

Those amazing folks with enough energy to jog after traipsing through the parks day after day will be glad to know that a nice variety of jogging and walking paths are to be found throughout the Walt Disney World property. Information and jogging maps are available at the front desk of each resort. At the Polynesian is a path laid out through its tropical grounds, the Grand Floridian has a pathway along the Seven Seas Lagoon, and the Wilderness Lodge offers miles of trails winding through the adjoining Fort Wilderness among pines and cypress trees. Epcot Resort guests should take advantage of the boardwalk-style walkway surrounding the 25-acre Crescent Lake, and at Old Key West picturesque pathways meander throughout the property.

Off-property, the Grand Cypress Resorts offer miles of jogging courses ranging from 1.3 miles to 4.7 miles winding through the extensive property. Celebration Hotel's beautiful jogging paths begin just outside the front door encircling Celebration Lake. Hard Rock Hotel and Portofino Bay Hotel are connected by attractive pathways that make their way to and from the theme parks.

DISNEY'S WIDE WORLD OF SPORTS

This 200-acre sports complex located in the heart of Walt Disney World is exclusively devoted to athletic sports. Built for both professional and amateur events, over 30 types of sporting activities take place, making this a must stop for sports fans.

This vast development holds a 9,500-seat baseball stadium, home to the Orlando Rays AA Baseball, a 30,000-square-foot field house accommodating basketball courts (training ground for the Harlem Globetrotters), volleyball, wrestling, martial arts, and inline hockey along with a 400-meter, nine-lane track and field complex with seating for 2,000. Four grass fields each seating up to 10,000 offer space for football, soccer, lacrosse, field hockey, and cricket, and the 11-court tennis complex accommodates up to 7,500 people. The baseball quadruplex along with the stadium is the spring training ground for the Atlanta Braves. You'll also find youth baseball fields and a softball quadruplex.

Cost is $9 for adults and $7 for children ages 3–9 and covers all nonpremium events. Advance tickets for premium events through TicketMaster at **407-839-3900** or online at **www.ticketmaster.com** as well as at the box office on the day of the event. For information call **407-828-FANS** or go online at **www.disneyworldsports.com.**

Getting There

Bus transportation can be time-consuming with a transfer at Disney–MGM Studios. You may want to consider a taxi instead of the lengthy bus ride. By car take Exit 64 off I-4 and follow the signs. Parking is complimentary.

Eating

The **Official All-Star Café**—Open daily 11:30 A.M.–8 P.M. with bar hours from 8–10:30 P.M. Admission not required to dine • chicken strips, burgers, sandwiches, steaks, pasta, quesadillas, nachos, potato skins, chili • cocktails, beer.

Concessions Stands—Hot dogs • light snacks • soda • beer.

Shopping

D-Sports Shop—NFL, NBA, and NHL merchandise • ESPN merchandise • Atlanta Braves memorabilia.

Disney's Clubhouse—Baseball merchandise.

RICHARD PETTY DRIVING EXPERIENCE

*Open daily 9 A.M.–5 P.M. Riders 16 or 17 years of age must be accompanied by a parent or legal guardian. Participants must wear closed toe shoes and socks. Call **800-BE-PETTY** for advance reservations.*

For those who dream of sitting behind the wheel of a race car, here's your chance. Lying next to the Magic Kingdom is this sometimes very loud speedway where white-knuckle rides in a NASCAR Winston Cup–style race car are offered. Each experience begins with a one-hour training session. All driving participants must have a valid driver's license and must know how to drive a stick shift. Spectators are welcome for no charge. Since the track sometimes closes due to inclement weather, it's always best to call ahead.

Getting There

With its location virtually in the parking lot of the Magic Kingdom, its necessary to either make your way to the Ticket and Transportation Center (TTC) and take the shuttle located near the kennels or enter the Magic Kingdom parking lot and follow the signs, driving through the tunnel to the infield.

Ride-Along Program

For $89, ride shotgun at speeds of up to 145 mph for 3 laps around the track with an experienced driving instructor. You must be at least 16 years or older to participate. This is the only program not requiring reservations.

Rookie Experience

Those ages 18 or older can drive the car themselves for 8 laps around the course. That is, of course, after an introductory class out on the speedway. The 3-hour program is $349.

King's Experience

You'll feel like a king after 4 or 5 hours of driving 18 laps around the speedway—for the princely sum of $699. Only those 18 years or older may participate.

Experience of a Lifetime

For $1,199 you drive 30 laps (3 sessions of 10 laps), improve your skills, and maybe change careers. Only for those age 18 or older. Lasts 4–5 hours.

CHAPTER 7

Shopping

For many, shopping is the best part of a vacation. The parks are loaded with something for everyone and in just about every price range. Detailed reviews have been included in the park sections themselves. But some folks would like to bring home something minus a Mickey Mouse or Cinderella motif. Here are some of the best options away from the parks:

Belz Factory Outlet World

There are 170 stores at this indoor, mega–outlet mall, including Calvin Klein, Bag and Baggage, Wolf Camera and Video, the Gap, Woolrich, Footlocker, Mikasa, Nautica, and Sunglass Hut. Located 12 miles from Disney World just across the I-4 and Kirkman Road interchange from Universal Orlando fronting I-4 (Exit 75A) and the Florida Turnpike. Open Mon–Sat 10 A.M.–9 P.M. and Sun 10 A.M.–6 P.M.; 407-354-0126.

Crossroads at Lake Buena Vista

Lots of shopping fun: Sunglass Hut, Electronics Plus (the closest place for camcorder needs), Goodings Market (the closest grocery store to Disney), Disney Character Connection, Foot Locker, Bath and Body Works, Hallmark, and Chico's. Located at the intersection of State Road 335 and Hotel Plaza Boulevard close to Downtown Disney; 407-827-7300.

Florida Mall

This 260-store mall is anchored by Saks, Lord & Taylor, Nordstrom, Burdines, J.C. Penny, Dillards, and Sears. Other stores include Williams-Sonoma, Pottery Barn, Brookstone, Banana Republic, Abercrombie & Fitch, Guess, Benetton, Express, Waldenbooks, Harry and David, MAC Cosmetics, Cutter & Buck, and Sephora. At the corner of South Orange Blossom Trail and Sand Lake Road. From Disney take I-4 East to Sand Lake Road and go east for 4 miles. From Universal take I-4 West to Sand Lake Road. Open Mon–Sat 10 A.M.–9:30 P.M. and Sun 11 A.M.–6 P.M.; **407-851-6255.**

Groceries

There are quite a few grocery shopping options. **The Gourmet Pantry** at Downtown Disney's Marketplace offers a small selection of staples along with wine, sandwiches, and beverages. **Goodings Market** at the Crossroads Shopping Plaza close to Downtown Disney has a full line of groceries. **Publix** on Vineland near the Orlando Premium Outlets is just 5 minutes from Disney property. **Winn Dixie** and another **Publix** are located at the intersection of Sand Lake Drive and Dr. Phillips near Universal Orlando.

Lake Buena Vista Factory Stores

Shop at Adidas, Gap Outlet, Calvin Klein, Murano Glass Factory, Oneida, Sony, Sunglass Hut, and Samsonite. Located 2 miles from Disney on SR 535, **407-238-9301.**

The Mall at Millenia

If you can make it to only one mall, make it this one. Just 1 mile north of the intersection of I-4 and Florida's Turnpike close to Universal Studios, this high-end mall is just a 15-minute drive from Disney. There are more than 50 stores anchored by Bloomingdale's, Macy's, and Neiman Marcus. Shop Chanel, Tiffany and Co., Gucci, Louis Vuitton, Burberry, Hugo Boss, Cartier, St. John, Giorgio's of Palm Beach, and Cole Hahn.

Orlando Premium Outlets

This 127-store designer outlet mall includes Burberry, Ermenegildo Zegna, Escada, Armani, Hugo Boss, Bottega Veneta, Versace, and Barney's New York Outlet. Located near I-4 and Vineland (Exit 68 or SR535) close to Downtown Disney; open Mon–Sat10 A.M.–10 P.M., Sun 10 A.M.–9 P.M.; **407-238-7787.**

Pointe Orlando

You'll find FAO Schwartz , Banana Republic, Abercrombie & Fitch, Victoria's Secret, Armani Exchange, B. Dalton Bookseller, Bath and Body Works, as well as an 18-screen Muvico Theater. More than 60 retail stores located near Universal Studios at **9101 International Drive; 407-248-2838.**

Winter Park

This quaint village is a 25-minute drive from Disney; take I-4 East to Exit 87, go east on Fairbanks Avenue for 3 miles to downtown Winter Park. There are beautiful gardens as well as three notable art museums. It is also the home of the first established college in Florida. Shop along Park Avenue in the historical district, where blocks of small boutiques (Solarte is my favorite with their excellent selection of linens and pottery from France), jewelry stores, and art galleries are scattered among well-known names like Ann Taylor and Banana Republic. Relax at any number of sidewalk cafes and restaurants.

The Charles Hosmer Morse Museum of American Art has an excellent Tiffany glass collection, including an exquisite Tiffany chapel interior built for the 1892 Chicago World Columbian Exposition. There is also a 12-mile scenic boat tour on the town's chain of lakes.

Celebration

Small town America is alive and well in Celebration, Disney's perfectly planned community located just minutes from the parks. Filled with a mix of delightfully nostalgic homes, palm tree-lined boulevards, great restaurants ringing a picture-perfect lake, and charming retail shops in its compact village, it's a perfect afternoon getaway or a great alternative to Disney lodging (see page 101 for a detailed review of the Celebration Hotel).

There are several shopping spots to go along with the great ambiance. Open Mon–Sat 10 A.M.–9 P.M., Sun noon–6 P.M. You'll find Orvis; Market Street Gallery for collectibles; Jerard International for home decor; Soft as a Grape for casual clothing; White's Books and Gifts; Village Mercantile, specializing in resort clothing along with Celebration logo merchandise; and Goodings Food Market, perfect for picnic items.

Dining choices in Celebration are excellent, with the Market Street Café, Columbia Restaurant, and Café D'Antonio being the best options (see pages 369-372 for a detailed review). After all that eating there's always the 3-story Celebration Fitness Center and Day Spa offering 60,000 square feet of weight training, cardiovascular equipment, aerobics, lap pool, and kids' gym. Or take in a movie at the two-screen AMC Theater on Front Street.

Golfers should consider the Celebration Golf Club where a Robert Trent Jones, Sr. and Jr.–designed course runs amid a park-like setting in a natural wetland environment. The rolling terrain winds through picturesque lakes and a landscape of native oak, pine, and magnolia.

To reach Celebration take I-4 to U.S. 192 East (Exit 64).

CHAPTER 8

Dining

Roasted striped bass with aromatic rock shrimp lemon grass risotto. 6-hour braised veal shank with orzo pasta and soy glaze. Cornbread stuffed quail with foie gras and sauce maltaise. Those are just a sampling of some of the incredible meals found at the over 270 dining spots on Disney property. A radical culinary transformation has occurred at Walt Disney World, evident in renowned restaurants like the **California Grill at the Contemporary Resort** and the AAA 5-Diamond Award–winning **Victoria and Albert's at the Grand Floridian**. It's a world of dining just waiting to be explored.

Disney's guests are becoming more sophisticated and more demanding in their search for creative and sumptuous cuisine. The challenge has been met quite nicely with the opening of many fine dining venues, particularly at the resort hotels. Top-notch chefs are now the norm, creating exciting menus at some of the highest-rated restaurants in the country. First-rate sommeliers have fashioned outstanding wine lists, particularly at **California Grill, Citricos,** and **the Flying Fish**. In fact, Disney sells over a half million bottles of wine a year.

Once just a hot dog and hamburger haven, Disney's reputation for dreadful theme park food is rapidly changing. What used to be a virtual wilderness when it came to appetizing food is now a pleasure with choices ranging from fine dining to more than palatable counter-service food. Although you'll always find burgers and chicken fingers, you'll also discover outstanding restaurants with beautiful theming, unique atmosphere, and the most obliging and friendly waiters (in fact, I've yet

319

to meet an unfriendly person in all of Disney). Children are treated as special guests; almost every restaurant along with all counter-service spots offers a menu just for kids. Meals are delivered quickly so if a quick meal is not your cup of tea, order an appetizer only and then your entree when you are finished with the first course.

Those in need of vegetarian or low-fat options will find plenty of choices both in the full-service restaurants and many counter-service spots where usually at least one vegetarian and one light option are offered. I've included many vegetarian choices in the sample entrees below. Those with special requests, such as fat-free, sugar-free, salt-free, lactose-free, and kosher, can be accommodated at full-service restaurants as long as they receive a 24-hour notice (it's probably best to do this when making your priority seating).

As for dress codes, casual is the word. All theme park restaurants are extremely informal; however, you will find that in many resort restaurants the dress is a bit more sophisticated. Smart casual clothing is usually fine, but I have noted the dress at each restaurant outside the four theme parks.

Reservations, particularly in busy season, are very important. Advance priority seating is available at theme park and resort full-service restaurants by calling **407-WDW-DINE**. Many of the restaurants at Downtown Disney offer priority seating; call their individual numbers listed below. Same-day priority seating may be made at each park, at the restaurant itself, through Guest Relations, or by picking up any public phone in Disney and dialing*88. Those staying in a Disney concierge room or suite may make reservations through the concierge staff.

Although there are many excellent restaurants in the city center of Orlando, I have not reviewed them. Most visitors to Walt Disney World or even Universal will probably not want to drive the 30 minutes or so it would take to reach these commendable dining spots. Instead, I've concentrated on the many excellent choices closer to the parks.

A wealth of admirable restaurants have sprung up near Universal Studios, particularly in the area of **Sand Lake Road** and **Dr. Phillips Boulevard**. Here you'll find **Roy's, Chatham's Place**, and **Christini's** with **Vito's Chop House** just around the corner on International Drive. All are worth the short drive from Disney and are only a hop away from the hotels near Universal. The Peabody has three excellent restaurants and Universal's hotels have outstanding choices particularly at Portofino Bay Hotel where you'll find **Delfino Riviera** and **Mama Della's.** And don't forget **Emeril's at CityWalk,** one of the best spots around.

PRIORITY SEATING PLANNING CHART

Priority seating is Disney's answer to dining reservations, a system whereby on arrival at the designated time you will receive the next table available for your party size. In other words, they won't save a table for you but will seat you as soon as possible, certainly before any walkups. This sometimes translates as a bit of a wait, but it is certainly better than simply taking your chances and walking in without any sort of seating reservation. All Disney-operated restaurants may be pre-booked, but each has a different advance-booking schedule. Use the chart below to plan ahead.

I cannot emphasize enough how important it is to make priority seating in advance; without it, you will be spending way too much time cooling your heels waiting for a table, particularly at Epcot where the demand for dining at World Showcase is high. This is especially true in the busier times of the year and for the more popular spots like **California Grill** and the **Flying Fish**, along with all character breakfasts. For priority dining call **407-WDW-DINE** unless otherwise noted.

Priority seating available 2 years in advance—Hoop-Dee-Doo Musical Revue • Polynesian Luau.

Priority seating available 1 year in advance—All American Barbeque.

Priority seating available 180 days in advance—Victoria and Albert's.

Priority seating available 120 days in advance—All Epcot restaurants except Bistro de Paris (30 days in advance) • Disney–MGM Studios for breakfast and lunch (dinner reservations are taken beginning 60 days in advance) • all Animal Kingdom restaurants for all meals • all meals at the Disney resort restaurants including the Swan and the Dolphin.

Priority seating available 60 days in advance—All Magic Kingdom restaurants • dinner at Disney–MGM Studios • Downtown Disney restaurants • Portobello Yacht Club (call 407-934-8888) • Wolfgang Puck's upstairs restaurant at Downtown Disney (call 407-938-9653).

Priority seating available 30 days in advance—Bistro de Paris at Epcot • Fulton's Crab House at Downtown Disney (call 407-934-2628).

Priority seating 14 days in advance—Wolfgang Puck's downstairs café (call 407-938-9653).

Priority seating at the theme parks may be made at: Magic Kingdom—City Hall • Epcot—Guest Relations • Disney–MGM Studios—Guest Information at the corner of Hollywood and Sunset. • Animal Kingdom—Guest Relations.

Best Restaurants

Best Italian—Palio (the Swan) • Delfino Riviera (Portofino Bay) • Christini's.

Best seafood—Flying Fish (Boardwalk) • Roy's.

Best steaks—Shula's Steakhouse (Dolphin) • Vito's Chop House.

Best for romance—Victoria and Albert's (Grand Floridian) • Delfino Riviera (Portofino Bay).

Best for kids—Rainforest Café (Animal Kingdom and Downtown Disney) • Whispering Canyon Café (Wilderness Lodge).

Best character meal—Cinderella's Royal Table (Magic Kingdom) • Crystal Palace (Magic Kingdom).

Best Disney view—Arthur's 27 (Wyndham Palace) • California Grill (Contemporary).

Best Disney resort restaurant—California Grill (Contemporary Resort).

Best Downtown Disney restaurant—Wolfgang Puck Café.

Best Universal hotel restaurant—Delfino Riviera (Portofino Bay).

Best CityWalk restaurant—Emeril's.

Best Epcot Illuminations view—Rose and Crown.

Best milkshakes—Beaches and Cream (Beach Club Resort).

Best pizza—Wolfgang Puck's (Downtown Disney) • Tony's Town Square (Magic Kingdom).

Best breakfast—Spoodles (Boardwalk).

Best Food at the Magic Kingdom—Restaurant: Liberty Tree Tavern for lunch; fast food: Pecos Bill Café.

Best Food at Disney–MGM Studios—Restaurant: Hollywood Brown Derby; fast food: ABC Commissary.

Best Food at Epcot—Restaurant: Bistro de Paris; fast food: Tangierine Café in Morocco.

Best Food at the Animal Kingdom—Restaurant: Rainforest Café; fast food: Tusker House.

Best Food at Universal Studios—Restaurant: Finnegan's Bar and Grill; fast food: Classic Monster Café.

Best Food at Islands of Adventure—Restaurant: Mythos; fast food: Thunder Falls Terrace.

SPECIAL DINING SHOWS

Combining brunch or dinner with a show is a Disney specialty, particularly popular with the little ones. Families love to attend the **Hoop-Dee-Doo Revue, Polynesian Luau,** and **Mickey's Backyard Barbeque,** shows so popular that reservations are taken 2 years in advance. Priority seating is a must and can be made by calling 407-WDW-DINE. For a change of pace consider the **House of Blues Gospel Brunch** on Sundays offering a Southern-style buffet along with foot-stomping gospel music.

Hoop-Dee-Doo Revue $$$$

Daily at 5 and 7:15 P.M.; in the busier months a 3rd show is offered at 9:30 P.M.; price includes tax and gratuity.

Located at Fort Wilderness' Pioneer Hall is an old-fashioned hoedown dinner with entertainment provided by country-western singers, can-can dancers, and slapstick comedians. The down-home chow served family style includes fried chicken, smoked pork ribs, corn, baked beans, salad, bread, strawberry shortcake, beverages, beer, and sangria. Since there is no parking at Pioneer Hall, those driving should park in the Fort Wilderness parking lot and take an internal bus to the Settlement Depot. Buses run from the Ticket and Transportation Center (TTC), but it will still be necessary to take an internal bus. Those staying at the Contemporary Resort or Wilderness Lodge can take a boat to Fort Wilderness with a short walk to Pioneer Hall.

Mickey's Backyard Barbeque $$$$

Tues and Thurs, 6:30–9:30 P.M., early Mar–late Nov and selected dates in Dec. Price includes tax and gratuity.

Have a rootin', tootin' time chowin' down on barbeque to the tunes of a live country-western band. The picnic-style festivities take place in an outdoor, covered pavilion near Pioneer Hall with line dancing and games led by your hosts Mickey, Minnie, Chip 'n' Dale, and Goofy. The fare is an all-you-care-to-eat buffet of barbeque pork ribs, baked chicken, hot dogs, baked beans, corn-on-the-cob, coleslaw, pasta salad, cornbread, watermelon, cake, draft beer, wine, iced tea, and lemonade. If you're mainly interested in seeing Mickey Mouse, a better choice would be one of the excellent character meals held at the resorts or parks. If barbeque and music are your cup of tea this might be the place for you. Allow plenty of time to take the internal resort bus from the Fort Wilderness parking lot or bus stop to the Pioneer Hall area (see directions above).

Polynesian Luau $$$$

Tues–Sat at 5:15 and 8 P.M.; price includes tax and gratuity; subject to cancellation in inclement weather.

The Polynesian Resort hosts a traditional luau with island dancing and music in an outside, covered dining area of candlelit tables. A special appearance by Mickey and Minnie comes with the all-you-care-to-eat Polynesian-style meal served family style featuring tropical-style appetizers, roasted chicken and pork, fried rice, sauteed vegetables, pineapple upside-down cake, and unlimited beverages including beer and wine. Children have additional options of mac 'n' cheese or PB&J sandwiches.

House of Blues Gospel Brunch $$$$

Sundays at 10:30 A.M. and 1 P.M. For reservations call the House of Blues box office at 407-934-BLUE.

On Sundays there's plenty of foot stomping and good old soulful music in the House of Blues at Downtown Disney. The bountiful Southern-style buffet includes rosemary marinated chicken breast, chicken jambalaya, rib fingers with a Jack Daniels barbeque sauce, roasted top round of beef, boiled shrimp, smoked salmon, fresh fruit salad, field greens salad, Italian pasta salad, an omelet station, roasted garlic potatoes, cheese grits, buttermilk biscuits, bacon, sausage, bread pudding with whiskey sauce, and peach cobbler.

DINING WITH THE DISNEY CHARACTERS

If you have a child in tow, at least one or two character meals are a must. These extremely popular dining spots, offered at both the theme parks and the Disney resort hotels, are a perfect way for your child to spend extra time with their favorite characters. Meals are offered in three ways depending on the restaurant: buffet-style, family-style, or pre-plated meals; regardless, it's essentially all-you-can-eat. Characters work the room, stopping at each table to interact with guests, pose for photos, and sign autographs (it's a good idea to pick up an autograph book for your child right away at one of Disney's gift shops). Book priority seating early, particularly for **Cinderella's Royal Table** and **Chef Mickey's** by calling **407-WDW-DINE.**

Magic Kingdom

Cinderella's Royal Table—Breakfast only; pre-plated meal • Disney's most popular character meal served high atop Cinderella's Castle • Cinderella, Jasmine, Aladdin, Belle, Fairy Godmother with an occasional appearance by Snow White and Peter Pan.

Crystal Palace—Breakfast, lunch, and dinner buffet • Pooh, Eeyore, Piglet, Tigger.

Liberty Tree Tavern—Dinner family style • Pluto, Goofy, Minnie, Chip 'n' Dale.

Epcot

Garden Grill—Lunch and dinner family style • Farmer Mickey, Pluto, Chip 'n' Dale • afternoon ice cream social at 3 P.M. with ice cream sundaes along with Mickey and Chip 'n' Dale.

Restaurant Akershus—Breakfast only; family style • on a rotating schedule are Snow White, Mary Poppins, Belle, Sleeping Beauty, Jasmine, Pocahontas, Mulan.

Disney–MGM Studio

Hollywood and Vine—Breakfast and lunch buffet • Minnie, Goofy, Pluto, Chip 'n' Dale.

Animal Kingdom

Donald's Prehistoric Breakfastosaurus—Breakfast buffet • Donald Duck, Goofy, Mickey, Pluto.

Disney Resort Hotels

Chef Mickey's—Breakfast and dinner buffet; Contemporary Resort • Mickey, Minnie, Pluto (Goofy replaces him at dinner), Chip 'n' Dale, Donald Duck (dinner only).

Ohana's—Breakfast family style; Polynesian Resort • Mickey, Goofy, Chip 'n' Dale.

1900 Park Fare—Breakfast and dinner buffet; Grand Floridian Resort • breakfast: Mary Poppins, Pinocchio, Geppetto, Alice in Wonderland, Mad Hatter • dinner: Cinderella, Prince Charming, the Fairy Godmother, Suzy and Perla, Lady Tremaine.

Cape May Café—Breakfast buffet; Beach Club Resort • Minnie, Goofy, Chip 'n' Dale.

Garden Grove (becomes **Gulliver's Grill** in the evening)—Breakfast on Saturday and dinner nightly; Disney Swan • breakfast: à la carte or buffet dining with Goofy and Pluto • dinner: buffet and à la carte dining with visits by Timon and Rafiki on Mon and Fri and Goofy and Pluto the other evenings of the week.

Coral Café—Breakfast on Sunday; Disney Dolphin • buffet or à la carte dining • Goofy, Pluto, Chip 'n' Dale.

WALT DISNEY WORLD THEME PARK DINING

Magic Kingdom

Cinderella's Royal Table $$$ to $$$

Contemporary American cuisine. Breakfast, lunch, and dinner.

Here's your chance for a feast in a fairytale castle. Through the massive door of Cinderella's Castle is the unique atmosphere of a medieval fantasyland complete with thick stone floors, shining shields, dazzling suits of armor, and resplendent medieval banners. At the top of a red-carpeted, spiral staircase is the grand dining room where through glittering leaded-glass windows is a bird's-eye view of Fantasyland. Rustic tables sporting purple runners and jolly napkins folded in the shape of jester hats are waited on by "royal attendants" clad in Renaissance clothing. While lunch and dinner à la carte offerings come with a respite from the throngs below, the food is only pleasant, not outstanding.

The restaurant's most popular meal is the plated all-you-care-to-eat character breakfast, delicious and well worth the high price tag if little ones are part of your vacation. To ensure a seat for this highly coveted meal, it's essential to call **407-WDW-DINE** 7 A.M. Eastern Time exactly 60 days prior. Reservations are usually gone in a matter of minutes. A $10-per-adult and $5-per-child deposit is required at time of booking (refunds made up to 24 hours prior).

Sample Menu Items

Pre-plated breakfast: Fresh fruit • breakfast breads • scrambled eggs • bacon • sausage • cheese Danish • French toast • potato casserole • waffles for children.

Lunch entrees: Spice-crusted salmon sandwich • Bruno's barbecue (apricot barbecue chicken breast with veggie slaw on apple cake) • Caesar salad with grilled herb marinated chicken • the Coachman (smoked turkey breast, ham, and Muenster cheese with beefsteak tomatoes on focaccia).

Dinner entrees: The Earl's poulet (roasted chicken on spinach and garlic bread, pudding) • spice-crusted salmon with aiolo on arugula and sweet corn mash • chili butter–coated double-cut pork chop with a chorizo and queso tamale • seared sea bass with two-olive relish • prime rib of beef served with roots smash horseradish cream.

Crystal Palace $$$

American cuisine. Breakfast, lunch, and dinner.

Winnie the Pooh, and his friends, Eeyore, Piglet, and Tigger are your hosts in this Victorian, skylit conservatory found at the castle end of Main Street. Patio-style wrought-iron furnishings, lofty windows, and ceilings hung with baskets of greenery create an al fresco atmosphere. A tasty and bountiful buffet is the fare, definitely one of the best spreads in the park. This is a popular dining choice, so make your priority seating early and on arrival ask for the dining room closest to Main Street with its charming view of Cinderella's Castle.

Sample Menu Items

Breakfast buffet: Juice • pastries • muffins • croissants • fresh fruit • cereal • oatmeal • sweet breakfast lasagna • breakfast meats • made-to-order omelets • roasted potatoes • biscuits and gravy • prime rib hash • scrambled eggs • puff French toast • pancakes • frittata.

Lunch and dinner buffet: Sliced meats and cheeses • salad bar • soup • chef-carved ham and prime rib • oven-baked chicken • herb-broiled tilapia • orzo seafood paella • chicken portobello Caesar pasta • pork fried rice • mashed potatoes • ratatouille with herbed mascarpone • asparagus with orange butter sauce • mushroom and artichoke Florentine • make-your-own sundae bar • strawberry and coconut cake • hot apple cobbler • chocolate torte • lemon bars • brownies.

Liberty Tree Tavern $$$

American cuisine. Lunch and dinner.

In an atmospheric tavern of period charm, dining rooms christened with the names of early American patriots are filled with colonial American reproductions. Planked flooring, thick leaded-glass windows, dark-paneled walls, servers in period attire, and even squeaky wooden stairs lend an air of authenticity to the cozy restaurant. Lunch offers updated American comfort food, exceptional by Magic Kingdom standards and dining here offers a pleasant, cool break from the park. Don't eat too many of the yeasty Sally Lunn rolls and the accompanying apple butter; save room for the appetizing food yet to come. Dinner fare is not as exciting when the restaurant turns into a standard fare, family-style meal hosted by patriots Chip 'n' Dale, Minnie, Goofy, and Pluto.

Sample Menu Items

Lunch entrees: Excellent roast turkey served with cornbread dressing and mashed potatoes • medley of fresh vegetables and white kidney beans tossed in herb olive oil • warm corned beef sandwich stacked with cole slaw and cheese served on molasses bread • maple cinnamon brined pork chop on applewood-smoked bacon mash • pasta of sauteed chicken breast, shiitake mushrooms, oven-dried tomatoes, pappardelle pasta, and arugula butter.

Family-style dinner: Roasted turkey breast • carved beef • smoked pork loin chops • mashed potatoes • garden vegetables • herb bread stuffing • mac 'n' cheese.

Tip: Even though Cinderella's Castle is more popular, this is probably the best sit-down meal in the Magic Kingdom. Lunch is especially nice for adults with its great selections and not a Mickey or Pluto in sight.

Plaza Restaurant $

American cuisine. Lunch and dinner.

A pleasant ambience permeates this informal restaurant located at the castle end of Main Street. Servers in Victorian dress mill about the Art Nouveau dining room serving simple but tasty sandwiches, hamburgers, and salads. From the verandah seats are impressive views of Cinderella's Castle and the moat surrounding it. If not for a meal, stop in for one of their famous ice cream specialties.

Sample Menu Items

Lunch and dinner entrees: Reuben sandwich • plaza club • chicken and strawberry salad (garden greens, grilled chicken, fresh strawberries, Gorgonzola cheese, and red onions tossed in a white zinfandel vinaigrette) • create-your-own hamburger • fresh vegetable sandwich.

Tony's Town Square Restaurant $$$

Italian cuisine. Lunch and dinner.

At the onset of Main Street sits Disney's delightful re-creation of Tony's Italian Restaurant portrayed in *Lady and the Tramp*. Romantic accordion music sets the mood in this Victorian-era trattoria of marble-topped tables, black-and-white checked floors, gaslights, and colorful stained glass. Portions are large, so come prepared with a hefty appetite or think about sharing an entree. The pizzas, some of the best in Disney, are called personal-size but one makes a meal for two with the addition of one of the best Caesar salads around. Other seating choices include the bright, airy solarium or the outdoor porch overlooking the Main Street square.

Sample Menu Items

Lunch entrees: Tony's pizza (grilled chicken, spinach, caramelized onions, sun-dried tomatoes, and mushrooms) • spaghetti and meatballs • grilled chicken breast sandwich topped with prosciutto and cheese • fettuccini tossed with pancetta, peas, onions, and tomatoes in an Alfredo sauce • pasta primavera.

Dinner entrees: Grilled pork chop topped with Italian sausage, peppers, onions, and a balsamic glaze • 8-ounce beef tenderloin topped with garlic spinach, sun-dried tomatoes, hollandaise, and caramelized onion • eggplant Parmesan • clams, mussels, and shrimp in a tomato fennel sauce over linguini.

EPCOT DINING

Future World

Coral Reef Restaurant $$$ to $$$$

Seafood at the Living Seas Pavilion. Lunch and dinner.

Feel like the Little Mermaid in this one-of-a-kind, softly-lit dining room filled with three tiers of leather banquettes lined with shimmering blue, wave-shaped mosaic tiles. Dominating the dining room and just a trident's throw away from all seats is the Living Seas' 6-million-gallon aquarium rife with coral reefs and sea life; use the handy reference guide at your table to help identify the wide assortment of underwater creatures. The former chef of Citricos has revamped the menu to one of super fresh seafood prepared with a flair. Lunch and dinner entrees are the same with dinner offering larger portions and heftier prices. The food will not disappoint although the view of the aquarium is worth the price of a meal alone.

Sample Menu Items

Lunch and dinner entrees: Whole roasted snapper with black beans, ginger, scallions, wine sauce, and roasted purple potatoes • pan-seared shrimp and andouille sausage with white bean cassoulet • blackened catfish with balsamic glaze over pepperjack cheese grits and smoked tomato compote • grilled New York strip loin with garlic potatoes and shiitake mushroom sauce.

Garden Grill $$$

American cuisine in the Land Pavilion. Lunch and dinner.

Slowly revolve through views of the ecosystems seen in the Living with the Land boat ride while seated in comfortable lime green and carrot-colored booths. An all-you-care-to-eat skillet meal of good old home-style cooking is prepared with many of the vegetables grown in the Land's own greenhouses. Farmer Mickey is host along with Pluto, Chip 'n' Dale, all dressed in jeans, overalls, and bandanas. The food is tasty if not outstanding, but the atmosphere is certainly worth a consideration. Take the boat ride before your meal so you'll know what you're looking at from above. An afternoon ice cream social with characters occurs daily here at 3 P.M.

Tip: Request a booth in the bottom-seating tier for the best views.

Sample Menu Items

Lunch and dinner skillet meals: Garden salad • sunflower seed grain bread • rotisserie pork and cornbread stuffing • fried catfish sticks • barbeque grilled flank steak • mashed sweet potatoes • seasonal vegetables • hot apple bread pudding with caramel sauce and vanilla bean ice cream • vegetarian option: roasted vegetable stew in marinara sauce served with grilled polenta, fried onions, and a smoked portobello mushroom • child's skillet: mac 'n' cheese, chicken fingers, steak fries, vegetables.

World Showcase

Biergarten Restaurant $$$

German cuisine in the Germany Pavilion. Lunch and dinner.

Set in a faux Bavarian village of cozy houses fronted with geranium-filled flower boxes and a working waterwheel is a year-round Oktoberfest. Live oompah-pah music, yodelers, and folk dancers clad in traditional Alpine clothing entertain while guests feast on a traditional German food buffet. Giant steins of Beck's beer and communal dining tables encourage introductions all around accompanied by plenty of singing and clapping. It's certainly fun but not the best food in World Showcase.

Sample Menu Items

Lunch buffet: Rotisserie chicken • assorted sausage • roasted pork with mustard sauce • bratwurst • mushroom salad • potato salad • sweet and sour cabbage • sliced beet salad • roasted red potatoes • braised red cabbage • sauerkraut • spaetzle.

Dinner buffet: Same as above with the addition of sauerbraten and chicken schnitzel.

Bistro de Paris $$$$

French cuisine at the France Pavilion. Dinner only.

Upstairs from Chefs de France is a charming Belle Époque dining room with an air of exclusivity. Here you'll find gilded mirrors, white linen tablecloths, crimson banquettes, and billowy white drapes framing windows overlooking the World Showcase Lagoon. Servers with delicious French accents roll out sensational dishes and proceed to plate them tableside. Only the freshest of ingredients are simply prepared in tantalizing sauces and crisp, bright vegetables accompany all entrees. The all-French wine list is a pleasure with many available by the glass. Afterward order a dessert of crepes prepared and flamed tableside while lingering over cordials and coffee in anticipation of the Illuminations spectacle.

Tip: Request one of the few window tables for a nice view of the lagoon and Illuminations.

Sample Menu Items

Dinner entrees: Double-cut chop of white veal accompanied by potato puree • honey roasted rack of lamb with a crispy goat cheese potato gratin • lobster served on shiitake mushroom fricassee with zucchini flower stuffed crab cake • roasted duck breast and duck confit with cherry brandy sauce • grilled filet mignon with wild mushroom sauce.

Chefs De France $$ to $$$

French cuisine at the France Pavilion. Lunch and dinner.

This Left Bank bistro will transport you to the Paris of your culinary dreams. It literally buzzes with festivity. Busy white-aproned waiters with romantic accents bustle about the cheerful Parisian restaurant. Choose from three distinctive dining areas: a brightly lit main dining room, a large glassed-in verandah with floor-to-ceiling windows offering a decent view of the lagoon and Illuminations, or the friendly corner bar accessible from the World Showcase walkway. Try the suggested wine pairings by the glass and sit back and enjoy a memorable meal.

Sample Menu Items

Lunch entrees: Salade nicoise (salad of greens with tuna, tomato, cucumber, potatoes, celery, eggs, and black olives with a light vinaigrette dressing) • quiche Lorraine of zucchini, eggplant, and tomato • grilled salmon served on grilled fennel and artichoke hearts • seared Angus strip steak topped with a shallot and vinegar sauce served with fries.

Dinner entrees: Traditional Mediterranean seafood casserole of grouper, scallops, and shrimp flavored with saffron • jumbo shrimp on fettuccini with garlic, tomatoes, and basil • a superlative grilled tenderloin of beef with a black pepper sauce served with a potato gratin • Roast breast of duck with sweet and sour orange sauce.

Tip: This is one of World Showcase's most popular restaurants and priority seating is highly recommended. The lunch menu will cost you less; however, the ambience is nicer in the evening. A verandah table here for the fireworks is relaxing, but don't expect a perfect view.

Le Cellier Steakhouse $$$ to $$$$

Steakhouse in the Canada Pavilion. Lunch and dinner.

An appealing wine cellar setting makes for cozy dining in the Canadian pavilion. What used to be a cafeteria-style restaurant is now lovely table service in low-ceilinged rooms with dark, windowless walls and snug fireplaces. Although the food is tasty with steaks as the house specialty, you'll find nothing very memorable. The cellar showcases a great selection of Canadian wines along with Old World–style craft ales and Canadian apple cider. My best suggestion is to simply stop in for a bowl of the best cheese soup on the planet and don't hesitate to request the recipe before leaving.

Sample Menu Items

Lunch entrees: Grilled steak burger topped with your choice of cheddar, Gruyere, or blue cheese • 10-ounce New York strip steak • cast iron–seared lake trout salad • spicy beef tenderloin salad • herb-crusted prime rib sandwich • classic Reuben.

Dinner entrees: The house specialties are the wild mushroom stuffed fillet and the crispy maple ginger glazed salmon • grilled porterhouse with flageolet bean stew • herb-crusted prime rib finished with an arugula butter sauce • mussel pasta with spicy chorizo and orecchiette pasta in a white wine butter sauce • oven-roasted beets and lentils • grilled veal chop with creamed leek fondue and red wine reduction.

Tip: This used to be an easy spot to obtain last minute reservations; however, this is rapidly changing as the restaurant gains in popularity. The don't-miss cheddar cheese soup is usually sold in winter from a kiosk in front of Canada on the World Showcase walkway.

L'Originale Alfredo Di Roma Ristorante $$$ to $$$$

Italian cuisine in the Italy Pavilion. Lunch and dinner.

In the waiting area of this elegant World Showcase dining spot you'll find framed photos of celebrities who dined at Alfredo de Lelio's original eatery in Rome whose claim to fame was their fettuccine Alfredo. Here, fittingly, the house specialty is the same. The ornate restaurant is a beauty with blazing chandeliers, trompe l'oeil muraled walls, and professional, white-coated waiters parading with giant silver trays of steaming food. Alas, the food does not live up to the atmosphere; it is a shame it's mediocre at best. Additional patio dining is a pleasant alternative with views of the piazza and its sparkling fountain of Neptune.

Sample Menu Items
Lunch entrees: Fettuccine Alfredo • lasagna baked with veal Bolognese and cream sauce, mozzarella, and Parmesan cheese • slow-roasted half chicken with aged white grape sauce served on Gorgonzola polenta • Italian sausage, onion, and green peppers in tomato sauce.

Dinner entrees: Tortellini stuffed with five cheeses served in a sauce of tomatoes, mushrooms, peas, prosciutto, and cream • grilled veal chop with Chianti and black truffle sauce • farm-raised chicken slow-roasted with rosemary and sage • red snapper roasted with a sauce of lemon butter, white wine, and sambuca topped with artichoke hearts over Gorgonzola sun-dried tomato polenta.

Tip: Pasta is cooked the traditional way here; if you are not an al dente fan, ask for yours to be prepared differently.

Nine Dragons $$ to $$$$

Chinese cuisine in the China Pavilion. Lunch and dinner.

Rich in beautifully carved rosewood decor, Oriental carpets, and Chinese lantern–style lighting is China's elegant restaurant. Here a gracious staff serves enjoyable dishes inspired by five different Chinese provinces. If you think it's a bit overpriced for Chinese food, consider that portions are large and shareable. At lunch the all-you-care-to-eat meal served family style offers a sampling of many dishes at a reasonable price.

Sample Menu Items
Family-style lunch: Shrimp and pork spring rolls • hot and sour soup • steamed dim sum • wonton soup • stir-fried shrimp with cashews • canton pepper beef • sweet and sour pork • honey sesame chicken • stir-fried vegetables • pork lo mein • vegetarian fried rice • red bean or ginger ice cream • hot Chinese tea.

Lunch and dinner entrees: Rainbow kung bao chicken • scallops with black bean sauce • beef with spicy sha cha sauce • stir-fried shrimp with garden vegetables • stir-fried seasonal Chinese vegetables • roast duckling with hoisin sauce • imperial pinecone fish for two (crispy whole

deboned fish glazed with a sweet and sour sauce) • lobster and sea treasure casserole (lobster tail, shrimp, scallops, and squid sauteed with ginger
and scallions in a white sauce).

*Tip: Stop in not for a full meal but to sample the savory appetizers and
fun specialty drinks. Ask for a front window table for a nice view of the
World Showcase Lagoon.*

Restaurant Akershus $$$

*Scandinavian cuisine at the Norway Pavilion. Breakfast, lunch, and
dinner.*

Those who love the idea of a buffet with a twist should try this
atypical one housed in a replica of Oslo's Akershus Castle. Inside, its
lofty, castle-like hall is adorned with massive iron chandeliers hanging
from rich wooden beamed ceilings. Lovely cut-glass windows arch above
the dimly lit dining room where blond-headed servers clothed in traditional Norwegian dress are patient and encouraging in describing the
many unfamiliar dishes. The buffet of over 40 selections of both hot
and cold fare is tasty and definitely a bit unusual; however, nothing is
outstanding. It is, nevertheless, well worth the reasonable price, particularly at lunch, to sample a bit of unfamiliar Scandinavian fare. At
breakfast is the newest character meal featuring Disney princesses.

Sample Menu Items

Family-style breakfast: Fresh fruit • cinnamon rolls • scrambled eggs
• cheese potatoes • French toast sticks • sausage • bacon.

Lunch buffet: Assorted cheeses • smoked mackerel • crab and eggs •
mustard herring • smoked salmon • cold roast beef and turkey • shrimp,
potato, crab, cucumber, beet, tossed, and tomato salads • steamed whitefish • pasta and cheese with ham casserole • meatballs in a rich brown
sauce • lamb and cabbage casserole • Norwegian sausage • braised red
cabbage • boiled red potatoes • mashed rutabaga • children's à la carte
menu available.

Dinner buffet: Same as lunch with the addition of peel and eat
shrimp, lamb fricassee, venison stew, and roasted pork.

Restaurant Marrakesh $$$ to $$$$

Moroccan cuisine in the Morocco Pavilion. Lunch and dinner.

The soul of Morocco is certainly captured in one of World Showcase's best dining venues. With the feel of a lavish palace, its lace-like walls, carved columns, and graceful arches are interspersed with vibrant mosaic tiles and a lofty inlaid ceiling. Gracious waiters in colorful silk clothing and fez hats work the two-tiered dining room around the hip-wiggling belly dancer and Middle Eastern musicians; it's even more entertaining when some of the audience gets involved. The Moroccan cuisine is extremely appetizing with its many exotic spices and delicate accompanying couscous that's part of each meal. Choosing a dish is difficult, so take a crack at one of the combination meals that offer a little of everything. This is one of the best and certainly the most authentic attempts in Epcot to re-create the atmosphere of international dining.

Sample Menu Items

Lunch and dinner entrees: Marrakesh feast and the royal feast (family-style meal with a sampling of appetizers, entrees, and dessert from the entire menu) • roasted lamb • shish kebab of beef • lemon chicken (braised half chicken seasoned with garlic, green olives, and preserved lemons) • broiled salmon marinated in Moroccan herbs and spices • vegetable couscous.

Tip: This is usually an easy place to dine without reservations.

Rose and Crown Pub and Dining Room $$$

Pub Food in the United Kingdom Pavilion. Lunch and dinner.

Nestled on the banks of the World Showcase Lagoon is an English pub with snug dining rooms and a rich wooden bar. Old-fashioned etched-glass windows, dark wood beams, gleaming brass, and pressed tin ceilings are surrounded by walls loaded with dartboards and family pictures. The delightful English accent of your server is worth the hefty price of the simple food the likes of thickly battered fish and fat chips and tasty cottage pies. Unlike most places in England, here you'll find your beverage filled with plenty of ice and your beer served frosty cold. Outside dining affords the very best panorama of the Illuminations fireworks.

Tip: Most, but not all of the outdoor tables give you a view of Illuminations.

Sample Menu Items

Lunch entrees: A super choice is the rich cottage pie (ground beef topped with mashed potatoes and cheddar cheese) • ploughman's lunch (sliced turkey, ham, cheese, pickle, and marinated salad) • fish and chips • chicken pot pie • sausage roll with baked beans and chips.

Dinner entrees: English pie sampler (pork pie, chicken and leek pie, and cottage pie) • pan-seared salmon fillet • fisherman's basket (battered and fried cod strips, prawns, and salmon cake) • prime rib with Yorkshire pudding • roasted half chicken with sage and onion stuffing.

San Angel Inn $$$

Mexican cuisine in the Mexico Pavilion. Lunch and dinner.

It's hard to find a more romantic restaurant than San Angel. It's perpetual nighttime here in this softly lit hacienda filled with flickering candlelit tables sitting alongside the inky Rio del Tiempo. Having grown up near the border, I call myself a Mexican food aficionado and I must say that the traditional dishes here are very good. The combination plates are the most popular, but consider branching out to the wonderful meat and seafood dishes prepared in a variety of piquant sauces. Those not used to spice may be in for a bit of a surprise, hopefully a pleasant one; however, not all dishes are prepared with chiles (your waiter can recommend a dish without the heat). Of course, you must try a frosty margarita and, if you're in luck, the fabulous Mariachi Cobre will be performing during your meal. My only disappointment was the basket of store-bought tostados served upon arrival, but the yummy red salsa accompanying it made up for the lack of authenticity.

Sample Menu Items

Lunch entrees: Sample several items by ordering the plato nacionale featuring a beef burrito, tamale, and beef flauta (beef rolled in a corn tortilla and crispy fried) each topped with a different tasty sauce • tacos al carbon (flour tortillas filled with grilled chicken or beef with peppers, onions, guacamole, and pico de gallo relish) • pollo a las rajas, (grilled chicken breast served over red peppers, onions, poblano chiles, Mexican sausage, and melted cheese).

Dinner entrees: Mahimahi à la Veracruzana (grilled fish fillet prepared with capers, olives, onions, and tomatoes) served with chipotle mashed potatoes • plato Mexicano featuring beef tenderloin tampiquena style, chicken enchilada, and beef burrito • beef tenderloin tips sauteed with onions and poblano chiles covered with roasted chile pasilla sauce • grilled shrimp served over angel hair pasta with tomatoes and peppers.

Tempura Kiku $$ to $$$

Japanese cuisine in the Japan Pavilion. Lunch and dinner.

Devotees of tempura will love this delightfully cozy space where they'll find the luscious, lightly battered, deep-fried meats and vegetables so popular in Japanese restaurants. Compensating for its compact size is charming sushi bar–style seating around a U-shaped counter rimming the cooking space allowing guests a view of the chefs as they prepare the tasty tidbits. On the menu is tempura along with a small offering of sashimi and sushi. Drinks include Kirin beer, sake, wine, and green tea.

Sample Menu Items

Lunch and dinner entrees: Tempura choices—chicken, shrimp, scallops, fish, and skewered beef served with tempura vegetables, sumashi soup, green salad, and steamed rice.

Teppanyaki $$ to $$$$

Japanese cuisine in the Japan Pavilion. Lunch and dinner.

A smoking hot, teppan grill is the centerpiece of each black-lacquered counter around which guests are seated to watch the show provided by a lightning-quick, multi-talented Japanese chef. In his tall white chef's hat, he chops, slices, and dices while stir-frying the meats and vegetables for his table of eight guests. Similar to the Benihana restaurants found around the country, it is well worth the money for the delicious, yet simple food and the unforgettable show that goes along with it.

Sample Menu Items

Lunch and dinner entrees: All entrees prepared on the teppan grill accompanied by grilled vegetables, mixed green salad, and steamed rice • entree choices: chicken, shrimp, scallops, sirloin, tenderloin, or simply a large portion of vegetables as well as numerous combinations • everyone's favorite: lobster and tenderloin steak.

DISNEY–MGM STUDIOS DINING

50s Prime Time Café $$ to $$$

American cuisine. Lunch and dinner.

Pass through a time warp into a 1950s family kitchen where guests dine watching *Leave it to Beaver* and *Father Knows Best* on black and white TVs sitting on the counter between the toaster and the blender. Linoleum floors, Formica tables, pull-down lamps, windows covered in venetian blinds, and tacky drapes are accompanied by a menu of savory renditions of good old American comfort foods like crackling-crisp golden fried chicken. "Mom" herself is your server, making sure everyone in the "family" observes good manners. No fighting at the table! No throwing spitballs! Mustn't forget to eat your vegetables! Our "mom" told us to set our own table; she didn't do chores. Check out the adjoining Tune-In Lounge for an appetizer and drinks before dinner.

Sample Menu Items

Lunch and dinner entrees: Spice-crusted pan-seared salmon • chicken pot pie filled with huge chunks of chicken and broccoli topped with phyllo dough • traditional meat loaf • old-fashioned pot roast • shrimp penne pasta, diced pancetta, and shiitake mushrooms in a Dijon cream sauce (vegetarian option available) • charbroiled pork tenderloin glazed with a chipotle barbeque sauce with cheddar cheese bacon mashed potatoes.

The Hollywood Brown Derby $$$ to $$$$

Contemporary cuisine. Lunch and dinner.

The Studio's best food is to be found at the illustrious Brown Derby, perfectly re-created right down to the collection of celebrity caricatures hanging on just about every square inch of wall space. Walk beneath the red awning and enter into 1930s Hollywood glamour seen everywhere from the rich mahogany walls and furnishings to the sway of potted palms. Its tuxedoed waiters, sparkling chandeliers, white linen tablecloths, plush ruby red banquettes, and derby-shaped lamps all set the mood for a sentimental waltz through the heyday of Hollywood. Although you'll find some of the original favorites on the menu, most entrees are definitely updated and accompanied by sumptuous sauces and creative sides. Of course, there's the famous Brown Derby Cobb salad (so finely chopped the lettuce resembles parsley) along with their signature grapefruit cake for dessert (a must-try). Choose to eat indoors or out, but opting for an outside table means missing the Brown Derby's special brand of ambience. It's also one of three restaurants here offering the Fantasmic Dinner Package (full details on page 236).

Sample menu items

Lunch entrees: Barbeque chicken Caesar salad • orecchiette pasta with spinach, zucchini, portobello mushrooms, and basil cream sauce • sesame-seared yellowfin tuna Cobb with avocado, chives, and cucumber tossed in a wasabi vinaigrette with spicy mango • grilled New York strip steak marinated in brown ale with chimichurri • pan-fired grouper over balsamic roasted asparagus, lemon butter sauce topped with a sweet onion marmalade.

Dinner entrees: Rotisserie half chicken served over warm spinach and bacon salad with roasted sweet potatoes and a maple whiskey glaze • pepper-grilled filet mignon with roasted shallot mashers • molasses barbeque pork tenderloin with a buttermilk corn pudding • mustard-crusted rack of lamb • grilled Atlantic salmon with savoy cabbage, applewood-smoked bacon, balsamic butter sauce, and horseradish aioli.

Tip: Your server won't mind providing you with the recipe for the Cobb salad and grapefruit cake; just ask. In the evenings a pianist entertains.

Hollywood and Vine $$$

American cuisine. Breakfast, lunch, and dinner.

A fun character buffet breakfast and lunch is served in an art-deco diner setting at Hollywood and Vine. Hosted by Goofy in a white zoot suit and a starlet-clad Minnie Mouse, they simply love to break out in a dance number with Goofy doing some fancy footwork. Naugahyde banquettes and Formica tables are accented by shiny chrome serving counters where diners choose from an array of pretty standard buffet items. Dinner is the same menu as lunch; however, no characters are on hand in the evening hours. This is one of three restaurants here offering the Fantasmic Dinner Package (full details on page 236).

Sample Menu Items

Breakfast buffet: Pastries • pastrami salmon with all the fixings • cereal • fruit • chocolate French toast • biscuits and gravy • sausage • skillet-fried potatoes • cheddar cheese grits • bacon • spinach and jack cheese frittata with caramelized sweet onions • pancakes • scrambled eggs • child's buffet: breakfast pizza, Mickey waffles with strawberry topping.

Lunch and dinner buffet: Salad bar • sage-rubbed rotisserie turkey • grilled flank steak • oven-baked chicken • chef's catch of the day • shrimp Alfredo penne pasta • vegetable lo mein • marinated tomatoes with buffalo mozzarella • mashed potatoes • roasted sweet potatoes with root beer and bourbon glaze • curry rice • corn with roasted peppers • chocolate and orange cream cake • soft-serve ice cream with toppings • child's buffet: barbeque meatballs, hot dogs, mac 'n' cheese, chicken strips.

Tip: One of the more available character meals and often just a short wait without a reservation.

Mama Melrose's Ristorante Italiano $$$

Italian cuisine. Lunch and dinner.

A New York–style Italian restaurant in a warehouse setting on Melrose Avenue in Hollywood might be a bit of a stretch even for Disney. Frank Sinatra and Dean Martin croon from speakers mounted on ceilings dripping with grape-laden vines, long salamis, strings of garlic, straw-wrapped Chianti bottles, and strands of twinkling lights; on the red brick walls are LP record covers, old movie posters, and Hollywood street signs. Food is tasty but not memorable with the exception of the wood-oven thin-crusted pizzas where Mama Melrose's excels. Lunch and dinner menus are the same only dinner comes with a bit higher price tag. This is one of three restaurants here offering the Fantasmic Dinner Package (full details on page 236).

Sample Menu Items

Lunch and dinner entrees: Grilled chicken pizza with pesto, spinach, pancetta, and Asiago cheese • penne alla vodka with pancetta, sweet onion and tomato basil cream • wild mushroom risotto • brick oven baked chicken Parmesan over capellini pasta • linguini Fra Diavolo with clams, shrimp, mussels, and calamari tossed with a spicy marinara sauce • grilled fillet of beef • pesto-crusted salmon • eggplant Parmesan.

Sci-Fi Dine-In Theater Restaurant $$$

American cuisine. Lunch and dinner.

Anyone lonesome for the drive-ins of their youth will go mad for this place. Eat in sleek, 1950s-era convertibles finished with lit taillights, whitewall tires, and sharp fins and watch B-movie sci-fi and horror trailers along with old cartoons. Waiters on roller skates carhop the darkened, starlit theater, occasionally interacting with the crazy happenings on the screen. Speaker boxes hang on the side of your car and, of course, popcorn and hot dogs dance on the screen during intermission. Though the food is just so-so, who cares when Godzilla is your entertainment!

Sample Menu Items

Lunch entrees: Reuben sandwich • blackened catfish sandwich • shrimp penne pasta with garlic, capers, tomatoes, and spinach • a thick, juicy, flame broiled all-American burger • slow-roasted BBQ ribs St. Louis style.

Dinner entrees: Pan-seared salmon with wild rice pilaf • brandy-glazed sauteed pork medallions with roasted apple and garlic mashers • New York strip with a maple-dipped loaded baked potato • vegetable potato bake.

Tip: Stop in during nonprime hours for a yummy milkshake and soak up the atmosphere in one of Disney's best themed restaurants.

ANIMAL KINGDOM DINING

Donald's Prehistoric Breakfastosaurus $$$

American cuisine in Dinoland U.S.A. Breakfast only 8–10 A.M.

Start your day at the Animal Kingdom with a delicious character breakfast buffet hosted by Donald Duck himself. He brings along fisherman Goofy and Scout troop leader Mickey with his dog Pluto in tow to this Digsite base camp for student paleontologists. Eat on rustic tables stacked with Melmac camping mugs in barracks-style dining rooms among dinosaur fossils, but beware of student waiters who love to tease and play tricks on unsuspecting visitors. After breakfast this restaurant reverts to a fast-food spot, offering burgers and Happy Meals from McDonald's.

Sample Menu Items

Breakfast buffet: Frittata • breakfast burrito • scrambled eggs • biscuits and gravy • hash browns • skillet potatoes • pancakes • French toast • sausage • bacon • oatmeal • grits • cereal • fresh fruit • muffins • donuts • coffee cake • bagels.

Rainforest Café $ to $$$$

American cuisine at the Entrance Plaza. Breakfast, lunch, and dinner.

Dine among the beasts of the jungle surrounded by crashing waterfalls, lush tropical foliage, dripping vines, and giant aquarium tanks while being bombarded with thunderstorms and noisy audio-animatronic wildlife. Although the atmosphere outweighs the food, it certainly is a delightful place, one that should definitely be on your Disney agenda. If you'd like a sampling of the atmosphere without a meal, stop for a drink at the Magic Mushroom to sip on specialty drinks, smoothies, juice, and coffee under a towering toadstool roof. An outside-the-park entrance allows dining without admission to the Animal Kingdom.

Sample Menu Items

Breakfast entrees: Tonga toast (baked cinnamon French toast surrounded by fresh strawberries and bananas) • Shangri-la frittata (eggs, mushrooms, peppers, and cheddar cheese encased in crispy potatoes and then baked) • jungle wrap (warm tortilla wrapped around scrambled eggs sauteed with peppers, andouille sausage, and creole sauce) • exotic juice and smoothies served at the Magic Mushroom Bar.

Lunch and dinner entrees: Hong Kong stir-fry • pot roast • Cobb salad • Caesar salad topped with sliced turkey and wrapped in a flour tortilla • linguini tossed with olive oil, garlic, and roma tomatoes in salsa marinara with fresh mozzarella • grilled chicken penne pasta with walnut pesto, broccoli, red peppers, and spinach tossed with Alfredo sauce • coconut shrimp • jambalaya • Maine lobster filled with crabmeat.

Tip: Priority reservations are taken and are highly recommended, particularly for lunch. Open for breakfast half hour before AK opening time.

Mammoth portions require either a big appetite or the need to split an entree.

WALT DISNEY WORLD RESORT DINING

The very best dining experiences in the "World" are to be found at Disney deluxe resorts. Back in 1996, the California Grill set the pace when it opened to rave reviews with an ever-changing menu of New American cuisine. One by one the deluxe hotels have launched a new breed of dining venues offering innovative cuisine and superior wine lists, one of which, Victoria and Albert's, boasts a AAA Five-Diamond Award.

Best restaurants at Disney Resorts

- California Grill perched high atop the Contemporary Resort with its picture-perfect views of the Magic Kingdom.
- Citricos at the Grand Floridian Hotel offering innovative Mediterranean cuisine.
- The Flying Fish at Disney's Boardwalk specializing in seafood and everything whimsical.
- Victoria and Albert's at the Grand Floridian for a special evening of romance.
- Artist Point's Pacific Northwest cuisine at the Wilderness Lodge.
- Shula's at the Walt Disney World Dolphin for the best steaks around.

Artist Point $$$ to $$$$

Contemporary cuisine at Disney's Wilderness Lodge. Dinner only; casual dress. Open nightly 5:30–10 P.M.

The rustic, U.S. National Park theme of the Wilderness Lodge continues into this attractive dining establishment. The intoxicating aroma of cedar wafts among the impressive expanse of fat ponderosa pine columns, lofty ceilings, Old West murals, and forest green slate floors. Oversized windows peer out on sparkling views of Bay Lake and the hotel's enchanting courtyard of giant boulders and cascading waterfalls;

on pleasant days tables spill out onto a picturesque terrace. The lovely decor takes a backseat to the Pacific Northwest cuisine of fresh seafood flown in daily, and the menu's game meats and fish are smoked on the premises. Choose the house specialty of cedar plank Alaskan King salmon paired with a bottle of Pacific Northwest wine finished with a fresh berry cobbler topped with sour cream drizzle and vanilla bean ice cream.

Sample Menu Items

Dinner entrees: Mixed grill of elk tenderloin, venison, and rabbit sausage with a root vegetable mash and port wine jus • air-chilled roasted free-range chicken breast with smoked bacon and two-potato hash • grilled buffalo top sirloin with sweet potato hazelnut gratin and sweet onion jam • pan-seared pork tenderloin on Tillamook cheddar mac 'n' cheese with Maytag crust.

Tip: If arriving before dark, ask for a view of Bay Lake. After dark request the knockout view of the illuminated courtyard waterfall. Take a post-dinner walk through the property to the edge of Bay Lake and wait for the geyser to erupt (every hour on the hour); it's quite a show.

Beaches and Cream $ to $$

American cuisine at the Beach Club Resort. Breakfast, lunch, and dinner; park casual dress. Open daily 6:30–11 P.M.

In this nostalgic 1950s-style soda shop are the best milkshakes and malts in all of Disney along with burgers and the best crispy onion rings around. Sit in a marble-topped booth or at the bar to watch the soda jerks at work while listening to the old-fashioned jukebox (the one on your table is just for looks). For a real treat order one of the thick, icy shakes served in a frosty fountain glass with the extras served in the stainless steel mixing cup; they're worth every calorie. Whatever, do not neglect to find your way to this adorable place. A light continental breakfast is available in the morning, and the walk-up counter allows a quick stop for ice cream or menu take-out.

Sample Menu Items

Lunch and dinner entrees: Burgers and cheeseburgers (single and double) • grilled prime rib sub sandwich with peppers, onions, and mozzarella cheese • grilled chicken sandwich • deli turkey sandwich •

veggie burger • hot dogs • chicken Caesar salad • chili • chicken noodle soup.

Desserts: Fudge mud slide (gooey chewy brownie covered with hot fudge, ice cream, Oreos, and whipped cream) • classic banana split • coke or root beer float • old-fashioned sundaes • Milky Way sundae • bundt cake topped with ice cream, hot fudge, butterscotch, whipped cream, and a cherry • the kitchen sink (eight scoops of ice cream smothered in every topping on the menu).

Tip: This very small place can really become crowded after the Epcot fireworks; come in the afternoon when it is not hopping with hungry, exhausted diners. It's only a 5-minute walk from Epcot's International Gateway.

Boma $$$

African cuisine at the Animal Kingdom Lodge. Breakfast and dinner; casual dress. Open daily 7–11 A.M. and 5–10 P.M.

The essence of Africa is potent beneath Boma's circular, thatched roofs where hearty foods prepared with an African flair (and a dash of American cuisine for the picky eater) are the fare. Earthy colors are dominant in the appealing dining room filled with hardwood chairs adorned with fanciful African-style designs, colorful textiles, and green leather booths topped with kraal fences. During breakfast the African servers sing beautiful native songs, a delightful start to your morning. At dinner the place comes alive with a bountiful spread of African soups and stews, savory wood-roasted meats, and an entire section (or pod) of meatless dishes, all served in a lively buffet setting. An evening here is highly recommended, a perfect place to sample African food.

Sample Menu Items

Breakfast buffet: Fru-nch (blend of lemonade, pineapple, guava, papaya, and orange juices) • fresh fruit • cereal • pastries • oatmeal • lamb and chicken-apple sausage • bobotie (curried African lamb and beef quiche) • carving station with roasted ham and cured pork loin • made-to-order omelets • scrambled eggs • roasted potatoes with peppers • bacon • brioche • waffles.

Dinner buffet: Moroccan seafood salad • watermelon rind salad with ginger and rice vinegar • South African melon salad • Moroccan couscous salad • chicken salad with chili cilantro • chicken pepper pot soup •

smoked tomato bisque • curried coconut seafood stew • Durban spiced roasted chicken • spit-fired prime rib • banana leaf–wrapped salmon • wood-roasted pork and lamb • spiced mashed potatoes • braised greens • vegetable lentil kofta • sweet potato pancakes • chocolate mousse zebra dome • coconut tiramisu • banana bread pudding • child's buffet: mac 'n' cheese, spaghetti and meatballs, chicken tenders.

Tip: Two delightful tables for two have a view of a bubbling, rock pool outside the window. It's a long shot, but go ahead and ask.

California Grill $$$ to $$$$

Contemporary cuisine at the Contemporary Resort. Dinner only; smart casual dress. Open nightly 5:30–10 P.M.

One of the toughest tables to obtain in the "World" is at the California Grill, a definite highlight for any connoisseur of cutting-edge cuisine. The modern decor and constant bustle of excited diners only adds to its drop-dead setting on the 15th floor of the Contemporary Resort. Through immense windows is an unbeatable panorama of the Magic Kingdom and the Seven Seas Lagoon and on many nights picture-perfect views of the Fantasy in the Sky Fireworks. From pristine fresh sushi to the exceptional New American cuisine to sensational desserts and the outstanding California wine list all served by the glass, this place has it all. The open show kitchen is a treat and the cocktail lounge has some of the best views in the house. Don't be discouraged if you don't get a coveted window seat; take a drink out onto the adjoining observation platform during the fireworks presentation and get a bird's-eye view of the extravaganza.

Sample Menu Items

Dinner entrees: Pot-braised lamb shank with fennel and apple gratin • grilled pork tenderloin with polenta and balsamic smothered cremini mushrooms • spit-roasted chicken with corn spoonbread souffle and smoked tomato broth • pan-roasted striped bass with aromatic rock shrimp lemon grass risotto (at the very least order a side dish of the risotto; it's the best I've tasted) • yellowfin tuna seared rare with fragrant mushroom-miso udon noodle bowl.

Tip: Either time your dinner to be finished before the fireworks and then move outside to the observation deck or arrive in time to pick up a drink from the bar before the show (be outside around 15 minutes prior to the presentation to get a place by the rail) and have your dinner afterward. I advise the latter if traveling without children; it makes for a much quieter evening. Reservations here go quickly, so plan ahead. Since Fantasy in the Sky is not a nightly happening in slow season, plan accordingly. If you're lucky enough to get a window seat and you time it correctly, the Epcot fireworks can also be seen in the distance.

Cape May Café $$$

Seafood at the Beach Club Resort. Breakfast and dinner; casual dress. Open daily 7:30–11 A.M.; and 5:30–9:30 P.M.

It's a day at the shore at Cape May Café. Colorful beach umbrellas, Victorian oceanside murals, and sandcastles create a New England seaside atmosphere that is bright and cheerful. Goofy's Beach Bash is a popular character breakfast buffet with his friends Minnie, Goofy, Chip 'n' Dale, all clad in bathing attire. If the idea of all-you-can-eat seafood is appealing, a New England–style clambake buffet is held nightly featuring a steam pit full of mussels, clams, and shrimp.

Sample Menu Items

Breakfast buffet: Juice • fresh fruit • scrambled eggs • roast beef hash • Mickey waffles • pancakes • grits • bacon• sausage • oatmeal • pastries • hash brown potatoes • biscuits and gravy • breakfast bread pudding with vanilla sauce.

Dinner buffet: Peel 'n' eat shrimp • mixed green and Caesar salads • potato and pasta salads • steamed mussels and clams • boiled red potatoes • corn-on-the-cob • baked fish • barbeque ribs • flank steak • marinated grilled chicken • mashed potatoes • snap peas • cornbread • raspberry mousse • chocolate cake • angel food cake with strawberries and whipped cream • assorted tarts • child's buffet: fried shrimp, chicken fingers, mac 'n' cheese, mini hot dogs.

Chef Mickey's $$$

American cuisine at the Contemporary Resort. Breakfast and dinner; casual dress. Open daily 7–11:30 A.M. and 5–9:30 P.M.

Join Chef Mickey for a lively buffet on the 4th-floor Grand Canyon Concourse of the Contemporary Resort. The decor here follows the mood of the resort with intense colors of purple and teal, sharp angles, and plenty of chrome. Super-sized flatware line the very noisy, very bright room where Goofy, Mickey, and Chip 'n' Dale attired in chef's clothing schmooze with guests (at dinner they are joined by Donald Duck and Minnie Mouse) while overhead the monorail glides by. Every 45 minutes or so it's a party when all the characters lead diners in a cheerful song accompanied by plenty of dancing and napkin-waving. Food is home-style cooking with plenty of choices, but nothing stands out unless you can count a heaping serving of the best Parmesan mashed potatoes around. If children are not a part of your vacation and steam tables leave you cold, I would definitely skip this one. Make early reservations for this extremely popular feast.

Sample Menu Items

Breakfast buffet: Fresh fruit • pastry bar • cereal • scrambled eggs • egg and sausage roulade • vegetable lasagne • cheese potatoes • bacon • sausage links • cinnamon-sugar dusted French toast • pancakes • buttermilk biscuits and gravy • made-to-order pancakes with toppings • warm bread pudding • juice.

Dinner buffet : Soup and salad bar with fruit, green salad, pasta salad, bean salad, chilled shrimp, crab salad • chef-carved oven-roasted prime rib and grilled flank steak • barbecue chicken • baked chef's catch with lemon-dill butter • roast pork loin with pear demi glace • four cheese pasta • Parmesan mashed potatoes • wild rice medley • broccoli au gratin • orange glazed carrots • make-your-own sundaes and cupcakes • lemon meringue pie • chocolate mousse cake • carrot cake • brownies • cobbler • cheesecake • cookies • child's buffet: mac 'n' cheese, pizza, fish nuggets, mini hot dogs.

Citricos $$$$

Contemporary Mediterranean food at the Grand Floridian Resort. Dinner only; smart casual dress. Open Wed–Sun 5:30–10 P.M.

An ambitious, ever-changing menu delivers innovative Mediterranean cuisine with admirable results. Combined with a sophisticated, contemporary dining room and exhibition kitchen reminiscent of the California Grill, this is a not-to-be-missed spot. In the too-bright room are comfortable upholstered chairs, starched white linens emblazoned with Citricos' logo, rich silk curtains, mosaic tiles, and swirling wrought iron. Picture windows afford views of the Magic Kingdom fireworks (though not the best) and the Seven Seas Lagoon along with the charming hotel courtyard and pool. A 2002 Wine Spectator Restaurant Award winner, its inspired California and French wine list shines in every category making it possibly the best in the "World." All in all an exceptional meal.

Sample Menu Items

Dinner entrees: Grilled salmon fillet with black olive tapenade and roasted fennel • seared tuna with saffron pappardelle, tomatoes, olives and capers • 6-hour braised veal shank with orzo pasta and soy glaze (their signature dish) • basil-crusted rack of lamb with a ragout of spinach, shiitakes, and white beans • roasted duck breast with rosemary polenta and sweet and sour pomegranate glaze; grilled fillet of beef and Maine lobster.

Concourse Steakhouse $$ to $$$

Steakhouse at the Contemporary Resort. Breakfast, lunch, and dinner; casual dress. Open daily 7:30–11 A.M., noon–2 P.M., and 5:30–10 P.M.

This space age steakhouse with its overly modern decor is open to the soaring Grand Concourse offering nice views of the monorail gliding overhead. Steaks are the specialty but also pleasing are the seafood and pasta choices; nothing fancy, just decent, fresh food. At breakfast are the usual suspects with the addition of yummy smoothies and shakes in eight varieties. Lunch, just a monorail ride away, is a good choice for a quiet respite from the Magic Kingdom.

Sample Menu Items

Breakfast entrees: Steak and eggs • breakfast quesadilla (eggs, peppers, onions, andouille sausage, cheese, hash browns, and salsa) • eggs Benedict • create-your-own omelet • steakhouse trio (two eggs, silver dollar pancakes, bacon or sausage, hash browns, and biscuits) • blueberry pancakes.

Lunch entrees: grilled salmon fillet salad • 16-ounce T-bone steak • Southwestern chicken pizza • cheese steak sandwich • seafood quesadilla.

Dinner entrees: Seared Yellow fin tuna with Manchego cheese, long grain rice, and tomato relish • spicy mandarin orange glazed pork ribs •

herb-crusted salmon • oak-roasted prime rib • 20-ounce T-bone • barbeque half chicken • oven-roasted mushroom linguini, spinach, and Parmesan cheese.

Flying Fish Café $$$ to $$$$

Seafood at the Boardwalk. Dinner only; casual dress. Open Sun–Thurs 5:30–10 P.M.; Fri and Sat 5:30–10:30 P.M.

Contemporary and trendy, yet whimsical, this restaurant will absolutely delight the senses. Dine in a festive room of flying fish mobiles, sea blue sparkling mosaic floors, and golden fish scale pillars where the open show kitchen is an entertainment in itself. Definitely the best food at the Boardwalk and one of Disney's greatest dining establishments, it offers top-notch and innovative seafood specialties like potato-wrapped Florida red snapper with a creamy leek fondue as well a few well chosen meat dishes such as a perfectly cooked oak-grilled pork chop paired with a cheddar potato gratin. Named a 2002 Wine Spectator Restaurant Award winner, it boasts an excellent international list. Don't forget to save room for the unforgettable desserts, especially the banana napoleon with warm caramel sauce.

Sample Menu Items

Dinner entrees: Oak-grilled wahoo with an excellent wild mushroom garlic risotto, truffle nage, and crispy leeks • handmade ricotta ravioli with tomato-olive sauce, capers, basil, and ricotta salad • oak-grilled Atlantic salmon with toasted pearl pasta, baby spinach salad, herb vinaigrette, and arugula pesto.

Grand Floridian Café $$ to $$$

Contemporary cuisine at the Grand Floridian Resort. Breakfast and lunch; casual dress. Open daily 7 A.M.–3 P.M.

Offering an appealing view from its large picture windows of the Grand Floridian Resort's courtyard and pool area is this cheerful, bright café of Victorian floral wallpaper, tufted banquettes, and a peaches and cream color scheme. Hop on a boat from the Magic Kingdom and head over to lunch for one of the delicious oversized sandwiches or the overflowing Cobb salad.

Sample Menu Items

Breakfast entrees: Vegetable frittata (a savory open-faced omelet with tomato, zucchini, onion, mushrooms, chives, and spinach) • eggs Benedict (the house specialty) • steak and eggs • corned beef hash and poached eggs • Belgian waffles with fruit.

Lunch entrees: Cobb Salad • New York–style Reuben sandwich • the fantastic earl of sandwiches (grilled ham and turkey on focaccia bread topped with Boursin cheese sauce, ham, turkey, tomatoes, and onion straws) • fried grouper sandwich • Asian grilled chicken salad • shrimp pasta primavera • fillet of striped bass topped with a tomato orange chili vinaigrette with spaghetti squash and wilted spinach.

Jiko $$$ to $$$$

Contemporary cuisine with an African flair at the Animal Kingdom Lodge. Dinner only; smart casual dress. Open nightly 5:30–10 P.M.

The Animal Kingdom Lodge's premier dining room is Jiko (Swahili for "cooking place"), one of the most seductive spaces yet at a Disney hotel. Floor-to-ceiling windows look out to a boulder-strewn stream and massive, mosaic tile columns are surrounded by blue leather banquettes, honey-colored walls, gleaming wood floors, and modern tables set with Italian glass. Soft, contemporary lighting, fantastically shaped in the guise of bird wings, hangs from a rich, blue ceiling giving the feeling of open space.

Giant, twin clay ovens draw the eye to the open kitchen where an eclectic blend of creations, prepared with an African flair in terms of spices and ingredients, are turned out in attractive presentations. Come early for a drink in the adjoining Cape Town Lounge and Wine Bar where knowledgeable bartenders are anxious to educate in the fine points of the all–South African wine list, the largest in North America. Don't leave without ordering the unbelievably wonderful chocolate-filled beggars purses with a honey dipping sauce, one of Disney's best desserts.

Sample Menu Items

Dinner entrees: horseradish-crusted salmon on red rice with vodka orange jus • oak-grilled beef tenderloin in a red wine sauce • rabbit leg confit with natural broth • chermoula roasted chicken with mashed potatoes, garlic, olives, harissa, and preserved lemons • wood-fired bone-in pork loin chop with sweet potato dumpling, asparagus, herb broth, and tomato jam • kamut, wheat berries, quinoa, black and pearl barley with brick baked vegetable and tandoori tofu.

Kona Café $$ to $$$

Pan Asian cuisine at the Polynesian Resort. Breakfast, lunch, and dinner; casual dress. Open Mon–Sat 7:30–11:30, noon–2:45 P.M. and 5–10 P.M.; Sun 7 A.M.–noon, 12:30–2:45 P.M., and 5–10 P.M.

This very simple, open dining room on the 2nd floor of the Great House at the Polynesian Resort, adorned with intricate ironwork and amber-colored pod lighting, looks out to the profusion of tropical foliage so dominant at this resort. Paddle fans softly turn overhead to the relaxing strains of South Sea music. Come at breakfast for the sinfully rich Tonga Toast stuffed with bananas and rolled in cinnamon sugar, but lunch and dinner will surely please with its reasonably priced and refreshing Asian-inspired cuisine. End your meal with a KoKo Puff, a pyramid of chocolate creme and puff pastry, and a cup of Kona coffee.

Sample Menu Items

Breakfast entrees: Eggs Benedict • ham and cheese omelet • beef tenderloin and eggs • blueberry or banana pancakes.

Lunch entrees: Blackened mahimahi sandwich • cheese ravioli tossed with shiitake mushrooms, red peppers, and arugula in a creamy Parmesan sauce • Asian noodle bowl (spiced beef broth with strip steak, snow peas, carrots, celery, and rice noodles garnished with chili garlic sauce and lemon) • kona wrap (lavosh rolled with turkey, cheese, tomatoes, lettuce, and miso-infused mayo) • beef teriyaki salad • barbeque pork sandwich with smoky mango barbeque sauce.

Dinner entrees: Beef teriyaki • seared scallops and shrimp with macadamia pesto • Pan Asian pasta (buckwheat soba noodles, chicken, vegetables, and stir-fry sauce of soy sauce, lemon grass, and ginger) • macadamia-crusted mahimahi in a lime-cilantro beurre blanc • Asian vegetable strudel • crispy tempura ahi tuna served rare.

Tip: Another great getaway from the Magic Kingdom, an appetizing alternative to park fare affording an opportunity to check out the Polynesian Hotel.

Narcoossee's $$$ to $$$$

Seafood at the Grand Floridian Beach Resort. Dinner only; smart casual dress. Open nightly 5:30–10 P.M.

This gazebo-shaped dining establishment nestled on the shore of the Seven Seas Lagoon offers a tranquil setting, inventive cuisine, and a magical view of Cinderella's Castle and the Magic Kingdom fireworks. The Key West ambiance of the softly lit, bi-level room is highlighted with shuttered windows, lazy ceiling fans, and beautiful wood ceilings. The chef's strategy here is the use of the freshest of ingredients in an ambitious menu dominated by fresh seafood; don't be surprised to see him taking a lap around the dining room making sure his luscious meals are up to snuff.

For a perfect culmination of your evening, step outside to the restaurant's wraparound deck or the adjoining boat dock for a prime viewing spot of the fireworks. After the show stick around for an after-dinner drink and a performance of the Electrical Light Parade that floats by on the lagoon directly in front of the restaurant.

Sample Menu Items

Dinner entrees: Coriander-crusted ahi tuna with Asian greens, ginger dressing, and wasabi sour cream • duet of lamb (grilled lamb loin and chop) served with mashed potatoes • jumbo seared scallops with herb polenta and caviar butter sauce • Maine lobster steamed with roasted asparagus and vanilla sauce • pan-roasted Alaskan halibut with Georgian sweet corn risotto and chili oil • shrimp with fettuccini, asparagus, mushrooms, garlic, tomato, and cream.

Tip: Request a window table along with your necessary priority seating and re-request it on arrival. The best strategy is to time your entree for a short move outside on the deck or the adjoining boat dock for a great view of the Magic Kingdom fireworks.

1900 Park Fare $$$

American cuisine at the Grand Floridian Resort. Breakfast and dinner; casual dress. Open daily 7:30–11 A.M. and 5:15–9 P.M.

The eminently colorful setting of this bright, whimsical place is a great start to your morning. Kaleidoscopic hot air balloons are your table's centerpiece, and the brightly striped walls are accented by carousel horses and framed Victorian circus prints. While the turn-of-the-century French band organ, Big Bertha, plays above your head, Disney characters roam the room signing autographs and taking pictures at each table. The breakfast buffet is hosted by Pinocchio, Mary Poppins, the Mad Hatter, Alice in Wonderland, Pluto, and Geppetto and in the evening hours the characters from Cinderella are in attendance for a bountiful prime rib dinner buffet. Breakfast is the better of the two meals, one of the best morning feasts at Disney.

Sample Menu Items

Breakfast buffet: Fresh fruit • oatmeal • cereal • bacon • sausage • waffles • French toast • sauteed potatoes • scrambled eggs • pancakes • made-to-order omelets • breakfast bread pudding • child's buffet: Mickey waffles, donuts, scrambled eggs.

Dinner buffet: Soup and salad bar • pasta and sauces • roast pork tenderloin • seafood newburg • baked fish • hand-carved ham and prime rib • assorted vegetables • mashed and roasted potatoes • creamed spinach • chocolate silk pie • key lime pie • warm cherry cobbler • warm bread pudding with vanilla sauce • soft-serve ice cream • child's buffet: fish nuggets, chicken nuggets, PB&J, mac 'n' cheese, mini hot dogs and hamburgers.

Ohana $$$

Polynesian cuisine at the Polynesian Resort. Breakfast and dinner; casual dress. Open daily 7:30–10:45 A.M. and 5–9:45 P.M.

Although I'm not a big fan of all-you-can-eat meals or even Polynesian food, I liked Ohana. Everything was more than pleasing and simply a hoot. The huge dining room is pleasant with batik fabric ceilings, banana-shaped upholstered rattan chairs, and torch-lit Tiki gods, and the massive picture windows offer fantastic views of the Seven Seas Lagoon, the Magic Kingdom fireworks, and the Electrical Water Pageant. Its focal point is the 18-foot, semi-circular fire pit where 3-foot skewers of marinated meat are grilled for the evening meal. Miraculously, given the amount of meat flaming away on the grill, nothing is overcooked or dry.

Each evening brings entertainment in the guise of coconut races, hula-hoop contests, and ukulele music. Adults looking forward to a quiet meal should arrive after 9 P.M. when the hullabaloo is over or request a seat in the side dining room away from the action. Breakfast is a family-style feast with Mickey, Goofy, and Chip 'n' Dale dressed in Polynesian regalia.

Sample Menu Items

Family-style breakfast: Scrambled eggs • fried potatoes with caramelized onions • pork sausage links • bacon • buttermilk biscuits and sausage gravy • fresh fruit.

Family-style dinner: Stir-fried vegetables • green salad with honey lime dressing • chicken and shrimp won tons • honey coriander chicken wings • stir-fried rice • barbeque pork loin • mesquite seasoned turkey breast • marinated sirloin steak • grilled jumbo shrimp.

Tip: Request a window seat when making your priority seating and re-request it on arrival.

Olivia's Café $$ to $$$

Florida cuisine at the Old Key West Resort. Breakfast, lunch, and dinner; park casual dress. Open daily 7:30-10:30 A.M., 11:30 A.M.–10 P.M.

This cheerful café's old Key West atmosphere is delightful. Soft pastel walls are covered with family photos, canoe oars, and mounted fish. Overhead paddle fans turn gently on the white pressed tin ceilings to the beat of soft Caribbean music. Lunch and dinner brings tasty food with an interesting Floridian flair, but breakfast is my favorite meal with huge omelets, fluffy biscuits, and irresistible hot cinnamon rolls.

Sample Menu Items

Breakfast entrees: Poached eggs over sweet potato and ham hash • steak and eggs • pancakes and eggs • a terrific three-egg omelet chockfull of your choice of numerous items • buttermilk pancakes with blueberry sauce.

Lunch entrees: Cuban sandwich • grilled smoked turkey Reuben sandwich • deep-fried buttermilk chicken breast • baked mahimahi on a bed of warm greens with sun-dried tomato caper vinaigrette and balsamic onions • garden veggie wrap.

Dinner entrees: Jumbo shrimp Alfredo • penne pasta tossed with Asiago cheese, sun-dried tomatoes, spinach, olive oil, and garlic • sauteed Florida snapper with mango butter over lobster risotto • grilled filet mignon paired with lobster stuffed shrimp • slow-roasted prime rib.

Palio $$$ to $$$$

Italian cuisine at the Walt Disney World Swan. Dinner only; smart casual dress. Open nightly 6–11 P.M.

Often overlooked, this atmospheric restaurant in the Swan Hotel certainly deserves attention. The draw of exquisitely prepared Tuscan cuisine along with a softly lit, high-ceilinged dining room of linen tablecloths, pleasant white-jacketed waiters, and the festive banners of "il Palio" (the drapes presented to the winner of Siena's famous horse race) make for pleasurable dining. Its terrific food and professional service has earned it the reputation of Disney's best Italian spot where wood-fired oven pizzas, authentic meat dishes, and fresh seafood along with a large Italian wine list can't be beat. Strolling musicians are a nice touch, although they seem to play more American than Italian songs.

Sample Menu Items

Dinner entrees: Ragout of lobster and tortellini sauteed in garlic, basil, and cream • pan-seared sea bass with a fennel and mushroom ragout in rosemary infused white wine sauce • saltimbocca (veal scallopini with prosciutto, sage, and porcini risotto with madeira sauce) • osso buco (braised veal shank in white wine and vegetable sauce with saffron risotto).

Tip: Because it's open until 11 P.M., it's a great dining choice after Epcot closes; however, you might be more comfortable changing out of park clothing.

Shula's Steakhouse $$$ to $$$$

Steakhouse at the Walt Disney World Dolphin. Dinner only; business casual dress. Open nightly 5–11 P.M.

Owned by Don Shula, this handsome restaurant is themed on the Miami Dolphins' 1972 undefeated season, well depicted in attractively framed black-and-white pictures embellishing the rich wood-paneled rooms. The dimly lit, dark hued interior is clubby and comfortable, outfitted in dark cherry wood, loads of shiny brass, cushy high-backed upholstered chairs, leather banquettes, and white linen-covered tables. What doesn't fit its sophisticated atmosphere is the menu printed on a pigskin football and the rolling tray of raw meat explained in detail (à la Morton's) by a member of the knowledgeable and friendly wait staff. However, the Angus beef steaks are sensational, done to perfection, and accompanied by mouthwatering sourdough bread.

Sides include sharing portions of Caesar salad, creamed spinach, oversized baked potatoes, great hash browns, or broccoli with hollandaise sauce. And with Frank Sinatra crooning in the background, what else could you ask for? Shula's outstanding California wine list was given a 2002 Wine Spectator Restaurant Award. Oh, and don't leave without lingering over a chocolate souffle or stopping in the adjoining clubby lounge, perfect for cigars and cognac.

Sample Menu Items

Dinner entrees: 12-ounce filet mignon • 24- or 48-ounce porter-house • 32-ounce prime rib • 22-ounce lamb loin chops • 4–5 pound Lobster surf 'n' turf • French-cut chicken breast • Norwegian salmon • 10-ounce Florida snapper.

Tip: Those traveling with small children should take advantage of the 2 hours of complimentary childcare at Camp Dolphin. Be sure to reserve ahead of time and enjoy your time alone.

Spoodles $$$

Mediterranean cuisine at the Boardwalk. Breakfast and dinner; park casual dress. Open daily 7:30–11 A.M. and 5–10 P.M.

Walls adorned with Italian ceramics, glossy hardwood floors (making this one noisy spot), a bevy of earthy colors, and a wood-burning pizza oven in an enormous open kitchen sets the stage for Mediterranean food and family fun at this bustling, appealing restaurant. On each rustic table is a bright stack of small plates for sharing the appetizing assortment of tapas and thin-crusted savory pizzas on the menu. The excellent arugula salad with apples, Gorgonzola, spiced walnuts, and warm smoky bacon vinaigrette combined with one of the tapas (try the sauteed chili garlic shrimp) is a meal in itself. Entrees are heartily prepared with robust sauces and sides of delicate couscous, grainy pilaf, or risotto.

In the mornings, fuel up at one of Disney's best breakfast spots with selections like wood-fired breakfast pizza or French toast made with challah bread topped with banana nut brittle.

Sample Menu Items

Breakfast entrees: Mediterranean breakfast platter (all-you-care-to-eat feast of scrambled eggs, Spanish-style breakfast potatoes, French toast, bacon, chorizo, vegetable rotollo, bread pudding, and breakfast bread) • roasted vegetable omelet • Moroccan pancakes (semolina pancakes rolled with a honey butter filling topped with almond granola) • breakfast flatbread topped with scrambled eggs, Italian sausage, and mozzarella cheese.

Tapas: Crispy fried calamari • roasted peppers with fresh mozzarella and basil • selection of Mediterranean dips • sampler platter (roasted peppers, Manchego cheese, lamb cigars, chorizo, and tapa of the day).

Dinner entrees: Grilled salmon with sweet onion risotto, red wine sauce, and crispy onions • rigatoni with Italian sausage, tomatoes, and portobello mushrooms • fettuccini with prosciutto, peas, and a Parmesan cream sauce • gratin of scallops with potato puree, sauteed mushrooms, and Parmesan bread crumbs • medallions of filet mignon with pancetta mashed potatoes, chive creme, and sun-dried tomato jam.

Tip: Another great alternative to Epcot dining, just a 10-minute walk from the International Gateway. Those wanting to take food back to their room should stop at the handy take-out window for pizza with a variety of toppings, calzones, meatball sandwiches, and salads.

Victoria and Albert's $$$$

Contemporary cuisine at the Grand Floridian. Dinner only; reservations mandatory; jackets required for gentlemen. Open nightly with two seating times: 5:45–6:30 P.M. and 9–9:45 P.M.

Fine dining in a stunning setting combined with virtually flawless service sets Victoria and Albert's apart. Awarded a AAA 5-Diamond Award for the 3rd year in a row (the only such restaurant in Orlando), dine on white linen–covered tables set with Royal Doulton china and Riedel wine glasses to the strains of the enchanting sound of harp music. The domed-ceilinged restaurant is tinted in soft hues of peach with marble columns, fabric walls, and oversized flower arrangements. Each evening the fare changes according to what is seasonal and fresh. Seven sumptuous, prix fixe courses are small, allowing enough room for a sensational dessert accompanied by a pot of coffee brewed at the table in an amazing vacuum pot.

Those seeking a special evening should book the newly-remodeled, 6-person chef's table set in a candlelit alcove in the kitchen, a spot perfect for an up-close, behind-the-scenes look at Disney's top chef in action. This table goes quickly (it can be booked up to 180 days in advance) so think ahead.

Although dining here is memorable, I just can't seem to get past the ridiculous butler and maid routine that persists throughout the meal with your waitress always named Victoria and your waiter playing the role of Albert. Why can't Disney just lose this silly act?

Sample Menu Items

Appetizers: Perigord truffle–stuffed poussin over lentils • lobster bisque • cured Canadian salmon with chipotle-lime vinaigrette • warm duck confit with fuji apple and warm sherry vinaigrette.

Entrees: Grilled prime beef filet with Vidalia onion risotto • rack of lamb with fresh herb gnocchi and natural jus • yellowtail snapper on a salsify gratin with champagne cream.

Desserts: Pyramid of chocolate mousse with glazed strawberries • kona chocolate souffle • vanilla bean creme brulee • caramelized banana gateau.

Tip: This is no place for children; be sure to book a babysitter.

Whispering Canyon Café $$$ to $$$$

Barbecue and smoked meats at the Wilderness Lodge. Breakfast, lunch, and dinner; casual dress. Open daily 7:30–11 A.M., noon–3 P.M., and 5–10 P.M.

Come prepared for plenty of hootin' and hollerin' and please, whatever you do, don't ask for the ketchup unless, that is, you like a lot of attention. Dedicated to hearty, not haute, cuisine, it's an all-you-care-to-eat blow-out of rib-stickin' barbecue served piping hot in iron skillets, or for those with smaller appetites, the option of an à la carte menu. In a setting reminiscent of Bonanza is the dining room of rustic lodgepole pines, metal wagon-wheel light fixtures, and tables laid with bandana napkins, jelly jar glasses, and lazy Susan barrel tops perfect for skillet sittin'. Here it's always a show where hobbyhorse-racing waiters in western attire love to make a huge production out of serving food, birthday celebrations, and those unfortunate enough to leave for the restroom.

The outside view of a cozy log cabin nestled in the woods only adds to the Old West atmosphere.

Sample Menu Items

Breakfast entrees: Skillet meal (scrambled eggs, hash brown rounds, bacon, sausage, fantastic buttermilk biscuits, sausage gravy, waffles, and breakfast bread) • steak and eggs • Kansas City hash (smoked beef brisket, au gratin potatoes, onions, peppers, and cheese topped with two eggs) • three-egg frittata • cinnamon swirl French toast • flapjacks • bread pudding topped with vanilla cream sauce.

Lunch entrees: Skillet meal (smoked pork ribs, barbeque chicken, smoked beef brisket, baked beans, corn-on-the-cob, coleslaw, roasted potatoes, breadsticks) • club sandwich of brisket, turkey, and bacon • little nutty chicken and cheese salad • smokin' St. Louis ribs • cowpoke pulled pork sandwich • fried chicken • grilled fish sandwich • seasonal vegetable platter.

Dinner entrees: Skillet meal (smoked pork ribs, smoked beef brisket, pulled pork, apple-rosemary chicken, pork sausage, smoked turkey leg, garlic potatoes, tossed salad, baked beans, cole slaw, corn, bread) • porterhouse steak • glazed pork chops • apple rotisserie chicken • pan-seared grouper • vegetarian pasta • nature's selection (marinated portobello mushroom, sauteed vegetables, roasted corn, and wild rice served with a vegetable ravioli).

Tip: Dinner here is extremely popular so make your priority seating early. Or beat the crowd and take the boat over from the Magic Kingdom for lunch, a time when the silliness is at a minium. Those desiring a more grown-up meal should request the smaller, more intimate dining room with its own cozy fireplace tucked away in the back of the restaurant, perfect for escaping the hustle and bustle of the main dining hall.

Yachtsman Steakhouse $$$ to $$$$

Steakhouse at the Yacht Club Resort. Dinner only; casual dress. Open nightly 5:30–10 P.M.

An atmospheric steakhouse setting of white linen–topped tables, red leather–cushioned chairs, and walls of framed pictures depicting the cattle drives of the Old West makes up for the too-bright lighting and loud hubbub of the bustling, but pleasant dining room. Here the mouthwatering steaks are cooked to perfection along with several seafood choices for the nonbeef-eater. Excellent accompaniments such as mushroom ragout, creamed spinach, or a platter of onions sauteed to a golden brown add to an already delicious meal, and be sure to choose the yummy au gratin potatoes as your side choice instead of baked. Their great California wine list was given a 2002 Wine Spectator Award.

Sample Menu Items

Dinner entrees: The don't-miss beef tenderloin medallions topped with baby spinach and tomatoes, Maytag blue cheese, and Cabernet wine sauce • charred Black Angus bourbon strip steak • Colorado rack of lamb in port wine black olive sauce • Black Angus prime rib with thyme garlic jus • pan-seared north Atlantic salmon in lemon thyme vinaigrette • land and sea (6-ounce fillet and 8-ounce rock lobster tail) • oak-grilled spring vegetables risotto.

Tip: Ask to sit in the circular dining room overlooking Stormalong Bay, the Yacht Club Resort's incredible pool.

DOWNTOWN DISNEY DINING

Bongos $$ to $$$$

Cuban cuisine at Downtown Disney's West Side. Lunch and dinner; reservations not accepted; casual dress. Open Sun–Thurs 11 A.M.–11:30 P.M.; Fri and Sat 11 A.M.–2 A.M.

Enjoy Disney's version of 1950s Havana with chairs and ceiling fans in the guise of banana trees, soaring palm tree columns, and walls glowing with glittering mosaics representing everything Cuban: paper money, Latino music, tourism, and Bacardi rum. This fun café is easily spotted by its 3-story pineapple, one of Downtown Disney's most defining landmarks. Have a seat on the festively tiled conga drum stools fronting the bamboo bar (one of three) and order a Mojito, an aromatic Cuban drink concocted of Bacardi rum, fresh mint, sugar, lime, and club soda. In the dining room, whopping platters of decent Cuban cuisine is served with mounds of white rice and black beans. Come late on weekends when the place is really hopping courtesy of a Ricky Ricardo–style band blasting out pulsating music for dance floor revelers.

Outside, the Café Cubano express window serves up Cuban sandwiches, croquettes, and empanadas.

Sample Menu Items

Lunch and dinner entrees: Ropa vieja (shredded beef in a light tomato sauce with onion and peppers) • churrasco, (tenderized skirt steak grilled and served with a side of chimichurri sauce) • Cuban sandwiches • zarzuela de mariscos (sauteed lobster, shrimp, scallops, calamari, fish, baby clams, and mussels in a creole sauce) • pollo asado (marinated, slow roasted chicken) • palomilla steak (but skip this bland rendition of a usually tasty meal).

Fulton's Crab House $$$ to $$$$

Seafood at Downtown Disney's Marketplace. Lunch and dinner; call 407-934-2628 for priority seating; casual dress. Open daily 11:30 A.M.–11 P.M. Stone Crab Lounge open until 2 A.M.

Don't expect wildly inventive dishes at Fulton's, but do expect the freshest seafood possible served in this replica of a Mississippi riverboat docked in the Lake Buena Vista Lagoon. Always delicious are the startlingly simple steamed crabs, lobster, mussels, and clams along with freshly shucked oysters and crab cakes full of pristine meat. Throughout the 3-story boat are nautical treasures in the form of buoys and lobster traps, ship wheels, and mounted fish. Butcher paper covers the crab motif tablecloths, and the window-filled dining rooms offer views of the water. What's more, Fulton's boasts one of the best bars in Disney, the Stone Crab Lounge, where the crowd is lively and the freshly steamed seafood and raw bar just can't be beat.

Sample Menu Items

Lunch entrees: Dungeness crab and spinach salad • Alaska king crab • shrimp club • Fulton's burger • North Atlantic snow crab • grilled Atlantic sea scallops • shrimp and seafood creole • mahimahi sandwich.

Dinner entrees: Sea scallop pasta with roasted red peppers, scallion, and spinach tossed with fettuccini and lobster butter • steamed twin Maine lobster • Alaskan king crab claws • grilled gulf shrimp • grilled Hawaiian ono • filet mignon served with roasted mushrooms • fried rock shrimp • cioppino • seafood boil (whole Maine lobster, clams, mussels, and snow crab with sweet corn and red skin potatoes).

House of Blues $ to $$$

Cajun/Creole cuisine at Downtown Disney's West Side. Lunch and dinner; reservations taken only for the Gospel Brunch and for groups of six or more at 407-934-BLUE; casual dress. Open daily Sun and Mon 11 A.M.–11 P.M.; Tues and Wed 11 A.M.–midnight; Thur–Sat 11 A.M.–1:30 A.M.

Inside the House of Blues' rusty tin facade is a funky dining room of wall-to-wall and floor-to-ceiling folk art, good old blues music, and some of the heartiest Mississippi Delta–style dishes around. They certainly make a mean jambalaya, full of shrimp, chicken, and fantastic andouille sausage topped off with a screaming hot habanero pepper, and you'll swear by the white chocolate banana bread pudding, one of the best desserts this side of the Mississippi. Thurs–Sat the pulse moves up a notch with live blues beginning at 11 P.M., and on Sundays they pack 'em in at the popular Gospel Brunch where plenty of foot stomping and good old soulful music is accompanied by a bountiful Southern-style buffet (full review on page 325). Next door you'll find the best live venue around with many concerts open to all ages.

Sample Menu Items

Lunch and dinner entrees: Seared ahi tuna salad • shrimp po-boy sandwich • slow-smoked baby back ribs with Jack Daniels barbeque sauce, mashed sweet potatoes and turnip greens • vegetarian lasagna • Louisiana crawfish and shrimp etouffee • Cajun meatloaf • penne pasta with a wild mushroom sauce, chicken, and smoked gouda.

Tip: On balmy days request a table outside on the pleasant back porch with perfect views of the Buena Vista Lagoon.

Portobello Yacht Club $$$ to $$$$

Italian cuisine at Downtown Disney's Pleasure Island. Dinner only; call 407-934-8888 for priority seating; casual dress. Open daily 5–11 P.M..

Excellent Northern Italian food in a seaside, nautical ambience attracts a loyal following at this Downtown Disney restaurant. The food consistently lives up to its good reputation; try the smoky-tasting, thin-crusted wood-oven pizzas or the mouthwatering rendition of pasta amatriciana robustly prepared with pancetta, onions, tomatoes, and fresh basil. Those with a hearty appetite may want to consider the four-course menu degusttazione consisting of an antipasti, salad, your choice of two entrees, and dessert. Many prefer to dine on the lovely outdoor patio overlooking the lake. Choose a bottle from Portobello's excellent international wine list, a 2002 Wine Spectator Restaurant Award winner. Or try the lively bar, which serves up good bellinis, martinis, single-malt scotch, and grappa.

Sample Menu Items

Dinner entrees: Scallops, shrimp, clams, and Alaska king crab with tomatoes, garlic, olive oil, wine, and herbs tossed with spaghettini pasta • charcoal-grilled center cut fillet of beef topped with white truffle butter • wood-roasted prosciutto and sage-wrapped tuna steak • veal scallopini sauteed with wild mushrooms and Marsala wine.

Rainforest Café $ to $$$

American cuisine at Downtown Disney's Marketplace. Lunch and dinner; call 407-827-8500 at least 24 hours in advance for priority seating; casual dress. Open Sun–Thurs 11:30 A.M.–11 P.M.; Fri and Sat 11:30 A.M.– midnight.

One of two Rainforest Cafés at Disney (the other is located at the Animal Kingdom), this one's the most popular with its prime Downtown Disney location and its rumbling and smoke-spewing 60-foot volcano. Visitors ooh and aah over the dining room's lush canopy of foliage, gushing waterfalls, massive aquariums, and menagerie of audio-animatronics wildlife that screech and growl when the intermittent thunderstorms pass over. Waits here can be ridiculous, so stop by and put your name on the list before browsing the Marketplace or checking out the Rainforest Café retail store filled with ecological souvenirs and clothing. For menu specifics see the Rainforest Café at the Animal King-dom on page 344.

Wolfgang Puck Café $$ to $$$$ (downstairs); $$$ to $$$$ (upstairs)

*Contemporary cuisine at Downtown Disney's West Side. Lunch and dinner downstairs, dinner only upstairs; casual dress downstairs and smart casual upstairs; call **407-938-9653** for priority seating. Open Sun–Thurs11:30 A.M.–11 P.M.; Fri and Sat 11:30 A.M.–midnight.*

Gastronomic fires are out of control at the exciting, ultramodern Wolfgang Puck Café. Long known for its innovative cuisine, savory thin-crusted pizza, and inventive pasta, the food is nothing short of divine with each explosively flavored bite evoking an automatic "wow." Every square inch is alive with vibrant colors seen in the vivid mosaic tiles, wacky lighting, and contemporary furnishings. The café features a startlingly fresh B's Sushi Bar, a downstairs café with additional outdoor dining, a Wolfgang Puck Express, and an upstairs dining room serving an ever-changing menu of fusion cuisine in a more formal, sophisti-cated atmosphere. With so many choices it's hard to decide which delectable dining venue to choose from.

Sample Menu Items

Downstairs café entrees: BLTA pizza (applewood-smoked bacon, mozzarella and Fontina cheeses, roma and sun-dried tomatoes, avo-cado, and chopped romaine) • spicy pad thai (the best pasta on the menu) • roasted pumpkin ravioli • coriander-crusted ahi seared rare with Asian vegetables and crispy noodles • bacon-wrapped meatloaf served with simply the finest garlic mashed potatoes on the planet • grilled wahoo with coconut-curry broth, Asian-style sticky rice, and vegetable stir-fry.

Upstairs restaurant entrees: Herb seared ahi tuna with roasted garlic and caper beurre blanc • "chinoise" lamb (Szechuan marinated domes-tic lamb with lobster and shiitake mushrooms, oyster sauce, and wasabi infused potatoes) • crispy chicken with lobster risotto cake and spicy lobster hollandaise • sauteed gulf white shrimp linguini with grilled artichokes, roasted tomatoes, Parmesan, and spicy lemon and garlic sauce.

Tip: If you like dining late, the view of the nightly Pleasure Island fireworks is great from the upstairs dining room.

OTHER NOTABLE RESTAURANTS NEAR DISNEY

Arthur's 27 $$$$

*Contemporary cuisine at the Wyndham Palace Resort near Downtown Disney. Dinner only; business dress; call **407-827-3450** for reservations. Open Mon–Sat 6–10 P.M.*

In a drop-dead setting high atop the Wyndham Resort is Arthur's 27, offering amazing views of Disney and the surrounding area along with fine dining in a sophisticated atmosphere. Tuxedoed waiters, soft lighting, classical music, pale pink linens, fine china, and gleaming crystal add to the romance of the evening where the presentation is worth the price and each dish receives a deserved "aah." The food is superb and extremely creative. The pricey wine list is small but interesting and a four- or five-course prix-fixe menu is offered for those with a larger appetite.

Sample Menu Items

Dinner entrees: Pistachio and spinach-crusted rack of lamb • fillet of turbot in a horseradish pastry crust • sauteed veal medallions, lemon basil capellini, grilled artichokes and gorgonzola sauce • pineapple-soy glazed breast of duck confit leg, Maui onion sauce • rack of elk, six onion risotto with sauce Grand Veneur • Tuscan bean agnolotti, shaved black truffles, braised arugula, madiera sauce.

Tip: The hotel's valet parking is complimentary for those dining at Arthur's 27. When making reservations (highly suggested) ask for a table with a view of Downtown Disney. From this vantage point you can see Spaceship Earth glowing in the fiery sunset along with the evening fireworks display at both Epcot and the Magic Kingdom. The view from the other side of the room, though very nice, also contains a not-so-lovely view of I-4. If you would like the panorama without the high price of dinner, have drinks in the adjoining sophisticated bar.

Black Swan $$$$

*Contemporary cuisine at the Villas of Grand Cypress. Dinner only; business casual dress; call **407-239-4700** for reservations. Open nightly 6:30–10 P.M.*

One of the Orlando area's best restaurants is this one hidden away in the Club House (of all places) at the Villas of Grand Cypress Resort. I knew it was going to be a perfect evening when before I could put my white linen napkin in the lap of my black dress, the waiter quickly replaced it with a black one to avoid the inevitable "white lint lap" syndrome. Tones of green and peach and lavish fresh flower arrangements, linen tablecloths, comfortable upholstered chairs, and sparkling crystal fill the small dining room. Tables have lovely views of the golf course's lush undulating greens and romantic lakes, service is impeccable, and the food, creatively prepared to perfection, is nothing short of divine.

Consider beginning with an Italian black truffle-filled tortellini topped with a pinot noir beurre rouge moving on to a melt-in-yourmouth sea bass wrapped in delicate hearts of palm nestled in charred mango chutney with a side of scrumptious coconut rice. Wrap up a perfect evening with a Grand Marnier souffle filled with Tahitian vanilla bean anglaise accompanied by a black swan cappuccino with Godiva dark chocolate liqueur. It's just as special as an evening at Victoria and Albert's without the silliness of a queen for a waitress and a prince consort for a butler.

Sample Menu Items

Dinner entrees: Grilled pink peppercorn-crusted New York prime strip with a red wine bearnaise • herb seasoned veal chop smothered with exotic mushrooms topped with a red wine demi-glace • chanterelle-crusted roasted rack of lamb and a rosemary burgundy sauce served with an applewood cheddar twice-baked potato.

Café D'Antonio $$ to $$$$

*Italian cuisine at **691 Front Street** in the town of Celebration. Lunch and dinner; call **407-566-2233** for reservations; casual dress. Open Mon–Fri 11:30 A.M.–3 P.M. and 5–10 P.M.; Sat 11:30 A.M.–10 P.M.; Sun 11:30 A.M.–9 P.M.*

A spare and uninspiring dining room tends to drive guests to the outside tables offering a soothing view of the surrounding town of Celebration. Waiters tend to be a bit abrupt, but the menu is tempting with authentic Italian recipes and brick oven pizza. And if al dente is not the way you like pasta, say so, or you may come away unhappy. In the pasta department the linguini mounded with fresh, succulent clams can't be beat; vegetarians should try the mouthwatering quattro pizza loaded with mushrooms, artichokes, pepperonata and mozzarella. A nice Italian and American wine list rounds out the extensive menu.

Sample Menu Items

Lunch and dinner entrees: Chicken roasted over a wood fire served on mixed greens with mushrooms, Fontina cheese, and roasted peppers • risotto porcini • penne pasta in a sauce of portobello and porcini mushrooms, pancetta, cream, and tomato • gnocchi with pomodoro sauce • fresh wood grilled salmon • veal chop sauteed with a sauce of spinach, walnuts, white wine, and prosciutto • papardelle tossed with crabmeat, leeks, cream, tomato, and white wine • lasagna Bolognese.

Columbia Restaurant $$$

*Cuban/Spanish cuisine at **649 Front Street** in the town of Celebration. Lunch and dinner; call **407-566-1505** for reservations; casual at lunch, smart casual at dinner. Open daily 11:30 A.M.–10 P.M.*

This fourth generation–operated family restaurant opened in 1905 in Tampa's Ybor City and has since become a legend expanding throughout Florida and, lucky for us, to the town of Celebration. A delightful atmosphere along with superb service and exceptional Spanish and Cuban cuisine are certainly the ingredients for success. White tablecloths, cane chairs, cushy leather booths, ceilings hanging with dimly lit Spanish lanterns, lush palm trees, and languidly turning wooden fans set the mood.

Start with several platters of tapas, little dishes of appetizers that are a Spanish tradition, or a bowl of tasty Cuban black bean soup followed by a must-have, table-side tossed, original "1905" salad of lettuce, smoked ham, Swiss cheese, tomato, olives, Romano cheese, and a tangy garlic dressing. Meals, all of which are plated at the table, include a hard-to-beat paella; don't neglect to order an accompanying pitcher of their specialty sangria or a bottle of rich Spanish red wine. A popular seating choice is the pleasant patio, and the adjoining cigar and tapas bar is a fun alternative to the main restaurant.

Sample Menu Items

Lunch entrees: Cuban sandwich • Havana club sandwich • arroz con pollo (chicken baked with yellow rice, green peppers, onion, tomatoes, and spices) • palomilla (thinly sliced marinated top sirloin, quickly grilled and topped with a mojo crudo of chopped onion, parsley, and lime juice) • deviled blue crab–filled pastry turnover • chicken salteado (boneless chicken sauteed with garlic, green peppers, onions, mushrooms, potatoes, chorizo, and red wine).

Dinner entrees: Paella à la Valenciana with clams, mussels, shrimp, scallops, grouper, calamares, chicken, and pork • roast pork à la Cubana • sea bass Bilboa baked with tomatoes, potatoes, onions, olive oil, garlic, and white wine • boliche criollo (eye round of beef stuffed with chorizo and roasted in a flavorful gravy).

Hemingways $$$ to $$$$

Seafood at the Hyatt Regency Grand Cypress Resort. Dinner only; call 407-239-3854 for reservations; smart casual dress. Open nightly 6–10 P.M.

Several small dining rooms adorned with brass hurricane lanterns and vases of fresh orchids are surrounded by long narrow windows overlooking the lush grounds of the Hyatt Grand Regency Resort. The casual Key West atmosphere is enhanced by Hemingway-style memorabilia and welcoming waiters in casual tropical-style attire happy to advise diners to start with the Key Wester Salad of romaine, capacolla ham, avocado, tomato, bacon, Parmesan, and blue cheese and to end with the coconut ice cream wrapped in Grand Marnier chocolate served over sponge cake. Ask to sit in one of the more intimate back dining rooms that hang over the pool (although you can't really see it from your table).

Sample Menu Items

Dinner entrees: Feast of the sea (2-pound Maine lobster, broiled, steamed, or crab cake stuffed) • shrimp and corn–stuffed ravioli served with jumbo prawns in a lemony sauce • beer battered macadamia and coconut shrimp served with pineapple guava sauce • grilled veal loin chop served over shell pasta, rock shrimp, Parmesan, and chives • Maryland-style crab cakes • paella Madrid.

La Coquina $$$$

Contemporary cuisine at the Hyatt Regency Grand Cypress Resort. Sunday brunch and seasonally for dinner; call 407-239-3854 for reservations; business casual. Open Sun 10:30 A.M.–2:30 P.M.; seasonally Thurs–Mon 6–10 P.M.

Take time away from the parks on a Sunday afternoon for the best brunch in the Orlando area in a striking dining room surrounded by floor-to-ceiling windows with views of the stunning Hyatt Regency grounds and Lake Windsong. At tables set with white linens, tropical fresh flowers, and cobalt blue chargers, the meal begins with freshly squeezed orange juice and Evian water. A talented pianist entertains guests who sip on glass after glass of Moet and Chandon and make trip after trip to the buffet in the restaurant's large kitchen. Here you'll find tables laden with fantastic starters: an entire table of stone crabs, oysters on the half shell, shrimp, and smoked fish, a salad table, sushi table, beef tenderloin, roasted peppers, egg rolls, fruit, terrines, waffles, pancakes, duck salad, and at least 50 more items to choose from. Next comes your choice of several entrees including rack of lamb, pheasant, elk chops, sea bass, and filet mignon, all prepared with delicious sauces and vegetables. The dessert table looks more impressive than it actually is, but choices include a large variety of truffles, mini tarts, fruit tarts, mousse, key lime pie, and more. Be sure to request a window seat when making your reservations. Resort valet parking is complimentary if dining at La Coquina. The restaurant is open seasonally for dinner in accordance with convention traffic.

Market Street Café $ to $$

American cuisine at 701 Front Street in the town of Celebration. Breakfast, lunch, and dinner; reservations not accepted; casual dress. Open daily 8 A.M.–10 P.M.

One of the most popular places in town and rightly so with a pleasant wait staff serving excellent classic meals with an updated twist. Eat inside in the booths of the art-deco style, chrome-lined diner or choose the patio facing the lake and town promenade. If not for a meal, stop in for the incredible homemade desserts or the perfect milkshake.

Sample Menu Items

Breakfast entrees: Baked potato omelet with hash browns, bacon, and cheddar cheese topped with sour cream • scrambled egg sandwich • breakfast burrito with scrambled eggs, pico de gallo, cheddar cheese, and sour cream • chocolate chip, blueberry, or apple pancakes • cinnamon-battered French toast served with strawberries.

Lunch and dinner entrees: Spinach salad tossed with a warm bacon vinaigrette, mushrooms, blue cheese, and chopped tomatoes • a fantastically rich buffalo chicken wrap (lettuce, tomatoes, chicken tenders, and cheddar cheese tossed in blue cheese sauce wrapped in a flour tortilla) • Shanghai stir-fry • ham and cheese casserole (penne pasta and ham tossed in a creamy cheddar cheese sauce topped with cracker crumbs) • salmon burger • veggie burger • open-face meatloaf sandwich.

Old Hickory Steakhouse $$$ to $$$$

*American cuisine at the **Gaylord Palms Resort**. Dinner only; call **407-586-0000** for reservations; smart casual dress. Open nightly 5:30–10 P.M.*

For sheer atmosphere this restaurant can't be beat. Dine in a rustic, tin-roofed hideaway over the swamps of the misty Everglades in the extraordinary Gaylord Palms Resort. Alligators growl and frogs croak while you feast on Black Angus steak and excellent fresh seafood. Those in the know will request one of the tables on the decks overlooking the swamp. My steak was tasty and cooked to perfection, but my dining companion's swordfish was the better of the two dishes. Stop in early for a drink at the rustic, candlelit bar with views over the swamp.

Sample Menu Items

Dinner entrees: all steaks are served with your choice of bearnaise, au poivre, Bordelaise, or diablo sauces • 16-ounce veal porterhouse steak • rack of lamb • surf 'n' turf of beef tenderloin and lobster tail • 21-ounce bone-in rib steak • center cut fillet • sea scallops with American caviar beurre-blanc • Maine lobster served with drawn butter and lemon • confit of Muscovy duck.

UNIVERSAL ORLANDO DINING

Finnegan's Bar and Grill $ to $$

Irish Food in Universal Studios' New York Area. Lunch and dinner; reservations not accepted.

Although Lombard's Landing is considered the premier restaurant in the Universal Studios park, stop here for a pint, much better food, and a bit of live entertainment. The casual, boisterous surroundings of this corner Irish pub make this the favored establishment for party-goers. Roost around an aged, dark-paneled bar with a pint in hand reveling in the live music (not necessarily Irish) amid old family photos and memorabilia. A full pub menu consisting of hearty, traditional Irish food along with some American choices is served in the bar as well as in the adjoining, more serene dining room of antique wood floors, wooden booths, dingy pressed tin ceilings, and vintage sports memorabilia. Start with the great Cornish pasties and order a yard of ale served in a glass so tall you'll need to stand up to drink it.

Sample Menu Items

Lunch and dinner entrees: Celtic chicken salad • Dublin pie (pot pie baked with chicken, mushrooms, and leeks) • shepherd's pie (casserole of ground beef and vegetables topped with a crust of potatoes) • fish and chips • corned beef and cabbage • bangers and mash • Irish stew • corned beef, sauteed onion, and Swiss cheese sandwich served on a pretzel roll • steak sandwich topped with sauteed peppers and onions • Gardenburger.

Lombard's Landing $$ to $$$

Seafood at Universal Studios in the San Francisco/Amity Area. Lunch and dinner; call 407-224-9255 for priority seating.

Dine in a Victorian-style warehouse reminiscent of old San Francisco among red brick walls, rich stained glass, and plenty of green cast iron. A Captain Nemo–looking aquarium sits center stage in the comfortable dining room where oversized picture windows afford a great view of the lagoon; in warm weather opt for the pleasant outside deck. Although the menu is agreeable, it isn't spectacular and certainly not a bargain. If you really need a quiet break, go for it; if not, opt for one of the nearby counter-service spots where the same fried seafood baskets can be had for around $10 less if you're willing to forgo table service.

Sample Menu Items

Lunch and dinner entrees: Seafood Cobb salad • charbroiled chicken sandwich • lo mein (stir-fried lo mien noodles with marinated grilled chicken breast, crispy vegetables, and fresh ginger) served with a shrimp and pork egg roll • five cheese ravioli • chargrilled 10-ounce sirloin steak • Gardenburger.

Mythos Restaurant $$ to $$$

Contemporary cuisine at Islands of Adventure in the Lost Continent. Lunch and dinner; call 407-224-9255 for priority seating.

Inside the stone sea cave dining room are dream-like, undulating rock walls interspersed with bubbling streams and fountains, carved ironwork railings, and red velvet chairs and banquettes. Food here is exceptional by park standards, certainly worth a gold star in Universal's crown. A must is the gratin of wild mushrooms served with a cheese crust, large enough as an appetizer for two or as a vegetarian entree. An admirable, mostly Californian wine list is accompanied by many specialty drinks including the restaurant's favorite Potion of the Gods made with 151 rum, raspberry liqueur, Cointreau, orange, pineapple, and cranberry juices served smoking over dry ice (only at a theme park could you not be embarrassed by a smoking drink).

Sample Menu Items

Lunch and dinner entrees: Chinese chicken salad • gnocchi with shrimp and roasted vegetables • grilled chicken club with applewood-smoked bacon and Vermont cheddar • cedar planked salmon • balsamic chicken served over a potato tart • shrimp and penne Alfredo style • risotto of the day.

UNIVERSAL RESORT DINING

Delfino Riviera $$$ to $$$$

Italian cuisine at Portofino Bay Hotel. Dinner only; business casual dress; call 407-503-3463 for reservations. Open Tues–Sat 6–10 P.M.

Perched above the piazza and overlooking the bay is the elegant Delfino Riviera. The overall tone is stylish, sophisticated, and soothing with massive floral arrangements, attractively appointed, candlelit tables, and upholstered chairs and sofas covered in apricot tones of floral and check. Walls are dotted with murals of Italian countryside scenes, and through the oversized, silk-draped windows are picturesque views of the twinkling harbor. Ligurian regional cuisine, splendidly presented by white-suited waiters, is imaginative and delectable although I had a miss or two with the soup and dessert; it was almost as if the chef was trying a bit too hard to be overly creative. The A+ wine list and the wandering singer is a definite plus. All in all it was a lovely evening if not a bit of a stuffy atmosphere. On balmy nights opt for the breeze-swept terrace overlooking the bay and piazza, the height of romance.

Sample Menu Items

Dinner entrees: Risotto with lobster and baby artichokes • tortellini filled with Swiss chard and fresh ricotta in a walnut sauce • grilled lamb loin with baby artichokes, garlic, and rosemary white wine sauce • breast of capon crusted with herbs in a balsamic reduction • jumbo prawns wrapped in prosciutto and grilled • marinated and grilled tenderloin.

Mama Della's Ristorante $$ to $$$$

Italian cuisine at Portofino Bay Hotel. Dinner only; call 407-503-3463 for reservations; casual dress. Open daily 5:30–10 P.M.

Dine well on old-world, hearty Italian food presented in the festive atmosphere of Mama Della's home. Mama has converted her house into a family-style restaurant where guests dine in different rooms, each with gaudy, flowery wallpaper and mismatched chairs, each with a roaming Mama in her housedress who encourages everyone to "eat, eat." Many of the earthy appetizers and entrees can be served family style on huge platters, with each additional portion at a bargain price. Wandering singers entertain amid an atmosphere of gaiety and good humor.

There's lovely outdoor dining on the piazza, but it's much more fun inside where all the action takes place.

Sample Menu Items

Dinner entrees: Rigatoni with Italian sausage, broccoli rabe, and garlic broth • linguini with red or white clam sauce • lasagna made with ricotta, meat sauce, and béchamel • veal Marsala • chicken cacciatore • frutti di mare with grilled shrimp, scallops, and snapper, roasted tomatoes, garlic, and olive oil • risotto with porcini mushrooms • grilled and sliced sirloin with caramelized onions and roasted potatoes.

The Palm $$ to $$$$

Steakhouse at the Hard Rock Hotel. Lunch weekdays and dinner nightly; call 407-503-PALM for reservations; smart casual dress. Mon–Fri 11:30 A.M.–11 P.M.; Sat 5–11 P.M.; Sun 5–10 P.M.

Orlando's branch of the famous New York steakhouse sits in the hip Hard Rock Hotel. Fortunately the blasting music from the hotel's public areas doesn't travel this far and the restaurant is blessedly quiet. The rich wood surroundings and private booths exude a clubby and sophisticated steakhouse atmosphere. Walls are adorned with caricatures of local celebrities, a Palm trademark. Long known for their specialties of divine but pricey jumbo lobsters and prime aged steaks and chops, additional choices include pasta, seafood, veal, and chicken dishes with sometimes disappointing and too-greasy sides of creamed spinach, string beans, hash browns, and fried asparagus. Stick with the steak, lamb, or lobster, and you can't go wrong. And head elsewhere for dessert.

Sample Menu Items

Lunch entrees: Sliced steak sandwich • open-faced meatloaf sandwich • Italian chicken sandwich • broiled crab cakes • grilled salmon fillet • filet mignon• linguini with clam sauce • broiled swordfish steak with black bean salsa and red pepper sauce.

Dinner entrees: Nova Scotia lobster • double-cut lamb chops • jumbo shrimp saute • prime aged porterhouse • rib eye steak • rib of beef • swordfish steak.

CITYWALK DINING

Emeril's $$$ to $$$$

Contemporary Cajun and Creole cuisine; lunch and dinner; call 407-224-2424 for reservations; smart casual dress. Open daily 11:30 A.M.–2 P.M. and 5:30–10 P.M.; Fri and Sat until 11 P.M.

CityWalk has been lucky enough to snag an outpost of one of the hottest restaurants in the nation, one that is absolutely intoxicating from the knowledgeable staff to the trendy decor to the unbelievable mouthwatering food. Reminiscent of the New Orleans warehouse district, the vibrant dining room is comprised of exposed pipe, stone walls adorned with contemporary art, sleek hardwood floors, a circular slate bar, and a 2-story, 12,000-bottle wine display.

Exploding with flavor and creativity is the beautifully presented and innovative Cajun/Creole cuisine. Start with the spicy smoked wild and exotic mushrooms in a home-cured tasso cream sauce over angel hair pasta and then move on to an entree of perfectly prepared lump crabmeat-crusted tournedos of beef in a red wine reduction sauce accompanied by saffron mashed potatoes. Top it all off with one of their extraordinary homemade desserts; I can never resist the rich white chocolate bread pudding with white chocolate whiskey sauce.

The preferred dining spots are in the Julia and Tchoupitoucas Room, a glass-enclosed space facing CityWalk, or the coveted counter seats perched in front of the exhibition kitchen. Hidden upstairs is a cozy cigar room of cushy leather easy chairs and a superb view of the lagoon. This is one restaurant that will leave you yearning for another night and yet another terrific meal. It is simply the best.

Sample Menu Items

Lunch entrees: Pecan-crusted Texas redfish in a Creole meniére sauce • confit of portobello mushroom served with saffron mashed potatoes • oyster-stuffed Mississippi farm raised quail served on cheesy grits with an andouille reduction sauce • grilled pork chop with red wine–braised cabbage, caramelized sweet potatoes, essence of tamarind, and a green chili mole.

Dinner entrees: Roasted rack of lamb with a creole mustard crust • grilled and roasted seasonal vegetable plate • smothered veal chop in a wild mushroom sauce served with melted Boursin cheese • saute of gulf shrimp with wood oven–roasted tomatoes, capacolla ham, savoy cabbage, beet nest, puff pastry round in a basil lemon broth.

Tip: Although no one would raise an eyebrow, you won't feel comfortable in park clothes. If you must come without changing, try sitting at the bar for your meal (the easiest way to eat without a reservation). Speaking of reservations, they are absolutely mandatory, even at lunchtime. Dinner usually requires thinking ahead 6–8 weeks; however, always call for cancellations in particular around 3 P.M. the same day, the time all diners must reconfirm for the evening meal. Children are scarce here so consider getting a babysitter. At lunchtime, use CityWalk's valet parking and have the restaurant validate your ticket (good for up to 2 hours).

Hard Rock Café $ to $$$

American cuisine. Lunch and dinner; call 407-224-3663 before 3 P.M. for same-day priority seating or through Hard Rock's Internet site (www.hardrock.com) beginning 30 days in advance; park casual dress. Open daily 11 A.M.–late night.

Yet another Hard Rock venue is located here at CityWalk, this one having the distinction of being the largest in the world (with seating for 750) and the only one built to resemble Rome's Colosseum. Wall-to-wall rock memorabilia is the draw along with blaring music and loads of drink choices. Stained-glass picture windows of rock and roll greats combined with plenty of gleaming brass and dark wood adds up to a good-looking, multilevel restaurant/club. The centerpiece of the main dining area is the pink-finned, 1961 Cadillac suspended over the huge circular bar surrounded by huge video screens featuring gyrating rock stars. Those in the know ask for a seat on the small outdoor dining balcony that comes with stellar views of CityWalk and the Universal theme parks. The reasonably tasty Southern roadhouse–style food takes a backseat to the zany atmosphere, but who comes here for the food anyway? Tours of the memorabilia collection are offered every half hour throughout the afternoon into early evening.

Sample Menu Items
Lunch and dinner entrees: Grilled Chinese chicken salad • haystack fried chicken salad (yum!) • hickory barbeque bacon cheeseburger •

veggie burger • hand-pulled pig sandwich • blackened chicken penne pasta • honey bourbon New York strip steak • grilled fajitas.

Tip: Access the café from inside Universal Studios behind Nickelodeon Studios. An attendant is on hand to stamp your hand for reentry into the park.

Jimmy Buffett's Margaritaville $ to $$$

American cuisine. Lunch and dinner; call 407-224-3663 before 3 P.M. for same-day priority seating; park casual dress. Open daily 11 A.M.–2 A.M.

Jimmy Buffett's joint here at CityWalk is literally overflowing with the sights and sounds of Key West and his famous hit songs. In the eminently colorful setting of the two-level dining room are coconut-studded palm trees, giant TV screens displaying Jimmy and his beach adventures, and speakers blaring just about every Buffett song imaginable. Suspended from the ceiling is a giant model of a floatplane with propellers spinning.

The cheeseburgers aren't exactly paradise so try one of Margaritaville's other festive dishes, many of them named after Jimmy's songs. At the restaurant's Volcano Bar is an 18-foot erupting volcano spewing forth molten margaritas into a Green Giant–sized glass or try the newly expanded Porch of Indecision for daily bar specials and a front row seat to CityWalk. The attached merchandise store is a must-stop for Buffett fans. After 10 P.M. live entertainment turns this spot into a hopping nightclub at which time a cover charge is assessed.

Sample Menu Items

Lunch and dinner entrees: Jerk chicken • grilled fish sandwich • veggie burger • Cuban meatloaf sandwich • blackened salmon salad • shrimp pasta of tomatoes, black beans, cilantro, and tequila lime sauce • jambalaya • coconut tempura-fried shrimp • crab cakes • blackened surf 'n' turf.

Latin Quarter $ to $$$$

Central and South American cuisine. Dinner only; call 407-224-3663 before 3 P.M. for same-day priority seating; casual dress. Open daily 5–10 P.M.; nightclub open until 2 A.M.

Latino cuisine housed in a bizarre attempt at a starlit Mayan temple gone wrong. I can't possibly figure out what kind of look the designer was striving for, but it doesn't work. However, the music is lively, the crowd happy, and the large portions of spicy food is pretty darn good. On the menu are a great variety of Nuevo Latino appetizers and entrees drawing from a wide range of Central and South America specialties. The earsplitting beat of nightly live Latino music gets the crowd moving on the roomy dance floor while onlookers sip on a huge variety of specialty drinks, Mexican and South American beer, and Chilean wine. After 10 P.M. Thurs through Sat a cover charge is imposed.

Sample Menu Items

Dinner entrees: Grilled marinated skirt steak with a chimichurri sauce • marinated roasted pork loin in a sour orange cilantro mojo • coconut snapper • paella (including a vegetarian version) • Caribbean crusted mahimahi with a roasted red pepper sauce • Cuban sandwich • barbeque salmon basted with a smoky sweet barbeque sauce topped with spicy popcorn shrimp.

Motown Café $ to $$$

American cuisine. Lunch and dinner; call 407-224-3663 before 3 P.M. for same-day priority seating; park casual dress. Open Sun–Thurs 11:30 A.M.–11 P.M.; Fri and Sat 11 A.M.–2 A.M.

It's the 1960s at Motown Café where vinyl booths wrap the walls and the music of the Supremes, the Temptations, and Marvin Gaye resounds. The Motown memorabilia is entertaining while overhead sits the world's largest record, a spinning 28-foot monster. A sparkling staircase lined with gold records spirals to the 2nd floor where tables line the balcony's edge overlooking the action below. On the 3rd floor is the late-night Big Chill Lounge with an adjoining outside balcony and great views of CityWalk. The food is pretty unforgettable, running the gamut from barbecue to catfish, but if you are a fan of soul music, this is your place. A cover charge is imposed after 9 P.M. on Fri and Sat with live music by the talented Motown Moments Wed–Sat.

Sample Menu Items

Lunch buffet: Pasta station • meatloaf • barbeque chicken • fried catfish • hot dogs • burgers • tossed salad • potato salad • cole slaw •

corn-on-the-cob • mashed potatoes and gravy • french fries • baked beans • mac 'n' cheese.

Dinner entrees: Smoked spareribs • barbeque chicken • New York strip • chargrilled filet mignon • deep-fried catfish • pan-seared salmon • crispy chicken salad.

NASCAR Café $ to $$$

American cuisine. Lunch and dinner; call 407-224-3663 before 3 P.M. for same-day priority seating; park casual dress. Open Sun–Thurs 11 A.M.– 10:30 P.M.; Fri and Sat 11 A.M.–11:30 P.M.

You have to be a NASCAR fan to appreciate the suspended race cars that rev up their engines and spin their tires with alarming frequency, the many walls of giant screens playing race after race, the red-and-white car seat booths, and particularly the blaring country music. If it's quiet you want, consider requesting a table on the outdoor balcony with fine views of CityWalk. The roadhouse fare consists of pretty decent burgers, salads, hand-pulled pork sandwiches, ribs, and steaks. Downstairs you'll find loads of memorabilia, a NASCAR merchandise shop, an arcade, and a bar with liquid fuel, high-octane drinks or alcohol-free high performance fuel for the younger set. And don't forget to take your picture next to the Winston Cup winning stock car sitting in front of the entrance.

Sample Menu Items

Lunch and dinner entrees: Variety of hamburgers, the best being the Thunder Road burger topped with homemade pimento cheese, grilled onions, and a jalapeno • fried chicken salad • club sandwich • veggie burger • hand-pulled pork sandwich • chicken-fried chicken • barbecue ribs • fresh catch of the day • chargrilled shrimp • chicken pot pie.

NBA City $ to $$$

American cuisine. Lunch and dinner; call 407-224-3663 before 3 P.M. for same-day priority seating; park casual dress. Open Sun–Thurs 11 A.M.– 10:30 P.M.; Fri and Sat 11 A.M.–11:30 P.M.

This 2-story restaurant/bar is a tribute to the stars and history of the NBA. With its bi-level basketball court decor, framed black-and-white pictures of the NBA greats, and colossal projection screens that run a nonstop barrage of championship highlights from the past, it's a dribbler's dream spot.

The food is one of the best of the many themed restaurants around; start with a perfect Caesar salad followed by a rich chicken bleu cheese pasta that can't be beat. Always hopping with revelers whooping it up over live sports is the upstairs SkyBox Lounge offering a view of CityWalk along with a full bar and menu items. Before leaving, compare your pint-sized hand with those of the NBA stars on the bronzed basketballs out front.

Sample Menu Items

Lunch and dinner entrees: Grilled chicken BLT sandwich • pastrami Reuben sandwich • grilled salmon and bow tie pasta in a roasted garlic cream sauce • barbeque chicken brick oven–baked pizza • grilled Caribbean jerk mahimahi • maple glazed pork chop • Southwestern Cobb salad piled high with romaine lettuce, roasted turkey, bacon, mushrooms, black beans, red peppers, avocado, and tortilla straws tossed with a savory honey citrus dressing.

Pastamore $ to $$$

Italian cuisine. Dinner only; call 407-224-3663 before 3 P.M. for same-day priority seating; casual dress. Open nightly 5–11 P.M.

Not all dining venues in CityWalk have a party atmosphere. Pastamore touts itself as a family-style restaurant; however, don't expect a bright, unsophisticated environment. Warm tones of terra-cotta, red, and green dominate the softly lit room filled with contemporary lighting, stained cement floors, and atmospheric Italian arias. All meals begin with a wonderful bubble bread chock-full of tomatoes. Follow that with your choice of thin-crusted pizzas baked in a wood-fired oven or flavorful, creative pastas and wood-roasted meats served à la carte or family style.

Sample Menu Items

Dinner entrees: Five-cheese ravioli • penne pasta puttanesca • wood oven–roasted chicken • grilled Italian sausage • white-water clams steamed with Italian sausage, garlic, white wine, and tri-color bell peppers served with fettuccini • mushroom and asparagus risotto • classic lasagna.

DINING NEAR UNIVERSAL

Café Tu Tu Tango $

Mediterranean food at 8625 International Drive. Lunch and dinner; call 407-248-2222 for reservations; casual dress. Open Sun–Thurs 11:30 A.M.–11 P.M.; Fri and Sat 11:30 A.M.–midnight.

The draw here are tapas in a funky atmosphere and fun entertainment in the form of flamenco and tango dancers, spontaneous belly dancing, stilt walkers, and artists at work. The menu of small plates of food meant to be shared allows a sampling of many different and delectable items. Begin with a complimentary, garlicky sample of hummus and then start ordering. And if you see anything on the walls that strike your fancy, it's all for sale.

Sample tapas: The don't-miss Cajun chicken egg rolls served with a Creole mustard sauce • Mediterranean spinach dip • seared tuna sashimi • crispy shrimp with chili pepper sauce • smoked ham and cheese croquetas on corn and chive sauce • grilled chicken and poblano thin crust pizza • beef napoleon layered with portobello mushrooms and spinach served with a dijon mustard sauce • crispy salmon wrapped in potatoes and horseradish.

Chatham's Place Restaurant $$$ to $$$$

Continental cuisine at 7575 Dr. Phillips Blvd. Dinner only; call 407-345-2992 for reservations; business casual. Open nightly 5:30–10 P.M.; closed the month of July.

For 13 years Chatham's Place has been a local favorite and rightly so. A darkened dining room combined with candlelit tables, white tablecloths, and fresh flowers softens the somewhat dated dining room and the strange courtyard office building setting. However, all is overshadowed by the very professional johnny-on-the-spot service and excellent cuisine.

Begin with a loaf of unbelievably wonderful sourdough bread stuffed with feta cheese and herbs and move on to one of their classic entrees such as black grouper sauteed in butter, pecans, and scallions or perhaps one of the nightly specials; our visit featured a fabulously fresh Dover sole, deboned tableside with a butter lemon and white wine sauce. The first-rate international wine list is particularly heavy on California vintages. All in all a more than enjoyable evening.

Sample Menu Items

Dinner entrees: Rack of lamb served with rosemary au jus • baked jumbo shrimp topped with seasoned bread crumbs in a spicy sauce • petit filet served with peppercorn cognac sauce • chicken piccata.

Christini's $$$ to $$$$

Italian cuisine at 7600 Dr. Phillips Blvd. Dinner only; call 407-345-8770 for reservations; business casual. Open nightly 6–11 P.M.

For wonderful old-world Northern Italian food and personalized service, head straight to this wonderful gem of a restaurant. Don't be put off by its location in a strip mall or its non-nouveau, classic menu; every morsel is mouthwatering, prepared perfectly with the very best and freshest of ingredients. For 18 years Chris Christini has wowed the locals with his award-winning restaurant; however, here tourists are treated as if they frequent this place on a regular basis. Expert tuxedoed waiters and a strolling solo musician roam the three intimate dining rooms of black tablecloths, flowered banquettes, and frosted glass.

Have Mauricio, Christini's expert and amiable wine steward, help you with picking a perfect bottle from among 400 plus selections to accompany your perfect meal. You'll leave with a feeling of total contentment as well as a long-stemmed red rose for the ladies.

Sample Menu Items

Dinner entrees: Don't miss the veal piccata (veal scaloppine sauteed in butter, white wine, and lemon juice served with a polenta cake) • fresh little neck clams linguini with red or white sauce • veal chop, broiled and seasoned with fresh sage, served with Calvados applesauce • filet mignon in a barolo sauce with caramelized pearl onions and mushrooms • jumbo shrimp flambeed with brandy and vodka, simmered in a spicy pescatore sauce, served with linguini.

Dux $$$ to $$$$

Contemporary cuisine at the Peabody Hotel. Dinner only; call 407-352-4000 for reservations; jacket and tie suggested for gentlemen. Open Mon–Thurs 6–10 P.M.; Fri and Sat 6–11 P.M.; closed Sun.

Dripping chandeliers, lavish arrangements of fresh flowers, and tuxedoed waiters set the mood for this special occasion spot where expert service and an exceptional and ever-changing menu of seasonal dishes are the norm. A subtle, yet elegant decor of soft, taupe-toned walls, cream-colored table linens, and tastefully upholstered seating and plush banquettes make for a lovely atmosphere. The Mobil 4-Star and AAA 4-Diamond Award–rated dining room led by Chef Christophe Gerard, previously of Taillevent in Paris and Lespinasse in New York, serves a combination of classic French and American nouveau cuisine with each dish perfectly prepared and skillfully presented. If the superb oven-roasted lobster with wine sauce is on the menu, go for it. If not, you will certainly be more than content with the array of delicate creations, all of which will leave you with a sense of money well spent.

Sample Menu Items

Dinner entrees: Yellowtail snapper served with mixed herb salad, olive oil, lemon, and artichoke and apricot chutney • vegetable tart with seasonal fruits • roasted rack of venison with baby turnips, rosemary, and lemon vanilla orange sauce • grilled veal chop and Belgian endive flavored with walnut, creme of lettuce, and port wine foie gras sauce.

Roy's $$$ to $$$$

*Contemporary cuisine at **7760 Sand Lake Road.** Dinner only; call **407-352-4844** for reservations; smart casual dress. Open Sun–Thurs 5:30-10 P.M.; Fri and Sat 5:30–10:30 P.M.*

Roy Yamaguchi originated Hawaiian Fusion cuisine in Honolulu and has spread his worldwide dining experience to his newest location on a stretch of West Sand Lake Road. Stylish locals as well as in-the-know vacationers flock to this ultra-trendy place where reservations are practically a must. You won't find any tiki torches, drinks in coconut shells, or Don Ho look-alikes here. Only a sleek, contemporary dining room dramatically lit by soft amber-colored lighting and partitioned by glassed walls of wine bottles and cushy banquettes that line the chunky stone walls.

Hands down the best appetizer is the lemon grass–crusted tiger prawns with pad thai noodles in a Malaysian golden curry sauce. Although beef is on the menu, go for one of the many fresh fish choices, superbly presented in a pool of luscious sauce. Some entrees are available in half orders for the smaller appetite or for those who would like to try more than one dish.

End with the signature chocolate souffle with raspberry sauce and vanilla bean ice cream. Many of the wines are Roy's private labels, most of which are served by the glass. And make sure you know that what Roy's calls butterfish is actually cod super-soaked in a miso and sake marinade, not the best thing on the menu unless your tastes run to the very different.

Sample Menu Items

Dinner entrees: Seared roasted macadamia nut–crusted Hawaiian whitefish with lobster butter • charred garlic honey mustard beef short ribs • seared jumbo sea scallops with wasabi sweet ginger butter • Chinese-style jade pesto steamed whitefish with sizzling ginger soy vinaigrette • coconut-crusted Atlantic salmon fillet with roasted banana cream thai curry sauce • oak-smoked and grilled New York–style buffalo strip steak.

Vito's Chop House $$ to $$$$

Steakhouse at 8633 International Dr. Dinner only; call 407-354-2467 for reservations; smart casual dress. Open Sun–Thurs 5–10:30 P.M.; Fri and Sat 5–11 P.M.

For a fun evening on the town consider Vito's, an excellent steakhouse with an Italian flair and loads of ambiance. The main dining room offers plenty of comfy red leather booths, low intimate ceilings, and brick walls festooned with fish tanks and bottles of wine. Excellent service is provided by tuxedoed waiters who present enormous and succulent aged steaks and fresh seafood cooked to perfection and your choice of over 950 selections of wine from a list given a 2002 Wine Spectator Restaurant Award.

One dish worth the trek from Disney is the marvelous filet mignon stuffed with Gorgonzola. Add to that one of the terrific side options such as fresh oak-grilled vegetables, garlic smashed potatoes, creamed spinach, green fried tomatoes, or jumbo asparagus with hollandaise sauce and you've got the makings of a perfect evening. And consider coming early or lingering after dinner for drinks and a cigar in the restaurant's atmospheric lounge.

Sample Menu Items

Dinner entrees: 24-ounce prime rib eye • the ultimate surf 'n' turf of a 50-ounce porterhouse with a 1½-pound lobster • 32-ounce Tuscan porterhouse seasoned with garlic and herbs served with Gorgonzola butter • 24-ounce porterhouse veal chop, oak and citrus–grilled basted with lemon parsley butter • swordfish au poivre • wood-grilled pork chops • king salmon cedar plank roasted • lobster fra diablo (twin lobster tails, fried and placed atop linguini and then topped with marinara and an assortment of peppers).

CHAPTER 9

Universal Orlando

Just 12 miles north of Walt Disney World is this whopper of a destination composed of two side-by-side theme parks, Universal Studios and Islands of Adventure, a dining, shopping, and entertainment venue, CityWalk, and three themed resorts where a few nights of pampering could only add to your vacation experience. Universal's rapid expansion has certainly given Disney a run for its money, and what it lacks in magic it more than makes up for in its certain brand of frenzied, high-speed intensity. Although Disney has the edge in service, attractions, and plain old customer satisfaction, the compact Universal Orlando is a great 2- or 3-day excursion.

With more thrill rides at the new Islands of Adventure theme park than Disney will probably ever have, a trip here is a must if you have a teenager or coaster addict in your party. Although it will never live up to the Magic Kingdom in the eyes of small children, Universal does offer fascinating child-oriented areas in each theme park as well as the very popular Nickelodeon Studios. Low-keyed adults love the working studio aspect of Universal Studios and are simply wowed by the creativity invested in the new Islands of Adventure. Take Universal for what it is, try not to compare it to Disney, and just enjoy.

Universal Orlando Admission

Take into account the variety of options when purchasing park passes. Consider how many days will actually be spent at the Universal theme parks and if visiting SeaWorld or Wet 'n' Wild are to be part of your plans. If many of these parks are of interest to you, buy one of the Orlando Flex Tickets, remembering they expire in 14 days. The Universal multi-park passes never expire. And with only a $15 difference between the 2- and 3-day pass, even if your plans only include 2 days at Universal, spring for the 3-day pass if a return trip is a strong possibility.

To avoid a lengthy wait in line your first morning at the park, prepurchase your passes by calling **800-711-0080** or at **www.universalorlando.com** where a slight discount is usually offered. In Orlando, tickets can be purchased at the entrance to both parks as well as at the hotels on Universal property. The prices below will most likely change given that price increases occur regularly. AAA members receive $4 off the 2-Day Pass and $5 off the 3-Day pass. Florida residents should always inquire about any special discounts offered.

- 1-Day/1-Park Ticket: Good for 1 day at either Universal Studios or Islands of Adventure. No park-hopping allowed.
- 1-Day/2-Park Ticket: Good for 1 day at both parks with hopping privileges.
- 2- and 3-Day Multi-Park Pass: Admission to both Universal Studios and Islands of Adventure with park-hopping privileges and a free CityWalk Party Pass.
- 4-Park Flex Ticket: Unlimited admission with park-hopping for 14 consecutive days to Universal Studios, Islands of Adventure, SeaWorld, and Wet 'n' Wild. Also includes a free CityWalk Party Pass. Parking fee is required only once a day at the first park visited. Pass expires 14 days after the first use.
- 5-Park Flex Ticket: Unlimited admission with park-hopping for 14 consecutive days to Universal Studios, Islands of Adventure, SeaWorld, Wet 'n' Wild, and Busch Gardens Tampa Bay. Parking fee is required only once a day at the first park visited. Also includes a CityWalk Party Pass and a complimentary Busch Gardens Express Bus. Pass expires 14 days after the first use.
- Preferred Annual Pass: 365 days of admission to Islands of Adventure and Universal Studios along with free self-parking and free admission to certain special and separately ticketed events. Special discounts are offered on companion passes, merchandise, restau-

rants, CityWalk Party Passes and seasonally up to 30% at Loews' Universal hotels.

- Annual Power Pass: Less expensive than the regular Annual Pass is this Power Pass good for both parks but minus the extra benefits of free parking, free admission to special events, and without the discounts. Blackout dates when admission is not allowed include several weekends in the summer, Christmas, and Easter Week. Quite a bargain when you consider a 2-day pass is $90.

Price Without Tax

	ADULT	CHILD (3–9)
1-Day/1-Park Ticket	$52	$43
1-Day/2-Park Ticket Less	$77	$67
2-Day Ticket	$97	$84
3-Day Ticket	$112	$97
4-Park Orlando Flex Ticket	$176	$143
5-Park Orlando Flex Ticket	$210	$176
Preferred Annual Pass	$170	N/A
Annual Power Pass	$110	N/A

Universal Orlando Basics

Getting There

From the airport take 528 West (the Bee-Line Expressway) then I-4 East to Exit 75A, Universal Boulevard and follow the signs. From Disney take I-4 East to Exit 75A and follow the signs. Parking is $8 per day; free to Annual Passholders. $11 for preferred parking closer to the main entrance (although it is still a 5–10-minute walk).

Do yourself a big favor and spend $14 to valet park. Instead of wide-open lots like those at Disney serviced by a shuttle, Universal Studios, Islands of Adventure, and CityWalk all share two gigantic high-rise parking facilities. The result is quite a jam-up in the mornings; more-experienced people or simply more people (believe it or not, many times only one person is moving all those cars along) directing traffic could certainly improve matters. From the parking lot proceed on long walkways (some of which are moving sidewalks) to CityWalk and then either straight ahead to Islands of Adventure or to the right for Universal Orlando. Either way it is about a 10- to 15-minute walk to the parks from your parking space. No trams are available.

Operating Hours

Both parks are open 365 days a year and normally open at 9 A.M. closing at 6 or 7 P.M. with extended hours during holidays and busy season. For special events the park may close as early as 4 or 5 P.M. Go online to **www.universalstudios.com** or call **800-837-2273** for up-to-date operating hours and information.

Alcohol—Alcohol is sold at both parks and CityWalk.

Child switch program—Available at each attraction is a child swap area allowing parents to take turns staying with a child while the other parent rides.

Pets—This day kennel, located in the parking structure, is $5 per day. No overnight boarding. Guests must provide proof of vaccination and food as well as return periodically to walk their pet.

Loews loves pets. Guests of the Portofino Bay and the Hard Rock Hotel can bring their pets in the room. Offered are special pet menus, pet walking and sitting services, and pet amenities. A veterinarian certificate no more than 10 days old is required and no more than 2 pets are allowed per room.

Smoking—Smoking is allowed in Universal theme parks except while in line, at shows, or riding attractions. Restaurants have separate smoking sections.

Transportation to Universal—From the airport use the same town car, limousine, and shuttle services as Disney (see page 16) for a slightly lower roundtrip fee. From Disney either take a taxi or for $12 per person utilize Mears Transportation shuttles (**407-423-5566**). If you are a guest of one of the Universal resorts, board the convenient water taxi or bus shuttle service to reach the parks and CityWalk.

Universal Express—Similar to Disney's Fastpass, the Universal Express system has literally taken over with almost every major attraction offering front-of-the-line access by reserving a time to return and ride. Simply take your park pass to the Universal Express Distribution Center found somewhere near each Express attraction and receive a time slot in which to return for less than a 15-minute wait in line. There is no charge for the service. Only one Express pass at a time; get another once you've used your existing pass, the time slot to return has passed, or 2 hours have passed from the transaction time. Registered guests at the Loews' Universal hotels may use their room key for all day front-of-the-line access at both parks.

VIP Tours—Call **407-363-8295** for information and reservations. Reservations must be made at least 72 hours in advance.

For $120 per person, a Universal guide will take you and up to 14 people on a 5-hour tour with front-of-the-line access on at least seven attractions. For a real splurge, opt for the $1,700 private Exclusive VIP Tour, an 8-hour tour behind the scenes of the parks with front-of-the-line access to the rides of your choice. A 2-Day/2-Park Exclusive VIP Tour is available for $3,000. Park admission is included along with bilingual guides, a VIP gift bag, and priority seating at restaurants. Remember that registered guests of Universal's hotels automatically receive front-of-the-line access.

UNIVERSAL STUDIOS

This 100-acre working motion picture studio, a theme park based entirely on the movies with over 100 back lot locations loaded with excellent attractions, is a must-see park. Here you'll find realistic facades and sets intermixed with an array of rides and live shows including stage sets and props, film production, mind-blowing pyrotechnics, and even twister re-enactments. Its immense appeal to adults sets it apart from many of Orlando's other theme parks, but child-oriented features like Woody Woodpecker's Kidzone and Nickelodeon will certainly charm the little ones. However, realize that many of the attractions can be intense and not appropriate for small children.

The Lay of the Land

Universal Studios is a bit confusing. Just beyond the park's main entrance you'll encounter a wide boulevard, Plaza of the Stars, with attractions on either side making up Production Central. Branching off to the right are four main streets leading to the other areas of the park, New York, San Francisco/Amity, World Expo, Woody Woodpecker's Kidzone, and Hollywood, all of which partially encircle a large lagoon.

Park Services

ATM machines—Four ATM machines are located at the park: just outside to the right of the main entrance, two just inside on the right, and one located in the San Francisco/Amity area near Lombard's Landing.

Baby facilities—A nursing room and companion restroom is located at Family Services. Diaper-changing facilities are available in all major restrooms.

Cameras and film processing—On Location located in the Front Lot near the main entrance sells cameras, film, and batteries. One-hour film processing is available.

Dining reservations—Make same-day dining reservations for **Lombard's Landing** at Vacation Services located on the left as you enter

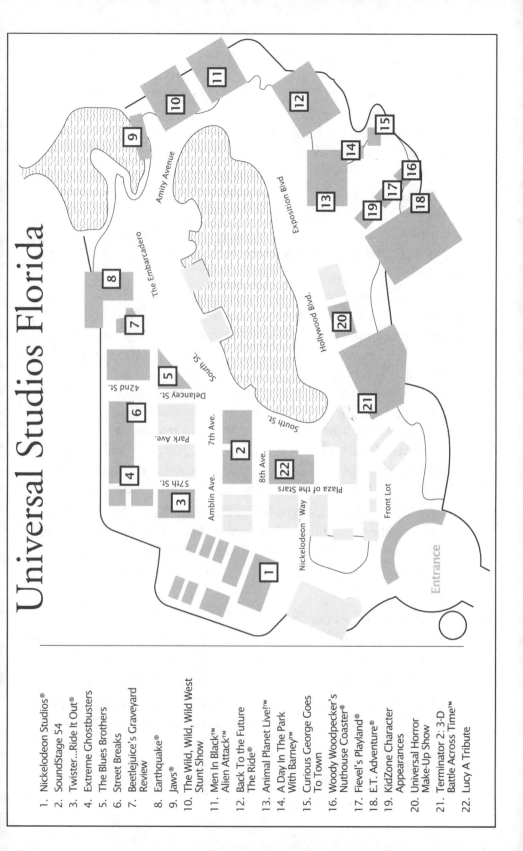

Universal Studios Florida

1. Nickelodeon Studios®
2. SoundStage 54
3. Twister...Ride It Out®
4. Extreme Ghostbusters
5. The Blues Brothers
6. Street Breaks
7. Beetlejuice's Graveyard Review
8. Earthquake®
9. Jaws®
10. The Wild, Wild, Wild West Stunt Show
11. Men In Black™ Alien Attack™
12. Back To the Future The Ride®
13. Animal Planet Live!™
14. A Day In The Park With Barney™
15. Curious George Goes To Town
16. Woody Woodpecker's Nuthouse Coaster®
17. Fievel's Playland®
18. E.T. Adventure®
19. KidZone Character Appearances
20. Universal Horror Make-Up Show
21. Terminator 2: 3-D Battle Across Time™
22. Lucy A Tribute

the park. If you would like to plan ahead, call **407-224-9255** no earlier than 30 days in advance.

First aid—First aid stations are located across from Beetlejuice's Graveyard Revue as well as near Guest Relations just inside the main entrance.

Guest relations—Located just inside the park entrance on the right is the place for information on studio production and special dining assistance along with guides for guests with disabilities, assistive listening devices and captioning services, foreign language maps, and lost children.

Guests with disabilities—Disabled guests may park in a special parking area; ask for directions at the toll plaza. All attractions plus shopping and dining facilities are wheelchair accessible with Woody Woodpecker's Nuthouse Coaster and Back to the Future the only rides where guests must be able to transfer to the ride's seating. Wheelchair accessible restrooms are located throughout the park and a companion-assisted restroom is located at Health Services near Beetlejuice. Call **407-224-5929** at least 2 weeks in advance to reserve a sign language interpreter. Closed captioning, Braille guides, assistive listening devices, a guidebook for guests with disabilities, and attraction scripts are available at Guest Relations. Guide dogs are allowed in the park.

Locker rental—Located on both the right and left sides of the Front Lot for $6 per day. Additional lockers are located outside the Men In Black attraction for $2 per hour with the first 60 minutes free.

Lost and found—Located at the Studio Audience Center just inside the main entrance.

Lost children—Look for a lost child at Guest Relations.

Package pickup—Purchases may be sent to the Universal Studios Store for pickup before leaving the park. Registered guests of Loews' Universal hotels may have purchases sent directly to their room.

Production information—Call the Studio Audience Center at **407-224-6355** or the Nickelodeon Production Hotline at **407-363-8000** for future production schedules.

Readmission—Have your hand stamped before leaving the park and retain your ticket for same-day readmission.

Stroller and wheelchair rentals—On your left as you pass through the turnstiles are stroller rentals for $9, double strollers for $14, and wheelchairs for $8. Electric convenience vehicles rent for $40 with a driver's license and a $50 refundable deposit. Call **407-224-6350** at least 48 hours in advance for ECV reservations.

Studio Audience Center—Located next to the bank on your right upon entering the park. Stop here for complimentary tickets to most studio productions distributed on a first-come, first-served basis. Tickets for Slime Time Live are usually only obtainable at Nickelodeon Studios, but stop here for information on times and the slim chance they will hand out a ticket or two.

Universal Orlando Vacations Services—The place for ticket upgrades, hotel and dining reservations, movie tickets for Cineplex at CityWalk, and special event passes. Located on the left as you enter the park.

Suggested 1-day itinerary at Universal Studios for adults and older children

- Be at the park before opening time (allow 30 minutes to park) and head straight to Back to the Future and then take in Men In Black: Alien Attack next door.
- Retrace your steps to Hollywood and see Terminator 2: 3-D (use Universal Express if necessary), the Gory, Gruesome and Grotesque Horror Make-Up Show, and walk through Lucy: A Tribute.
- Universal Studios offers many scheduled attractions, but only two are really worth it—the Wild Wild Wild West Stunt Show and Animal Planet Live; see the others only if there's time.
- Sometime during your day pick up lunch at a counter-service spot. My favorites are the Classic Monster Café and Richter's Burger Co.
- Move to New York and pick up a Universal Express pass to Twister (if necessary) and during your wait see Earthquake in the nearby San Francisco area.
- Ride the Jaws attraction and work in the Wild Wild Wild West Stunt Show if possible. Avoid seeing Jaws just after the Wild Wild

Wild West Stunt Show lets out when everyone makes a beeline to the next-door attraction.

- Swing over to Woody Woodpecker's Kid Zone (this might be the time to pick up the Animal Planet Live Show) and ride the E.T. Adventure. Walk back to the Curious George Goes to Town area and get wet if it's a hot and steamy day.
- Head back to your hotel or plan an evening at CityWalk.

Suggested 1-day itinerary at Universal Studios for adults with young children

This park has enough to keep kids busy for part of a day, but remember that many of the attractions with major scare factors are not suitable for little ones.

- Go straight to Woody Woodpecker's Kidzone and ride the E.T. Adventure first followed by Woody Woodpecker's Nuthouse Coaster. Work in the Animal Planet Live show and A Day in the Park with Barney when you can during the day.
- Break for lunch at the Classic Monster Café and then visit Nickelodeon Studios.
- Go back to Woody Woodpecker's Kidzone for playtime at Fievel's Playland and Curious George Goes to Town.
- If your children are not too young and have a high tolerance for scary attractions, you may want to try Jaws, Earthquake, and Twister.
- Parents may want to utilize Universal's Child-Switch Program for rides with a high scare factor whereby one parent can watch the children while the other rides an attraction and then the other parent hops aboard leaving the first rider with the children.

Universal Studios don't-miss attractions

- Twister: Ride It Out
- Back to the Future: The Ride
- Men in Black: Alien Attack
- Terminator 2: 3-D Battle Across Time
- Jaws

Production Central

Formed around a front lot are a series of industrial-looking ware-houses holding several attractions including the ever-popular Nickelodeon Studios and two soon to open, brand-new attractions—a Jimmy Neutron ride and a Shrek 3-D movie.

NICKELODEON STUDIO***

Take a guided studio tour of the #1 cable network for kids. Your excursion of Nickelodeon land begins with a peek at the production stages through soundproof windows. Like all backstage tours, if there is a show in progress it can be fun but without one it's a bit of a yawner. Move downstairs to Production Alley where the wardrobe, hair, and makeup department is viewed and a discussion on props and the finer points of Goo, Gak, and Slime takes place with one of Nickelodeon's "gak meisters." A young volunteer even gets to taste a sample of the supposedly delicious gak. The final stop is the Game Lab where all the fun takes place. Here the audience (kids and adults alike) participate in silly games from Slimetime Live ending with one "lucky" child chosen to be slimed. **45-minute scheduled show.**

Tip: Nickelodeon is a working studio where visitors can participate on a limited basis as members of the live studio audience. Before arrival call **407-363-8000** *or, once in Universal, stop at the Studio Audience Center located near Guest Relations for information on Slime Time Live production schedules. Filming is normally from 2–5 P.M. each weekday (seasonal) and tickets are available on a first-come, first-served basis near the Green Slime machine, distributed approximately 2–3 hours before the shoot.*

Shopping in Production Central

Studio Sweets—Ever-popular confectionery • homemade fudge • Rice Crispies treats • cookies • cotton candy • fudge-dipped apples.

It's a Wrap—Gifts • mementos • t-shirts • hats • small souvenirs.

Nickelodeon Kiosk—Small shop located outside Nickelodeon Studios • green slime • Nickelodeon activity sets, toys, posters, books, videos • Rugrat dolls • green slime t-shirts.

Universal Studios Store—Just about every souvenir imaginable having anything to do with Universal Studios.

New York City

The New York City streets are so authentic you'll feel as if you're really in the Big Apple. Sit on the brownstone stoops to watch the world go by or perhaps cool off in a spouting fire hydrant on a hot muggy day. Cigar stores, newsstands, neighborhood shops, and an Irish bar front the manhole-filled streets edged with dingy, cracked sidewalks. Fire escapes and awnings line the brick and cast iron buildings, and traffic lights protect each corner. Picture-takers love 57th Avenue where a faux facade features the Guggenheim, Macy's, the New York Public Library, and plenty of pigeons to give it all authenticity.

TWISTER. RIDE IT OUT***

In the waiting area for this hair-raising attraction is film footage of actual twisters wreaking their devastation. Move inside a soundstage to view clips of *Twister* narrated by Helen Hunt and Bill Paxton who relay many frightening experiences during the filming of the movie, some of which you will soon have the opportunity to take part in. Walk through the set of a twister-ripped house where another video explains the logistics of how some of the more intense portions of the film were created. Then on to the grand finale, a re-creation of a scene set in a small Midwestern town, one in which visitors will actually feel the power of a 5-story twister. The wind and pelting rain builds and darkness and cold descend as the funnel cloud approaches. The entire set shakes as trees are torn apart, a drive-in screen is sent flying, windows break, power lines fall, a truck and cow soar through the air, and a gas tank explodes. Just a small testimony to the majesty and mystery of nature. **15-minutes.**

Tip: Rated PG-13 due the intensity of the twister demonstration. Those in the back and immediate front get the wettest, although no one actually gets drenched. Don't stand too far to the side or you might not get the full effect of the wind and rain.

Entertainment

The Blues Brothers—This hopping street show performed on the corner of Delancey Street really gets the crowd rocking. Jake and Elwood sing and dance accompanied by a piped sound track, a talented sax player, and a one-woman showstopper with an Aretha Franklin–like voice. The Blues Brothers renditions of "Soul Man," "Everybody Needs Somebody to Love," even their version of "Rawhide" entertain the hand-clapping crowd.

Extreme Ghostbusters: The Great Fright Way—The guys from *Ghostbusters* and *Beetlejuice* team up for a comedic song and dance routine in front of the New York Street facade.

Street Breaks—Young troupe performing acrobatic break dancing on the streets of New York.

Shopping in New York

Aftermath—Plush toys, hats, t-shirts, even cow-spotted underwear • miniature pet tornado machine • hardhats • books on weather and tornadoes • *Twister* videos and DVDs.

Second-Hand Rose—Bargain Universal merchandise.

San Francisco/Amity

The waterfront setting of San Francisco and the coastal Maine town of Amity make for one of the most charming areas of the park. In San Francisco imagine yourself at Fisherman's Wharf as you stroll the dock area lined with red brick warehouses, wharf-side canneries, rows of Italianate Victorian houses, and an Earthquake attraction. Of course, Tony Bennett croons over the loudspeakers with the familiar tune "I Left My Heart in San Francisco."

In Amity coastal birds swoop and cry overhead as you wander between lobster shacks, lighthouses, and clapboard shops and cottages with exteriors strewn with weathered buoys and lobster traps. A typical boardwalk with games of skill (for an additional cost) lines the street. And shark-lovers (or haters) won't want to miss taking their picture with their head inside the jagged mouth of the defeated Jaws.

BEETLEJUICE'S ROCK 'N' ROLL GRAVEYARD REVUE*

The only exciting aspect of this attraction is the hilarious preshow with Marx Brothers look-alikes hamming it up with the waiting crowd; the rest is a ho-hum program of monster rock and roll. Creepy song and dance numbers are performed by hip versions of Frankenstein and his Bride, Wolfman, Dracula, and the Phantom of the Opera with Beetlejuice serving as master of ceremonies. Plenty of steam, really loud music, and a few pyrotechnic displays don't save the show from extreme tedium. **18-minute show.**

Tip: This is my least favorite show in the park. Unless you have preteens in tow or just happen to be a huge fan of cavorting monsters, skip it. Rated PG-13.

EARTHQUAKE—THE BIG ONE***

Earthquake is a 3-part attraction allowing a glimpse of how disaster movies are created. Begin with a somewhat antiquated clip of Charlton Heston explaining how the special effects used in the movie Earthquake were produced using high-speed cameras to shoot the destruction of a miniature model city. Afterward the curtain rises to reveal part of the actual model used in the film. Next enter a soundstage where, with the help of audience volunteers, a Los Angeles mall sequence from the movie is recreated using a blue-screen background, and a stunt demonstration offers a bit of a surprise. Then board a BART subway train for a ride across San Francisco for the final disaster scene. On approach to Embarcadero Station—wham! A big one hits at 8.3 on the Richter scale and soon the station is literally coming to pieces. A propane tanker comes crashing down in a fiery explosion, ceilings collapse, platforms crack, there's a near collision with a runaway train, and 65,000 gallons of water hurtles down the stairs into the station. **20 minutes. Expectant mothers, those with heart, neck, and back problems, and those sus-**

ceptible to motion sickness should skip the train part of this attraction.

Tip: The final part of this attraction is too intense for young children; utilize the child switch option here.

JAWS****

Your boarding point for a sightseeing trip around the harbor of the coastal New England town of Amity seems calm enough as you load into 40-passenger boats for a ride through memory lane, shark memories that is. Of course, something is amiss in Amity. A crackly distress call from another tour boat sounds over the radio, warning of a shark sighting; soon what's left of the unfortunate boat comes into view as your boat is jarred and the dorsal fin of Jaws is spotted. The guide makes a quick decision to escape into the so-called safety of a gloomy boathouse, but Jaws soon finds you; his huge head and sharp, jagged teeth pierce the water, scaring the daylights out of everyone. There's barely enough time to recover before onshore gas tanks explode and the 30-foot wall of fire results in a massive fish fry when Jaws bites a dangling high voltage wire. The relieved passengers clap as the boat makes it back to safe harbor. A fun ride guaranteed to get a few giggly screams out of even the most daring of adults. **7-minute ride. Expectant mothers should not ride this attraction.**

Tip: Although too frightening for young children, adults find it to be quite a riot. You'll most likely get wet on this one, but the right side of the boat is usually a bit drier. Most of the action takes place on the left for those who dare. If you rode this ride years ago and thought it was too hokey, try it again; they've livened it up a bit since then. If you want to avoid crowds, steer clear of here immediately after the Wild Wild Wild West Stunt Show next door lets out. And for heightened enjoyment try it at night when the special effects really dazzle the eye.

THE WILD WILD WILD WEST STUNT SHOW***

The old-fashioned stunt show is alive and well at Universal in an Old West setting complete with saloon, stable, barn, and dry goods store. Anyone who frequents theme parks will certainly have many times over seen a version of this type of production, but this one takes the cake. Rootin'-tootin' tough gal Ma Hopper and her less-than-precious "twin" boys (otherwise know as Dumb and Dumber) are out to cause trouble for the regular stuntmen who simply want to demonstrate to the audience what they do for a living. What results is a bang-up show with plenty of shootin', hollerin', bullwhip crackin', and fist-fightin' along with death-defying 3-story plunges, searing hot dynamite explosions, and dazzling pyrotechnics, all accompanied by plenty of humor. **18-minute show.**

Tip: Some of the gunshots and explosions may be startling to young children. If you'd like to cool off a bit, sit in the splash zone located in the lower bleachers near the water well.

Shopping in San Francisco/Amity

San Francisco Candy Factory—Bulk candy • fudge • chocolates.

Quint's Surf Shack—Island print clothing • beach hats • swim attire • flip-flops.

Shaiken's Souvenirs—Universal logo attire • souvenirs.

World Expo

This futuristic area, the smallest in the park, is supposedly a World's Fair Exposition Park. Because of the excitement of the attractions here, no one really notices the humdrum contemporary buildings, mundane look, and total lack of imagination.

BACK TO THE FUTURE. THE RIDE****

When you catch sight of the silver DeLorean parked outside, you'll know you've made it to one of the best rides Universal has to offer. Meet up again with the crazy Doc Brown and bully Biff at the Institute of Future Technology where Biff has surreptitiously appeared in a time-travel vehicle. He now wants to return to the 1950s via a stolen test DeLorean, planning a bit of a joyride on the way back. Doc Brown asks you to save the universe by catching Biff before he alters the past. You're mission is to bump his car and send him reeling back to the institute.

Strap into an 8-passenger DeLorean motion simulator vehicle and prepare yourself for the ride of your life. Suspended above an IMAX-size screen, you'll fly back to the Ice Age (get ready for a blast of cold air), have a run in with a man-eating dinosaur, and plunge down fiery volcanoes. As your body jerks, dips, and dives, your brain's thinking you're flying through space at heart-stopping speeds. **5-minute ride. Height requirement 40 inches. Expectant mothers, those with heart, neck, and back problems, and those susceptible to motion sickness should not ride.**

Tip: This ride really jerks you around and is probably not for you if you tend to get motion sickness; do not eat before riding unless you possess a stomach of steel. If you start to feel sick, take your eyes off the screen and look at the cars on either side (your attention is so affixed to the screen you won't even notice them at first) immediately easing the nausea.

MEN IN BLACK: ALIEN ATTACK***

The MIB training facility is searching for several good agents to protect the Earth from the galaxy's evil aliens in this interactive, video game thrill ride. Two 6-passenger cars depart together and meet up again several times as they speed through New York streets and alleyways playing laser tag along the way, blasting away at as many lifelike aliens as possible with zapper guns. The team that creams the most extraterrestrial creatures is the winner. Look up, down, and sideways for the little green guys: in trash cans, dumpsters, sidewalk hot dog stands, upstairs windows, on top of buildings, and hanging from lampposts; there's even a baby alien in a carriage. Zip, tilt, and spin as your score builds. What makes this ride interesting is that contestants find themselves in battle with the other vehicle as well as the aliens themselves who react when they are shot and even shoot back; when your vehicle is zapped it goes into a 360-degree spin. The last creature you encounter is a 50-foot wide, 30-foot tall alien bug (the world's largest animatronic figure). This is similar to the Buzz Lightyear ride at the Magic Kingdom, but quite a bit more sophisticated and exciting. **5-minute ride. Height requirement 42 inches; children between 42–48 inches must be accompanied by an adult. Expectant mothers, those with heart, neck, and back problems, and those susceptible to motion sickness should not ride.**

Tip: If you don't mind riding without other members of your party, go for the singles line. This process is used to fill empty seats and will greatly cut your time in line. Carry-on bags are not allowed; use the free (for the first 60 minutes) lockers out front to store your gear.

Shopping at World Expo

Back to the Future: The Store—*Back to the Future* merchandise • futuristic toys • Hill Valley High class rings • DeLorean radio-control cars.

MIB Gear—Out-of-this-world souvenirs • MIB apparel, videos, toys • books on UFOs and aliens • glow-in-the-dark aliens, t-shirts, and futuristic toys.

Woody Woodpecker's Kidzone

What Universal lacks in attractions for preschoolers, it makes up for with some of the most superb children's areas around. This one, along with Seuss Landing at Islands of Adventure, is exceptional. Kids could spend hours here and be perfectly content with their own roller coaster, water play area, and playground not to mention a live Barney show.

ANIMAL PLANET LIVE***

Universal Studios has teamed up with the cable network Animal Planet to bring you its newest stage show, an updated version of the old Animal Actors attraction. Enter the fascinating and entertaining world of animals with video clips from the Animal Planet's network interspersed with live and lovable trained animals. A demonstration of the games usually shown on Animal Planet Sports includes a wacky competition between two dogs, Bentley and Goliath, with the addition of human volunteers to liven up the contest. You'll see a video camera–toting pig, a swinging orangutan, a precious baby chimp, a bird from the film *Ladyhawk,* even Lassie. And unless you love snakes, think twice about volunteering for the segment with Tina, the boa constrictor. All in all it's an animal's world and a pretty silly one at that. **22-minute show. Check your guide map for times.**

CURIOUS GEORGE GOES TO TOWN***

The naughty monkey of storybook fame continues his pranks at this super play area. Follow the yellow paw prints and come along on an adventure with George. You'll encounter different play areas for the little ones along the way, but the action begins when you make it to the back of the attraction and the buildings of town. Now it is time to have fun. In the town square is a barrage of water: everything from squirting sidewalks, rain drains, and broken pipes to enormous barrels of water that dump on unsuspecting visitors every few minutes (a clanging bells warns of the imminent downpour). Follow the red footprints to explore and still stay dry. Those who love mischief can climb behind the building facades and relentlessly shoot water cannons on soggy revelers below. Behind the square you'll find a 2-story Ball Factory brimming with thousands of soft, foam balls. Giant vacuums suck them upstairs to blasters where the truly impish can shoot visitors below.

Tip: Though it looks very tame from the entrance, don't neglect to take a stroll through the best play area in the park. A towel and a change of clothes will allow your children to splash to their heart's content.

A DAY IN THE PARK WITH BARNEY***

Who can resist a famous purple dinosaur and all the songs kids love best? Not anyone under 5, that's for sure. A quick preshow features Mrs. Peekaboo who introduces the parrot Bartholomew and her quirky, funny house. Soon you'll stroll underneath a soft, sparkling waterfall and into Barney's perfect indoor park, a cozy setting of tall trees, soft blue skies, colorful flowers, singing birds, and gentle breezes. Sit in the circular room where Barney, at center stage, comes to play and sing all the familiar songs along with precious Baby Bop and BJ. Autumn leaves float, trees sparkle, stars twinkle, frogs croak, and rain and snow falls. Children who would like to meet Barney may do so after the show. Although I was not very familiar with the Barney show, the setting was so beautiful it was worth sitting through all the silly songs.

As you exit, stop and play in Barney's Backyard, a park-like, indoor play area. Frolic in a tree house, ring wind chimes, try the interactive games, slip down slides, build a sandcastle, and find plenty of places to explore. Those who just want to play may enter from the Barney Store. **25-minute show. Check your guide map for times.**

E.T. ADVENTURE***

In the screening room, Steven Spielberg informs the audience that E.T.'s beloved planet is in trouble; all his friends are dying and only his healing touch can save them. And guess who can help get him home? Wind your way through a nighttime forest amid the sound of crickets, the pine smell of the woods, and soft moonlight shining through the treetops (probably the best part of the attraction) before boarding a 9-passenger bicycle powered by a ski-lift contraption with none other than E.T. hiding in the front basket. Soar through the woods with the police in hot pursuit then high above the moonlit city and off through the stars to the Green Planet. Soon E.T.'s healing power changes the dry and dusty landscape to one that is green and blooming with flowers. You will be personally thanked by E.T himself at the conclusion (listen carefully). Although not exactly a high-tech thriller, it's a wonderful children's attraction and certainly fun for low-speed adults. **5-minute ride.**

Tip: Upon entering the screening room at the start of the attraction, move all the way to the opposite side, which will put you first in line for the second waiting area (that's right, there are two waiting areas). Request a front seat for the very best view; back seats are partially blocked by the heads of folks in the front rows.

FIEVEL'S PLAYGROUND**

While exhausted parents rest their feet, children may romp to their heart's delight at this outdoor play area of giant Wild West props from Fievel's movie setting in *An American Tale.* Play, slide, and splash amid colossal saddles, a 100-gallon cowboy hat, oversized cactus, giant buckets, and enormous sardine cans. Crawl through mammoth books, slip down slides of all shapes and sizes, climb on a very tall net climb, and splash in buckets of water. Particularly fun is the lofty water pipe slide offering a wet ride down on rubber rafts. **Children must be 40 inches or taller or accompanied by an adult to slide down the waterslide.**

Tip: Perfect for a hot, steamy day. Bring a change of clothes for little ones and before they dry off, sidle on over to Curious George Goes to Town for a real soaking.

KIDZONE TROLLEY CHARACTER MEET AND GREET**

This wacky-looking trolley loaded with kids' favorite cartoon characters zips up at scheduled times to the stage in front of the E.T. Adventure. Fred Flintstone, Yogi Bear and Boo Boo, Woody Woodpecker, and Scooby-Doo all hop out to perform a song-and-dance routine and then sign autographs for the kiddies. **Check your guide map for times.**

WOODY WOODPECKER'S NUTHOUSE COASTER**

Board crate-like cars for a quick zip through Woody's nut factory on a bright red roller coaster. **1-minute ride. Height requirement 36 inches. Expectant mothers should not ride this attraction.**

Shopping in Kidzone

The Barney Store—Barney and friends merchandise.

Cartoon Store—Hanna-Barbera, Animal Planet Live, and Nickelodeon merchandise.

E.T.'s Toy Closet and Photo Spot—E.T. merchandise • have your picture taken with E.T.

Hollywood

A re-creation of Hollywood in its heyday with more-than-realistic facades of famous landmarks facing the palm tree–lined Hollywood Boulevard. So very authentic-looking are the Mocambo Club, Café Montmarte, and the Hotel Beverly Wilshire that you just might find yourself trying a door that leads to nowhere. Hollywood stars are embedded in the sidewalk in front of Schwab's pharmacy, and the Garden of Allah Villas, a 1940s-style motel, is so convincing you'll want to inquire where to check in. Nostalgia at its best.

THE GORY, GRUESOME AND GROTESQUE HORROR MAKE-UP SHOW**

Learn the secrets behind the blood, guts, and gore of a typical horror and crime show. Your hosts are two witty fellows who keep the show moving with jokes, puns, and audience participation. Demonstrations involving fake blood, prop knives, creepy creatures, gruesome masks, mechanical heads, makeup effects, and computer-generated imagery are interspersed with plenty of humor. Especially interesting are the Academy Award–winning mechanical heads from *An American Werewolf in London*. Film clips accompanying many of the presentations explain how each process is incorporated into well-known movies such as *The Godfather, The Mummy,* and *The Thing*. The grand finale is a comical teleportation presentation involving the pods from *The Fly*. **25-minute show.**

Tip: Rated PG-13 because of unsavory film clips, subject matter, and a few slightly raunchy jokes.

LUCY—A TRIBUTE**

Fans of the famous redhead will love this captivating walk-through exhibit. Display windows present an array of memorabilia: numerous awards including her Emmys, a model of the *I Love Lucy* set, letters, old telegrams, scripts, and costumes. True enthusiasts could spend plenty of time watching the continuously running videos of famous friends reminiscing about Lucy and short clips of her TV shows. There is, of course, a shop at the end of the exhibit selling *I Love Lucy* videos, Lucy and Desi dolls, even Lucy and Desi pajamas with matching slippers.

TERMINATOR 2: 3-D BATTLE ACROSS TIME****

You're on a tour of Cyberdyne's corporate headquarters when, during a briefing on the new SkyNet program, John Conner and his mother Sarah from *Terminator 2* seize the video screen. They're here with a warning that SkyNet's newest scheme is a threat to the human race and must be destroyed before it destroys us. There's only 5 minutes to get out before the building is obliterated. The video is quickly stopped and the ditzy tour guide smoothes over the interruption by escorting visitors into the huge Cyberdyne theater.

Slip on your 3-D glasses and be prepared to watch one of the best 3-D shows around. The original stars of *Terminator 2* appear on giant-size screens along with live 8-foot Cinebotic T-70 Soldiers, stunt actors, and a rip roaring Harley Davidson "Fat Boy" motorcycle. Fantastic 3-D special effects and colossal explosions accompanied by loads of smoke and a rocking theater will leave you reeling. I guarantee your mouth will be hanging open when it's all over. **20-minute show. Expectant mothers or those with heart, neck, or back conditions may sit in stationary seats.**

Tip: Rated PG-13 and a pretty darn intense show for young children due to loud and startling noise. All seats are decent, but hang back a little and enter the doors on the right to sit front center. At one point all the seats in the theater jerk abruptly; those with back or neck problems should take heed.

Entertainment

Double Date—In front of Mel's Drive-In you'll find this harmonious quartet performing music à la *American Graffiti*.

Shopping in Hollywood

Brown Derby Hat Shop—Some of the coolest hats around • toppers in every shape and size: some serious, some absolutely goofy, and plenty in-between • silly wigs • stylish fedoras • straw sunbonnets • putting green caps • Woody Woodpecker heads • outrageous Elton John–style sunglasses.

Cyber Image—*Terminator 2* t-shirts and videos • black leather jackets • Harley-Davidson apparel.

Movietime Portraits and Celebrity News—Have your portrait taken in your choice of costumes and movie props.

On Location—Cameras • film • batteries • postcards • sunglasses • suntan lotion • gifts • two-way radio rentals • purchase photos taken by park photographers here.

Silver Screen Collectibles—Hot pink Betty Boop, Lucy and Desi, and Marilyn Monroe memorabilia • Red Racer pedal cars.

Restaurants and Counter Service at Universal Studios

Production Central

Universal Studios Classic Monster Café—Saturday afternoon fiends from baby boomer's childhoods are glorified here at this special café for monster movie fans • purchase your frightfully decent grub in Frankenstein's lab and proceed to your preference of monster dining rooms • chopped chef's salad, chicken or shrimp Caesar salad, cream of broccoli soup, four-cheese ravioli, linguini primavera, wood-oven pizza, rotisserie chicken, penne pasta with pesto, Italian sausage, and sun-dried tomatoes • devil's food cake, deep-dish apple pie, strawberry shortcake, butterscotch chocolate parfait, fresh fruit cup.

New York

Finnegan's Bar and Grill—Lunch and dinner • Irish pub dining with live entertainment • full review on page 374.

Louie's Italian Restaurant—Visit Little Italy at this counter-service café • pizza (cheese, pepperoni, veggie, and BBQ chicken), lasagna, fettuccine Alfredo, spaghetti Bolognese, spaghetti and meatballs, panino sandwiches, meatball sub, minestrone soup, chicken Caesar salad • tiramisu, Italian custard, cannoli, cream horns, cappuccino cheesecake, gelato (cappuccino, pistachio, chocolate, and chocolate-hazelnut), Italian ice in lemon, cherry, and grape flavors • Italian beer and wine, sodas, espresso • Starbucks coffee stand.

San Francisco/Amity

Boardwalk Funnel Cake Co.—Funnel cakes • soft-serve ice cream.

Brody's Ice Cream Shoppe—Soft-serve and hand-scooped ice cream • frozen yogurt • Haagen Dazs • ice cream bars • sundaes • banana splits • floats.

Captain Quint's Seafood and Chowder House—Fried seafood baskets eaten at outdoor picnic benches • fish and chips, fried shrimp, fried scallops, chicken tenders, combination baskets, clam chowder, lobster bisque, slaw, fries.

Chez Alcatraz—Outside seating on the waterfront • crabmeat cocktail, peel 'n' eat shrimp, smoked turkey croissant, chili, seafood chowder • frozen specialty drinks, beverages, beer.

Lombard's Landing—Lunch and dinner • seafood is the specialty here in a San Francisco warehouse setting • full review on page 374.

Midway Grill—Eat on one of the picnic tables and watch the activity of the Boardwalk • hot dogs, grilled Italian sausage sandwich with peppers and onions, chicken fingers, Philly cheese steak sandwich.

Richter's Burger Co.—Good burgers complete with all the trimmings inside an earthquake-damaged, brick-walled warehouse • plenty of inside seating, but outside offers a pleasant view of the lagoon • single and double hamburgers, grilled chicken sandwich, Gardenburgers, toppings bar.

San Francisco Pastry Co.—Wide assortment of pastries and sweets • ham and cheese or turkey croissant sandwiches, fresh fruit plate, salad plate • specialty coffees, beverages, beer.

World Expo

International Food and Film Festival—Counter-service food court • Italian: lasagna, penne pasta with marinara sauce, chicken Parmesan, pizza, minestrone soup • America: fried chicken, hot pressed sandwiches • Asian: Szechuan orange chicken, shrimp lo mein, stir-fried beef and peppers, sweet and sour chicken, wonton soup • ice cream and yogurt stand outside offering Haagen Dazs soft frozen yogurt, soft-serve ice cream, sundaes, root beer floats, banana splits.

Hollywood

Beverly Hills Boulangerie—Pastries, giant cookies, muffins, pies, cake, croissants • croissant breakfast sandwiches • coffee, cappuccino, espresso • smoked turkey, roast beef, vegetarian, or baked ham and cheese sandwiches, soup, salad.

Café La Bamba—Hollywood mission-style fast-food eatery • rotisserie chicken or salad, barbeque baby back ribs, chicken and rib combo plate, barbeque pork sandwich platter, cheeseburgers, barbeque chicken wrap, garden salad, corn-on-the-cob • Cantina Bar accessible from both inside and out serving frosty margaritas, strawberry daiquiris, wine, beer on tap • half-price drinks 3–5 P.M.

Mel's Drive-In—Authentic-looking 1950s-style burger joint à la *American Graffiti* • naugahyde booths, curved picture windows, vintage jukebox • outside are rows of gleaming 1950s cars and bobby sox–era entertainment • counter-service instead of gum-smacking waitresses • burgers, chicken sandwiches, blue plate chili with cheese and onions, chili dogs, hot dogs, Gardenburger, chili cheese fries, onion rings, garden salad • apple pie, shakes, root beer floats.

Schwab's Pharmacy—Semi-stab at re-creating the famous Hollywood pharmacy where Lana Turner was discovered at the soda counter • sit outside on tables lining the star-studded sidewalk or inside on twirling barstools underneath nostalgic Coca-Cola signs and black and white photos of the original Schwab's • hand-dipped ice cream, banana splits, sundaes • apple pie à la mode • sandwiches.

Special Events

For information and tickets call the Special Events hotline at **407-224-5500**.

Mardi Gras—Late winter into early spring experience the festivity of New Orleans with nightly parades, live music, street entertainment, and Cajun and Creole food. Included in the price of admission.

Fourth of July—Colossal fireworks show accompanied by an orchestra playing favorite Universal movie themes.

Rock the Universe—For 2 nights on a weekend in early September the latest in contemporary Christian music is on the agenda. $35 for 1 night or $50 for 2 evenings; $40 per night at the gate. Music and attractions from 4 P.M.–1 A.M.

NBC Soap Fanfest—In early November, favorite soap stars from NBC converge at Universal Studios for a 2-day weekend gala, signing autographs and participating in interviews. If you're not a soap fan, avoid the park on these days or pay the consequence of spending your day with hoards of excited fans. Included in the price of admission.

Holiday Festivities—The park is merry with plenty of Christmas decorations, a Macy's holiday parade, carols, Santa Claus sightings, and even snow on Delancey Street.

New Year's Eve—A spectacular fireworks presentation along with special entertainment rings in the New Year.

ISLANDS OF ADVENTURE

When Universal's newest theme park opened in May of 1999, it was an immediate hit with more state-of-the-art attractions and amazing thrill rides than any other park in Orlando. Totally different from its next-door sister park Universal Studios, it's worth the price of admission simply for a glimpse of its six distinctive islands, each more imaginative and outrageous than the next. Everywhere the eye rests there's a barrage of zany color and immense creativity.

Although the park has something for every age, it's a sure lure for coaster junkies and the teenage set. Many of the attractions have height restrictions; however, with Seuss Landing and Camp Jurassic there is

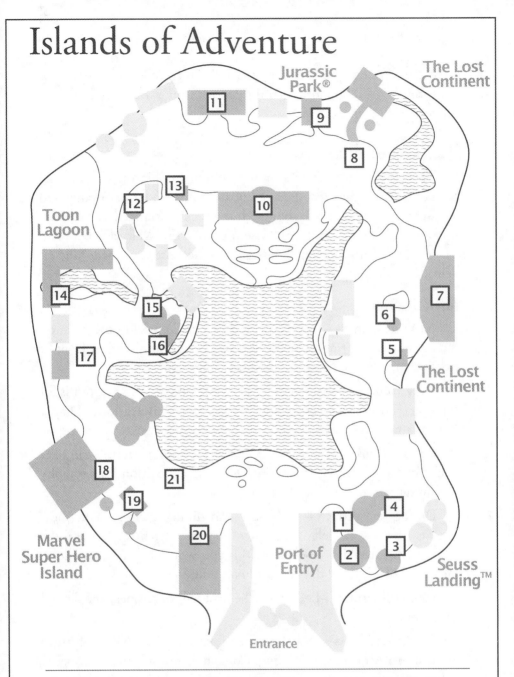

Islands of Adventure

Jurassic Park®

The Lost Continent

Toon Lagoon

The Lost Continent

Marvel Super Hero Island

Port of Entry

Seuss Landing™

Entrance

1. If I Ran the Zoo™
2. The Cat In The Hat™
3. One fish, Two Fish, Red Fish, Blue Fish™
4. Caro-Seuss-el™
5. Poseidon's Fury®
6. The Mystic Fountain
7. The Eighth Voyage of Sinbad®
8. Dueling Dragons®

9. The Flying Unicorn®
10. Jurassic Park Discovery Center®
11. Jurassic Park River Adventure®
12. Camp Jurassic®
13. Pteranodon Flyers®
14. Dudley Do-Right's Ripsaw Falls®
15. Popeye & Bluto's Bilge-Rat Barges®

16. Me Ship, The Olive
17. Toon Lagoon Beach Bash Show
18. The Amazing Adventures of Spider-Man®
19. Doctor Doom's Fearfall®
20. Incredible Hulk Coaster®
21. Meet Spider-Man™ and the Marvel Super Heroes!

plenty to keep the little ones happy as well. And if roller coasters are not your thing, you'll be more than thrilled with the variety of attractions offered for the tamer crowd.

The Lay of the Land

This park is laid out in a more traditional fashion than Universal Studios with a main street, Port of Entry, leading from the entrance and dead-ending into a large lagoon with the islands arranged in a circular fashion around it. Moving clockwise you'll first find Marvel Super Hero Island, then Toon Lagoon, Jurassic Park, the Lost Continent, and finally Seuss Landing.

Park Services

ATM machines—Two ATM machines are located in the park: on the right after entering the park next to the restrooms and in front of the Enchanted Oak Tavern in the Lost Continent.

Baby facilities—A nursing facility and companion restroom is located at Family Services located within Guest Releations. Diaper changing facilities are available in all major restrooms.

Cameras and film processing—Cameras, film, batteries, and one-hour film processing is available at De Foto's Expedition Photography just inside the entrance on the right.

Dining reservations—Make same-day dining reservations at Vacation Services on your left as you enter the park (currently Mythos is the only restaurant taking reservations). If you would like to plan ahead, call 407-224-9255 30 days or less in advance.

First aid stations—Located in the Lost Continent near the Sinbad attraction.

Guest relations—Located on the right-hand side of Port of Entry in the Open Arms Hotel building. Come here for information, special dining assistance, guides for guest with disabilities, assistive listening devices and captioning services, and foreign language maps.

Guests with disabilities—Special parking areas for disabled guests are available; ask for directions at the toll plaza. All shops, dining facilities, and attraction queues are wheelchair accessible. However many rides require the ability to transfer from wheelchair to the ride's seating (check the guide map for details). Wheelchair accessible restrooms are located throughout the park and companion-assisted restrooms are located near Guest Relations and in the Lost Continent. Call **407-224-5929** at least 2 weeks in advance to reserve a sign language interpreter. Closed captioning, Braille guides, assistive listening devices, a guidebook for guests with disabilities, and attraction scripts are available at Guest Relations. Guide dogs are allowed in the park.

Lockers—Located on the left upon entering the park and available for $6 per day. Lockers are also located at the entrance to Incredible Hulk, Dueling Dragons, and Jurassic Park River Adventure for $2 per hour with the first 60 minutes free.

Lost and found—Located at Guest Relations next to the park entrance.

Lost children—Locate lost children at Guest Relations.

Readmission—Have your hand stamped before leaving the park and retain your ticket for same-day readmission.

Strollers and wheelchairs—Rentals are located on the left-hand side as you pass through the turnstiles. Strollers rent for $9, double strollers $14, and wheelchairs are $8. ECVs are $40 with a driver's license and a $50 refundable deposit. Call **407-224-6350** at least 48 hours in advance for ECV reservations.

Universal Orlando Vacations Services—If after purchasing your tickets you decide to upgrade to a multi-day or annual pass, stop here on the right as you leave the park. Also the spot for annual pass processing.

Suggested 1-day itinerary at Islands of Adventure for adults and older children

- Be at the park before opening time (allow 30 minutes to park) and head straight to Marvel Super Hero Island to ride the Amazing Adventures of Spider-Man, then the Incredible Hulk, and finally Doctor Doom's Fearfall before heading over to the Jurassic Park area.

- Pick up a Universal Express pass (if necessary) for the Jurassic Park River Adventure. While waiting, see Triceratops Encounter and if there's time take a spin around Camp Jurassic, one of the neatest kid play areas around (don't miss the cave that leads to the amber mine). Return to ride the Jurassic Park River Adventure.
- Pick up a Universal Express pass for Dueling Dragons if necessary and during your wait have lunch at Mythos Restaurant.
- After lunch see Poseidon's Fury and then ride Dueling Dragons. If there's time, see the Eighth Voyage of Sinbad.
- Walk through quirky Seuss Landing and if you are still a child at heart ride the Cat in the Hat and Caro-Seuss-el.
- Now that you are hot and sweaty, go back to Toon Lagoon to ride Popeye and Bluto's Bilge-Rat Barges and if time allows, take in Dudley Do-Right's Ripsaw Falls before heading home.

Suggested 1-day itinerary at Islands of Adventure for adults with young children

- Begin your day at Seuss Landing and make One Fish, Two Fish, Red Fish, Blue Fish your first stop. Proceed to the Cat in the Hat, then Caro-Seuss-el, and stop to play at If I Ran the Zoo.
- Have an early lunch and see the show at Circus McGurkus Café Stoo-pendous and then proceed to the Lost Continent to ride the Flying Unicorn. If your children are not too young for loud noises, work in the Eighth Voyage of Sinbad.
- Next comes Jurassic Park where the Triceratops Encounter and Jurassic Park Discovery Center is a must for dinosaur-loving kids followed by a romp in the super Camp Jurassic, one of the best play areas for kids in the Orlando area. If lines are short, ride the Pteranodon Flyers.
- Work your way over to Toon Lagoon and let the kids have fun at Me Ship, The Olive and work in the Toon Beach Bash Show.
- Parents may want to utilize Universal's Child-Switch Program for attractions with a high scare factor whereby one parent can watch the children while the other rides an attraction and then the other parent hops aboard leaving the first rider with the children.

When to Come and What to Wear

Because of the popularity of this park with local teenagers, avoid the weekends. Even in the fall when most parks are slow, this park is crowded Sat and Sun with locals who receive special end-of-the-year discounts for Florida residents beginning in September.

This is one park that requires a bit of forethought in park attire. If you plan on riding Popeye and Bluto's Bilge-Rat Barges you will, and I repeat, will become thoroughly soaked. Depending on where you sit, Dudley Do-Right's Ripsaw Falls and Jurassic Park River Adventure can cause quite a drenching. Come wearing fast-drying clothing, water footwear of some sort, and in cooler months perhaps a rain poncho to remain somewhat dry. A change of clothes might also be helpful. And remember, if you're a coaster fan, flip-flops cannot be worn on Dueling Dragons.

Port of Entry

A soaring lighthouse representative of ancient Egypt leads the way to adventure and Universal's newest theme park. As you enter the gates you'll find yourself in the Port of Entry's fantasy surroundings reminiscent of the ancient Middle East. Visitors wander in awe through the bazaar-like atmosphere where they'll find Vacation and Guest Relations, lockers, stroller and wheelchair rentals along with exotic-looking shops and eateries.

Shopping at Port of Entry

De Foto's Expedition Photography—Film • cameras • camcorder tapes • batteries • postcards • hats • sunglasses • pick up your pictures taken by the Island of Adventure's photographers here.

Island Market and Export Candy Shoppe—Chocolates • fudge • jellybeans • saltwater taffy • candy apples • peppermint sticks • bulk candy • jams.

Islands of Adventure Trading Company—One-stop souvenir store selling a cornucopia of merchandise representing each area of the park.

Ocean Trader Market—Exotic, tented shop selling Far East merchandise • batik clothing • silk pillows • sarongs • wind chimes • Indonesian wooden sculptures and masks.

Port of Entry Christmas Shoppe—Ornaments from around the world • tree skirts • Christmas candles • angels • stockings • teddy bears • favorite find: Grinch and Cat in the Hat tree ornaments.

Port Provisions—Islands of Adventure logo t-shirts, sweatshirts, backpacks, hats.

Don't-miss attractions

- The Incredible Hulk
- The Amazing Adventures of Spider-Man • Popeye and Bluto's Bilge-Rat Barges
- Dueling Dragons

Marvel Super Hero Island

Ultramodern and ear-shatteringly loud, this is the teen crowd's favorite hangout. Massive icons of Marvel super heroes and villains are mounted atop every vibrantly colored structure in this futuristically wild and zany area. Over the blaring rock music, unremitting screams can be heard coming from the highly visible Hulk coaster and the looming Dr. Doom's towers. Stick around until you catch sight of muscle-bound Spider-Man quietly and mysteriously crouching on a recycling can or his other Marvel friends and foes who zip around in their siren-blaring four-wheel ATVs.

Offering over 50 exciting games, the immense Kingpin's Arcade is a big hit with the youngsters; stop out front to watch the face painting as would-be villains stretch out to be transformed.

THE AMAZING ADVENTURES OF SPIDER-MAN****

Hands down, this is the most remarkable attraction in the Orlando area, the first to combine 3-D film, special effects, and moving vehicles. On your very long wait, snake your way through the office of the Daily Bugle where you'll find that the dastardly Sinister Syndicate has absconded with the Statue of Liberty using their new levitation ray gun. Since all of the staff reporters have mysteriously disappeared, you are recruited by the gruff editor, J. Jonah Johnson, to go out into the devastated streets of New York and get the big scoop.

Board your 12-passenger, state-of-the-art "scoop vehicle," actually a 3-D simulator that moves along a track and rotates 360 degrees for the ride of your life. You'll scream with delight at each encounter with Spider-Man and his foes as they spring onto the hood of your car in amazing 3-D causing your vehicle to gyrate and pitch off to the next crazy encounter. Move through more than a dozen New York scenes, plowing through warehouses, dropping below the streets to the city sewers, and flying through towering skyscrapers. Feel the heat in mind-boggling 3-D explosions accompanied by a state-of-the-art sound system (each vehicle has its own proprietary system) that offers an intense audio along with the excitement of the ride. The most amazing scene is one in which you plunge down a 400-foot simulated drop (pure illusion but scary just the same). Don't worry, Spider-Man plans on catching you in his net at the bottom. Disney could learn a few lessons from this utterly state-of-the-art attraction. (I'm sure the Imagineers are already hard at work to top this one.) **5-minute ride. Height requirement 40 inches; children 40–48 inches must be accompanied by an adult. Not recommended for expectant mothers, those with back or neck problems, or those prone to motion sickness.**

Tip: This is the most popular ride in the park. Show up early and go directly to this attraction or be ready to wait at least an hour in line. The front seat is the best choice; just ask. This is an intense ride for young children; even though there are no actual drops it certainly feels as if you're falling at a high rate of speed. If you want to save huge amounts of wait time use the singles line; just don't expect to ride in the same vehicle with your party.

DOCTOR DOOM'S FEARFALL**

Dual, imposing-looking towers rocket you straight up 150 feet in open-air seats and then free-fall drop you bungee-style in Dr. Doom's Fearfall Sucking Machine. It's over so fast you won't know which one of the Sinister Syndicate has hit you. This thrill ride is similar to Disney's Tower of Terror minus a great storyline. **Less than a 1-minute ride. Minimum height 52 inches. Not recommended for expectant mothers or those with heart, back, or neck problem.**

Tip: This is an incredibly slow-loading ride; each tower shot holds only 16 people. If lines are long, skip it and try later or never. If you want to save some wait time use the singles line; just don't expect to ride with your party.

INCREDIBLE HULK COASTER****

An eruption of gamma rays from Bruce Banner's (better known as the Hulk) studio launches you straight up from a near standstill to a whiplashing 40 mph in just 2 seconds on this green giant of a steel roller coaster. Immediately roll into a gut-wrenching 128-foot, zero-G dive, accompanied by a feeling of weightlessness and an adrenaline rush beyond belief, straight down toward a misty lagoon. With speeds of up to 60 mph, loop through inversion after giant inversion and twice underground before you finally come to a halt on this unbelievable monster. This is one of America's most thrilling rides and not to be missed if you are a fan of big, bad coasters. **2-minute ride. Minimum height 54 inches. Not recommended for expectant mothers or those with heart, back, or neck problems.**

Tip: This is an extremely popular ride, so try for first thing in the morning after riding Spider-Man. You can't possibly hold on to your valuables; make use of the short-term lockers located at the attraction entrance, free for the first 60 minutes. If you'd like to ride in the front seat there's a line just for that purpose but be ready for a long wait. If you want to save huge amounts of wait time use the singles line; just don't expect to ride in the same row as the rest of your party.

STORM FORCE ACCELETRON*

Universal didn't give much thought or cash outlay to this twirling, stomach-churning carnival-style ride. Grape and banana-colored, saucer-shaped vehicles spin, twirl, and twist along at a zippy speed on a rotating circle. Similar to the Mad Tea Party at the Magic Kingdom. **2-minute ride. Not recommended for expectant mothers, those with back or neck problems, or those prone to motion sickness.**

Shopping at Marvel Super Hero Island

Comic Book Shop—Comic book fan's delight • Marvel Comics action figure clothing • trading cards • X-Men Monopoly game • walls of comic books.

The Marvel Alterniverse Store—Marvel Comics character merchandise.

Spider-Man Shop—Everything you ever wanted to buy with a Spider-Man logo and were afraid to ask.

Toon Lagoon

Visit the funny papers at Toon Lagoon where Blondie and Dagwood, Popeye and Olive Oyl, Boris and Natasha, Dudley Do-Right, Betty Boop, Heathcliff, and a slew of other nostalgic characters greet you in a barrage of quirky, giant-size blowups and whimsical statues on Comic Strip Lane. Entertaining music plays amid an overwhelming choice of photo opportunities and chances to splash in the fire hydrants of Marmaduke or under Hagar's boat. The Toon Beach Bash Show brings all your favorite characters like Popeye, Olive Oyl, Bluto, Beetle Bailey, and Woody Woodpecker together for a song and dance seaside routine. Also the soggiest area of the park where attractions like Dudley Do-Right's Ripsaw Falls and Popeye and Bluto's Bilge-Rat Barges dump water by the barrelful on unsuspecting visitors.

DUDLEY DO-RIGHT'S RIPSAW FALLS***

Although this is a fun flume ride ending in a wicked plunge, Splash Mountain it isn't. Float along in a 6-passenger log boat through Ripsaw Falls amid not exactly state-of-the-art melodramatic scenes of Dudley, Nell, and the unscrupulous Snidely Whiplash. Then hang on for the final doozy of a drop, one that's amazingly fast and steep culminating 15 feet underwater. Don't panic; the water is contained so you won't need to practice holding your breath, although you will get plenty wet. If you have any question about riding, stand outside for a preview of the final descent. **5-minute ride. Height requirement 44 inches; children 44-48 inches must be accompanied by an adult. Not recommended for expectant mothers.**

Tip: Hang on tightly to the bars on the big plunge; your rear end raises off the seat quite a bit.

ME SHIP, THE OLIVE**

Explore Popeye's boat in this children's playhouse. Three levels of slides, interactive noisemakers, and water cannons perfect for shooting unsuspecting riders on the Bilge-Rat Barges below are all part of the fun. For adults there's a great view of the park from up top.

POPEYE AND BLUTO'S BILGE-RAT BARGES****

Perhaps the funniest barge ride you'll ever have the pleasure of encountering. You can't help but get entirely soaked on this absolutely hilarious attraction as you swirl and twist over white-water rapids in 12-passsenger circular rafts accompanied by the tooting and bellowing of boat horns, renditions of "Blow the Man Down," and Popeye's theme song. Sail through scenes of Popeye and Bluto in their fight for Olive Oyl's love while water swirls close to your knees. Rendezvous with a squirting, giant octopus and ride through Bluto's Boat Wash for a good cleaning. Of course, Popeye saves Olive Oyl in the end but is none the drier in the process. Don't miss this super attraction, even if you have to wear a rain poncho to keep dry. **5-minute ride. Minimum height 42 inches; children 42–48 inches must be accompanied by an adult. Not recommended for expectant mothers.**

Tip: Place your valuables in the watertight containers located in the center of the raft and make sure the snaps are tightly shut. You must wear footwear to ride, so come prepared in fast-drying shoes or water sandals. Even if you prop your feet off the floor, they'll still get soaked from above.

Shopping at Toon Lagoon

Gasoline Alley—Island-related merchandise • Hawaiian-print shirts, dresses, and sarongs • grass hula skirts • straw bags • sunglasses • comic strip character beach towels and t-shirts.

Toon Extra—Comic strip character merchandise and souvenirs • precious Swee' Pea infant clothing • Betty Boop merchandise.

Jurassic Park

Begin your adventure in the wilds as you walk under the imposing arched gates of Jurassic Park. The dramatic strains of the movie's theme song plays among the steamy, dense foliage of towering palms and tropical plants. While the mist rises, an ominous feeling of danger lurks around every corner; the sporadic roars of dinosaurs accompanied by the chatter of a multitude of tropical birds and insects in the thicket don't do much to dispel your jitters. See life-size dinosaurs on the Jurassic Park River Adventure, climb and frolic through Camp Jurassic, or pet a seemingly alive triceratops. Just watch out for those high voltage fences, the only thing between you and disaster!

CAMP JURASSIC***

Orlando's very best play area for children is this one in Jurassic Park. Kid's will want to spend hours exploring this very extensive and maze-like prehistoric romping ground of rushing water, rocky pathways, and a creepy cacophony of dinosaur and jungle sounds. Here they will encounter plenty of places to climb over and under with various stairways and bridges lined in jungle netting and tree roots leading to a multitude of slides. Look carefully when rounding corners or risk encountering dinosaur spitting water cannons manned by children from both below and above. The very best spot here and one not to be missed is the dark, cave-like passageway leading to a glowing, bubbling amber mine.

Tip: Although it's a children's playground, adults will enjoy a walk around.

JURASSIC PARK DISCOVERY CENTER**

This bi-level, interactive, walk-through attraction houses a counter-service restaurant and shop on the top floor and a must-see attraction for dinosaur-lovers combining fiction and fact in a scientific-like atmosphere on the lower level. A life-size skeleton of a T-Rex thrusts its head above the circular stairwell central to the building. Downstairs attractions include the Nursery where dinosaur eggs can be scanned to view the growing embryos inside; try to be around when a baby raptor hatches from its shell. DNA Sequencing allows visitors to mix their own special DNA with a dinosaur of their choice, and at Discovering Dinosaurs is an actual rock formation from the North Sea area embedded with a unique blend of dinosaur fossil bits that can be observed through a "Neutrino Scanner." The Beasaur exhibit allows a look at the world through the eyes of a dinosaur, and You Bet Jurassic is a competitive quiz show for those with a brain full of dinosaur trivia. Out back is a terrific terrace offering panoramic vistas of the lagoon.

JURASSIC PARK RIVER ADVENTURE***

This ride brings you gently into the middle of a lost world and then roughly lets you out. Load up into oversized, 25-person rafts to travel deep into the lush rain forest of Jurassic Park. Float past gentle 5-story dinosaurs (some of the largest audio-animatronics in any theme park) who ignore the passing traffic as they breathe, roar, and munch on plants. Soon, however, the sweetness turns to fighting when visitors come across the more aggressive breeds (even a few who spit), particularly a nasty T-rex who forces the raft into the Raptor Containment Area where a few hairs might rise on the back of more than one passenger's neck. The only way out of this mess is up and over, and by over I mean by way of a pitch-dark, 80-foot, very steep plunge at speeds of 50 mph ending in a tremendous splash guaranteed to douse each and every person in the boat. **6-minute ride. Minimum height 42 inches; children 42–48 inches must be accompanied by an adult. Not recommended for expectant mothers or those with back or neck problems.**

Tip: Use the short-term lockers, free for the first 60 minutes, located outside the attraction for loose articles or valuables. This ride is notorious for breakdowns, so come prepared. To the right of Thunder Falls Terrace Restaurant is a walkway leading to a great splash zone/observation spot where the chicken-hearted can watch as others drop down the final descent. If you want to save huge amounts of wait time use the singles line; just don't expect to ride in the same vehicle with your party.

PTERANODON FLYERS**

Quietly soar 40 feet above the ground beneath the wings of a 2-seater flying pteranodon that's suspended from a curving track high above Camp Jurassic. Feet dangle while riders get a terrific bird's-eye view (no pun intended) of the park, but lines can be lengthy since only a few flyers are in movement at any given time. A child must accompany adults wishing to ride; if you didn't come with one, either borrow someone else's child or forget it. If this is high on your list come first thing in the morning to ride. Although this is considered a children's ride, the two seats are separate and young ones could possibly become a bit frightened with Mom or Dad not seated next to them; the ride tends to swing out a bit on curves, doing nothing to calm the little one's nerves. **1-minute ride. Designed for children 36–56 inches tall. Guests over 56 inches tall must be accompanied by a child who meets this requirement. Not recommended for expectant mothers.**

Tip: Lines tend to be excruciatingly slow and just may not be worth it.

TRICERATOPS ENCOUNTER***

Come face-to-face with a seemingly real triceratops. First walk a lengthy but beautiful queue through a jungle paradise past research stations, camps, and labs. Throughout, monitors transmit the "Jurassic Journal," Jurassic Park's information channel, broadcasting from the interior of the fascinating world of dinosaurs. Sooner or later you'll enter a paddock where a technician is conducting a checkup with a 10-foot tall resident triceratops that has been supposedly sedated. The beast's routine and preferences are discussed while this remarkably realistic audio-animatronics creature moves, breathes, groans, and responds to the "veterinarian" giving the exam. On the way out visitors are given a chance to pet her. **5-minute show. Not open until late morning in slower seasons.**

Tip: Though lines may be long, I can't imagine a bigger thrill for a dinosaur-loving kid than to be able to pet, to all appearances, a real dinosaur. Be patient or come early to really enjoy this attraction.

Shopping at Jurassic Park

Dinostore—Found inside the Discovery Center • dinosaurs books, model kits, and toys • Jurassic Park logo attire.

Jurassic Outfitters—Jurassic Park logo clothing • dinosaur-related merchandise • safari clothing • binoculars • rubber snakes • dinosaur boxer shorts.

The Lost Continent

It's a mixture of fantasy and medieval reality in this festive area of the park where beastly, armored griffins greet you at the bridge into the Lost Continent and silently watch you as you depart. You're never really sure if you're somewhere in the Middle East, perhaps in ancient Greece, or in a mythical land. Whatever, it seems to work its spell here where fantastical music plays and wild displays of color abound amid structures straight out of an Aladdin storybook.

DUELING DRAGONS****

You'll notice as you board either one of these two terrifying roller coasters, Fire and Ice—surprise! surprise!, there's no floor. On the world's first inverted, duel track, near-miss coasters, two dragons are in a dog-fight and you're along on the back of one for the battle. Your legs dangle free as you loop and twist along and at certain points you'll swear your feet almost touch those of the opposite dragon as it goes roaring by (supposedly they are only a scant foot apart). Ride one first and then the other for comparison; they are two different experiences. This is not for the faint-hearted. **2-minute ride. Minimum height 54 inches. Not recommended for expectant mothers or those with heart, back, or neck problems. Flip-flop footwear not permitted.**

Tip: If waits are short it won't be necessary to go all the way back to the entrance to ride the other coaster; just look for an opening on the way out for the turnaround to the second coaster. Daredevils should try for the front row in order to get a clear shot of the oncoming train. Use the short-term lockers (free for the first 60 minutes) located outside the attraction for loose articles or valuables. If you want to save huge amounts of wait time use the singles line; just don't expect to ride in the same row as the rest of your party.

THE EIGHTH VOYAGE OF SINBAD**

This live-action stunt show of innumerable explosions, erupting water, and free-falling performers takes place in a cave-like theater setting. Sinbad is off on his eighth adventure seeking even more riches when he finds a beautiful kidnapped princess in an evil sorceress's cave and fights alongside her and his comic sidekick Kabob to gain the magical ruby known as "the Sultan's Heart." Over and over again, the pyrotechnic effects dazzle; however, the story line is somewhat weak and the comedy fairly lame. The grand finale involves a 22-foot dive into a pool of water by a living fireball, a stunt performer engulfed in flames. **20-minute show. Check your guide map for times.**

Tip: Those who want to cool off should sit in the middle front for the water action. On your way out, pause at the bubbling and gurgling Mystic Fountain; just don't be surprised if it talks and squirts on occasion.

THE FLYING UNICORN**

This enchanted kiddie coaster was contrived by a wizard who used a unicorn's horn to create the charmed contraption. Board a 14-person car led by an armored unicorn for a ride that's loads of fun, perfect for those who have not quite graduated to the likes of Dueling Dragons. No dips, just a short ascent and then a very quick, corkscrew ride down as the wizard warns "get ready to fly." You'll be surprised how fast it travels. **1-minute ride. Minimum height 36 inches; children under 48 inches must be accompanied by an adult. Not recommended for expectant mothers, and those with heart, neck, or back problems.**

POSEIDON'S FURY: ESCAPE FROM THE LOST CITY***

Pass through the ruins of the lost city of Atlantis where a lagoon is strewn with the vestiges of a toppled statue of Poseidon before winding down a dark, narrow passage to the main attraction. In this newly revised show, the Global Discovery Group is working to excavate the remains of Poseidon's underwater city, allowing you to tour the site. As your group, led by a dig site assistant, moves through a secret passage, Darkenon, an evil high priest and Poseidon's archenemy, seals the room. Escape is made possible by the discovery of Poseidon's ancient trident that unlocks the portal to the heart of a hidden temple entered through an amazing tunnel of swirling water. Here Poseidon and Darkenon battle it out in a massive 350,000-gallon watery clash with countless pyrotechnic effects. **25-minute show. Children under 48 inches must be accompanied by an adult.**

Tip: The final battle scene of loud explosions and hurling fireballs is pretty intense for young children. You'll be standing throughout this attraction so don't expect to rest your feet. Some think this is one of the park's best attractions while others are not as impressed; although the first half of the tour tends to be a bit tedious, the grand finale more than makes up for it.

Shopping at the Lost Continent

Chimera Glass—Sparkling crystal figurines and pendants • glassblower at work.

The Coin Mint—Medieval medallions, hand-minted on a drop hammer forge • refillable quill pens.

The Dragon's Keep—Everything a dragon community could need is right here • plastic bats (the Dracula kind) and bugs • toy warrior swords • Dueling Dragon apparel • wizard caps • medieval costumes • magic tricks and games • crystal balls.

Historic Families—Family crest and coat-of-arms • shiny daggers • beautifully carved chess sets • coats of armor.

Mystic Henna—Sparkling Middle Eastern clothing • henna body art • silk scarves • soft slippers • exotic jewelry.

Star Souls—Fortunes read.

Treasures of Poseidon—Underwater merchandise • frames decorated with marine creatures and shells • books on Atlantis and mythology • seashells • marine sculpture • marine plush toys • beach towels.

Quiet Places

Behind Cats, Hats, and Things in Seuss Landing is a quiet courtyard with crooked benches and an invitation to sit on Horton's egg • in the Lost Continent, walk toward the lagoon beside Mythos restaurant for a hidden sitting area with a view of the entire park, the same panorama you'd receive while dining at Mythos • downstairs behind Jurassic Park Discovery Center is a beautiful terrace overlooking the lagoon and the entire park.

Seuss Landing

What a challenge it must have been for the folks at Universal to interpret the unbelievable imagination of Dr. Seuss into an actual three-dimensional setting. Step inside Dr. Seuss's whimsical world, a wild conglomeration of color and sound, where there's not a single straight line (even the palm trees are bent) and, believe it or not, every building is made completely of carved and shaped Styrofoam. If you're not already feeling discombobulated, the zany music playing over the speakers will certainly get you there. The name of every store, snack bar, and attraction comes straight from Dr. Seuss's fascinating tomes; you'll see a forest of truffulo trees, the street of the lifted Lorax, Horton's egg, and McElligot's pool. The Cat in the Hat and his zany sidekicks, Thing One and Thing Two, roam the streets with Sam I Am to the delight of all. And look up for an occasional glimpse of Sylvester McMonkey McBean circling overhead on his Very Unusual Driving Machine. Who couldn't love a place where all you want to do is giggle.

CARO-SEUSS-EL***

This is probably the most unique carousel you'll ever ride! Mount a slew of fanciful Seuss characters, all with bright, silly faces plodding along in various shapes and crooked sizes. Pull on the reins and watch their ears wiggle, heads bounce, tails wag, noses twitch, and eyes blink along to the madcap music. It's enough to make your day! Visitors with disabilities will love the special loading platform for wheelchairs. **2-minute ride. Children under 48 inches must be accompanied by an adult.**

THE CAT IN THE HAT***

Anyone who's ever read and enjoyed *The Cat in the Hat* will love this amusing ride. Sit on powder-blue sofas and ride, spin, and swoop along to the hilarious story of the famous cat that comes to visit two children home alone for the day. Your journey includes the Cat along with the naughty Thing One and Thing Two and the tormented family goldfish who tries but fails to keep order while the parents are away. Every creature and object moves, flies, and bounces along to the frenzied beat of the crazy narration. Laugh along as you move through scene after scene of this celebrated children's book and be enchanted with the re-creation of a simply great story. **3-minute ride. Children under 48 inches must be accompanied by an adult. Not recommended for expectant mothers, those with back or neck problems, or those prone to motion sickness.**

Tip: Regrettably, this ride seems to break down with frequency; if so, don't wait it out since it usually takes a bit of time to restart.

THE CIRCUS MCGURKUS SEUSSIAN SING-A-LONG**

Taking place in the Circus McGurkus Café throughout the day is a sing-a-long show geared to little ones. Ringmaster McGurkus is joined by the Cat in the Hat, Thing One and Thing Two, the Grinch, and other Seuss characters in an interactive song and dance performance accompanied by a zany pipe organ. Shows are conveniently planned around mealtimes, so order up something from the counter and sit back to be entertained while you chow down. **30-minute show. Check your guide map for times.**

IF I RAN THE ZOO**

The creatures from the book of the same name are featured in this interactive play area for kids. Presided over by Gerald McGrew, the various areas of fun include the Cave of Kartoom for crawling in search of the Natch, the tunnels of Zomba-ma-tant for sliding, the Island of Yerka for water play, and tic-tac-toe with Joe. Scraggle Foot Mulligatawny emits a big sneeze while a bubble bath creature likes for others to be wet too. Simply loads of fun!

ONE FISH, TWO FISH, RED FISH, BLUE FISH**

Your children will delight in Universal's version of the Dumbo ride, one with a few twists. The Star Belly Fish officiates above this soaring, kaleidoscopic attraction composed of an assortment of 2-passenger fish cars, all with goofy smiles. Control the loftiness of your creature with the handle inside and, if you want to stay dry, take care to avoid the spitting fish lying in wait on the sidelines. **2-minute ride. Children under 48 inches must be accompanied by an adult.**

Shopping at Seuss Landing

Cats, Hats and Things—Fun store totally dedicated to the Cat in the Hat • plush toys • books • apparel • souvenirs • green-striped, stove-pipe cat hats • bright blue Thing One and Thing Two wigs.

All the Books You Can Read—Marvelous collection of Dr. Seuss storybooks, videos, cassettes, and software • kids t-shirts • games • banks • Seussian plush toys • children can relax and read in kid-sized benches and chairs.

Mulberry Street Store—Every piece of Seussian merchandise imaginable • kids love their very own tiny entrance door • Cat in the Hat beach towels, hats, and clothing • Grinch house slippers and Christmas stockings • Horton and Yertle the Turtle plush toys • Dr. Seuss trivia game.

Picture This—Fun family photos taken in Dr. Seuss storybook sets.

Snookers and Snookers Sweet Candy Store—Bulk candy • lollipops • Circus McGurkus animal cookies.

Restaurants, Counter-Service Meals, and Snacks

Islands of Adventure has a huge array of food choices, many of them extremely tasty. They have one-upped the image of park food with creative dining areas, many with delightful views, and plenty to eat besides the typical hot dog and burgers.

Port of Entry

Arctic Express—Funnel cakes with a variety of toppings • waffle ice cream cones • sundaes.

Cinnabon—Hot, delicious cinnamon rolls dripping with icing • Minbons (a smaller version of a Cinnabon) • caramel Pecanbons • Cinnabon Stix.

Confisco Grille—Lunch and dinner • full-service restaurant offering light meals • chicken tenders, buffalo wings with blue cheese dipping sauce, confisco fries served with dipping sauces, nachos, Tex Mex wrap, chicken Caesar salad, Greek salad, fajitas, open-faced turkey sandwich, burgers, croissant club sandwich • adjoining Backwater Bar offers a full bar and happy hour daily 3–5 P.M.

Croissant Moon Bakery—Pastries, tarts, pies, muffins, cookies, breakfast sandwiches • deli sandwiches of roast beef, ham and swiss, and turkey, Caesar salad, fruit, soup • specialty coffees.

Marvel Super Hero Island

Café 4—Space-age diner sporting blue-tinted windows and neon lighting with convenient door opening directly into Kingpin's Arcade • pizza, spaghetti and meatballs or sausage, barbeque chicken and Boursin, lasagna, garlic cream fettuccini, chicken Caesar salad, Italian hoagies, meatball subs, minestrone soup, pasta salad.

Captain American Diner—All-American modern eatery • indoor seating overlooks lagoon, outdoor seating offers a great view of the Hulk coaster • burgers, chicken sandwich, chicken fingers.

Toon Lagoon

Blondie's: Home of the Dagwood—A towering, multilevel sandwich topples over the entrance of this counter-service, stacked sandwich shop • the Dagwood (loaded with ham, salami, turkey, bologna, and

Swiss and American cheeses piled high with lettuce and tomatoes), Tootsie's Favorite (smoked turkey and cheese), Vegi Choice (tomatoes, mozzarella cheese, and lettuce), hot meatloaf sandwich, jumbo hot dogs, chili, chef's salad, cream of tomato soup, potato salad, slaw.

Cathy's Ice Cream—Waffle cone sundaes • root beer and creamsicle floats.

Comic Strip Café—Food court café—Pizza and Pasta: pizza, lasagna, spaghetti and meatballs, fettuccini Alfredo, deli subs, meatball sandwich, Caesar salad • Mexican: soft tacos, fajitas, Southwestern club wrap, tostado salad, nachos, rice, beans, salad • Chinese: sweet and sour chicken, beef and broccoli, shrimp and scallop lo-mein, vegetable stir-fry, egg rolls, fried rice, wonton soup • Fish and Chicken: fried fish, chicken fingers, Cajun popcorn shrimp hoagie, Philly cheese steak, fried shrimp.

Wimpy's—Wimpy, the famous hamburger-lover himself, claims he personally supervises the culinary construction of each burger here at this counter-service shack • tables offer a fun view of the Popeye and Bluto Bilge-Rat Barges • burgers, chicken sandwiches, hot dogs, chili dogs, chicken tenders.

Jurassic Park

Burger Digs—Indoor seating overlooks the Discovery Center's huge T-Rex skeleton while outdoor balcony tables come with super views of the lagoon and park • burgers, grilled chicken sandwich, chicken tenders, topping bar.

Pizza Predattoria—Only outdoor, covered seating at this counter-service prehistoric spot • pizza (cheese, pepperoni, barbeque chicken and pineapple), sandwiches (meatball, Italian sausage, or deli-stacked), Caesar salad in a pizza crust.

Thunder Falls Terrace—A jungle lodge setting with huge picture windows affording views of the final plunge of the adjoining Jurassic Park River Adventure • one of the better fast-food stops in the park • conch chowder, rotisserie chicken platter or salad, chargrilled baby back ribs, barbeque-glazed chicken wings, roasted corn and potatoes, cream of chicken soup, black beans. Open seasonally.

The Lost Continent

Enchanted Oak Tavern and Alchemy Bar—Cavernous counter-service restaurant in the base of a gnarly, ancient tree • delightful eating terrace out back with lagoon views • smoked chicken, ribs, and turkey legs, bacon-cheeseburgers, smoked chicken salad, corn chowder, roasted corn, corn muffins • adjoining Alchemy Bar serves frozen margaritas, beers, specialty drinks with daily happy hour 3–5 P.M.

Fire Eater's Grill—Middle Eastern–style snack bar • gyro sandwiches, chicken fingers, spicy chicken stingers, hot dogs • juice, sodas, coffee, beer.

Mythos—Lunch and dinner—remarkable sea cave dining room offering the best food in the park • great lagoon views • full review on page 375.

Seuss Landing

Circus McGurkus Café Stoo-pendous—Quirky circus tent counter-service café literally bursting with color. Catch the Circus McGurkus Show while dining on kid-friendly food • fried chicken, pizza, lasagna, spaghetti and meatballs, spaghetti marinara, chicken Caesar salad, alphabet soup, fruit and chicken salad • McGurks Soda Fountain inside for soft-serve ice cream cones, root beer floats, milkshakes.

Green Eggs and Ham Café—Green eggs (they get their color from parsley) and hamwich sandwich, burgers, chicken sandwich, chicken nuggets • seating is outside, but covered.

Hop on Pop Ice Cream Shop—"Walk Away" Sundaes on a stick dipped in chocolate and rolled in sprinkles • waffle cone banana split • upside-down sundaes (chocolate brownie topped with vanilla ice cream, caramel, whipped cream, and upside-down sugar cone).

Mouse Juice Goose Juice—Moose Juice (tangerine concoction) and Goose Juice (sour green apple brew), fresh or frozen • fresh fruit cup • Jello parfait • homemade cookies • churros • hot pretzels.

Lounges

Alchemy Bar—Located within the Enchanted Tavern in the Lost Continent • dark, pleasant lounge offering a full bar, frozen margaritas, beer, specialty drinks • daily happy hour 3–5 P.M.

Backwater Bar—Adjoins Confisco Grille at Port of Entry • happy hour daily 3–6 P.M.

The Watering Hole—Outdoor bar amid the roar of dinosaurs in the Jurassic Park area • margaritas, island coolers, frosted drinks.

Special Events

Halloween Horror Nights—Have a spooky evening on selected nights during the month of October featuring five haunted houses, live entertainment, ghouls and monsters roaming the park, Halloween-theme stage shows, and a Festival of the Dead parade. $50 admission. Weekdays 7 P.M.–midnight; Fri and Sat 7 P.M.–2 A.M. Young children are not encouraged to attend. No costumes allowed.

Grinchmas—From the end of Nov to the end of Dec, Seuss Landing is transformed into the Christmas town of Whoville featuring the Grinch, live stage shows, impromptu street performances, and Mt. Crumpit Snow Plummet, a 60-foot slide with snow at its base. Included in the price of admission.

CITYWALK

Universal's energetic answer to Downtown Disney is quite a good one. Though not as extensive, it's a nice alternative to park fare for daytrippers and a sparkling mirage of twinkling lights, delicious dining, tempting shops, and unique and happening nightclubs for evening partygoers. The 30-acre complex, conveniently positioned between Universal Studios and the Islands of Adventure, is a definite lure for those making their way to and from the parks. The picturesque lagoon that runs through the complex offers an opportunity for a boat ride to the Universal resorts hotels where even more dining and entertainment possibilities exist.

Admission

Unlike Pleasure Island, there is no charge to enter CityWalk; however, there are individual cover charges at each club. If you plan to party in several spots, consider the CityWalk Party Pass for $9 which allows unlimited entry for 1 night to all clubs (excluding Hard Rock Live).

Any Universal multi-day pass comes with a CityWalk Party Pass good for 7 consecutive days beginning with the first day of use. The $12 CityWalk Party Pass and Movie buys unlimited 1-night club admission plus a movie at Universal Cineplex. Purchase a Meal and Movie Deal for $18 for dinner at one of several CityWalk restaurants and a movie. A Meal and Party Deal is $18.

Parking

Parking is $8 during the day, free after 6 P.M.; valet park for $14. At lunchtime most full-service restaurants will validate your valet parking ticket for 2 hours or less.

Dining Reservations

Call 407-224-3663 before 3 P.M. for same-day priority seating or stop by the CityWalk Information kiosk on the walkway in front of the movie theater. Registered guests of the Loews' Universal hotels may show their room key for the next available table at all CityWalk restaurants excluding Emeril's (not available on Fri and Sat). Call 407-224-2424 up to 3 months ahead for Emeril's reservations.

Information

Call 407-363-8000 or visit www.citywalk.com for upcoming event information.

Full-Service Restaurants

Full CityWalk restaurant reviews on pages 378-383.

Emeril's—CityWalk's best dining spot, a spin-off of New Orleans' hottest restaurant.

Hard Rock Café—World's largest Hard Rock Café.

Jimmy Buffett's Margaritaville—Cheeseburgers in paradise at this popular Key West–style hotspot.

Latin Quarter—Central and South American specialties along with lively Latino music.

Motown Café—Soul food amid Motown memorabilia and music.

NASCAR Café—Dine on roadhouse fare under the roar of suspended racecars.

City Walk

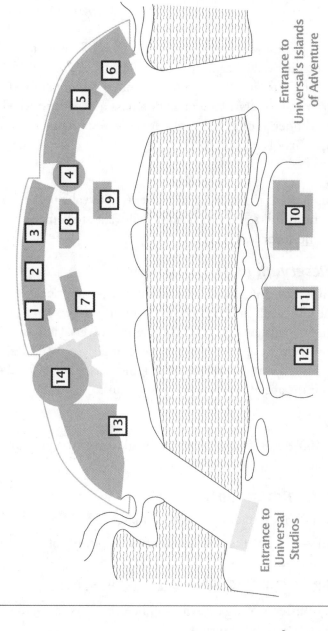

Entrance to Universal's Islands of Adventure

Entrance to Universal Studios

1. Motown® Cafe Orlando
2. Bob Marley - A Tribute to Freedom
3. Pat O'Brien's® Orlando
4. The Groove
5. Latin Quarter™
6. Jimmy Buffett's Margaritaville®
7. Pastomoré
8. CityJazz®
9. Emeril's® Restaurant Orlando
10. NBA City
11. Hard Rock Cafe® Orlando®
12. Hard Rock Live® Orlando®
13. NASCAR Cafe™ Orlando
14. Universal Cineplex

NBA City—Good food and a nonstop barrage of NBA championship highlights.

Pastamore—Italian specialties in a contemporary family atmosphere.

Counter-Service Eating

Big Kahuna Pizza—Walk-up window • pizza whole or by the slice • beer, beverages.

Cinnabon Bakery—Hard-to-resist warm cinnamon rolls oozing with icing.

Pastamore Market Café—All-day café annex adjoining the main Pastamore restaurant • breakfast: scrambled egg platter, breakfast pizza, pastries • lunch and dinner: antipasto, sandwiches, salads, pizza, meatball sub, lasagna, spaghetti • margarita Italiano, sangria, wine • Happy Hour 3–7 P.M. daily.

St. Augustine Sausage—Walk-up window • burgers, coney island dogs, hot dogs, jerk chicken sandwich, chicken wings • beer, beverages.

Universal Cineplex Movie Theater

When you are weary of walking and are ready to relax, head here for your choice of 20 extra-large screens of entertainment. Along with stadium seating and high-back rocking seats are wine and beer at the refreshment stand. Box office opens at 12:30 P.M.

Nightclubs at CityWalk

Bob Marley—A Tribute to Freedom— *Open 4 P.M.–2 A.M.; live entertainment nightly 8 P.M.–1:30 A.M.; cover charge after 8 P.M.; only those ages 21 or older allowed entrance Fri–Sat nights* • replica of Bob Marley's Jamaican home • two levels face an open-air courtyard holding gazebo-shaped bandstand • live reggae on tap every evening along with Red Stripe beer • appetizers and light meals: oven-roasted sweet peppers stuffed with fresh vegetables and rice, smoked whitefish dip, Jamaican beef patties, Jamaican jerk mahimahi sandwich, fried red snapper in a Red Stripe tempura batter, smoky white cheddar cheese fondue spiked with Red Stripe, jerk marinated chicken breast with yucca fries.

CityJazz—*Open Sun–Thurs 8 P.M.–1 A.M. ; Fri. and Sat 7 P.M.–2 A.M.; appetizer menu available Mon–Sat.; live music nightly; cover charge* *after 9 P.M.; for information call 407-224-5299* • live R&B, soul, and rock combines with the classiest club at CityWalk • over 500 pieces of jazz memorabilia • full bar, martinis • fine cigars.

The Groove—*Open 9 P.M.–2 A.M.; cover charge; 21 years of age or older for admittance* • DJ-driven tunes and live bands • five bars and three specialty lounges surround the hopping dance floor, each offering a different setting and specialty drink menu • super sound system, special effects, video wall • predominately young crowd.

Hard Rock Live—*Concerts normally begin at 8 P.M. with ticket prices varying from free for local bands to as high as $150 for big names; purchase tickets at Hard Rock Live box office, from Ticketmaster at 407-839-3900, or online at www.ticketmaster.com; call 407-351-5483 or go online at www.hardrock.com/live for information on upcoming events* • live entertainment arena • big names as well as local bands • can be configured as either a large rock concert venue accommodating over 2,000 or converted to an intimate nightclub setting.

Jimmy Buffett's Margaritaville—After 10 P.M. the restaurant turns into a hopping nightclub with live entertainment at which time a cover charge is assessed • bands play from one of several stages • margaritas flow • choose from full menu until midnight; after that appetizers only.

Latin Quarter—Thurs–Sat this restaurant turns into a Latin nightclub with live entertainment, dancing, and floor shows; cover charge after 10 P.M. • combination restaurant and dance club.

Motown Café—*Cover charge after 9 P.M. Fri. and Sat* • combination café and nightclub featuring the music of Motown • live music by the talented Motown Moments Wed–Sat.

Pat O'Brien's—*Open 4 P.M.–2 A.M.; after 9 P.M. guests must be 21 or older with a cover charge* • replica of the world-famous New Orleans watering hole • three bars: Piano Bar where the concept of dueling pianos originated, laid-back Main Bar with its neighborhood gathering place atmosphere, and the romantic, candlelit courtyard with flaming fountains • over 100 varieties of specialty drinks • light meals: crawfish nachos, po' boy sandwiches, spicy shrimp gumbo, jambalaya, coconut-crusted shrimp, muffuletta sandwich.

Shopping at CityWalk

Although shopping here could not exactly be described as spectacular, it is entertaining with a wide range of merchandise for all ages. In addition to the shops below, many of the nightclubs have their own retail shops with specialty items ranging from Motown memorabilia to Rastafarian t-shirts.

All-Star Collectibles—Team logo-adorned jackets, t-shirts, and jerseys • sports collectibles.

Cartooniversal—Universal cartoon merchandise store.

Cigarz at CityWalk—Atmospheric cigar shop and bar reminiscent of Cuba.

Dapy—Hodgepodge of collectibles and unique toys.

Elegant Illusions—Lab-created gemstones in gold or silver settings are perfect for those who love jewelry but possess small pocketbooks.

Endangered Species Store—National Geographic t-shirts • animal plush toys • leopard print clothing • New Age CDs • nature books.

Fossil—Fossil merchandise galore • watches • sunglasses • purses • wallets • belts • t-shirts.

Fresh Produce—Casual clothing line in a rainbow of lively pastels for women and girls.

Glow—Glow-in-the-dark clothing, Frisbees, even underwear.

Quiet Flight Surf Shop—Cool shades • Tommy Bahama, No Fear, Quiksilver, Billabong, and Roxy clothing.

Silver—Sterling silver jewelry.

Universal Studios Store—Universal Studio merchandise store.

CHAPTER 10

Other Nearby Theme Parks

SEAWORLD

You may think you've landed in Maine on your approach to SeaWorld's gate when you encounter a quaint lighthouse and boulder-strewn pool engulfed in crashing waves accompanied by the screech of seabirds and the wail of foghorns. It's the perfect setting leading to a day of adventure at this first-rate marine park. Lovingly landscaped and sparkling-clean, its 200 acres of fun is certainly worth a day away from Mickey. And if you think Shamu is the only show of real interest here, think again. Show after show and exhibit after exhibit leads you through the fascinating world of marine life and their connection with mankind. All of it's done at a more laid-back pace, a welcome respite from the breakneck speed of Disney and Universal's theme parks.

SeaWorld is undergoing a major expansion with new retail stores and restaurants set to open this summer around the lagoon. Look for a new and better SeaWorld.

Divided into two sections, the north and the south area almost separated by a 17-acre lagoon, visitors will find 5 different live shows and 15 continuous exhibits or rides. With a bit of planning and lots of speed walking, it's possible to go from one show to the next with a short break for lunch although this doesn't leave much time for seeing the continuous exhibits, many of which are even better than the live shows. If time allows, plan 2 days for a relaxed tour of the park and all it has to offer.

Getting There

SeaWorld's entrance is on Central Florida Parkway just off I-4 (Exit 71) or the Beeline Expressway (528).

Admission

Turn in your 1-day ticket before departure and receive a second day (to be used within 7 days) free. Tickets purchased at **www.seaworld.com** come with a slight discount.

Price Without Tax

	ADULT	CHILD (3–9)
1-Day/1-Park Ticket	$52	$43
4-Park Orlando Flex Ticket	$176	$143
5-Park Orlando Flex Ticket	$210	$176
SeaWorld/Busch Gardens Value Ticket (1 day at each park)	$86	$73
Silver Passport (seniors and children)	$85	$75
Gold Passport	$130	$120

Park Operating Hours

Open at 9 A.M. with closing times varying according to the season. Call **407-351-3600** for up-to-date information.

Services

ATM machines—Six ATM machines are scattered throughout the park: just outside the main entrance, just inside, across from Stingray Lagoon, across from Terrors of the Deep, across from Penguin Encounters, and next to Mango Joe's.

Baby care services—A nursing area is located next to the ladies restroom near the Penguin Encounter. Baby changing stations can be found in most women's restrooms and the men's restroom near the entrance.

Cameras and film—Film and disposable cameras are located in most stores throughout the park.

First aid—Two locations: behind Stingray Lagoon and in Shamu's Harbor.

Guest relations/information counter—Look here for lost children and lost articles.

Guest with disabilities—Most of SeaWorld's attractions are easily accessible for guests in wheelchairs. Wheelchair accessible restrooms are found throughout the park and companion-assisted restrooms are near the main entrance, in the Village Square across from Polar Parlor, and near Terrors of the Deep. All restaurants are wheelchair accessible. Guide dogs are permitted. Interpreters are available for the hearing-impaired with at least a two-week notice; call **407-363-2414** for reservations. Guides for guests with disabilities and in Braille are available at the Information Center at the park. Call **800-432-1178** for information.

Information and reservations—Go to **www.seaworld.com** or call **800-432-1178** for advance information. Just past the entrance gate is the information booth offering guide maps and information in addition to reservations for behind-the-scenes tours.

Lockers—Located just inside the main gate and near Kracken available for $1–1.50 per day depending on the size.

Parking—$7 per day; free for Annual Pass holders. Preferred parking for $10 within easy walking distance to the entrance. Parking is directly in front of the park with rows 1 through 37 within walking distance; all others serviced by tram.

Pet kennels—Located immediately outside the main gate next to the tram stop. Daily fee is $6. Proof of vaccination required.

Soak zones—Some of the live shows have clearly marked soak zones. Avoid them if you wish to stay dry and/or are carrying expensive camera equipment. When they say you will get wet, believe them; you may even get soaked and that's with ice cold saltwater.

Stroller and wheelchair rentals—Single strollers rent for $10, doubles $17, wheelchairs $8, and ECVs $32.

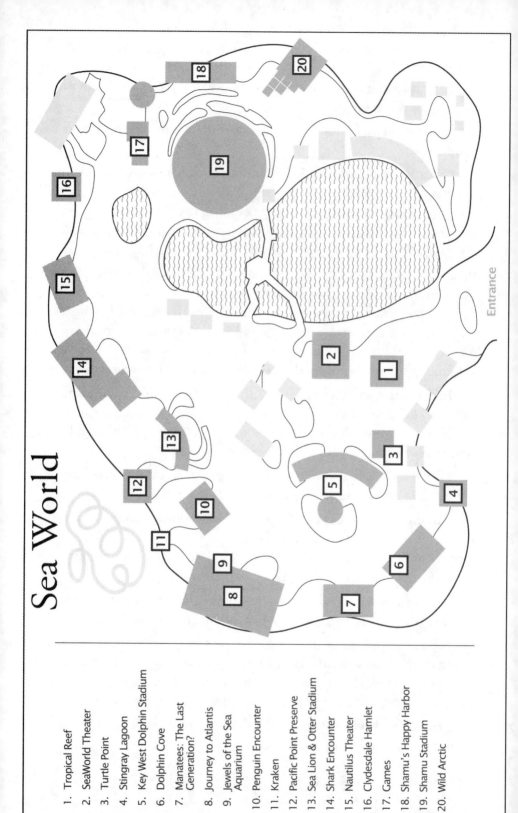

Sea World

1. Tropical Reef
2. SeaWorld Theater
3. Turtle Point
4. Stingray Lagoon
5. Key West Dolphin Stadium
6. Dolphin Cove
7. Manatees: The Last Generation?
8. Journey to Atlantis
9. Jewels of the Sea Aquarium
10. Penguin Encounter
11. Kraken
12. Pacific Point Preserve
13. Sea Lion & Otter Stadium
14. Shark Encounter
15. Nautilus Theater
16. Clydesdale Hamlet
17. Games
18. Shamu's Happy Harbor
19. Shamu Stadium
20. Wild Arctic

Entrance

Northern Area
Continuous Viewing
DOLPHIN COVE***

Be prepared for crowds at this popular dolphin interaction area. Hoards of visitors line the edge of the rocky, reef-like pool to watch and hopefully pet the many bottle-nosed dolphins who come right up to their outstretched hands. Fish may be purchased for the dolphin feeding sessions, perfect for enticing them to get really close. A member of the education department gives frequent talks and answers questions. Afterward stroll around the pool to the underwater viewing area.

JOURNEY TO ATLANTIS****

Travel on water as well as high-speed rails in a special effects battle between good and evil at this one-of-a-kind attraction. Riders are lured by sirens into the Lost City of Atlantis where, with the use of lasers and holographics, they encounter hundreds of special effects and several surprises along the way including two very steep and wet drops, one of which is totally unexpected. Pump up your heart for the final 60-foot plummet and be prepared for a good soaking. **6-minute ride. Height requirement 42 inches; guests 42–48 inches must be accompanied by an adult. Expectant mothers or those with heart, neck, and back problems should not ride.**

KRACKEN****

A legendary sea monster held in captivity by Poseidon is released in all its fury at the tallest, fastest, and longest coaster in Orlando. And what's more, it's floorless and open-sided. All that's holding you in are your bench and shoulder harness. Ascend to the top of the steepest drop in Central Florida before plunging 149 feet (15 stories) to the bottom at speeds of 65 mph. You'll find yourself upside down seven times and underwater three times before shooting through a tunnel immediately before screeching to a halt. It's so fast you won't know what hit you. **3½ minute-ride. Height requirement 54 inches. Expectant mothers or those with heart, neck, and back problems should not ride.**

MANATEES: THE LAST GENERATION?***

This excellent exhibit and short film is a must, one that is highly entertaining but essential if simply to educate the public on the gloomy plight of the gentle manatees attempting to coexist with man. Manatees have been around in great numbers for 15 million years, but now less than 2,000 remain in the state of Florida. Those seen here have been injured by the propellers of boats, fishing lines, and the polluted waterways of encroaching civilization, and all have been rescued by SeaWorld where they are treated and rehabilitated before being released.

On your walk to the entrance, stop for your first glimpse of the manatees in a Florida waterways habitat, much like the ones in which they live. The languid, plant-eating mammals slowly swim through this delightful cove of greenish water joined by fish, egrets, turtles, and ibis surrounded by wetlands filled with cattails, live oaks, sable palms, fallen logs, and the soothing sounds of insects and birds. Move on to the Manatee Theater to view a 3-minute film on their history and sad dilemma and learn what you can do to ensure these animals do not vanish from the earth. Then to the underwater viewing area to get up close and personal with the astonishing creatures.

PACIFIC POINT PRESERVE***

Be transported to the rocky shores of the Pacific coast at this 2½-acre outcropping where waves crash and lap the giant boulders of a realistic pool overflowing with sea lions and seals, each attempting to outbark the others. Overhead seabirds soar and squawk and soon a feeling of contentment overwhelms you, tempting you to stay longer than time allows. Stick around for the feeding frenzy when fish may be purchased.

PENGUIN ENCOUNTER***

Step on a moving sidewalk for a short view of SeaWorld's playful penguins frolicking in their 34-degree, 160,000-gallon icy abode. The speed in which these playful birds swim through the water, some as fast as 20 mph is quite a sight to see; too bad they're some of the most pungent-smelling creatures around. The separate puffin exhibit is definitely worth a stop. If you haven't got your fill of these tuxedoed creatures, there's a stationary viewing platform above the moving sidewalk where you may watch to your heart's content.

SKY TOWER**

Ride to the top of this 400-foot tower for a circular, revolving view of SeaWorld and the surrounding landscape. The panorama extends as far as Walt Disney World and over to downtown Orlando. Closed during inclement weather or high winds. Don't waste your money on overcast days. **$3 additional charge.**

STINGRAY LAGOON**

Waist-high pool filled with gliding, gentle stingrays just waiting to be fed by you. Purchase a small tray of food (early in the morning when they are good and hungry is best) and enjoy.

TROPICAL REEF**

Cool and dark, this delightful aquarium is loaded with glowing tropical fish, most of which you probably didn't know existed. Look for cardinal fish, coral shrimp, pufferfish, geckos, lionfish, seahorses, giant clams, and much, much more. No tropical reef here, just individual aquaria dramatically backlit in the darkness while soothing music plays.

TURTLE POINT**

Sea turtles weighing as much as a Volkswagen Beetle are the display at this natural pool area edged by a sandy beach. Though they're not high entertainment, it's fascinating to watch them lazily swimming about. An outdoor display educates visitors on the plight of these marvelous creatures.

Live Shows

CLYDE AND SEAMORE TAKE PIRATE ISLAND***

In a loose plot involving pirates, a treasure map, and a search for gold, Clyde and Seamore, two of SeaWorld's cleverest resident sea lions, entertain while slipping and sliding through their antics as they mimic their way around the stage. A sneaky sea otter only adds to the fun. And if you're in luck, a 2,000-pound walrus will make an appearance making the entire show worth the wait. (Be careful, he spits!) **25-minute show.**

KEY WEST FEST***

Bottlenose dolphins and false killer whales (members of the dolphin family but larger and darker than the bottlenose variety) are the stars here at the Key West Stadium as they cavort and leap in the air accompanied by plenty of "oohs" and "aahs" from the audience. Nothing is more entertaining than when they push their trainers through the pool and into the air at amazing speeds. There's an amusing segment involving a young member of the audience who interacts with a dolphin accompanied by a few comical moments. And beware the grand finale resulting in a few soggy visitors. One of the best shows here. Don't miss it. **12-minute show.**

PETS AHOY***

Worth a bit of planning, this comically entertaining show set in a harborside village features 130 animals, including dogs, cats, birds, rats, and even a pig. Considering most have been rescued from local animal shelters, you'll be amazed at their skillful performance in a variety of fun skits and tricks. You'll see cats walking tightropes, pigs driving cars, dogs jumping rope, and ducks flapping their way across the stage. All in all one cute act. **25-minute show.**

North Side Restaurants and Snacks

Captain Pete's Island Eats—Chicken fingers • conch fritters served with key lime mustard sauce • coconut pineapple with orange sauce • funnels cakes • tropical smoothies.

Cypress Bakery—Cookies, pastries, cupcakes, muffins, cake, Rice Crispies treats • specialty coffees, hot chocolate.

Mama Stella's Italian Kitchen—Chicken parmigiana • pasta primavera • pizza • spaghetti with meat sauce • opt for the outdoor seating overlooking a soothing pond.

Polar Parlor Ice Cream—Waffle ice cream cones.

Smoky Creek Grill—Mesquite-grilled chicken, baby back ribs, beef brisket • sides of fries, corn-on-the-cob, coleslaw, baked beans.

Waterfront Sandwich Grill—Nice waterfront deck makes this one of the more pleasant stops for lunch • burgers, smoked turkey breast sandwich, club sandwich, fries, potato salad.

North Side Shopping

Bud's Shop—Budweiser souvenirs.

Coconut Bay Traders—Island clothing for adults and children • marine plush toys • straw bags • bathing suits • sarongs • flip-flops • Sperry topsiders • colorful beach bags.

Conch City Leather Works—Kiosk selling leather products • belts, key chains, and wallets.

Crosswalk Gifts—SeaWorld logo clothing and souvenirs.

Cruz Cay Market—Open-air market • grass skirts • island print clothing • sandals.

Flamingo Point Gifts—Florida flamingo souvenirs • stylish straw hats • SeaWorld logo t-shirts.

Friends of the Wild—Marine life souvenirs for the home • framed pictures of marine animals • dolphin clocks • glass sculpture • jewelry • plush toys • porcelain figurines.

Manatee Cove Gift Shop—Manatee logo clothing and plush toys • wind chimes • marine sculpture.

Sand Castle Toys 'n' Treats—Children's SeaWorld logo clothing • plush animal toys • hats • clothing.

Shamu's Emporium—SeaWorld merchandise • plush marine toys.

Shamu Souvenir—Everything Shamu including t-shirts, hats, beach towels, postcards.

Sweet Sailin' Candy—Fudge • salt-water taffy • lollipops • caramel apples • boxed chocolates.

Special SeaWorld Behind-the-Scenes Tours

Call **800-432-1178** (press 5) for advance reservations for the False Killer Whale Interaction Program or the Animal Care Experience. All other tours can be booked by calling **800-406-2244** or by e-mailing SeaWorld at **education@seaworld.org**. Once inside the park reservations may be made at the Behind-the-Scenes Tour counter.

False Killer Whale Interaction Program

Get up close and personal with false killer whales, a species of dolphins, during this 2-hour program where you'll help conduct animal training and even have a session in the water with them. Cost is $200, which includes lunch, t-shirt, souvenir photograph, and 7-day pass to SeaWorld. Participants must be at least 13 years old and 52 inches tall.

Animal Care Experience

New 8-hour program designed for those interested in the care, feeding, rescue, and rehabilitation of SeaWorld's animals. Work alongside marine mammal experts who interact and care for seals, walruses, whales, and manatees. $389 including lunch, t-shirt, souvenirs, and 7-day pass to SeaWorld. The program begins at 6:30 A.M. Up to four guests per day; only those age 13 years and older may participate.

Trainer for a Day

Spend an entire day with a SeaWorld animal trainer. Dress in a wetsuit and meet Shamu, help with food preparation and cleanup, and learn training techniques while getting up close to sea lions, otters, and a walrus. $389 including lunch. Must be at least 13 years old and at least 52 inches tall to participate. Call 407-370-1382 information. Limited to only 6 people per day.

Adventure Express Tour

Enjoy a 6-hour guided tour with back-door access to Kracken, Journey to Atlantis, and the Wild Arctic along with reserved seats at two of the seated shows. Also included are dolphin and sea lion feedings plus a chance to go behind the scenes to pet a penguin. $80 for adults, $75 for children ages 3–9, including lunch. Park admission not included.

Predators Tour

In this 1-hour tour, learn about the mystery and behavior of sharks with a chance to touch one. Then move backstage at Shamu Stadium and learn about killer whales. $10 for adults, $9 for children plus park admission.

Polar Expedition Tour

This 1-hour tour goes behind-the-scenes at the Wild Arctic attraction to learn about polar bears and beluga whales. You'll even get to pet a penguin. **$10 for adults, $9 for children plus park admission.**

To the Rescue Tour

This 1-hour program offers a glimpse of SeaWorld's animal rescue and rehabilitation program. **$10 for adults, $9 for children plus park admission.**

Sharks Deep Dive

Two-hour program immerses guests into the fascinating world of sharks. Don wetsuits and either snorkel or scuba dive in a shark cage smack dab in the middle of more than 50 sharks. **$125 to snorkel, $150 to scuba. Includes 2-day park admission. Proof of certification is required. Must be 10 years or older.**

Southern Area
Continuous Viewing
ANHEUSER-BUSCH HOSPITALITY CENTER***

Not only can you stop here for a taste of the many beers that make Anheuser-Busch famous, but garden-lovers will be awed by the sight of misty waterfalls, flowering plants, and soothing ponds and streams. Inside the pavilion is a super hospitality center where visitors partake of complimentary samples of a wide assortment of brews while relaxing at one of the tables complete with fabulous views. The Anheuser-Busch Beer School is offered several times a day for those interested in the history and process of beer brewing. To sign up, arrive 15 minutes before the times listed on your guide map.

CLYDESDALE HAMLET***

The chance to see the pristine lodgings of the famous Clydesdale horses (each weighing close to a ton) should not be missed. If only my house were this clean and shiny. Stalls of rich hardwood filled with fresh hay and not a hint of horse smell open out to a rich, grassy pasture where the impeccably groomed beauties are allowed to roam. Photo and petting opportunities occur at intervals throughout the day (see your guide map for times). A team of Clydesdales complete with a Dalmatian companion parade twice daily into the park for pictures.

SHAMU'S HAPPY HARBOR***

Here is the place for kids to romp and play, a place all their own. They can bong on steel drums, climb aboard a fun ship, scale a vinyl rope mountain, have fun in sandy play areas, run through a water maze, and romp to their heart's content on one of the best net climbs around, a huge 4-story affair. Boogie Bump Bay is the exclusive area for those 42 inches and under with sand play, a mini vinyl rope climbing mountain, a ball crawl, and a mini bounce. For a fee try your hand at the remote-controlled cars and boats.

TERRORS OF THE DEEP****

Definitely the best exhibit here, fear-inspiring yet fascinating. Begin your exploration by traveling on a moving sidewalk through an acrylic aquarium tunnel filled with fish and moray eels. Look closely at the reef; the eels love to find cozy hiding places. If you're in luck, one might swim slowly over your head.

Proceed to individual tanks filled with scorpionfish, barracuda with razor-sharp teeth, the poison puffer fish, and the lion fish with its toxic spines, then on to the best part of the exhibit, the shark tunnel. Utilizing the same type of construction as the eel tank, this 124-foot tube supporting more than 2,232 tons (the weight of 372 elephants) is simply unbelievable. Five varieties of shark swim slowly around you, a sight guaranteed to raise the hair on the back of your neck. The accompanying ominous music only adds to the tension. As I moved through the tunnel, a sawfish sat above my head, quite a sight to behold.

WILD ARCTIC***

The fascinating animals of the Arctic have come to sunny Florida. Your adventure begins with either a jetcopter adventure film (by air) in a motion simulator setting or a viewing in stationary seats (by foot) minus the stomach churning. The line for the walking show is always shorter. After the film, proceed to the chilly Base Station Wild Arctic where beluga whales, polar bears, and walruses in ice cold pools can be viewed both from above and after winding your way down ramps, from under the water. **The by-air simulator ride has a 42-inch height re-**

quirement and is not recommended for expectant mothers, anyone with heart, neck, or back problems, or those prone to motion sickness.

Tip: The simulator ride is even a bit more gut-wrenching than Disney's Body Wars; those with even a bit of motion sickness should beware.

Live Shows
CIRQUE DE LA MER**

What this show has to do with SeaWorld is certainly a question many visitors ask. Here you'll find a combination of pulsating fire dancers, daring acrobatics, high-flying ballet, and more, all with a Peruvian backdrop. Go figure! In between each act a Harpo Marx-type comedian entertains; his most hilarious scene is one in which male volunteers from the audience participate under his guidance in a Rocky-style boxing match.

Tip: This show is scheduled to close sometime in 2003.

SHAMU ADVENTURE SHOW****

This high-tech killer whale show is by far the best in the park. A huge "ShamuVision" screen suspended behind the giant pool displays film clips and live footage of the show in progress. On the screen, Jack Hanna of TV fame introduces the audience to the natural habitat of the Orca killer whales with beautiful footage of the hunting habits of these powerful predators. Then out come the glorious creatures themselves. Listen to the screams of delight that sound throughout much of SeaWorld as the audience witnesses these magnificent whales propelling their trainers around the pool, riding them 30 feet in the air, leaping and diving as they perform an absolutely amazing show.

Those members of the audience who choose to sit in the "splash zone" will get soaked throughout the show; however, nothing compares to the grand finale when the largest killer whale in any marine life facility in the world, weighing in at over 12,000 pounds, sends enormous waves of ice cold water (up to 30 rows high) over unprepared spectators. Just sit back and watch the mind-changing audience run up the stadium steps to higher and drier ground when they realize the true power in the tail of this huge creature. After leaving the show, walk around the other side of the stadium to Shamu: Close Up!, where you'll find the whales' training facility and below a super underwater viewing area. **35-minute show.**

Tip: Think twice before seating very young children in the splash zone. The water that hits the audience can be pretty powerful and could intimidate an adult much less a small child. A major advantage that might possibly overshadow the soaking is the spectacular underwater view of the whales through the glass-walled tank from the lower seats. In busy season arrive 30 minutes prior to show time to assure yourself a spot for this most amazing of shows.

South Side Restaurants and Snacks

The Deli—Located inside the Anheuser-Busch Hospitality Center • overstuffed top round of beef, oven-roasted turkey, and club sandwiches all served with potato salad • delicious chicken Caesar salad.

Dine With Shamu—A chance to dine with Shamu trainers alongside killer whales in a backstage area • question-and-answer session as well as a training session in progress • all-you-care-to-eat seafood buffet served poolside • salads, pasta, seafood, and chicken. Call **407-351-3600** for preferred seating.

Dock Side Café—Barbecue grilled chicken, hot dogs, barbecue beef sandwich, chicken strips, fries • cookies.

Mango Joe's Café—Loads of open-air seating with terrific views of the SeaWorld lagoon • fried fish, club sandwich, shrimp tortilla wrap, fajita salad, chicken and beef fajitas.

Sharks Underwater Grill—Dine in front of the amazing shark tank at SeaWorld's newest full-service restaurant featuring a "Floribbean" menu with an accent on seafood • flatbread pizza, pan-seared red snapper, oak-grilled filet mignon. Lunch and dinner; call **407-351-3600** for preferred seating.

South Side Shopping

Gulf Breeze Trader—Island clothing • straw hats • plush toys • beach towels • Hawaiian-print shorts • bathing suits.

Ocean Treasures—Linen dresses • great assortment of beautiful beach bags • lighthouse lamps • island clothing.

Wild Arctic Gift Shop—Plush polar bear toys • Wild Arctic logo clothing • figurines • Arctic videos by National Geographic • SeaWorld Viewmasters.

Special Shows

Aloha Polynesian Luau—The Aloha Polynesian Dinner Show includes a family-style dinner of salad, fresh fruit, sweet and sour chicken, smoked pork loin, and mahimahi in pina colada sauce along with steamed vegetables, rice, dessert, one cocktail, and nonalcoholic beverages. Entertainment consists of 2 hours of island music and dance including a Samoan Fire Knife Dance. I am not even a fan of luaus in Hawaii, much less one at SeaWorld in Florida. But if luaus are your thing, have at it. **Presented nightly at 6:30 P.M. $38 for adults, $28 for juniors ages 8–12, $17 for children ages 3–7. Park admission not required. Call 800-327-2424 or 407-351-3600 for reservations.**

DISCOVERY COVE

Swim with the dolphins at the one-of-a-kind Discovery Cove.

Much controversy surrounds the park as animal rights activists protest the exploitation of these amazing creatures, making the decision to participate one not to be taken lightly. However, if there is one place to do a dolphin swim, Discovery Cove is probably it, a place where extreme caution is taken to ensure the animal's safety.

That said, here is one of the best places to spend your vacation dollars. And dollars you will spend with a full day costing as much as $229. But it is a chance to get in the water with a dolphin, snorkel in tropical coves loaded with fish and rays (sharks and barracudas are safely behind Plexiglas), and sit on relatively uncrowded white-sand beaches. Only 1,000 guests per day are allowed to enter this 30-acre park, built at a cost of $100,000,000.

Discover a tropical paradise overflowing with palms and flowering plants, dripping bougainvilleas, crystal-clear blue lagoons, waterfalls, aviaries, and marine life galore. It has the feel of a Caribbean island in which only a limited amount of people are allowed to visit. Interact with tropical fish, stingrays, colorful birds, and of course, dolphins. Lie on lounge chairs scattered under luxurious umbrellas around the white sandy beaches fronting the boulder-strewn, sparkling blue dolphin lagoons while sipping tropical drinks to your heart's content. It has the makings for a great day in the Florida sun.

Getting There

From Disney take I-4 East toward Orlando to Exit 71 (the same exit as SeaWorld). Turn right on Central Florida Parkway. Discovery Cove is on the right just past the entrance to SeaWorld. From Universal take I-4 West to Exit 71 and turn left on Central Florida Parkway.

Hours

9 A.M.–5:30 P.M. Doors usually open at 8:30 A.M. for those who would like an early jump on the park. This is definitely one place where the early bird gets the worm, the worm being one of the first in the lagoon with the dolphins. Arriving early assures a much less crowded park, your pick of beach chairs, and a dolphin swim first thing in the morning allowing time to explore the other areas of the park at your leisure.

Parking

Complimentary parking is just a short stroll away from the lobby. Valet parking, offered for $10 ($7 if purchased in advance), is surely a waste of money given the small size of the parking lot. Those with a disability tag receive free valet parking.

Admission

The cost is an all-inclusive price of $219–229 including a dolphin swim or $119–129 (depending on the season) minus the dolphins. Only those ages 6 and older may participate in the dolphin swim. I personally don't think the park is worth the money if there is no interest in the dolphins. Although it's certainly a beautiful spot, there isn't enough activity for a full day unless you love the idea of suntanning on a white-sand beach. Your money would be better spent at one of the many spectacular water parks in the area.

If the price seems unreasonably high, consider what is included: all attractions, lunch, a 5-by-7 photo of your party, parking, lockers, snorkeling equipment, wetsuit, towels, fish and bird food, and a special bonus of 7 consecutive days admission to SeaWorld (must be used consecutively with your visit—either right before, after, or a combination of both). It's really quite a bargain.

Reservations

Reservations are a must. In busy season try to plan your visit 6 months in advance. Off-season allows for a bit more flexibility. If the day you wish to visit is sold out, keep checking for cancellations. **Call 877-434-7268 or go online at www.discoverycove.com. 25% deposit required at time of booking with full payment due 45 days prior.**

Cancellation Policy

Full refund up to 45 days prior, 75% refund 30 to 45 days prior, 50% refund 8 to 29 days prior, and no refund if cancelled within 7 days of your visit.

Discovery Cove only closes in case of lightning; once your payment is made, rain or shine, you'll not receive a refund. Date changes are allowed up to 5 P.M. the day before if space is available. So if stormy weather threatens, try for an alternate day. The first date change is complimentary; after that a $50 fee is assessed.

When to Come

Discovery Cove is open year-round; however, the warmer months in Florida make it easier to dip into the chilly 70-degree saltwater pools. Although winter days in Florida can be warm and sunny, some are downright cold, not exactly conducive to relaxing on the beach or swimming in the bracing water. If you want to avoid rain, stay away during the peak hurricane season Aug through the end of Oct. Spring and late fall are the best times to visit.

Park Basics

Lay of the Land

This is one park where you won't need a guide map. It's compact and simple to maneuver. Just follow the pathways and consult the large maps located throughout.

Guests With Disabilities—Those who can maneuver up to the wading areas may participate in the dolphin swim as long as they need limited help or have personal assistance. Specially equipped wheelchairs with oversized tires for beach maneuvering are available and can be reserved in advance.

Lockers and changing rooms—Complimentary lockers are located near Dolphin Lagoon and Ray Lagoon. Leave your sunscreen at home—special, dolphin-safe sunscreen is provided. Near the lockers are showers and changing rooms with complimentary towels, toiletries, even hairdryers.

Eating—Your admission price includes lunch at the Laguna Grill. You'll find it to be just so-so, really only glorified fast food. Included is an entree, side salad, beverage, and dessert. Entree choices are fajitas, chicken pasta, salmon, chicken or vegetarian stir-fry, burgers, roast beef sandwich, chicken Caesar salad, chef salad, Gardenburger, hot dogs, and chicken fingers. Snacks may be purchased at one of two spots, each with the exact same menu of nachos, pretzels, ice cream, fresh fruit, smoothies, beer, wine, tropical drinks, and sodas. From 8:30–11 A.M., a breakfast of fresh pastries, cereal, juice, and coffee is offered.

Shopping—At Tropical Gifts are bathing suits, hats, sandals, resort clothing, Discovery Cove merchandise, and gifts galore.

"Trainer For a Day" program—New to Discovery Cove is this behind the scenes program allowing up to 12 guests per day to work with the trainers, feeding, training, and caring for many of the animals in the park. Cost is $399 per person; participants must be in good physical condition and at least 6 years old. Those under age 13 must be accompanied by a paying adult. The price also covers everything included in the cost of regular admission, consisting of a enhanced dolphin encounter and training session, lunch, and the 7-day SeaWorld pass.

Attractions
DOLPHIN ENCOUNTER****

The superstar of adventures here is the dolphin swim. In groups of no more than ten people with two trainers you'll meet your bottlenose dolphin and the fun begins! What gentle yet unbelievably strong creatures. You're introduction begins with a dolphin rubdown; you'll be amazed at how clean and rubbery their bodies are. Those timid about being in the water with dolphins (as I was) will find their worries soon evaporate. The trainers do not allow any sudden movements, kicking, or hand-slapping that might scare the animal. Continue with hand signals that get an instant reaction, such as chattering, spinning, or flips, and receive a big dolphin hug for a great photo that can be purchased later.

Then comes the part you've been waiting for as two people at a time along with a trainer swim out to deeper water to "play" one-on-one with the dolphin. What you do depends on the trainer but always ends with each person hanging on for dear life to the dolphin's back and a fin for a tow into shore. What a ride! Your session ends with a big smooch on your new friend's nose.

CORAL REEF**

This is where your snorkeling equipment comes in handy as you swim through a man-made reef and underwater shipwreck filled with 10,000 tropical fish, rays, and coral reefs. Sharks and barracuda are kept behind Plexiglas walls allowing an illusion of swimming with them minus the danger. This was the only place in the park where I felt crowded. Even though it looks large enough and I jumped in early before the crowds arrived, I felt hemmed in by fins in my face and bumping bodies. Try it but don't expect to feel as if you are in the middle of the ocean.

TROPICAL RIVER**

When you're ready to get away from the rest of the park, head straight for the beautiful and much warmer waters of the Tropical River. Explore caves and waterfalls while circling the park with stops along tranquil banks loaded with lush foliage and rocky outcroppings. If you're worried about your adolescents taking off on their own here, never fear. A barrage of lifeguards at every turn makes this super safe and worry-free. The river is also the best way to enter the aviary where you must pass under a waterfall bird barrier. My only complaint is how shallow the water is in most areas making it difficult to float and swim along.

AVIARY***

Almost worth the price of admission is the aviary, where over 250 tropical birds wander and literally eat right out your hand. A Discovery Cove employee is on hand to distribute bird feed (some of it pretty gross looking) and offer advice on exactly how to attract these colorful creatures. If you're holding a handful of food be prepared; the birds seem to come at you from out of nowhere. A new Small Bird Sanctuary allows visitors to hand-feed hundreds of birds including finches and hummingbirds. Oh, and enter from the Tropical River instead of walking in; it's a kick.

RAY LAGOON***

Swim among hundreds of southern and cownose rays in this small cove. Go ahead and touch them; they're gentle and most importantly have had their barbs removed.

WET 'N' WILD

Near SeaWorld and Universal Studios is 25 acres of watery fun called Wet 'n' Wild. Owned by Universal; what it lacks in a cutesy theme it more than makes up for in mega-thrills galore. This was the original Orlando thrill water park and has since been copied throughout the nation particularly at nearby Disney in their concepts for Typhoon Lagoon and Blizzard Beach.

Getting There

Just 2 miles from both SeaWorld and Universal Orlando where International Drive meets Universal Boulevard. From I-4 take Exit 75A to Wet 'n' Wild at 6200 International Drive.

Admission

$32 for adults, $26 for children ages 3–9. Also part of the Orlando FlexTicket Packages. Additional fees: tubes $4, towels $2, and lockers $5, all including a $2 deposit. Life vests are complimentary. Advance tickets may be purchased at **www.universalorlando.com**.

Hours

10 A.M.–5 P.M. with extended hours in the busier months of the year. Open year-round with heated pools in the cooler months. Call 800-992-WILD for up-to-date operating hours.

Parking

$5 per day.

Attractions

BLACK HOLE

A 2-person raft makes a twisting 500-foot trip in almost complete darkness. **Those 36–48 inches tall must be accompanied by someone at least 48 inches tall.**

THE BLAST

Jets and gusts of water propel riders through Wet 'n' Wild's newest ride.

BLUE NIAGARA

From 6 stories up take a 300-foot trip to the bottom in intertwined looping and twisting tubes that ends in quite a splash. **Minimum height 48 inches.**

BOMB BAY

Be dropped like a bomb almost straight down a 6-story slide at 30 mph. **Minimum height 48 inches.**

BUBBA TUB

The entire family can ride down a 6-story, triple-dip slide in a 5-person tube. **Those 36–48 inches in height must be accompanied by someone over 48 inches tall.**

BUBBLE UP

Just for kids, climb up a large balloon and bounce down the side into a 3-foot pool. **Only for those 36–54 inches in height and under 12 years old.**

DER STUKA

A 250-foot, 6-story, free-fall slide reaching speeds of up to 50 mph. **Minimum height 48 inches.**

THE FLYER

A 4-passenger toboggan course propelled by wild water zips along 450 feet of banked curves. A minimum of two people must ride together. **Those 36–48 inches tall must be accompanied by a person over 48 inches tall.**

HYDRA FIGHTER

Two people seated back-to-back on a bungee-style swing regulate high-pressure water cannons that control how high and fast they go. **Minimum height 56 inches.**

KID'S PARK

Children 48 inches and under will find miniature versions of some of the park's rides including their own Wave Pool with 1-foot waves, Mach V, Raging Rapids, and Lazy River as well as kid-size beach chairs and a mini-food kiosk.

KNEE SKI

Test your kneeboarding skills pulled by a cable-operated ski tow on a ½-mile course around the Wet 'n' Wild Lake. **Seasonal attraction. Minimum height 56 inches.**

LAZY RIVER

Float down a slow-moving, mile-long, winding river.

MACH 5

Ride headfirst on toboggan-style mats down three slippery flume rides (a total of 1,700 feet) that twist, dip, and turn their way to the bottom.

THE STORM

Wet 'n' Wild's newest attraction, a swirling body coaster where riders wash down a chute into a huge open bowl that spins them in circles at high speeds to the pool below. **Minimum height 48 inches.**

THE SURGE

Whoosh over 580 feet of curves and flumes in 5-person rafts.

WAVE POOL

A 17,000-square-foot wave pool with 4-foot-high waves.

WILD ONE

Waverunners tow up to two people on inner tubes at this 5-minute course on the Wet 'n' Wild Lake. **$4 additional fee. Minimum height 56 inches.**

Eating

Surf Grill—Burgers • hot dogs • chicken • barbeque beef sandwich • salad • vegetarian burger.

Bubba's Barbeque 'n' Chicken—Barbeque chicken, ribs, beef, and pork platters • wings • chicken fingers • corn dogs.

Pizza 'n' Subs—Pizza • calzones • spaghetti and meatballs.

Sidewalk Sweets—Soft-serve ice cream • sundaes • cookies • funnel cakes.

KENNEDY SPACE CENTER

Set smack dab in the middle of the largest wildlife refuge in the state of Florida is the fascinating home of the U.S. Space Program. An extensive Visitor's Center and exciting bus tour to the outlying areas of the property make for a wonderful side trip from Disney with a one-way travel time of approximately 1 hour and 15 minutes. To fully enjoy your visit, get an early start and plan on spending at least 6–8 hours at the center. Once there, the best strategy is to take your tours first and then explore the extensive Visitor's Center afterward.

Try timing your visit to coincide with a shuttle launch, visible from the Visitor's Center and for many miles around; an additional $15 ticket will get you within 5 miles of the launch. Call **321-449-4444** or buy tickets online at **www.ksctickets.com**. For one of the best viewpoints, travel to the beaches of Cocoa Beach or Titusville.

Getting There

From Disney or Universal take I-4 to Highway 528 (a toll road) to Highway 407 North to Highway 405 East and follow signs to Spaceport USA.

Admission

To enter the Visitor's Center you must at least buy the Maximum Access Badge priced at $33 for adults and $23 for children ages 3–11. This entitles you to the Kennedy Space Center Tour of restricted areas, IMAX movies, and exhibits. Add on $20 for each of the special tours, definitely worth the extra money (see below under Add-On Special Interest Tours). A 12-month pass for adults at $46 and $30 for children includes unlimited visits to the Visitor Complex and priority purchase of launch transportation tickets. To avoid the sometimes very long lines, tickets may be prepurchased online at **www.kennedyspacecenter.com**. AAA members receive a discount if pre-purchased from AAA.

Guests with disabilities

Wheelchair accessible buses are available; ask crew members for departure information. Call **321-449-4400** for American Sign Language interpreters and tours for visitors who are blind for advance reservations.

Hours

Daily 9 A.M. to dusk except for Christmas Day and certain launch days. Call **321-452-2121** for specifics.

Kennels

Complimentary kennel service at the center.

Parking

Complimentary parking located directly in front of the Visitor's Center.

Strollers and wheelchairs

Free of charge.

Attractions at the Kennedy Space Center Visitor Complex

ROBOT SCOUTS

Walk-through sessions introduce robots who explore distant planets where human astronauts cannot yet go.

EARLY SPACE EXPLORATION

Walk-through exhibit featuring a historical display of the Mercury Mission Control Room and Mercury and Gemini space capsules.

EXPLORATION IN THE NEW MILLENNIUM

The history of exploration unfolds from the age of the Vikings to the Mars Viking Lander. Visitors may also touch an actual piece of Mars!

ASTRONAUT ENCOUNTER

Actual astronauts speak to the audience in this open-air area. Includes a question-and-answer session along with personal stories about space travel. See your daily schedule guide for times.

SHUTTLE EXPLORER

Walk through full-scale replica of the space shuttle Explorer (you'll be amazed at how small the crew quarters actually are). Outside are solid rocket boosters, each weighing 1,300,000 pounds.

UNIVERSE THEATER

A 15-minute film exploring the possibility of life on other planets.

ROCKET GARDEN

Guided tour of historical space rockets including a Mercury Atlas, the same type that launched John Glenn into space.

ASTRONAUT MEMORIAL

Touching, black granite memorial dedicated to all astronauts who have died in the name of space exploration.

LAUNCH STATUS CENTER

Interesting briefings occur throughout the day explaining in layman's terms the intricate details of a shuttle launch and the International Space Station. See daily schedule guide for times.

IMAX THEATERS

Two 40-minute films on 5½-story IMAX screens. *The Dream Is Alive,* narrated by Walter Cronkite and filmed from the space shuttle by astronauts, offers unbelievable panoramic shots of the earth's landmarks from 280 miles up. In *L-5: First City in Space*—experience for yourself how it would feel to live in space in this fictional story of a futuristic space settlement and its inner workings, all in 3-D. **See daily schedule guide for times and arrive at least 10 minutes prior to show time.**

KENNEDY SPACE CENTER TOUR

Included in the cost of your Maximum Access Badge is this self-paced tour of the outlying areas of the Space Center. Buses depart from the Visitors Center, stopping at points of interest. Visitors are allowed as much time as they would like to explore before reboarding at their convenience. The last bus departs 4 hours prior to closing. Stops include the following:

International Space Center—Full-scale replicas of Space Station modules along with a viewing gallery from which to watch NASA technicians readying actual components for launch.

LC-39 Observation Gantry—60-foot viewing tower affords great vistas of the space shuttle launch pads, the crawlerway over which shuttles are transported to the launch pad, and the gigantic Vehicle Assemble Building, the second largest building in the country.

Apollo/Saturn V Center—Genuine 363-foot Saturn V moon rocket (its sheer size is absolutely mind-boggling) inside a massive building. View a re-creation of the dramatic launch of the first Apollo mission with the actual consoles from the original control room. And don't forget to touch a piece of moon rock before leaving.

Add-On Special Interest Tours

Add-on price of $20 each. Last tour commences 2 hours prior to closing. In order to see everything at the Visitors Center and take both tours you will need to arrive first thing in the morning and plan well. Both 2-hour guided bus tours, led by a space program expert, are highly recommended.

Cape Canaveral Then and Now Tour—Perfect for nostalgic space fans. Tour Hangar S where the Mercury astronauts lived and trained, the Gemini launch pad, the launch site of the Explorer 1 satellite, the Air Force Space and Missile Museum and Rocket Garden, the historic Cape Canaveral Lighthouse, and the launch pad where Alan Shepard first left for space.

NASA Up Close Tour—Visitors get up close to the space shuttle launch pads as well as the Vehicle Assembly Building, the shuttle landing strip, the giant Crawler-Transporter used to move the shuttle to the launch pad, and the press-site launch countdown clock.

Eating

There are quite a few dining choices here at the Visitor's Center; however, don't expect gourmet cuisine. Most are either fast food or cafeteria style with only one full-service spot, Mila's Restaurant. Snack bars are also located on the tour stops at both the Apollo/Saturn V Center and the LC-39 Observation Gantry.

Lunch Pad—Burgers, fried fish, barbeque beef sandwich, hot dogs, chicken fingers, grilled chicken salad.

Orbit Café—Cafeteria-style dining • rotisserie chicken, lasagna, baked ziti, pizza, spaghetti and meatballs, soup, mashed potatoes, mac 'n' cheese, vegetables.

Mila's Restaurant—Full-service in a 1960s-style diner • quesadillas, salads, sandwiches, burgers, fajitas, baked chicken, pot pie, catch-of-the-day.

New Frontier Café—Barbecue sandwiches.

Planetary Pizza—Pizza, calzones, hot dogs, ice cream.

Milky Way Parlor—Ice cream treats.

Shopping

Space Shop—World's largest space memorabilia store.

CHAPTER 11

Disney Cruise Line

Combining a land package with a Disney cruise is the best of both worlds. Departing from nearby Port Canaveral are 3- and 4-night cruises to the Bahamas as well as 7-night cruises to both the western and eastern Caribbean. All are perfect for extending your vacation on a trip to sea. While mainly geared to adults traveling with children, the ships do offer many adults-only experiences including special programs, a special area at Castaway Cay, and an adults-only dining room and spa. But do be prepared to cruise along with hoards of little ones; it can't be avoided. Those traveling with children can look forward to many shared as well as adults-only activities, and kids will love the supervised children's programs and many character appearances onboard.

Both ships are lovingly designed in an art-deco style, basically identical varying only in itinerary. Each holds 2,400 passengers with 877 staterooms, many with verandas. Staterooms are spacious by cruise standards with 73% of them outside cabins and 44% with private verandas. Call **800-951-3532** or go to **www.disneycruise.com** for information and reservations.

Accommodations

Choose from accommodations ranging from an inside cabin to 2-bedroom suites with oversized verandahs, media libraries, walk-in closets and whirlpool tubs. Twelve categories make it easy to choose what's best for you and your family. Of course the larger the staterooms the higher the price. You'll also pay a premium for outside versus inside rooms and for a higher deck versus a lower one. In the winter, spring, and fall, Disney offers discounted rates; ask for the Sunshine Sailaway, Springtime Magic, or the Fall Fantasy promotions. If you'd like to sail at another time of the year, book far in advance and receive an early booking discount.

Even the least expensive of Disney's staterooms are larger than most ships. All are nautically decorated with natural woods, brass fixtures, and imported tiles. Bedding is either a queen or two twin beds and all rooms (at the very least) have a sitting area with a sofa and curtained divider. Each offers satellite TV, telephones, safes, a cold box for drinks, and low-powered hairdryers. No smoking is permitted except on verandahs, outside decks, and a few of the lounges. Concierge service is included in categories 1–3 with full room-service breakfast, snacks throughout the day, CD and video rental, special gifts, and the services of a concierge staff to help with dining, spa, and shore reservations.

Category 1

Two luxurious suites fit this category offering two bedrooms and two and a half baths with a separate 8-person dining table, media library, walk-in closets, Jacuzzi tub, wet bar, and even a baby grand piano. The very spacious verandah is the length of the cabin. Sleeps seven with 1,029 square feet. Includes concierge service.

Category 2

Two bedroom, two-and-a-half-bath spacious suites with an extended balcony. In the living area is a queen sleeper sofa, 6-person dining table, and wet bar. The master bath offers a whirlpool tub, double sinks, and a walk-in closet. Sleeps seven with 945 square feet. Includes concierge service.

Category 3

In this one-bedroom, two-bath suite is a separate parlor with double sleeper sofa as well as a pull-down bed, wet bar, 4-person dining table, and extra-large verandah. There are two closets, one a walk-in. Sleeps four to five with 614 square feet. Includes concierge service.

Category 4

These are called family suites although they are simply a large state-room with one bath. The sitting area, separated from the bed area with a curtained divider, contains a sofa and a wall pull-down bed. All come with a verandah. Sleeps four to five people with 304 square feet.

Category 5 and 6

Category 5 cabins are located one deck higher than 6. Both have verandahs and a curtain-divided sitting area with a sofa and vanity. Sleeps three to four people with 268 square feet.

Category 7

The same as Category 5 and 6 except they come with a Navigator's Verandah, an enclosed verandah with a large open porthole. Sleeps three to four people with 268 square feet.

Category 8, 9, and 10

Category 8 are outside cabins on higher decks with Category 9 cabins outside but on the two lowest decks; neither has a verandah. Category 10 is an inside cabin on the two lower decks. Each has a curtain-divided sitting area with sofa and vanity. Sleeps three to four people with 214 square feet.

Category 11 and 12

Category 11 are inside cabins located on the upper decks; Category 12 is inside on a lower deck. The sitting area has a curtain divider with sofa and vanity. Sleeps three to four people at 184 square feet.

Itineraries

Although each type of sailing offers a different itinerary, all include a stop at Disney's own private island where an entire day is dedicated to fun in the sun. Here guests can swim, cruise around on paddle boats, sail, sea kayak, snorkel around special Disney-created "shipwrecks," snooze in a hammock, shop a Bahamian marketplace, and dine at a barbeque buffet on the beach. Trails and bike paths are laid out for the exercise-minded, and those who really want to relax can book a massage in one of the private beach cabanas. (This should be done immediately after boarding the ship; they go quickly.) **Castaway Jo Pavilion** is the place for pool, foosball, ping-pong, shuffleboard, horseshoes, and basketball. Several bars scattered throughout the island offer alcoholic tropical drinks.

Four separate beaches cater to the needs of children, families, teens, and adults. Kids have their own special area called **Scuttle's Cove** where a program of activities is sure to please. **Serenity Bay** is the adults-only beach for those 18 and older where private cabana massages can be prearranged. **The Family Beach** is perfect for those who want to spend the day with their children, and **the Teen Beach** offers floats and rope swings as well as a supervised activity program.

At each stop a variety of shore excursions is offered, and the good news is they may now be booked before your cruise begins.

3- and 4-Night Bahama Cruises

Sail on the *Disney Wonder* to **the Bahamas**. The 3-night itinerary departs on Thursday and includes stops at **Nassau** and **Castaway Cay.** The 4-night cruises depart on Sunday with the addition of either a day at sea or on alternating stop at **Freeport.**

7-Night Caribbean Cruises

New 7-night cruises to the western Caribbean alternate weekly with an eastern Caribbean itinerary on the *Disney Magic*. All depart on Saturday with the western itinerary including **Key West, Grand Cayman, Cozumel,** and **Castaway Cay,** and the eastern itinerary including **St. Maarten, St. Thomas,** and **Castaway Cay.**

Recreation

Arcade—Quarter Masters is the ship's arcade with the latest in video games.

Deck fun—All ages enjoy the shuffleboard and ping-pong tables, and the exercise-minded will love the outdoor jogging track on Deck 4.

Pools—Three heated pools are found on Deck 9, all with fresh water. Forward is the adults-only Quiet Cove pool with two adjacent whirlpools, mid-ship is the Goofy Pool perfect for families with two adjacent whirlpools (one hot and one cold), and aft is the shallow Mickey Pool with a fun waterslide for young children.

Wide World of Sports deck—Recreation area on Deck 10 offering basketball, volleyball, and badminton.

Entertainment

It's doubtful you'll ever be bored with the multitude of entertainment choices on board.

Beat Street/Route 66—On the Disney Magic you'll find Beat Street, an entertainment area offering three different nightclubs for adults (ages 18 and older) only. At the Rockin' Bar D are live bands playing rock and roll, Top 40s, and country music in a small town honky-tonk setting; Off-Beat features comedic dueling piano players; and Sessions jazz club offers live piano music along with specialty coffees, champagne, wine, liqueurs, and even caviar.

On the Disney Wonder it's Route 66. Clubs include Wavebands where dancing to a live band or DJ-driven music playing the hits of a span of generations is the agenda; the Cadillac Lounge for romantic piano music and a sophisticated setting; and Barrel of Laughs, with dueling piano comedians and sing-along entertainment.

Buena Vista Theater—Watch your favorite films here in this 268-seat theater where Disney classic movies as well as first-run feature films are shown with plenty of popcorn.

ESPN Skybox—Live sporting events on big-screen TVs, a great view, and a menu of stadium food is a recipe for success at this floating sports bar.

Fantasia Reading and Game Room—Check out games and books for your enjoyment.

Internet Café—Surf the web, e-mail a friend, or find out more about your cruise activities here. A fee is charged for Internet services. Open 24 hours.

Promenade Lounge—Lobby lounge featuring live easy-listening music each evening.

Studio Sea— This family nightclub offers game shows, karaoke nights, cabaret acts, and dancing for all ages.

Walt Disney Theater—3-level, 1,040-seat theater offering original stage productions that change each evening.

Dining

Disney's dinner system, which rotates through each of three dining rooms, is unique. Seating is assigned, and although you will be moving to a different restaurant each evening, your servers as well as table guests will travel with you each night.

At **Parrot Cay** there's island-style cuisine along with Caribbean music and tropical decor, and at **Animator's Palate** the room changes as the night progresses from black and white to a barrage of color with animated scenes from classic Disney movies. On the *Disney Magic,* the third dining room is **Lumiere's,** where there's fine dining and a Beauty and the Beast twist on the evening. On the *Disney Wonder,* it's **Triton's,** where seafood and a Little Mermaid underwater-style setting is the theme.

Tables are tough to come by at **Palo,** the reservations-only, adults-only (ages 18 and over) dining room. Featured is Northern Italian cuisine, fine wines, and an air of romance accompanied by 270-degree views of the ocean. Since reservations fill up quickly, make them immediately after boarding. Dining is from 6–11 P.M. and an additional $5 service charge per guest is added to your final bill. Palo also features a reservations-only champagne brunch on 7-day cruises for a $10 charge.

Anytime the stomach starts to rumble head to **Pluto's Doghouse** for hot dogs, tacos, grilled chicken sandwiches, and burgers; **Pinocchio's Pizzeria** for a slice of pizza; or **Scoops** for soft-serve ice cream. Room service is offered 24-hours a day with continental breakfast served from 7–10 A.M. and sandwiches, salads, soup, pizza, pasta, and dessert the remainder of the day and into the wee hours of the morning. Those staying in a suite may order a full breakfast.

Dinner is served at either 5:30 or 7:45 P.M. Disney tries to put adults with other adults and families with children with other families. Evening attire for adults in Animator's Palate and Parrot Cay is resort casual (no shorts, t-shirts, or jeans except on young children), while jackets for men and pantsuits and dresses for women are suggested in Lumiere's, Triton's, and Palo. On 7-night cruises there are two formal evenings.

Breakfast and lunch is open seating served at either Parrot Cay and Lumiere's on the *Disney Magic* and Triton's on the *Disney Wonder.* A casual breakfast and lunch buffet is offered at **Topsider's** on the *Disney Magic* and at **Beach Blanket Buffet** on the *Disney Wonder.* Beverages such as coffee, tea, soda, juice, and milk are served complimentary with meals only. Anywhere else beverages, both alcoholic or non, may be charged to your room.

Services

Vista Pool and Spa—This adults-only 9,000-square-foot spa, salon, and fitness center offers a long list of luxurious services perfect for a great day at sea. Spa services include many types of massage, body treatments, and hydrotherapy, while the salon offers manicures, pedicures, cut, and color. Couples love the Surial Bath, where they are provided with three types of medicinal mud in a private steam room. The Tropical Rain Forest offers saunas, steam rooms, and a rain forest treatment for a nominal fee. For an additional fee, personal training, aerobic classes, and body composition analysis are available.

At the complimentary fitness center you'll find treadmills, stair climbers, exercise bicycles, rowing machines, exercise machines, and free weights that come with a super ocean view.

Children's Programs

With nearly an entire deck dedicated to children, there are a wide range of age-specific programs for kids. We all know what Disney does best and that is catering to the needs of children. And when children are happy so are their parents. It's a perfect combination of family time and playtime with other children their own age. The children's programs run from around 9 A.M. to about midnight and are complimentary (with the exception of Flounder's Reef Nursery). They can even eat with their group if they desire. Beepers are provided to parents in case their children need them for any reason.

Flounder's Reef Nursery—Hours have been expanded here giving parents more free time to enjoy the adults-only activities offered on board. The fee of $6 per hour per child ($5 per additional child per hour) with a 2-hour minimum for children ages 12 weeks to 3 years old. Those 3- and 4-year-olds not potty trained, and therefore not eligible for the Oceaneer Club, may be accommodated here. It's best to make advance reservations since only a limited amount of infants and toddlers are accepted at one time. Although hours vary, the service is generally provided from 1–4 P.M. and again from 6 P.M.–midnight while in port and 9:30–11:30 A.M., 1:30–3:30 P.M., and again from 6 P.M.–midnight while at sea.

Children ages 3–7—At the **Oceaneer Club**, in a setting reminiscent of Never Land, potty-trained children ages 3–7 have plenty to keep them occupied and happy. For 3- and 4-year-olds are such activities as training to be a Mouseketeer, visits from Mickey Mouse, searching for Tinkerbell with clues along the way, a Never Never Land party, and swinging with Tarzan. Ages 5–7 will enjoy pirate story adventures, trying out new experiments in the Oceaneer Lab, taking tea with Wendy and Peter Pan, learning animation techniques, and having a dig at Castaway Cay. And all have a stage performance for the entire ship. This plus much, much more. Open 9 A.M.–midnight.

Kids ages 8–12—At Disney's ultramodern **Oceaneer Lab**, children will find Nintendo played on a giant screen and 10 terminals of computer games. Divided into two age groups, children ages 8–9 will participate in lab workshops, learn the secrets of Disney animation, take part in a TV production, solve a mystery involving teamwork, make a radio commercial, and play glow-in-the-dark games. Ages 10–12 participate in such activities as making a soundtrack, building a bridge out of only pasta and glue, finding treasure on Castaway Cay, making a mouse pad, and producing a newscast. Open 9 A.M.–midnight.

Teens—Teens ages 13–17 can hang out in a New York–style coffee shop, **Common Grounds**, where games, a large-screen TV, Internet, and music are the entertainment. There's karaoke, pool parties, photography, teen-only movies, a pizza party, bamboo boat building, and a farewell party. Open 10 A.M.–1 A.M.

INDEX

Give the Gift of

The Luxury Guide to
Walt Disney World
to Your Friends and Colleagues

CHECK YOUR LEADING BOOKSTORE OR ORDER HERE

❏ **YES**, I want _____ copies of *The Luxury Guide to Walt Disney World* at $19.95 each, plus $4.95 shipping per book. (Texas residents please add $1.57 sales tax per book; Ohio residents please add $1.25 sales tax per book.) Canadian orders must be accompanied by a postal money order in U.S. funds. Allow 15 days for delivery.

❏ **YES**, I am interested in having Cara Goldsbury speak or give a seminar to my company, association, school, or organization. Please send information.

My check or money order for $_____ is enclosed.

Please charge my ❏ Visa ❏ MasterCard
❏ Discover ❏ American Express

Name _____

Organization _____

Address _____

City/State/Zip _____

Phone_____ E-mail _____

Card # _____

Exp. Date_____ Signature _____

Please make your check payable and return to:

BookMasters Inc.
30 Amberwood Parkway • Ashland, OH 44805

Call your credit card order to: 1-800-247-6553
Fax: 419-281-6883

www.luxurydisneyguide.com